Social Thinking–Software Practice

Social Thinking–Software Practice

edited by Yvonne Dittrich, Christiane Floyd, and
Ralf Klischewski

The MIT Press
Cambridge, Massachusetts
London, England

This book was set in Sabon on 3B2 by Asco Typesetters, Hong Kong.

Library of Congress Cataloging-in-Publication Data

Social thinking–software practice / edited by Yvonne Dittrich, Christiane Floyd, and Ralf Klischewski.
p. cm.
ISBN 978-0-262-04204-8 (hc. : alk. paper), 978-0-262-53813-8 (pb.)
1. Computer software—Development—Social aspects. 2. Human-computer interaction. I. Dittrich, Yvonne, 1964– II. Floyd, Christiane. III. Klischewski, Ralf, 1962–
QA76.76.D47 S597 2002
005.1—dc21 2001054634

Contents

Introduction ix
Ralf Klischewski, Christiane Floyd, and Yvonne Dittrich

I **Deconstructing 1**
Christiane Floyd

1 **Developing and Embedding Autooperational Form 5**
Christiane Floyd

2 **On Foundational Categories in Software Development 29**
James M. Nyce and Gail Bader

3 **Making Use of Social Thinking: The Challenge of Bridging Activity Systems 45**
Victor Kaptelinin

4 **Challenging Traditions of Inquiry in Software Practice 69**
Hans-Erik Nissen

II **Informing 91**
Chris Westrup

5 **On Retrieving Skilled Practices: The Contribution of Ethnography to Software Development 95**
Chris Westrup

6 **Representing and Modeling Collaborative Practices for Systems Development 111**
Marina Jirotka and Paul Luff

7 **The Locales Framework: Making Social Thinking Accessible for Software Practitioners 141**
Geraldine Fitzpatrick

8 What Doesn't Fit: The "Residual Category" as Analytic Resource 161
Eevi E. Beck

III Grounding 181
Yvonne Dittrich

9 On the Intertwining of Social and Technical Factors in Software Development Projects 185
Urs Andelfinger

10 Software Practice Is Social Practice 205
Jacob Nørbjerg and Philip Kraft

11 "Yes—What Does That Mean?" Understanding Distributed Requirements Handling 223
Kari Rönkkö

12 Doing Empirical Research on Software Development: Finding a Path between Understanding, Intervention, and Method Development 243
Yvonne Dittrich

IV Organizing 263
Jesper Simonsen

13 Changing Work Practices in Design 267
Keld Bødker, Finn Kensing, and Jesper Simonsen

14 Information Systems Research and Information Systems Practice in a Network of Activities 287
Mikko Korpela, Anja Mursu, H. Abimbola Soriyan, and Anne Eerola

15 Reaching out for Commitments: Systems Development as Networking 309
Ralf Klischewski

16 Participatory Organizational and Technological Innovation in Fragmented Work Environments 331
Bettina Törpel, Volker Wulf, and Helge Kahler

17 Large-Scale Requirements Analysis as Heterogeneous Engineering 357
Mark Bergman, John Leslie King, and Kalle Lyytinen

V **Reorienting** 387
Olav W. Bertelsen

18 **Useware Design and Evolution: Bridging Social Thinking and Software Construction** 391
Horst Oberquelle

19 **Discontinuities** 409
Olav W. Bertelsen and Susanne Bødker

20 **Localizing Self on the Internet: Designing for "Genius Loci" in a Global Context** 425
Sara Eriksén

21 **Intent, Form, and Materiality in the Design of Interaction Technology** 451
Thomas Binder

List of Contributors 469
Index 471

Introduction

Ralf Klischewski, Christiane Floyd, and Yvonne Dittrich

Software practice is everywhere: software development, design, and use as well as related management are shaping today's technology and changing the way we engage in social relations at work and at home, in small groups and in the larger society. Scientific reflection on software practice aims at understanding and improvement; at the same time the motives for understanding and the direction of improvement are also subjects for reflection and discourse. Whereas the discipline of software engineering is mainly concerned with the formal principles, technical basis, and methodological support for software development, reflection on software practice as social activity needs to go beyond a traditional engineering framework.

Social thinking is used here to refer to scientific reflection guided, informed, and/or inspired by social science approaches. Theories and methods developed with no specific concern for computing (e.g., ethnomethodology, activity theory) provide a starting point for inquiry into a variety of issues in software practice. In the last two decades, interdisciplinary cooperation between social scientists and computer professionals in areas such as human-computer interaction or computer-supported cooperative work has already produced a rich body of knowledge. But research in this field is still impeded by segregation according to different schools of thought and by the difficulties of relating engineering and social science research traditions. Therefore, efforts to understand and improve software practice need to go beyond simply applying traditional social science precepts and methods.

This book seeks to promote the discourse about and the interrelationship of social science–based approaches that shed light on the social aspects of software practice. In focusing on software practice as social activity, it allows for a variety of social science approaches to be applied and takes a close look at how humans act in relation to software.[1] Each of the twenty-one contributions takes up and relates social thinking and software practice in a unique way. All the authors offer perspectives for reflection on and guidance to software practice, based on extensive experience with projects and interdisciplinary research.

The book is the result of a joint effort over three years. It started with planning a seminar on the same topic, which was held in Schloss Dagstuhl in Germany in September 1999. Initiated by Christiane Floyd together with Nimal Jayaratna, Finn Kensing, and Lucy Suchman, the seminar was organized by Olav Berthelsen, Yvonne Dittrich, Viktor Kaptelinin, Helena Karasti, Ralf Klischewski, Jacob Nørbjerg, Jesper Simonsen, Chris Westrup, and Volker Wulf—an international and interdisciplinary group of researchers. (The position papers of all the participants are available in Dittrich et al. 2000.) The seminar provided a framework for intensive discussion and for interrelating this community of authors. At the end of the seminar most participants agreed to engage in a joint authoring process and to strive for a book with interrelated contributions using the Dagstuhl discussion as a starting point. The first step, then, was to cluster the expected contributions into five parts and to engage spokespersons for each part with a view to coordinating communication within the respective group of authors (this planning session was held in Aarhus in October 1999). To enhance the book's quality, mutual reviewing was encouraged both within and partly across the clusters. This was also supported by frequent e-mail postings to the authorship community and a Web site providing access to all drafts. The final structure was established on the basis of an authors' meeting in Copenhagen in June 2000.

Each part of the book contains several chapters, introduced by the spokesperson. The titles for the parts were chosen so as to point to different ways of relating social thinking and software practice. These are:

- *Deconstructing:* Looking for underlying paradigms in software practice and related research; questioning established paradigms for reflecting on software practice; pointing out new concepts and/or new areas for applying existing approaches

- *Informing:* Analyzing how social aspects of software use are conceptualized within the development process; creating social science–based representations of the workplace; questioning prescriptions and retaining a sense of critical and reflective appraisal
- *Grounding:* Promoting a broader understanding of the software development process by empirical research as well as theoretical concepts; adapting social thinking for developing and improving software development methods
- *Organizing:* Relating software practice to organizational change; opening places of thought for reflecting on software management issues; focusing on how to integrate different groups of actors and their perspectives in information systems development and research
- *Reorienting:* Focusing on use-oriented design; providing rich case descriptions and concepts for understanding software; evaluating software usability and providing innovative directions for use orientation and design in connection with technological advances

This book is written for readers with personal experience in the field of computing, such as software researchers, teachers or practitioners on a student or professional level, and social scientists closely involved with software practice. We, the editors, hope that you, the reader, will easily find your way through this book, according to your own background and priorities. The book's structure and chapter sequence, together with the index, may help you take advantage of the individual contributions in whatever way you find most useful. We welcome your feedback; at the end of the book you will find contact information for all the contributors.

Finally, we would like to express our gratitude to all who helped make this book possible. We thank the Schloss Dagstuhl Computer Science Foundation for enabling face-to-face discourse in a pleasant environment; the "spokespeople" Olav Berthelsen, Jesper Simonsen, and Chris Westrup for helping with the editorial work by coordinating the communication among the authors of parts II, IV, and V; Olav Berthelsen, Jacob Nørbjerg, and their research groups for hosting the Aarhus and Copenhagen meetings; and all the authors for engaging in the joint effort to produce this collection of valuable writings.

Note

1. The title is inspired by Peter Checkland's influential book, which offers a coherent approach relating "systems thinking" to "systems practice" (Checkland 1981).

References

Checkland, P. 1981. *Systems Thinking, Systems Practice*. Chichester, England: Wiley.

Dittrich, Y., C. Floyd, N. Jayaratna, F. Kensing, and R. Klischewski, eds. 2000. *Social Thinking—Software Practice: Approaches Relating Software Development, Work, and Organizational Change*. Dagstuhl Seminar Report 250, September 5–10, 1999. Wadern: Schloss Dagstuhl International Conference and Research Center for Computer Science.

I

Deconstructing

Christiane Floyd

What are the paradigms underlying software practice? What are their origins and consequences? To what extent can they be transformed by social thinking? These questions can be asked from a variety of angles to shed light on different issues. It is not surprising, then, that the first part of this book is heterogeneous. By *deconstruction* we refer to taking apart the interleaved levels of concern involved in software practice in order to take a closer look at a given aspect of software practice, at the same time, drawing on social thinking in a distinct way. Common to all the contributions in this section is an attempt to identify and challenge existing assumptions and ultimately to suggest richer paradigms.

The emphasis of the book is on practice involved in software development. There are many diverse settings for this practice. The object of work may be to develop new software, to enhance or adapt existing software, to find solutions for how to embed software as infrastructure in organizations, and so on. Beyond the immediate concern with products, software development is concerned with promoting the successful use of software. Thus, the practice of software development must be understood in terms of learning and communication processes. Through these processes it is intertwined with software use.

It is questionable whether the use of software should be considered a form of practice in itself. If so, the focus is on the use of one specific product or form of technology. But, beyond that, wherever it occurs, software use is intimately connected with whatever type of work or communication the users are engaged in. This means software developers need to learn enough about the practice of their clients to be able to advise them on appropriate software solutions.

How developers view their own work influences the priorities they set and the course of their development efforts. The views and values of software practitioners are shaped partly through education and partly through the communities of practice they are part of. Of particular relevance in this book is the contrast between the practice of software developers and that of social scientists cooperating with them, whose work proceeds on entirely different premises. To facilitate mutual understanding it is important to look at the scientific and philosophical background reflected in the paradigms adhered to by both groups.

Of the four contributions grouped in this part of the book, two are by computer professionals and two are by social scientists representing different influential schools of thought. Thus, both members and observers reflect on the paradigms underlying software practice.

Chapter 1, "Developing and Embedding Autooperational Form," attempts to provide a conceptual framework for understanding the nature of computer artifacts in the context of human practice. Contrasting action and operation, it reveals a field of tension inherent in design: the unique way that human activity unfolds in the situation and the need to describe operations with a view to automation. To bridge the gap between the social world of situated activity in development and use and the formal and technical world of computer artifacts, designers need to reconstruct the area of interest in terms of what is called *operational form*. Through implementation, autooperational form is made available that is interpreted by users in their situated action.

In chapter 2, "On Foundational Categories in Software Development," software development is viewed by two ethnographers as exhibiting culture and embodying cultural assumptions. As a basic paradigm, design relies on "problem solving"; in other words, it views the world in terms of problems and solutions, ignoring other alternatives. Moreover, design approaches reflect specific cultural assumptions. A case in point is the Scandinavian approach to participatory design that relies basically on discourse and negotiation between the parties involved and thus attributes a positive value to the spoken word. This is quite different from approaches that prevail in the United States. Thus, design approaches need to be embedded in their surrounding culture.

Chapter 3, "Making Use of Social Thinking: The Challenge of Bridging Activity Systems," is centered on the relevance of social theory for software practice. The school of thought under discussion here is activity theory. This approach offers a rich conceptual framework for understanding human activity and the idea of goal hierarchies to shed light on complex activity. So far, activity theory has been successfully tailored to efforts to understand the practices of software use. Now, the suggestion is to also rely on it in order to get a better appreciation of software development. But cooperation between social scientists and software developers is difficult because different goal hierarchies are involved with the two practices. Overcoming these discrepancies will be a major challenge in future development efforts.

Finally, chapter 4, "Challenging Traditions of Inquiry in Software Practice," focuses on how the paradigms shaping the way software practitioners think about human beings in relation to computers affect their communication with customers and users. The chapter draws an analogy between the work involved in requirements analysis and user-oriented design on the one hand and therapeutic work on the other. In both practices, experts need to come to deeper insights in communication and cooperation with a view to helping their client. Two lines of research are sketched. The first—the logical/empirical tradition emphasizing objectivity and rational thought—tends to equate human beings and computer functions. The second—the hermeneutic/dialectical tradition—goes further by bringing into play the subjective horizon of the parties involved and the interchange between perspectives—for example between developers, users, and managers—in various ways. As an example of a key distinction, Maturana and others have introduced the term *autopoietic* to denote living beings, in contrast to *allopoietic* technical devices.

Part I shows that the paradigms underlying software practice cannot be highlighted without utilizing applied epistemology and social theory. These disciplines bring to bear ideas on human thinking, learning, and activity whose relevance goes far beyond software development and use. The chapters in this section contribute to the foundational discussion relevant also for the sections to follow.

1

Developing and Embedding Autooperational Form

Christiane Floyd

Relating social thinking and software practice as we set out to do in this book is a complex endeavor. What do we mean by software practice? How do we want to deal with it? What kind of social thinking do we have in mind? How do we see social thinking related to software practice? Each contribution in this book provides its own answers to these questions. The objective of this chapter is to propose a conceptual framework for the discussion of computer artifacts in connection with human activity. First, I will provide some orientation on how social thinking and software practice can be related to one another.

1 Computing: Bridging the Gap between the Social, the Technical, and the Formal

In what follows the term *software practice* refers to the sum total of activities involved in developing and promoting the use of software. The focus is on *software embedded in social contexts* such as human work and communication. This is not meant as a distinction between these systems and other types of software, but rather as a vantage point from which to look at software. The relevant actors are software developers, managers, vendors, buyers, and users, who, in turn, are engaged in practices of various kinds. The assumption that software practice can be meaningfully considered on its own is not at all obvious. One implication is that the hardware required belongs to a separate area of concern; another is that it is necessary to draw a fuzzy borderline between software practice and related areas such as work design and organizational development. Finally, it should be emphasized that software practice includes all activities promoting software use (for example by coaching, involving key users, or providing technical infrastructure), but not software use as a whole, which occurs as part of diverse human practices.

Software practice varies greatly from one setting to another. For example, we can distinguish research from industry, technology innovation from technology application, the production of new software from the adaptation and enhancement of existing software, the development of standard software from the customization for individual use sites, and so on. Questions of scale also matter: in large firms, software practitioners tend to be in highly specialized work settings, while in small firms generalist jobs are more common, or the firm as a whole is specialized. Also, software practice is shaped by how individual firms cooperate with one another on a local or global scale.

The present discussion is not primarily concerned with portraying the variety of activities involved in software practice. Instead the emphasis is on the objective of software practice: software as artifact to be designed, developed, introduced, or promoted within software practice.

Therefore, cutting across the distinctions made above, I propose to distinguish *levels of software practice* depending on the complexity of the social context relevant to software. These levels of concern, coexisting in time and often nested in one another, require different kinds of skills and give rise to different areas of work for both computer professionals and users. They also entail quite different problems for social reflection, so I suggest viewing social thinking in connection with these levels of software practice.

Against this background I address my topic, which is a conceptual framework for understanding computer artifacts in connection with human activity, highlighting how computing is anchored and how computer artifacts are embedded in human activity. I hope to contribute to ongoing discussions on the nature of the discipline of computing—its object, its scientific core, and its methods—with a view to promoting a discourse with social theory. The sheer diversity of names (*computer science*, *computing science*, *informatics*, *datalogi* ...) as well as the separation in some countries, for example between computer science and information science, point to the fact that there are various complementary or even conflicting views of this discipline. To avoid these terminological difficulties, I will use the term *computing* throughout this chapter in a very general sense.

I will portray computing as a constructive discipline around the development and use of computer artifacts that at its core is concerned in a specific way with form. The notion of form relevant here needs to connect organized human activity and technology development with the strictly logic-based idea of formalization inherent in theoretical computer science. Bridging the gap between the social, the technical, and the formal realms, with the concept of *operation*, I will introduce the notion of *operational form* as a key to understanding what can be reified in computer artifacts. On that basis, I will argue that computing is concerned with producing and embedding *autooperational form*. This means (1) making operational form explicit in the area of interest and (2) making autooperational artifacts available for human use.

In connection with this, I will uncover *operational (re-) construction* as the basic method associated with computing. That is, when engaged in computing, we perceive the area of interest—any part of the natural, the social, or the technical world or a formal universe of discourse—in terms of operational form. Of this we develop a decontextualized model, which, implemented as a program, becomes autooperational when executed on a computer. Thus, choices in design reflect *how* we perceive the area of interest in terms of operational form. While computer artifacts may be designed, for example, as tools, media, or agents, the distinguishing property of these tools, media, or agents is that they are autooperational. When embedding computer artifacts, we create conditions for recontextualizing autooperational form and open up spaces of opportunities for situated human activity.

The view proposed here brings out the inherent connection between design and scopes for choice. While human activity is not determined by computer artifacts, because autooperational form is always interpreted in the use situation, it unfolds in the space of opportunities open to technology users. Thus we make decisions on available options in design. This clearly relates to issues of responsibility to be negotiated as part of software development.

The double purpose I pursue in this chapter is reflected in the structure of the text. Section 2 may be considered a metatheoretical contribution: I will introduce the field of relating software thinking and social practice in a general way, indicating basic questions of interest and distinctions between different social theory approaches as they pertain to software practice. In sections 3 and 4 I present my considerations on developing and embedding autooperational form. Section 5 ties the two parts together by locating the specific conceptual framework I propose in the overall territory of social thinking and software practice sketched earlier.

In both the metatheoretical and the conceptual framework sections, the discussion relates to the works of many authors in computing, social theory, and the philosophy of science, far too many to refer to in an introductory chapter. As an alternative and not without regret, I opted for presenting the argumentation itself, and just point to connections with theoretical stands taken elsewhere. I know this to be problematic but I hope to make the text more intelligible this way.[1]

2 Viewing Software in Social Contexts

For some orientation on how social thinking can be related to software practice, we need to look at software in social contexts. Software development and use, even in everyday settings, necessitate taking a stand on basic questions relating computers and human beings—such as: Can computers, in principle, be likened to human beings? How can the social world be modeled in computing terms? How should computers be allowed to interface with human activity? These questions arise at different levels of complexity in design, and the stand we take on them is embodied in design decisions. On the other hand they are dealt with by social theories in different ways. In what follows, I try to characterize the problems at hand in terms that will hopefully enable the reader to gain a deeper understanding of his or her own questions.

2.1 What Is a Computer?

Let me start with a little anecdote. At a conference on social changes related to information technology the lecturer, a computer scientist, gave an excellent overview of the most recent technical developments, focusing on advanced Web applications. But the first question in the discussion was simply "What is a computer?" Raised by a white-haired gentleman who has lived through the whole era of computing, this question caused considerable embarrassment. Asked in the twenty-first century, it seemed unbelievably naive. Or was it?

After some hesitation the lecturer described the computer as a technical device that can do computations "and of course much more." Clearly he was trying to condense his technical and formal knowledge into a few simple words suitable for a nonspecialized audience. His aim was to describe the computer as an entity in itself, endowed with capabilities provided through programming. As seen from his angle, the basic paradigm of computation, extended from the numeric to the symbolic and the structural realms, gives rise to the whole spectrum of possible programmed behavior.

I interpreted the question instead as relating to issues such as: What parts of the real world can be modeled in computer programs? What kind of reduction is implied? How can computer programs become effective in the area of interest? How are computers perceived in interaction? These issues are fundamental to understanding computers *in use*. They need to be addressed in a way that permits people to make a connection between the full world of human activity and experience and the abstract world of the computational paradigm. I also gave a simplified answer, describing the computer as a technical device capable of storing and executing predefined plans for action.

The gentleman did not speak up again and I do not know which answer came closer to what he had in mind. It struck me how difficult his question was to reply to in spite of some fifty years of debate on humans and computers. Also, his concern was still with "the computer"—perceived as an individual technical agent exhibiting quasi-intelligent behavior—rather than with information technology as a whole.

This incident again confirmed my suspicion that all social reflection on computing rests on understanding computers in the human context. But unlike the lecturer just referred to, I am not interested in dealing with these questions in ontological terms, attributing to the computer an existence of its own. Instead, I prefer to see computers as artifacts and propose to bring in human beings involved in programming them, interacting with them, using them, and so on, as the frame of reference. This implies keeping track of two distinctions. One is Heidegger's distinction of experiencing something as "thing-in-use" (*Zeug*), as "ready to hand" while being immersed ("thrown") in an ongoing activity, as opposed to understanding it as "thing" (*Ding*): an entity "present at hand" with properties that can be described and studied on their own. The other is that between the *development* and *use* perspectives. For software professionals the object of their work is to find and implement a computational structure meeting the needs of users. For users the results of these efforts provide the technical means or environment for performing their own work. Thus, following Leigh Star, software can be regarded as border object shared among different communities of practice.

To appreciate how software mediates between developers and users, we need to be concerned with software development as a human activity, software as a means of reifying aspects of human activity, and software use in the context of human activity. On the theoretical level, this will necessitate an encounter between formal theory underlying the computing field, and social theory about human activity in software development and use.

2.2 Formal and Social Theory Perspectives on Computing

As we have seen, it is not easy to find appropriate general terms for what is of interest. Should the focus be on "the computer"? This is misleading, since it gives the illusion of a stand-alone agent, and obscures how the computer as an agent is instructed by a multitude of interleaved programs. "Software"? No, software is never experienced in itself. "Computer-based system"? Then there is the suggestion of a system, comprising technical elements and more—very problematic. I opt for "computer artifact," but again, there are problems.

From a computing point of view, the term *computer artifact* is not customary. Programs appear as formal, symbolic objects, capable of causing computers to exhibit specified behavior. The emphasis is on the development of hardware and software *systems* or *products*; there is little consideration for their embedding in the human world. The term *system* is used in a technical ("hard") sense, referring to a combination of components on different technological levels that, when active, can assume a large but finite number of possible states, brought about by external inputs and the effect of programs. The term *product* emphasizes that software is a sellable commodity. It entails a host of connotations known from industrial production such as division of work, profit, product quality, and the distinction between product development and maintenance. The category relating products with human activity is *usability*. Thus, people communicating or performing their work with the help of computer artifacts are simply users, regardless of their field of expertise, the context of their work, and their connection with others.

From a social science point of view, the term *computer artifact* conveniently integrates the levels of hardware and software and the connection to other technical components required for a program to become effective, their distinction being of no interest at a use-oriented level of analysis. Social theories provide a conceptual basis for analyzing computer artifacts in the context of human activity, considering them as objects of, means to, or constraints on human communication and work or as constitutive for social change on a large scale. But these theories originate in other fields of interest such as the study of ethnic cultures or of traditional industrial production, they relate to older forms of technology, and they offer no specific concepts for the computing realm. Also, they use their own jargon. For example, the terms *artifact* and *human activity* belong to the vocabulary of different social theories. Can they be used outside specific theoretical frameworks?

These observations suggest that we need to work toward a common language, or rather to find ways of deconstructing and reconstructing concepts used in the different disciplines. But beyond terminology, there is the challenge of bridging the gap between worldviews embodied in the disciplines involved. Computing technology implements the ideal of abstract, objective knowledge, while social theory is faced with the place of this technology in situated and unique human activity unfolding in time.

The formal theory underlying computing is based on foundations in logic, abstract mathematics, and formal linguistics. Also, in the discipline of computing, there are fundamental views equating humans with computers. Even in formulating his basic theoretical concepts, Alan Turing, the most influential thinker inspiring the mathematical science of computation, explained the functioning of his universal machine by likening it to a human being proceeding according to rules. This worldview is shaped by the history of formalization in Western culture since the beginning of Greek philosophy and strongly relates to the philosophical program established by Descartes that eventually gave rise to the rationalistic tradition.

Computing emerged at a time when the discussion throughout the humanities was dominated by the rationalistic tradition. Positivistic philosophy, formal approaches to linguistics, behaviorism as a mechanistic approach in psychology, taylorism in organizations as a way of rationalizing human work, and many other developments provided a scientific environment conducive to extending the central notions of computing into the human and social realm. But while formal theory remains firmly rooted in the rationalistic tradition, the relevance of this tradition to understanding human thinking and activity is subject to hot debate. In the last few decades there has been a tremendous surge of theories challenging its basic assumptions.

Social theory at all levels has rediscovered the situated nature of human activity, shaped by history and tradition and creatively engaged in shaping further development. Not only is the rationalistic tradition unable to account for perspectives related to social relations and power struggles; its assumptions on knowing and acting have also been questioned. The instance of knowing is no longer the individual but the community drawing on a tradition of practice and relying on artifacts. Knowing does not take place "in the head" but is enacted in the body as a whole. Human thinking is no longer seen as essentially governed by rules, but is thought to be rooted in bodily action through images, experience, and intuition. The ideal that all knowledge is explicit, general, static is being given up in favor of assumptions about tacit, situated, dynamic ways of knowing. Strangely enough, computing technology itself and the changes in society triggered by it contribute to shaking the very foundations it was originally built on.

Since software practitioners have to go back and forth between the formal and the social world, a suitable treatment of software practice must comprise both theoretical perspectives. In what follows, I will not argue for combining these perspectives into one common supertheory but for creating a dialogical framework, taking both perspectives into account. Such a framework has to allow for the formal properties of software on the one hand and for the social context of their development and use on the other.

2.3 Levels of Software Practice and Social Reflection

In keeping with the proliferation of computing technology, software practice is all around us. As initial orientation for relating software thinking to social practice I propose to distinguish technology levels according to the complexity of relevant social contexts for software. These levels can be associated with the emergence of technologies in time, but from a current perspective, they coexist and often are nested or linked in one system. They will be outlined here in terms of the basic technology, the skills required of software practitioners, the guiding metaphors used in development, and the social context relevant to theoretical reflection.

The basic level is that of *programs* for automating specified computations or algorithms, designed to solve a formal or a real-world problem. Programming relies on a clear separation of the human and computer elements. While this is the oldest form of software practice, it still survives today in the form of automata or agents performing a function as part of an encompassing system. The essential demand is that the program fulfills the functional and technical requirements. The basic skills required are to master the programming language and the programming environment. There is hardly any social context. Machine, system, and automaton are guiding metaphors. The computer is used to automate separable parts of individual work in both scientific and commercial computation. The social reflection involved pertains to likening or contrasting human faculties of individuals with those of computers.

Interactive workplace systems enable a close intertwining of human work steps and computer functions and give rise to choices in design. Beyond personal computing, local networks allow for providing computer support for groups. This is the realm of systems design with users. In addition to the skills required for programming, this requires an understanding of human cognitive faculties, of ways and styles in performing and structuring work, and of the place of artifacts in human problem solving. On the technical level, interface and local network technology come into play. Questions of usability arise in connection with the need to design the human-computer interface. The relevant social context is human work and communication processes, and the guiding metaphors for computer artifacts are tool and medium. Thus, it is here that we find reflection on computers in the context of human activity.

Enterprise information systems codify structural aspects of organizations. They come with problems of integration and (organizational) standardization on a large scale. Usually it is not a question of developing new systems but of adapting existing systems, so design pertains to how to introduce the system in the organization at hand. Technical challenges lie in using components for tailoring systems to specific needs. The relevant social context is organizational development. Software practitioners are engaged in organizational intervention, being perceived as agents of change. They also have the role of mediators between organizations and vendors. There is less scope for design, because existing structure within organizations provides constraints on choices, and the introduction of software also promotes standardization across organizational boundaries. The relevant social reflection pertains to technology as upholding structures in organizations.

Computational infrastructure is the basis for the networking of communities within or across sites. The emphasis shifts from the individual computing artifact to families or landscapes of artifacts, accessible from particular technical platforms and allowing or inhibiting communication and cooperation. Infrastructure is associated on the one hand with technical standardization and compatibility; on the other, it is closely related to working styles and the culture of communities, which is embodied in shared practices of technology use. A community can be well defined and localized in one physical setting, or it can be spread out geographically and be a loose assembly of people sharing some kind of interest. Associated with infrastructure is the notion of ecology, emphasizing the coevolution of individual components or parts and the close intertwining of the technical and social levels. In keeping with this, there is the notion of "growing" rather than of designing infrastructure.

Networks of humans and computers provide open spaces for opportunities shared globally with unknown participants. The basic technology is the Internet and the World Wide Web, associated with as-yet poorly defined Web-engineering methodologies. Technological challenges include security problems, data communication on a large scale, and mass data management. Information technology becomes a cultural technology, comparable to book printing or mass media, and gives rise to profound social changes, making information a commodity and allowing communication to overcome space and time, thus giving rise to globalization. This level of software practice involves developing Web sites and Web applications in keeping with the needs of the emerging information society. Through suitable portals and links, it becomes possible to access a seemingly unlimited world of nodes that provide knowledge and services of various kinds. Social reflection on technology pertains to the nature of networking and the interlinking of human and technical nodes in networks.

As shown, individual theories can be related to different levels of software practice. In what follows the emphasis will not be on any specific level, but on how to relate the technical and the social realm.

2.4 Theoretical Stands in Relating Computers and the Social Realm

In this section we look at social theory as inspiration or guidance for understanding problems arising in software practice and bring out differences between families of theories, as they become relevant to computing. Several distinctions or fields of tension are elaborated so as to show how they become influential in software practice.

Logical/empirical or Hermeneutic/dialectical This distinction between families of social theory approaches is made by Nissen in this volume (see chapter 4) and is in keeping with the one made earlier in this chapter. As we have noted, viewing the social world in the spirit of the rationalist tradition creates conditions of uniformity that encourage the use of computing concepts in the social world or the modeling of parts of the social world in computing terms. Also, in the logical/empirical tradition technology development appears to be governed by objective facts or constraints. Adopting a hermeneutic/dialectical viewpoint on the other hand leads to an inherent field of tension and necessitates bridging the gap between two worldviews in software practice. Many authors who take a critical stand in the hermeneutic/dialectical tradition tend to subordinate the formal/technical world to the social world, so that technology appears plastic and molded according to the interests and values of its owners.

Objective/realist or Subjective/constructivist This distinction in social theories is related but not identical to the one made above and has a special significance for software practice. Unlike social reflection, software practice is not content with observing, but is concerned with bringing about change. It is in itself constructive, in that it is oriented toward developing, introducing, and enhancing computer artifacts. A basic distinction is between approaches that suggest that technological change essentially mirrors and reinforces social structure and views that concentrate on the innovative and inventive character of software practice. This field of tension also relates to relying on ontological argumentation or taking an epistemological stand. Typically, the former will emphasize the constraints resulting from things as they (supposedly) are while the latter will point to opportunities related to design. The two approaches thus imply different role models for software practitioners.

Abstract or Concrete Social theories relevant to computing differ in terms of their methodological stance. In particular, some theories aim at staying close to the situated phenomena as encountered in the field of observation, while others use abstractions for categorizing these phenomena. In connection with software practice, relying on abstract categories is closely related to modeling. Since any program embodies a computational model of the area of interest, modeling is inherent in computing. But the computational model is not necessarily derived from an explicit model of the application area. Social theory approaches providing inspiration for methods in software development will suggest quite different ways of proceeding. On the one hand, explicit modeling creates more distance from the social world and brings about distortions, since the abstract categories used in modeling shape the view of reality represented in the model. On the other hand, explicit modeling is an opportunity to negotiate how the model should be constructed, as well as what features of reality should be represented and how.

Actor-oriented or Systemic This distinction relates to how social theories portray the social world. Actor-oriented approaches bring out the scope of influence, highlight the opportunities and commitments of individual or collective actors, and clarify the relationships and conflicts between them. Systemic approaches emphasize the integration of actors into a coherent whole and concentrate on emergent systemic properties. In connection with software practice, these theoretical approaches are often perceived as being connected to interests of different groups. While actor-oriented approaches are usually associated with bringing out the interests of the different parties involved and are fundamental to participatory design, systemic approaches are taken to stand for management positions. A new category, particularly relevant for studying social changes around information technology, is the *network*. It can be used with either an actor-oriented or a systemic interpretation and has the potential for mediating between them.

Technology as Structure or Agent To understand software in social contexts, it is also important to see what status technology is assigned in the theoretical approach. Again, there are two extremes with a field of tension. Is technology considered part of the environment of the social world (and vice versa)? If so, how are they related to one another? Or are technology and the social world seen as integrated into one whole? And if so, what is their mutual dependency and what do they have in common? There are at least two ways of looking at technology in connection with the social world. One approach emphasizes its potential for *reifying structural aspects* of human activity. Here, technology has the essentially passive role of an external memory for human learning and action, freezing routines that become "alive" only in the context of situated use of technology. The other dimension is *agency attributed to technology*, recognizing that artifacts have their own way of becoming effective. If so, is technical agency taken to be similar to or different from that of human beings?

The reader may use these distinctions and fields of tensions as ways of deconstructing and assessing proposals for understanding software in social contexts. The last field of tension takes us directly to the conceptual framework I am about to present in the rest of this chapter.

3 Developing Autooperational Form

The need for a conceptual framework first became clear in looking closely at the problem of establishing requirements for interactive software systems. These systems involve three types of entities, which have to be understood in different terms: organizations (in terms of tasks), people (in terms of activity), and computers (in terms of functions). Whenever we make design decisions on the functionality and interface of computer-based systems, we affect the fields of tension between these entities and we take a stand—often implicitly—on the nature of their relationship. It seemed important to develop a terminology that allowed us to mediate between them without blurring their differences. Later, this conceptual framework was elaborated and expressed in more general terms so as to be applicable to other areas of computing as well.

3.1 Bringing out Operational Form

In what follows, I use the concept of operational form as a key to understanding how human activity can be computerized and how computer artifacts can be embedded in social contexts.

Let us first look at the concept of *operation*, which is established in different domains, all relevant to the discussion here. In organized human activity (ranging from the military, to medicine, to enterprises of different sorts), it refers to proceeding in the situation based on planning with a specified objective. In mathematics, it denotes a computation step in a formalized and interpretation-free manner. In connection with technology, it refers both to the working of machines and to making a machine work. In activity theory, it refers to quasi-automated routines acquired by people through experience with action, the idea being that the levels of action and operation can be analytically separated through scientific observation.

Common features of the concept of operation as used in these domains are:

- Operations are rooted in repeated human action of individuals or groups.
- Fundamental to operations is the separation of description and performance.

- The description of operations makes well-defined ways of proceeding possible that can be taught, planned, and enforced.
- The performance of operations is embedded in situated human activity.

In what follows, we will concentrate on developing a concept of operation suitable for the realm of computing, and focus on the interplay of description and performance already implied in other uses of the term.

The description of an operation requires an observer. This does not necessarily imply an individual carrying out the observation ad hoc; more often there is a tradition of description used as a reference for common action. Descriptions allow for disconnecting operations from human beings acting in situations in a unique way.

Through description operations are given a name, they are characterized and distinguished from other operations or actions. Individual operations are described in terms of material or abstract objects to be dealt with, of prerequisites needed for the operation to be performed, of effects to be obtained, of rules that govern the operation, and of means to be used. Descriptions are always made for a purpose. They can be used for teaching, planning, and coordinating human activity.

Operational form results from connecting the descriptions of individual operations in terms of temporal, logical, and causal relations. This connection again needs an observer. Operational form can itself be considered an operation on a higher level, thereby leading to complex, interdependent structures of operational form.

The performance of described operations requires tailoring situated activity with a view to fitting the conditions and constraints specified in the description. Thus, operational form does not specify the activity itself, but the demands on activity in terms of well-defined results.

The emergence of operational form is essential for all organized human activity in our culture, so much so that "operational thinking" evokes the basic paradigm of the Western way of dealing with the world. Computing relates to operational thinking in a particularly poignant way:

- Operational thinking in mathematics, philosophy, and language has led to the notion of algorithm, which is fundamental to expressing operational form through programming.

• Operational thinking in science and technology has given rise to new ways of understanding nature and to the development of machines on the basis of specified operational form.

• Operational thinking in organizations is at the root of professional training and standards in diverse fields of human practice.

Before shedding further light on how computing connects the world of human practice, formal method, and technology through operational form, we need to look at artifacts making operational form available to human activity.

Description of Operational Form through Symbolic Artifacts Though operational form can be traced in oral tradition, it becomes vastly more effective when codified in writing. Thus it can be transferred through symbolic artifacts across space and time.

Operational Form in Situated Action Predefined operational form is interpreted in situated action, thereby bridging the gap between situational needs and specified objectives and constraints. Also, operational form is constantly refined and revised through human action. The more generally applicable operational form is intended to be, the more its description will need to be unambiguous and interpretation-free, and the more emphasis is likely to be placed on making it unchangeable.

Performance of Operations by Technical Artifacts If operations and their connections are described in an interpretation-free manner by specifying only formal properties (such as input and output, rules for performing the operation, and so on), they can be mechanized and therefore executed by technical artifacts like machines. Unlike human actors, technical artifacts as nonhuman agents merely execute operations; they only interpret them to the extent that this interpretation itself is specified as operational form.

Artifacts Opening Spaces of Opportunities for Situated Action On the one hand, operational form is reified through artifacts; on the other, when used in situated human activity, the same artifacts give rise to new opportunities, conditions, and constraints for human activity. The result can be perceived in cyclical terms, with situated activity leading to operational form, this being reified in artifacts, these opening new spaces of opportunities, which unfold through situated action, again leading to operational form, and so on.

Thus, operational form is associated both with symbolic artifacts through description and with technical artifacts through performance. The distinctive feature of software is that it is symbolic and technical at the same time. Thus, software can be studied along both dimensions suggested in the previous section. As symbolic artifact it has the potential of codifying operational form, which is taken to correspond to the part of the social, technical, or natural world of interest. As a technical artifact, it has the potential to execute formally specified operations. Some important steps are still needed, however, to tailor the general arguments proposed so far to the realm of computing:

- Computing is concerned with informational operations, dealing with informational objects and associated with prerequisites, effects, conditions, and rules that can be specified in terms of information.
- Computing rests on making operational form explicit and decontextualized. That is, where operational form is already found, for example in social contexts, it needs to be specified in detail. Otherwise it needs to be invented so as to fit or simulate the area of concern.

To sum up, I suggest that the software computer as a technical agent can replace a human being in terms of operations, not in terms of actions. The question then is, what is new about a computer as opposed to other machines executing operational form? This will be pursued in the next section by showing that computer artifacts are not tied to fixed operational form but are instructed by modeled operational form embodied in computer programs.

3.2 Operational (Re-)construction and Autooperational Form

In the field of computing, method tends to refer to prescriptions like top-down or bottom-up design procedures or to the use of certain higher-level languages and diagrams, which may be incorporated into a comprehensive approach to software development. Instead we will reflect on the basic paradigms implicit in software development so as to meet the needs of an application. The crucial step to be taken is to *model* operational form. This constructive activity relies on modeling concepts and on ways of applying these concepts to the area of interest. The overall process of modeling operational form will be called *operational (re-)construction.* We start from the following assumptions:

- In connection with computing, the relevant area of interest is considered in terms of operational form.
- Modeling, a constructive process, is inherent in computing.
- Computing is concerned with reproducing existing operational form and inventing new operational form, the boundary between these two concerns being indistinct.

Operational form can be (re-)constructed in different ways or styles, which have been consolidated in modeling concepts belonging to so-called programming paradigms. The *procedural style* rests on modeling operational form through standardized procedures or functions operating on collections of informational entities. The *object-oriented style* views informational entities or objects as the starting point for modeling, and provides a repertoire of connected operations associated with objects that can be combined in flexible ways. The *constraint-oriented style* is only concerned with specifying the desired effect of operations on informational entities and leaves the operations themselves open. Irrespective of the modeling style adopted, operational reconstruction implies specific ways of dealing with the area of interest.

Building Informational Objects and Operations This involves deciding what should be included in the model, how it should be represented, and how it should be connected to the surrounding world in informational terms. Relevant objects may be abstract or material things in the natural or social world or in a formal universe of discourse. Operations need to be chosen so as to bring about observable changes by natural or technical processes or by human activity. Where computing is used to deal with problems of the real world, informational objects and operations are often used to substitute for their material counterparts. Considering something informational means making explicit an informational content that so far has been implied, often replacing sensual or bodily ways of dealing with the world with abstract, intellectual ones. This in turn is the basis for deciding which phenomena and events should be used as data to represent the informational content and attributes of objects and operations.

Specifying Objects and Operations in Discrete Terms Computing invariably has to do with identifying and standardizing discrete operational steps and grouping them into complex formalized procedures, which give rise to algorithmic structures to be executed on a computer. Objects need to be specified in terms of discrete attributes. Both space and time are modeled in discrete terms. Classifications are used to separate related cases in the area of concern or to distinguish states. Thus, discretizing is not only implied by the digital nature of technology but inherent in the process of modeling operational form.

Integrating Objects and Operations into a System In computing two levels of system formation need to be distinguished and related: the *computer system*, consisting of hardware and software parts, and the *referent system*, consisting of the part of the technical, natural, or social world that is modeled, affected, manipulated, or simulated by the computer system. Forming a computer system is inherent in computing. On the software level it consists of the informational objects and operations obtained through modeling and their connection to the technical environment through technical signals. The notion of a referent system is less obvious. Clearly, a referent system can and must be considered when computer systems are used to simulate or control natural or technical processes. But where software is embedded in social contexts, it is a question of the social theory adopted, and more specifically, whether the social world is considered as a system and if so, how.

The result of operational (re-)construction is an operational model of the area of interest that can be reified through description in a suitable symbolic form. To bring about the operation of a computer, such descriptions must be expressed in programming language, allowing for the unambiguous statement of operational structures (algorithms and data structures) corresponding to the operational model, thus leading to *autooperational form*. The term *autooperational* is deliberately chosen by analogy to the term *automobile* for "car," denoting a technical device moving on its own. The suggestion is that the computer is a device operating on its own (energized by electricity, of course), instructed by operational form described in programs, and triggered by situated human activity in use.

4 Embedding Autooperational Form

Embedding autooperational form in social contexts has a structure and an agency dimension. On the one hand, autooperational form is interpreted in human activity; on the other, it becomes effective when executed on a computer. Note that a clear distinction between *actors* and *agents* is implied, the former term being reserved exclusively for humans, while the latter is applied to nonhuman technical agents.

The common feature of all computer operation is that it is based on a model representing a system of discrete, interacting informational elements. How these are modeled, and how this model is related to the social context of use, accounts for the tremendous variety of existing computer artifacts and is the central issue in design. Since all operational form rests on reductionist models of entities carrying informational attributes, the modeling concepts shape the way we think about the world. The relation of formal models to reality is not given but constructed in the design process. This involves deciding which aspects are included in a model and how the model is to become operational in use.

Perhaps the most important question is the following: What kinds of interaction between human actors and autooperational agents do we allow for? We cannot discuss this without taking a stand of our own, referring to our basic values. Since we are manipulating the scope for humans to take responsibility in situated action, serious ethical considerations are at stake. In the rest of this section, we touch on some fundamental concerns that relate to embedding autooperational form.

Design and Scopes of Choice A basic concern in design is modeling operational form with a view to human use. This requires that the entities to be modeled are perceived in their social context and that the human-computer interaction fits the needs of the situated activity. Design rests on the possibility of making *choices*. And through design, the choice parameters of users are influenced. For example, if computer artifacts are designed as tools or media, the idea is usually to increase the scope of choice for human users. This is not so obvious in workflow systems, where the idea may be more to constrain the scope of choice available to users. Also, when we consider computers as artifacts, they are designed to mediate human activity. Here, autooperational form is inevitably interpreted in situated action, leading to creative forms of computer use. On the other hand, designing software as intelligent agents is associated with the idea of allowing them rights and a scope of operation comparable to those of humans. Thus, design influences but does not determine the available options.

Autonomy versus Rules Since software design rests on bringing out operational form, it is intimately connected with rules. There is an entity responsible for setting up rules, a human who makes or identifies rules (for example, the software developer complying with the wishes of the customer), an entity that imposes rules, often a nonhuman agent (the computer controlling work processes or technical systems), and an entity that carries out rules, either human or technical. Imposing automated, formalized procedures through computers brings about a new quality. While in general, the rules imposed on human activity have to be sufficiently clear and unambiguous for humans to follow, here they must be formulated in machine-interpretable terms. While humans interpret rules as they apply to the needs of the specific situation, programs always operate according to their predefined model. And while humans tend to associate rules with exceptions, computers do not.

Automating or Informing To allow for the use of computer artifacts in different situations, the designer must have a mental picture of all possible situations and a sufficiently rich understanding to allow for any potentially relevant activity at any time. There are two basic options for embedding formalized procedures in the richness of human situations. One is to attempt to accommodate all possible use situations in a formal model and to automate a set of rules for how to proceed according to this model. The other is to leave the use context open and to offer a repertoire of resources to use in self-organizing work, thus contributing to making the situated activity more informed.

Ways that Autooperational Form Becomes Effective In use, autooperational form becomes effective in different ways. For example, it may be supportive or controlling, informative or instructive, simulative or directly affecting reality. I do not know a good classification scheme, but we need to work in this direction, as the proliferation of computing technology proceeds further and further. Perhaps we need something akin to speech act theory in the philosophy of language: an operational model–effect theory that would provide us with conceptual categories for discussing how computers interfere with human activity in situated use.

Populating the World with Autooperational Agents In my view, computer programs in operation belong to a novel category of entities. If I were a Popperian interested in ontology, I would call for a "fourth world" consisting of human-made autooperational artifacts. Staying close to software practice, I would rather point out that by making a host of interconnected software systems of different types available, designers enable complex styles of human-machine interaction where the full consequences of human action triggering computer operation, and the mutual rights of human actors and technical agents in networks, are clear only to specialists. This calls for increased attention to security and transparency.

Viewing computing in terms of making autooperational form available does not, in itself, suggest a way of dealing with these ethical issues, but it does make it possible to discuss them appropriately so as to raise awareness of the problems involved.

5 Autooperational Form as a Way of Viewing Software in Social Contexts

As this chapter comes to a close, the conceptual framework offered here needs to be related to the different levels of software practice distinguished and assessed in terms of the theoretical positions proposed in section 2.

The idea of developing and embedding autooperational form is relevant for all levels of software practice distinguished according to their social contexts. But of course, operational form comes about in different ways, and the design scope is not always the same. In particular, complex social and technical contexts are associated with standardization, usually imposing limits on design. Programs describe and execute operations on informational objects in a largely decontextualized way. Interactive systems reflect operational form pertaining to how individual work steps can be interrelated with computer functions and how cooperation and coordination can be carried out in groups. Enterprise information systems codify operational form underlying, for example, workflows and business processes. Infrastructure embodies operational form related to combining the use of different artifacts and components. Networks provide operational form for relating different human actors and technical agents.

Although the position taken here does not claim the status of a social theory, it can be located in the territory of social reflection. It belongs to the hermeneutic/dialectical tradition, bringing out, as it does, the complementarity of situated action unfolding in time in unique ways and operational form, stating general decontextualized principles. It is constructivist in that it portrays software development as a creative process in terms of the scope of choice available, but it does not blind itself to existing structures that are expressed in terms of operational form. It is certainly abstract, since it provides analytic categories for connecting computer artifacts to human activity. Operational form lends itself to an actor-oriented or a systemic view, depending on whether the emphasis is on how it is interpreted in human activity or on how it is constitutive for integrating the elements of the system into a whole.

The main purpose of the framework, however, is to contribute to an understanding of technology as both structure and agency. The concepts offered here make it possible to discuss these dimensions concretely as they relate to software. On the one hand, operational form is a specific way of codifying structure that can subsequently be interpreted in human activity. On the other hand, understanding technical agency in terms of operation rather than in terms of action offers a way of relating human and technical agency that avoids the strong symmetry implied in regarding the two as equivalent.

My aim in this chapter has not primarily been to urge adoption of the terminology proposed, but to increase awareness of the distinctions implied. For software practitioners, this discussion should provide a better idea of the social context, as it relates to what is modeled in computer programs. Social thinkers reflecting about software practice may acquire a richer understanding of the way software relates to the social world. Above all, I would like to promote a view of the computing discipline that makes it possible to address the connections between the formal, the social, and the technical worlds in a suitable way.

Notes

The conceptual framework reported here was deeply influenced by several doctoral theses that I had the privilege of supervising. In particular, I have been inspired by the work of Reinhard Keil-Slawik, Fanny-Michaela Reisin, Reinhard Budde, Heinz Züllighoven, Guido Gryczan, Ralf Klischewski, and Yvonne Dittrich, listed here in chronological order, from earliest to most recent dissertation projects.

The reflection on how to relate social thinking and software practice has benefited greatly from discussions with Wolf-Gideon Bleek, Ralf Klischewski, Bernd Pape, and Ingrid Wetzel, all associated with the groups for Applied and Social Informatics and Software Engineering at the University of Hamburg, while I was writing this chapter.

1. The conceptual framework presented here has been published only in German so far, first as a contribution to a workshop on the philosophy of science (C. Floyd, "Autooperationale Form und situiertes Handeln," in C. Hubig, ed., *Cognatio Humana-Dynamik des Wissens und der Werte*, 237–252 (Berlin: Akademie Verlag, 1997) and then as part of a study text for students in informatics (C. Floyd and H. Klaeren, *Informatik als Praxis und Wissenschaft*, Tübinger Studientexte Informatik und Gesellschaft (Tübingen: University of Tübingen, 1999). For those who are interested and who read German, I would like to point out that this study text goes well beyond the scope of the present chapter. It demonstrates connections to the origin and history of computing and discusses the contributions of many authors who have dealt with issues relating to my line of argument.

2

On Foundational Categories in Software Development

James M. Nyce and Gail Bader

Anderson (1994) describes the design-and-development process (and community) as bounded by a preoccupation with "problem and solution." In other words, this process is seen as a relatively straightforward problem in information engineering and one for which a more-or-less "elegant" solution can be arrived at. The design-and-development process, for those who take part in it, represents a "scientific" problem that can be solved using methodical information gathering and rule-bound (processing) procedures.

Anderson (perhaps because he assumes this is inevitable) spends little time on ends and goals. He more or less equates the design-and-development process with a technological agenda. "Problem" and "solution" in the design-and-development community do default almost immediately to questions of technology—that is, to questions about kind, number, and procedure. This step by step process defines and redefines what the technological constraints are and in this way leads to a particular choice. As this occurs, what gets forgotten is that "any account that takes the properties of a particular technology as its starting point . . . becomes caught up in . . . practices that generate and sustain the objectively given quality of those" technologies (Wynn and Katz 1997, 306). In other words, once solution and problem coincide with technology, there is little reason to look elsewhere. In short, technology, not the social world whose product it is, frames both the questions and the answers designers and developers come up with.

In this chapter, we will draw on some of the software development projects that we have worked on over the past seventeen years. Our role in these projects was typically that of "ethnographic observers," documenting the design, development, and use of software programs. On some projects, we took a more active role in design and development; we will identify those projects when we discuss them in more depth. The majority of these projects focused on education and the development of software for teaching and learning. What all these projects have in common is that they focus on the software development process and the interaction between "developers" and "users." Sometimes these were "technical" developers (i.e., software engineers) and "content" developers (i.e., teachers developing the educational material and requesting particular technical capabilities). Sometimes the categories of developer and user were collapsed, as when teachers both "develop" (i.e., create software design) and "use" the software as they teach to their students. In all these cases, we studied what happens when developers and end users together create, evaluate, and make use of (software) tools.

Much of the material in this chapter comes from the Access Project (Bader and Nyce 1998; Graves 1995; Nyce and Bader 1995, 1993). In this chapter we will focus on the "teacher developers/users," the design and development of a multimedia corpus for American history and literature, and the high school student users. Data will also be drawn from the Brown University Library project (Graves 1995). This project was a study of work practices by university librarians in relation to the manual card catalog just prior to the introduction of an electronic, online card catalog.

Data will also be drawn from the Intermedia Project (Beeman et al. 1987). This project studied the development of two large multimedia corpora for use in the college classroom. The data used in this chapter will focus on the design team and university faculty as developer/users. Our role in this project was not merely that of observers. As members of the design-and-development organization, we were also involved in formative assessment.

Data is also drawn from some ten years' observation of participatory design (PD) efforts in Sweden. In particular, we will use data from a series of medical informatic projects (Sjöberg and Timpka 1998; Timpka, Sjöberg, and Svensson 1995; Timpka et al. 1992). Here again we both studied and took part in a series of design-and-development efforts.

In these studies, three qualitative methods (participant observation, informal as well as structured interviews, and document analysis) were used. Participant observation is a set of methods based on learning the subjects' world by participating in, observing, and questioning them about their routine actvities. At times, survey data was collected and used as well.

For designers and developers, the need to understand design and development as a scientific, engineering problem is self-evident. When design and development are framed this way, members of this community tend to think about and to use ethnography as a means of "solving problems." In the design-and-development community, however, the definition of "problem" takes an instrumental and pragmatic turn. Because of this, the purpose of ethnography as the design-and-development community sees it is to provide "usable" information that will allow "better," more "elegant" systems and applications to emerge. However, ethnography can bring to the design-and-development community something more valuable than this. A strong ethnography can help designers and developers become more aware of the framework within which they operate. Rather than assume homogeneity and thereby reduce failure to a series of accidents (individual and collective), ethnography can raise questions about the categories, resources, and rules that inform what we call design-and-development work and makes particular forms of them (we will use PD as an example) seem legitimate and credible.

The Development Process

The development process for designers and developers represents a natural frame of reference. What this means is that work divisions, methods, and procedures are seen as logical and reasonable ways of proceeding with the task at hand. Further, the idea that the development process is an eminently rational procedure is confirmed, reaffirmed, and validated through all the work designers and developers do. This natural order of things is so constituted that for designers and developers "analysis," "problem," and "solution," as well as the social, are read, equated, and satisfied through technology. In other words, software designers and developers define design and development as a scientific, engineering problem, and this is taken to be the natural order of things.

As a result, designers and developers are very concerned with problem identification and problem solving. This is typically where they see the usefulness of social science research. "Thick description" or, even better, a numerical description of behavior, provides designers and developers with a richer, more detailed set of information—one they believe can lead to correct problem identification and solution. The idea that everyday as well as scientific knowledge, stance, and action are always variable and context dependent is rarely taken into account. If this line of thought is considered at all, it is dismissed as "fluffy" social science double-talk that flies in the face of "real science" and common sense. This stance toward knowledge reflects, at least in the United States, how computer science is taught.

The result is that what designers and developers do is *first-order* work. By first-order work we mean that for developers and designers, the world is unquestioningly a place where engineering knowledge "works" and issues like epistemology are defined as irrelevant. Here, critical inquiry is reduced to questions of "how to do it better," and answers to this question rely more on common sense and introspection than anything else. To give but one example, this is where developers and designers involved in instructional technology derive their understanding of what students "need" in the classroom and what they "are like." Designers believe that by talking to teachers, they have reached the bottom of the epistemological barrel. Teachers, they think, know or should know what goes on in their own classrooms.

Developers and designers typcially view knowledge acquistion as a problem of getting enough information to clearly identify the "correct" problems and solutions. For example, in the Intermedia Project considerable effort and cost were expended to make certain that communication "went well." One staff person helped developers understand faculty and helped faculty understand designers. It was felt that few problems of interpretation would crop up if only staff would ensure that clear communication could take place. This may be one reason that software development teams add more and more specialized specialists to development projects. These "specialized specialists" are thought to increase the chances of achieving clear understandings. They can, it is believed, break down the different kinds of work routines or processes involved in tasks, thus providing the hidden information that will (finally) allow a clear view of the practice developers want to know more about. In the Intermedia Project, for example, the content development team included not only the faculty members teaching the courses but also the teaching assistants or undergraduate assistants who worked with the faculty. Teams can involve any number of specialists in the process, including instructional designers, content experts, other teachers, and even, as a last resort, a few students.

This multiplication of knowledge experts would seem to improve the knowledge base for software developers, but, we argue, in fact it does not do so. At least one reason the knowledge base is not improved with the addition of more specialists is that simple addition (1 expert + 1 expert and so on) does not necessarily yield analytic insight. This is particularly the case when it comes to knowledge about one's own practices, because we often cannot articulate exactly how we do things. Experts, like the rest of us, do not know (or cannot say) exactly what they themselves do when it comes to specific elements of practice.

Besides the problem of "taken-for-grantedness," there is the problem of the difference between a domain of culturally defined meaning and an individual enactment of that domain. While one may routinely incorporate a positive remark into a correction given to a student who makes a factual error in the classroom, this one instance of "good teaching" does not begin to cover the whole domain of "good teaching." In fact, one instance of good teaching may involve "supporting" a student, while another may involve challenging students to look beyond themselves. In short, domains of cultural ideology, like the domain that encompasses our enactments of things like "teaching" and "learning," are beyond the grasp of any one person.

What developers and designers in the United States have finessed in their dependence on individual instances is any careful consideration of what consitutes a cultural domain. Current software development practice, for example, implies that working with informants (experts) is the best way to get to the bottom of the epistemological barrel. However, though the addition of different kinds of content experts may seem to partially clear up what is in the barrel, it still leaves us knowing little or nothing about the barrel itself. What informs the domain of teaching itself? Why is something considered, when it comes to teaching, good or bad, effective or ineffective? Do students and teachers even share the same ideas about teaching and learning?

Education theory today does not support merely designating the teacher as the ultimate authority in the classroom or the final arbiter of learning effectiveness (see for example Giroux 1983; Gilligan, Ward, and Taylor 1988). Recognition of the students' role in a teaching relationship requires some attention to their active participation in the teaching and learning relationship (Shulman 1986). All these factors—which are beyond the knowledge of any one individual or even one set of actors—constitute the domain of teaching. Because issues of this nature have not been a priority in the design-and-development community, we tend in analysis essentially to just take our informants' word for it. After all, who knows more about teaching than a teacher? Or who knows more about medicine than a physician?

The relationship between individuals and what they know and practice has been a central issue in anthropology at least since Edward Sapir tackled it in "Why Cultural Anthropology Needs the Psychiatrist" ([1938] 1951). When confronted with a kinship chart (a rule-derived, rule-bound description of familial relations), an Omaha (one of Dorsey's informants) denied that these "universal" rules applied to him (Dorsey 1884). This brought to the surface the issue of which informants (experts) and rules we can "trust," in turn raising the more general issue of whether rule-bound description can be adequate at all when it comes to human action—something most designers and developers take for granted. It also raises, at least for anthropologists, the most interesting issue of all.

Individuals are often unaware of their own basic cultural assumptions and of the relations of power and authority that govern their lives. They are unaware of these things, of course, because they are immersed in them. As Kenneth Burke ([1961] 1996) has argued, few of us believe Edgar Allan Poe when he claimed to have first deduced the principles of ideal poetic form and then, on the basis of those principles, to have written "The Raven." As members of a culture we are busy living our lives, not analyzing or deducing the structure of that life.

To give an example of how practice and thought disjoin in everyday life, let's look for a moment at eating and dieting. People who wish to lose weight are often asked to keep a "food diary." The purpose of this diary is to help them become aware of the routine, taken-for-granted aspects of their life like how, when, where, and why they eat the way they do. We would assume that a person would be aware of this most basic of all activities. Yet a surprising number of people are not.

Taking a "problem-solution" approach toward what users do in their everyday practice ignores these issues and indeed assumes that definable rules must exist somewhere. The result is that the everyday practice of users gets compressed into engineering concepts by the design-and-development community. More precisely, it is framed in terms of "a problem and a solution," and what end users (as well as expert user/developers) say is taken literally at face value. When this occurs, problems about the nature and structure of knowledge and human practice never come to the surface. Instead they are transformed into engineering questions. In having their issues framed as engineering questions, some users are empowered and others are not. Some practices are legitimated; others are not. Some choices are conventionalized and some are not. Structures and practices are represented in certain ways rather than in other ways that could be more useful.

When design and development are framed this way, members of this community are induced to think about and to use ethnography as a means to "solve problems." Also, as Westrup (chapter 5, this volume) has noted, ethnography here is reduced to a realistic strategy (it collects things and "answers" questions). In the design-and-development community, what a "problem" is takes an instrumental, pragmatic turn. In particular, what a "problem" is and how to "solve" it get reduced to a series of practical interventions and practical outcomes.

No longer do software developers have to be concerned with experts who provide "expert knowledge" that other "experts" will deny. Problems of partial social and cultural domain awareness either "disappear" or are banished. Because of this, the function of ethnography, as the design-and-development community sees it, is to provide "useful" information at essential points in the design-and-development process (practical interventions) that will allow "better" systems and applications to emerge (practical outcomes). This is a point that Jirotka and Luff (chapter 6, this volume) make. This turn to realism often reduces ethnography to method (see Bødker, Kensing, and Simonsen, chapter 13, this volume).

The Practical Contribution of Ethnography

We reject this characterization of ethnography. Anderson (1994, 170) suggests that what ethnography can bring to the design-and-development community is something more valuable than "the detailed description of work routines and daily life with which to fix the features of the design." Ethnography can, and has, made a number of contributions of this kind. Nevertheless if ethnography is to contribute in any strong way to design, it must move beyond this stage. What ethnography should do is help designers and developers look at their own, culturally constructed practice of software development.

Anderson (1994, 170) suggests (and we agree) that ethnography can reveal and so challenge "the taken for granted assumptions embedded in the conventional problem-solution framework." Shapiro (2000) makes much the same point when he suggests that ethnography can help solve the problem of what requirements capture "is." The CSCW community's interest in invisible work has so far not extended to the work of design and development itself (Nardi and Engeström 1999). For example, a central trope that informs this work—the notion of "intervention"—is still something we know little or nothing about. In the design-and-development literature "intervention" is portrayed as something much like a scientific "solution" to a technical problem—a logical, disinterested proposal or procedure whose objectives serve everyone equally well. But interventions are not necessarily neutral or value free. Nor is it enough to acknowledge (as the PD literature does) that these interventions reflect power, structural, and ideological differences.

The task is to tease out what intervention "means" for those involved with a technical problem and how this "occurs." Central tropes that define the nature of design-and-development work, like the notion of intervention, are something strong ethnography can bring to the surface.

However, there may be no single or universal answer to this question. This not only casts doubt on whether a basic definition of *intervention* is possible. It also takes us a step closer toward asking what interests and principles in the design-and-development community customarily define both what an intervention is and what success is.

The task, given these ethnographic considerations, is to help both software designers and those who hire them (a link that can no longer be casually dismissed) become aware of the frameworks within which they are operating. The social relations of the design-and-development process can be productively explored using ethnography. The general failure to explore these kinds of issues has led to considerable misunderstanding. For instance, staff critiques of design-and-development agendas are often misinterpreted as resistance to technology per se (in the sense of resistance to technology by nineteenth-century "Luddites"). As an example, our study of the research library was initially informed by the often-repeated fear of some administrators that their staff unreasonably rejected any kind of technology. Although we found no such fears among the staff other than fairly clear-cut and specfic concerns about the ability of the technology to perform essential work tasks, the adminstrators seldom admitted that their staff had, when it came to technology, reasonable, work-related concerns.

We need to ask in analytic and precise terms questions like these: Who is the end user and what is the end user's relationship to the "client" or the representative of an organization paying for the process? Are the two the same? Who has a stake in maintaining or "reengineering" work processes? For example, in the design-and-development community, who is the "user"? Is the user the contracting person (i.e., the authorized agent) who signs papers, authorizes payments, and meets with software developers to establish specifications? Is the user the employee who will be required to use the software or be terminated? Is the teacher or the student the user? If there are conflicts of interest (and there will be conflicts of interest between employees and employers in the United States), whose interests do we speak for?

From this line of inquiry we can move to questions like what consequences does the problem-solution paradigm have for designers/developers and their clients? What is obscured when this paradigm is taken as the natural order of things? What happens when one particular world-view is assumed to be the "natural" or only way to look at things? This is why (and how) things like power, autonomy, culture, hierarchy, and money get muted, masked, or disappeared in the doing of design and development. We would like to argue that we need take a close look at foundational categories—ones that both uphold and have received little acknowledgment within the problem-solution paradigm. Again, a starting point, as Anderson (1994) suggests, would be to look at what the design-and-development community itself defines as "intervention," the kinds of resources that members of this community believe are "necessary" to apply in an intervention, and what constitutes the beginning and end (that is, the solution) of a particular intervention.

To illustrate how ethnography can help answer questions about what informs particular design-and-development agendas (see also Bader and Nyce 1998; Forsythe 1999), we will look at PD. There is little evidence that PD "works"—that is, succeeds in its stated goals (Whitaker, Essler, and Östberg 1991). Given this, it is time perhaps to ask some questions about what supports PD and why it is seen as "effective" (Carmel, Whitaker, and George 1993). It is too easy, once when we start down this road, to reduce PD to an ideological construct (a kind of mirage, perhaps). However, rather than treat PD as essentially an epiphenomenon, one that reflects (and is a product) of a particular historical moment, we will argue instead that it rests and "works" on the basis of some fundamental Scandinavian assumptions (Nyce and Löwgren 1995). In particular, these have to do with rationality, speech, and action.

Participatory Design

PD makes use of prototypes and mock-ups. Nevertheless, it assumes that group work and rational discussion are essential for design and development because it is from them that mutual understanding, consensus, and agreement among stakeholders emerge. Here, consensus or agreement (or discussion by all "stakeholders" in the work situation) results in both an adequate understanding of local work processes and a robust design-and-development cycle (Greenbaum and Kyng 1991; Bjerknes, Ehn, and Kyng 1987; Docherty et al. 1987).

PD, then, rests on a set of Scandinavian assumptions about language and speech. For example, in Sweden speech has the potential to triumph over differences in power, authority, and hierarchy. Because all stakeholders are brought to the table and are allowed to voice their own positions and perspectives, it is believed that inequalities in status, power, and knowledge can be banished, or at least overcome through "rational" discussion.

Often this takes place through an appeal to rules. If a set of meeting rules regarding things like turn taking, making alliances, subject choice, and tone can be agreed on, all the issues that might be problematic (particularly those that might be interpreted as structural like rank and authority) no longer matter or are overcome. To frame a sociotechnological intervention in these terms is very much what PD in Sweden is all about. The end result is that the solutions that emerge from these discussions are, by definition, "rational." That some members have more expertise or power than others is denied because each stakeholder had his or her say.

This makes little sense in the United States. First, the idea that discussion can lead to any change at all would be regarded with skepticism. What is effective and efficient, when it comes to change in U.S. terms, is action, not speech. In fact speech has little or nothing to do in the United States with agency and change. Folk sayings ("Show me you're a man," for example) make this point over and over again.

The idea that speech and discussion necessarily have anything to do with rationalism is equally suspect. Persuasion in American terms, while it may make use of speech, is seldom dependent on (or seen as a voicing of) rationality. Persuasion and argument are seen as having more in common with what salesmen "will do" to make a sale (think of the role the used-car salesman has in America). Thus, unless proven otherwise, speech and argument are seen as having little to do with rational expression.

Then there is the problem of self-interest. Almost any discussion in the United States will invariably turn to a discussion (and accusations) of self-interest. In short, far from overcoming differences and inequality, discussion and negotiation for participants in the United States are seen as horse trading and making deals that entitle some and leave others out. In the United States, having one's say may not matter. Or it may not be "enough." After all, backroom deals do happen and public meetings can be nothing more than a theater piece staged to confirm (display) any number of private agreements.

What is privileged in the United States is any kind of technical discourse. These kinds of discourse are not privileged in and of themselves (for their words or rhetoric). They are privileged because, in the United States, this discourse reveals the factual world as it is. They offer the possibility, Americans believe, of strong, useful revelations about what goes on in the world. In effect, they are privileged because they rest on and embody what Americans take to be scientific knowledge. Scientific knowledge is typically thought of as knowledge that has strong claims to the "truth." This kind of knowledge is taken to be more impartial and fair, because it reflects not special interests but the nature of the world. As a result, in the United States, technical discourse stands the best chance of being taken seriously. In American terms, this is about as close as it ever gets to rational, impartial descriptions of the world.

Claims to "rationality" play a powerful role in design and development in the United States. Workers who refuse to use information technologies "correctly"—that is, as "designed"—or question the wisdom of automating work processes in general or in particular (as in the library example) are often labeled "irrational." Then there is the problem of end-user "failure." Further, struggles between designers/developers and end users can alienate end users (and devalue their vision of the technology under development) or devolve into clashes between different kinds of expertise (e.g., competencies of workers and professionals vs. hardware, software competencies).

Design-and-development efforts in the United States often take the form of negotiating who can make the strongest rhetorical claims about "solution," "rationality," and "technical" competence. This of course privileges designers and developers who believe (and others do too) that design-and-development work and its results have much to do with engineering and science. Also, given that in the United States, development-and-design efforts narrow down almost immediately to issues and questions of technology, it is not surprising that end users, no matter how competent, generally come off second best (for a PD effort in the United States where this occurred, see Blomberg 1990).

In both Scandinavia and the United States, we want to develop software that will be useful and support work processes. Yet we have very different ways of attempting to create a "level playing field"—one that can overcome differences in hierarchy, authority, and power so that both structure and knowledge can emerge that will enable useful, appropriate software to be built and accepted.

To build applications of this kind, PD assumes that a level playing field is necessary, that this can be achieved, and that to do this is comparatively simple. From a Scandinavian point of view, this at best requires only some language work. At worst, it will require a design-and-development effort to come to some agreement about what principles in this linguistic exchange will "guarantee" participant parity and equity.

This is not the case in the United States. The way language is viewed (i.e., it represents a weak, if not suspect, form of action), and the strong, privileged role technical discourse has, throw into doubt whether PD can level the playing field. This raises the question in turn of whether PD can provide either the structure or knowledge necessary to build useful and acceptable applications for the workplace.

This leads us to the question of whether PD is, as it has so often been portrayed, a rational, neutral instrument. Greenbaum (1993, 47), to give an example, writes that the "pragmatic look at things and theoretical reflections [of PD] are largely independent of cultural conditions." In principle and on the ground, however, PD emphasizes equity, reason, reform, and democracy—themes that directly link it to social democracy. Likewise, PD also denies the constitutive power of history and culture (Nyce and Löwgren 1995). As such, PD is both heir to (and part of) the modernist tradition—a tradition that asserts that rule, principle, and procedure are sufficient to understand and govern human events. All this has left PD "ignorant of how power works and therefore open to being dominated by power" (Flyvbjerg [1991] 1998, 234). In short, to rely on rationality and its bedfellows (rule, procedure, appeal, and "fairness"), as PD does in the workplace, does not necesarily make power and hierarchy "go away." In fact, taking the stance PD does risks exacerbating the very problems it wishes to solve (Flyvbjerg [1991] 1998).

PD brings to the workplace, it is believed, institutional reform (Greenbaum and Kyng 1991; Bjerknes, Ehn, and Kyng 1987; Docherty et al.

1987). In theory and practice, institutional reforms are central to the modernist strategy (Flyvbjerg [1991] 1998). This is particularly the case when it comes to making democracy "operate" as PD wishes to do in the workplace. Institutional reform provides rules, resources, and principles (in Sweden these define among other things "right" speech) that presumably help to level the playing field. However, when it comes to PD and the workplace (regardless of what its proponents believe), this is still more a hypothesis than an axiom (Flyvbjerg [1991] 1998).

The question all this raises is whether we should derive methodology only from the design-and-development community's ideology, a culturally and historically specific statement that describes and treats particular things as "real." Or would a design-and-development agenda be stronger (of more use to developers and end users) if it rested on something other than common sense? The issue here is what holds together, informs, and makes design-and-development work (in the abstract and the particular) seem credible. These are questions we have started to answer about other forms of work; it is time, we believe, to start to ask the same questions about design-and-development work.

We have used PD here to illustrate why it is important to look at the foundational categories that underlie the development process (Nyce and Löwgren 1995). We have also shown that ethnography, a strong analytically informed ethnography, can take on problems of this kind. As our example has made clear, the design-and-development process is a set of social relationships, not simply a set of pragmatic operations. As such, this process is not just informed by but is the result of history and culture. As a result, not only do development and design goals differ, but the way we go after these goals, the evidence we use, and the appeals we make, reject, and accept can differ as well.

If the design-and-development community was more aware of what in its own terms defines "legitimate" action, method, and thought, it would be possible to make design-and-development choices on the basis of something other than "common sense." The kind of ethnography we are arguing for would help designers and developers become aware of what they take to be self-evident in their own work and practice. In turn, this would help us all make more reflective choices about the technology we need and how we should build it.

References

Anderson, R. 1994. Representations and requirements: The value of ethnography in system design. *Human-Computer Interaction* 9: 151–182.

Bader, G., and J. Nyce. 1993. When freedom of choice fails: Ideology and action in a secondary school hypermedia project. In F. Dubinskas and J. McDonald, eds., *Electronic technologies and instruction: Tools, users, and power*. National Association for the Practice of Anthropology, Bulletin 12, 66–72.

Bader, G., and J. Nyce. 1998. When only the self is real: Theory and practice in the development community. *Journal of Computer Documentation* 22(1): 5–10.

Beeman, W., K. Anderson, G. Bader, J. Larkin, A. McClard, P. McQuillan, and M. Shields. 1987. Hypertext and pluralism: From lineal to nonlineal thinking. *Hypertext'87 Papers*, 1–20. New York: ACM Press.

Bjerknes, G., P. Ehn, and M. Kyng, eds. 1987. *Computers and democracy: A Scandinavian challenge*. Aldershot: Avebury.

Blomberg, J. 1990. Reflections on participatory design: Lessons from the Trillium experience. In *Proceedings of the Conference on Human-Computer Interaction*, 353–359. New York: ACM Press.

Burke, K. [1961] 1996. Poetics in particular, language in general. In *Language as symbolic action: Essays on life, literature, and method*, 25–43. Berkeley: University of California Press.

Carmel, E., R. Whitaker, and J. George. 1993. PD and joint application design: A transatlantic comparison. *ACM Communications* 36(4): 40–47.

Docherty, P., K. Fuchs-Kittowski, P. Kolm, and L. Mathiassen, eds. 1987. *System design for human development and productivity: Participation and beyond*. Amsterdam: Elsevier North-Holland.

Dorsey, James Owen. 1884. *Omaha sociology*. BAE Third Annual Report. Washington DC: Government Printing Office.

Flyvbjerg, B. [1991] 1998. *Rationality and power: Democracy in practice*. Chicago: University of Chicago Press.

Forsythe, D. 1999. "It's just a matter of common sense": Ethnography as invisible work. *Computer Supported Collaborative Work* 8: 127–145.

Gilligan, C., J. Ward, and J. Taylor. 1988. *Mapping the moral domain: A contribution of women's thinking to psychological theory and education*. Cambridge, MA: Harvard University Press.

Giroux, H. 1983. *Theory and resistance in education*. South Hadley, MA: Bergin and Garvey.

Graves, W. III. 1995. Ideologies of computerization. In M. Shields, ed., *Work and technology in higher education: The social construction of academic computing*, 65–87. Hillsdale, NJ: Erlbaum.

Greenbaum, J. 1993. PD: A personal statement. *ACM Communications* 36(4): 47.

Greenbaum, J., and M. Kyng, eds. 1991. *Design at work: Cooperative design of computer systems*. Hillsdale, NJ: Erlbaum.

Nardi, B., and Y. Engeström. 1999. A web on the wind: The structure of invisible work. *Computer Supported Collaborative Work* 8: 1–8.

Nyce, J., and G. Bader. 1993. Fri att välja? Hierarki, individualism och hypermedia vid två amerikanska. In L. Ingelstam and L. Sturesson, eds., Brus over landet. om informationsoverflodet, kunskapen och manniskan, 247–259. Stockholm: Carlsson.

Nyce, J., and G. Bader. 1995. To move away from meaning: Collaboration, consensus, and work in a hypermedia project. In M. Shields, ed., *Work and technology in higher education: The social construction of academic computing*, 131–139. Hillsdale, NJ: Erlbaum.

Nyce, J., and J. Löwgren. 1995. Towards foundational analysis in human-computer interaction. In J. Thomas, ed., *The social and interactional dimensions of human-computer interfaces*, 36–47. New York: Cambridge University Press.

Sapir, E. [1938] 1951. Why cultural anthropology needs the psychiatrist. In D. Mandelbaum, ed., *Selected writings of Edward Sapir in language, culture, and personality*, 569–577. Berkeley: University of California Press.

Shapiro, D. 2000. Technologies for self-organisation. In Y. Dittrich, C. Floyd, N. Jayaranta, F. Kensing, and R. Klischewski, eds., *Social thinking—software practice*. Dagstuhl Seminar (Schloss Dagstuhl, September 5–10). Seminar Report 250, Wadern, Germany, 76–79.

Shulman, L. 1986. Paradigms and research programs in the study of teaching: A contemporary perspective. In M. Wittrock, ed., *Handbook of research on teaching*. 3rd ed. London: Collier.

Sjöberg, C., and T. Timpka. 1998. Participatory design of information systems in health care. *Journal of the American Medical Informatics Association* 5(2): 177–183.

Timpka, T., J. Nyce, C. Sjoberg, P. Hedblom, and P. Lindblom. 1992. Developing a clinical hypermedia corpus: Experiences from the use of a practice-centered method. In *Proceedings of the Annual Symposium on Computer Applications in Medical Care*, 493–497.

Timpka, T., C. Sjöberg, and B. Svensson. 1995. The pragmatics of clinical hypermedia: Experiences from 5 years of participatory design in the MEDEA project. *Computer Methods and Programs in Biomedicine* 46(2): 175–186.

Whitaker, R., U. Essler, and O. Östberg. 1991. *Participatory business modeling*. Research Report 31. Luleå University, Luleå, Sweden.

Wynn, E., and J. Katz. 1997. Hyperbole over cyberspace: Self-presentation and social boundaries in Internet home pages and discourse. *Information Society* 13: 297–327.

3

Making Use of Social Thinking: The Challenge of Bridging Activity Systems

Victor Kaptelinin

This chapter deals with potential obstacles to utilizing social science methods and concepts in software development. It is claimed that one of the main obstacles is the underlying metaphor of "delivery," an assumption that social scientists can present potentially relevant ideas and empirical analyses to systems developers and expect the latter to take up the insights and translate them into their field. The chapter criticizes this assumption. It claims that usually there is no preexisting social and organizational context of cooperation that would ensure that the contributions of potentially useful social sciences will have an impact on the process of software development. In many cases such a context needs to be created by way of coordinating two fundamentally different practices, those of social scientists and of systems developers respectively. Activity theory is proposed as a theoretical framework that can help social scientists identify relevant software practices and find appropriate strategies of influencing them. The chapter outlines the ways activity theory can be applied for understanding: (1) the structure of software development as an activity that constitutes the object of collaboration between social scientists and software developers, and (2) the structure of users' activities, which are intended to be supported by the system to be developed.

Bridging the Gap between Social Thinking and Software Practice: Success or Failure?

In recent years a number of theoretical, empirical, and applied papers explicitly aiming at bridging the gap between the social sciences and software development have been published (e.g., Bowker et al. 1997;

Button and Dourish 1996; Ehn 1988; Lancaster University and Manchester University 1994; Nardi 1996; Nardi and O'Day 1999; Suchman 1987). It appears the idea of finding ways to establish cooperation between the above areas is becoming widely accepted and is currently attracting more and more attention. The conference titled "Social Thinking—Software Practice" (Dagstuhl, Germany, September 1999) and the present collection of chapters, based on that conference, can also be considered indications of a growing interest in the issue. Paradoxically, however, there is also increasing awareness that research advances, measured by the number of studies conducted, papers and books produced, and so on, have not been paralleled by corresponding changes in actual software practice. About ten years ago Ehn (1988) reflected on whether participatory design projects, such as DEMOS or UTOPIA, could be considered successes. He concluded that those projects could be interpreted both as successes, in terms of raised social awareness of the problems and recognition by the international research community, and failures, from the point of view of development of actual systems. There are reasons to believe that many more recent projects can be characterized the same way.

The lack of tangible practical outcomes of numerous initiatives appears confusing. On the one hand, it is almost self-evident that insights coming from the social sciences can potentially be transformed into design of more useful and usable systems. There are good reasons to believe that the social sciences, with their theories, concepts, and methods, can provide a better understanding of the reality of human use of information technologies. Such insights can help systems developers take into account factors they otherwise tend to overlook, and thus help them avoid serious problems with systems they develop. Therefore, it appears social scientists and systems developers alike are interested in making social science work in software development. Should it be assumed that the limited progress in achieving this goal is perhaps just a temporary problem that can be solved by continuing to follow existing approaches? From my point of view, the answer is negative. The fact that the goal of fruitful cooperation between the social sciences and software development has proved so elusive calls for reflection on the reasons the cooperation has not been more successful and, perhaps, for a reframing of the whole issue.

In this chapter I focus on one potential obstacle that should be dealt with. There is often an assumption, either implicit or explicit, that the division of labor between social scientists and software practitioners can be considered a sort of "delivery" of social science insights. In other words, it is assumed that social scientists are responsible for developing theoretically and empirically based insights into the social reality of the use of technology. Further, they are supposedly responsible for delivering these insights, as well as related information on general requirements, to software practitioners, who are charged with implementing them in actual systems. This position has been criticized before (Rogers 1997) but still appears influential. This chapter calls for a different approach, based on understanding a complex relationship between two practices—those of social scientists and of software developers respectively—each of which has its own underlying theoretical principles, methods, concepts, interests, and priorities. In most cases there is no preexisting division of labor within which the social sciences could take responsibility for certain subtasks within the whole structure of systems development and hope their work will be integrated into the common outcome—that is, better software products.

Therefore, there is a need for the social sciences to reflect on the ways the two practices just discussed can be coordinated. In my view, to be useful the social sciences should be applied at two levels. Studies of how people actually use information technologies have the potential to inform and improve software practice. However, this potential cannot be realized unless appropriate conditions for contributions from the social sciences are created. This, in turn, can be facilitated if social science approaches are applied in order to understand the context in which the process of informing (and, hopefully, improving) software practice is taking place. In this chapter I will present a brief outline of how one particular social science framework, namely, activity theory, could be applied in the two types of analyses: understanding the use of information technologies and analyzing how such understanding can be utilized in software practice.

Activity theory is a conceptual approach that brings into focus socially determined, developing, hierarchically organized, mediated human activities (Leontiev 1978, 1981). According to activity theory, understanding phenomena related to individuals, groups, and organizations requires identifying actors and how they interact with the world and each other. This approach has become the theoretical foundation for a number of studies in the areas of information systems, human-computer interaction, and computer-supported cooperative work (see Nardi 1996). The contemporary interest in activity theory appears to have been spurred largely by a need for an alternative (or, perhaps, a complement) to the currently dominant approach—that is, ethnomethodology. The requirement of presuppositionlessness, associated with an ethnomethodological perspective on studies of the use of technology (Lancaster University and Manchester University 1994), imposes severe limitations on the use of models and concepts. However, there is a need for models and concepts that can capture the social reality in which technology is used, in particular for making the outcomes of social science research understandable and applicable by systems developers. This need explains the ongoing efforts to find a conceptual framework rich enough to capture the complexity of the real-life use of technology but at the same time structured enough to make that complexity manageable and communicable. For instance, several contributions to this volume explore the potential benefits of applying a structured theoretical social science approach (see Bertelsen and Bødker, chapter 19; Fitzpatrick, chapter 7; Korpela et al., chapter 14).

Before moving to the next section I want to emphasize that the perspective outlined in this chapter is limited to specific fields involving the application of social science to software development, namely, human-computer interaction (HCI) and computer-supported cooperative work (CSCW). Other fields, such as information systems, may require different conceptualizations. Also, this chapter is written from a social scientist's perspective, which may explain its focus and concerns as well as possible biases.

Creating Prerequisites for Collaboration

As mentioned, the relationship between the social sciences and software practice cannot be limited to social scientists supplying systems developers with knowledge about users that can be utilized in systems design. According to Rogers (1997), systems developers have their own methods, tools, and expertise to inform their work practice, and, therefore, might resist methods and tools that come from a different domain and sometimes exclude an awareness of the details of software development as an area of practice. It would be appropriate to claim that the relationship between the social sciences and software development can be represented as an interaction between two distinct practices that can be contrasted along a number of dimensions: the settings in which these practices take place, the main objectives of the practices and criteria for success or failure, and the underlying theoretical approaches, concepts, and methods.

There is no preexisting context within which social scientists and systems developers collaborate with each other. They belong to different communities, which have different, sometimes conflicting, values and priorities. Even though they might have common interests, these interests are subordinated to higher-level priorities, which are different for the respective practices. Therefore, the context of such collaboration should be reflected on and possibly constructed anew in each individual case. The context of collaboration can be established in a variety of ways.

The aim of "bridging the gap," for instance, can entail possible organizational arrangements for bringing two settings closer together. In that case the most central issues would be the underlying reasons and the actual and potential forms of promoting cooperation between academia and industry, including the necessary regulations, sources and forms of financing, and organizational structures (intermediaries, venture enterprises, company-oriented education, and so on). If the focus were on the conceptual gap between software development and the social sciences, the central issues would be quite different. They would include the mutual impact of two practices at the highest theoretical level, such as application of information processing metaphors of the human mind in cognitive psychology (Johnson-Laird 1989), the consequences of spreading those metaphors in society in general (Nissen, chapter 4, this volume), or the use of the metaphor of society in artificial intelligence (Minsky 1988). A legitimate issue would also be a comparison of user study methods developed by social scientists as opposed to those developed by software practitioners. For instance, in a comparative analysis of two approaches to user involvement in the design of information technologies, participatory design and joint application design, Carmel, Whitaker, and George (1993) conclude that the difference between these two approaches can to a large extent be attributed to the fact that one of them has its roots in academia, while the other originates in the software industry.

To sum up, "bridging the gap between social thinking and software practice" can mean different things depending on what exactly is meant by the "gap," who is aiming at bridging it, and for what reasons. In my view, to avoid possible confusion it is essential to explicitly address the above questions. One possible way to do so, proposed in this chapter, is by looking at the relationship between the social sciences and software development as influences that reciprocally change their respective practices. Such influences appear to be asymmetrical. Apparently, academics are more concerned with software practice and its actual and potential development than people working in industry (who have other urgent things on their minds) are with social science issues. This makes bridging the gap mostly a concern of academics, both social scientists and computer scientists interested in social science approaches. It must be understood that the context of the social science contribution is not a given. As mentioned above, it should be constructed by those who intend to make the contribution. First, social scientists must be aware of their own reasons for dealing with software development. Such an understanding can help to clearly identify topics of mutual interest and draw an explicit line between what social scientists are and are not interested in. Second, which is even more important, social scientists should realize that software practitioners have their own goals, concerns, values, and priorities. Social scientists' insights can only be heeded if they fit into this system of goals and concerns. Therefore, in order for collaboration with systems developers to be productive, social scientists should have a clear idea of whose practices they want to influence, what is important for those people and organizations, and why those people and organizations might be interested in the collaboration.

It is possible to identify at least three general ways for the social sciences to have an impact on software practice: by (1) providing more efficient techniques for understanding users and translating such an understanding into design, (2) extending software developers' view on how people use technology, making sure potentially relevant aspects are not overlooked, and (3) trying to change the values underlying software development, if necessary. The social sciences have a long history of trying to understand people in real-life situations, and that history shows that acquiring such an understanding is much more difficult than it might seem. These difficulties are often underestimated by systems developers, who by their training are inclined toward an overrational, straightforward view of how people use technology. The social sciences can potentially supply methods and techniques that can be more advanced than the ones currently being used in software development. As noted, these techniques cannot be accepted unless software practitioners realize that their existing tools are not good enough. However, there are reasons for believing that today many practitioners do feel a need to improve their techniques. The recent success of practical methods, such as contextual design (Beyer and Holzblatt 1998) or MUST (Kensing, Simonsen, and Bødker 1998), might indicate that increased competition, high development costs, and increased awareness of the need to understand users all make software developers willing to try new methods.

Another way to influence software practice is to bring to practitioners' attention problems and issues they tend to overlook because of their tendency to ignore what is not directly relevant to the immediate concerns of systems design. The contribution of the social sciences can be to demonstrate that a richer understanding of the social context of using technology can result in more successful designs. Such discussions (which I will later refer to as "constructive criticisms") can improve software practices if they are carefully targeted, in terms of both content and audience. It is critically important that constructive criticisms are offered within a context meaningful for systems developers, such as product development or reflections on systems design.

Finally, a potential way for the social sciences to change software practice is to influence the goals of systems design and its underlying values. A social science perspective on software practice is often not "ideologically" unbiased. In many cases it does not take much effort to reveal an intention to support the users and make sure their needs and interests are taken into account in the design, evaluation, and implementation of information technologies. This attitude was heavily emphasized during the early days of participatory design (Beck, chapter 8, this volume; Ehn 1988), and it has always been a central issue in the area of HCI. According to Cooper and Bowers (1995, 50), "A pervasive, fundamental and highly visible feature of HCI discourse has been its representation of the user and his or her needs." It would be logical to assume that advocacy of users' interests will continue to be a social science concern in the future.[1]

Viewing the social sciences and software development as two distinct practices leads to a conclusion (reflecting an intuitive, commonsense understanding) that simply calling on software developers to make certain values a priority in systems development can hardly be the most effective way to change software practices. As mentioned above, social science contributions are likely to be ignored if they are not considered relevant to the goals of software practitioners. Therefore, ways need to be found for making sure that software developers do consider them relevant. Possible strategies include education and support of computer users, both individuals and organizations, in selecting technologies that really serve their needs. It can be done by helping customers to "vote with their money" for the products that take their needs seriously, or by helping people reflect on how their work can be changed by technology and make appropriate decisions when formulating requirements for a new system or implementing an existing one. The latter approach has been successfully applied, for instance, within developmental work research projects (Engeström 1990). The most radical way for social scientists to make sure their values are actually influencing software development is to take the initiative and directly lead software development projects. The best-known examples of such an approach are early participatory design projects (Ehn 1988).

The above discussion is just an outline of potential ways of ensuring that social science contributions make a difference in the area of software development. To make it more specific, one needs a conceptual framework for representing the two practices and the ways they can influence each other. In the next section I will discuss activity theory as a possible approach that can help develop such a framework.

Framing HCI: A Case for Activity Theory

The relationship between the social sciences and software development became a concrete and specific concern in HCI and related areas in the late 1980s.[2] There seem to be three reasons why it happened at that time. The first was general agreement that high expectations associated with the cognitivist approach as the dominant theoretical framework for HCI turned out to be unrealistic, so that there was a need for extending the conceptual foundations of the field (Carroll 1991). During that time, there was hardly any gap between social thinking and software practice in the area of HCI, since social science—specifically, psychology—was represented by the cognitivist approach based on the information processing metaphor borrowed from computer science. However, an understanding of the limitations of the cognitivist approach stimulated a search for an alternative framework, and possible candidates included those focusing more on the social aspects of computer use.

The second reason was the emergence of a new research field, CSCW, which required explicit attention to the social nature of work. In this field the relationship between the social sciences and software development was a major concern from the outset.

The third reason was Suchman's (1987) criticism of the notion of plans as it had been used in cognitive science, the criticism that led to the idea of the situated nature of human actions, which was convincingly advocated by Suchman.

Both CSCW research and the situated-action approach relied heavily on ethnomethodology as a framework for understanding the flexible, contingent, socially coordinated nature of the human use of technology. As a result, the relationship between software practice and the social sciences, at least in HCI and CSCW, is now often considered the relationship between systems design and ethnomethodology. Arguably, ethnomethodology has been used in the best-known examples of the successful application of social science that have provided deep and useful insights into the reality of everyday work. However, the application of ethnomethodology in HCI and CSCW is not without serious problems (Button and Dourish 1996; Hughes et al. 1994).

The main limitations of ethnomethodology as an approach to understanding actual or potential users of information technologies, as they have been discussed in the literature (Button and Dourish 1996; Lancaster University and Manchester University 1994; Rogers 1997), can be summarized as follows. First, the outcomes of ethnographic fieldwork are difficult to understand for systems developers, because those accounts "are textually discursive and, on their own, offer little guidance as to system requirements" (Lancaster University and Manchester University 1994, 9). Second, ethnomethodological studies pay close attention to the minute details of existing practices. This focus of ethnography creates the potential of finding subtle but important aspects of users' practices that software engineers can overlook. On the other hand, this is exactly why it is difficult to apply the data in systems design, since implementation of a system can cause large-scale transformations of users' practices, which leaves open the question of how relevant the conclusions based on the fieldwork may be for the future.

These limitations appear to be serious enough to raise a general concern about just how useful ethnomethodology can be for systems design. This concern is substantiated by the fact that no systematic strategy for dealing with the above limitation has been proposed so far. The most widely accepted proposals are perhaps to make social scientists actually participate in systems development projects and to make systems developers become familiar with basic ideas underlying ethnography, thus enhancing their understanding of the social organization of work (Button and Dourish 1996; Rogers 1997; Nyce and Löwgren 1995; Cooper et al. 1995). Undoubtedly, having individuals cross the border between computer science and the social sciences provides an extremely valuable resource for both specific systems design projects and the development of interdisciplinary studies (see Bowker et al. 1997). However, it is hardly possible to delegate the task of bridging the gap between the social sciences and software practice to individuals who have backgrounds in two disciplines. The gap does not mysteriously disappear if it is placed "in the head" of an individual. If the differences between the disciplines are so fundamental that in the literature they are often referred to as a "great divide" or "The Northern Passage" (e.g., Bowker et al. 1997), how can individuals manage to reconcile them? On the other hand, if individuals can do that, doesn't that mean the gap can be bridged in interdisciplinary discourse as well?

In my view, other social science frameworks—less atheoretical ones—are needed to complement ethnomethodology in establishing a more productive cooperation between social thinking and software practice. Not only can such approaches help formulate generalizations related to the social aspects of the use of technology and make them more understandable for systems developers, they can also help generate strategies for bringing social scientists and software developers closer together. As mentioned above, several conceptual approaches are being considered as possible frameworks for areas such as information systems, HCI, and CSCW. In this chapter I will discuss activity theory, an approach originated by the Russian psychologists Vygotsky, Rubinshtein, Leontiev, and others (see Nardi 1996; Leontiev 1978), with work beginning in the 1920s. During the last decade activity theory has become the theoretical foundation of considerable research in information systems and HCI, especially in Scandinavia (e.g., Bødker 1991; Engeström 1990; Kaptelinin 1996). Several chapters in the present volume apply this approach to an analysis of the relationship between social thinking and software practice (see Bertelsen and Bødker, chapter 19; Korpela et al., chapter 14).

The basic ideas underlying activity theory were formulated by Alexey Leontiev in his study of the origins of the human mind (Leontiev 1981). Leontiev concluded that the mind emerged in the process of evolution as a special organ that helped organisms survive. Development of the mind, from the simplest evolutionary forms to the human mind, was shown to be determined by the logic of successful adaptation to more and more complex environments. This evolutionary perspective had led Leontiev to the conclusion that the most basic fact that can help understand the nature of the mind is that living beings have needs that make them actively interact with their environment to survive. This interaction creates the context that should be taken into account when attempting to understand the mind, its functioning and development.

This conclusion served as a starting point for Leontiev's analysis of the human mind. This analysis required a different approach, since the notion of biological evolution could not be of much help any longer.

Important as it is, this notion cannot explain the dramatic development of the human mind since the emergence of civilization because this development has not been associated with any substantial changes in human biology. To explain the development of the human mind Leontiev relied on cultural-historical psychology developed by Lev Vygotsky (Vygotsky 1978). As a disciple of Vygotsky, Leontiev played a central role in the cultural-historical psychology of the 1920s and 1930s. This background was undoubtedly a major factor influencing the development of activity theory by Leontiev between the 1940s and 1970s.

I do not intend to give an overview of the basic concepts and applications of activity theory here. Detailed expositions of this approach can be found in Leontiev 1978, Bødker 1991, and Nardi 1996. Space limitations do not allow anything but a brief mention of some of the main ideas underlying activity theory.

The most fundamental assumption of activity theory is that the unit of analysis in studies of mental and social phenomena should be agents (which are called *subjects*, according to the terminology accepted in activity theory) accomplishing their goals by interacting with the world. These interactions, or activities, are hierarchically structured and reflect the functional subordination of subgoals to higher-level goals. By accomplishing progressively higher-level goals, subjects eventually meet their needs. It is impossible to separate the subjective and the objective, because the history of interactions between subjects, who actively and purposefully transform objects and the world, is the process of development during which subjects become what they are. It is of special importance to research in such areas as information systems and HCI that activities are considered to be mediated by socially developed artifacts. Human beings do not need to evolve biologically to increase their potential for adaptation and survival. External "extensions," such as clothes, hammers, eyeglasses, or computers, help people enhance their physical and mental capabilities without changing their biology.

These main ideas determine the general strategy of approaching complex social phenomena. According to activity theory, such phenomena can be understood by identifying subjects, their needs and goals, the structure of their interaction with the world (including other subjects) and the social context in which this interaction takes place, mediational artifacts used by the subjects, and the developmental transformation of activity as a whole.

Software Practice as an Activity

Even though some important software developments take place outside software companies (for instance, in universities), it seems logical to identify software companies as key actors in the area of systems development. Accordingly, a central issue for applied social science approaches in this area is changing the practice within such organizations. That is why the structure of activities in software development deserves a closer look. The structure of the activity of a software company, as of any other activity, is defined by the hierarchy of goals. A simplified hierarchy of the goals of software development in a company can be characterized as follows.

The most obvious goal of software development is writing program code and making sure the program actually works. Accomplishing this goal does not mean the software development is successful, even though it is a basic requirement. However, if this requirement is not met, it is meaningless to apply higher-level criteria, because it is clear that the product cannot be successful. One level up is the goal of making the system usable. Again, accomplishing this goal is just a precondition for moving on to higher-level goals. However, if the system is not usable, one can immediately draw the conclusion that the product is not successful.

Having a functional computer program that also meets usability criteria is necessary but not enough. The next goal is the development of a useful system, a system that meets users' needs. Development of a potentially useful product does not mean, however, that this product will actually be used. If people prefer other products because these products are better—that is, less expensive, more familiar, more compatible with other applications, and so on—potentially useful systems can never be used. Actual use of a system constitutes the basis for accomplishing the top-level goal of the activity in question: development of a profitable product. Profitability in this case is not limited to direct revenues from selling copies of the product. An application can be given away for free but still bring substantial earnings to the company in indirect ways (the Netscape Web browser is perhaps the best-known example).

The hierarchy of goals presented in table 3.1 is very sketchy and incomplete. A detailed analysis of goals and subgoals of the activity of software development in a company would require a substantial effort and would take far more space than is available here. This structure could be elaborated, for instance, by analyzing roles assigned to various people within collective activity as a whole. Also, it should be emphasized that the goals are definitely not accomplished in a linear, bottom-up fashion. Ideally, the sequence of goals should follow the opposite, "top-down" path, but this rarely happens. Software development takes place on several levels at the same time. Finally, the extent to which a software product should meet a criterion to be considered "sufficiently" good in this respect can vary depending on higher-level criteria. Some products are used by a small number of people and still can be very profitable because of their high price. Many widely used and profitable applications are not the most useful ones on the market, can lack usability, and crash far more often than users would prefer. They are being used anyway, since for a number of reasons the users have no choice. However, there are certain minimal requirements according to the above criteria that the product should meet to be regarded as successful.

Simple as it is, the hierarchy in table 3.1 helps identify several possible concerns for a social science–based analysis of software development in a company. Basically, there are three aspects of social science research, namely, focusing on software practice as (1) a business, (2) meeting

Table 3.1
Aspects of software quality

Aspects of software quality	Area of concern	Key actors
Profitable	Business	Company
Used	Competition	Company and competitors
Useful	Functionality	Users
Usable	Interface design	Users
Functional computer program	Programming	Software engineers

users' needs and requirements, and (3) programming (in a broad sense). It is important to keep in mind that these three aspects are related to each other. In particular, understanding users' needs and requirements (taking care of functionality and usability) should be considered within the context of a company's activity as a whole. It means that attempts to change current practices of user studies by systems developers in a certain company should be related to both the business environment of the company and the social organization of the process of code writing.

Therefore, an applied social science project aiming at having an impact on software development can only be successful if its goal is defined as a transformation of the existing practices of systems design. Certain prerequisites should be met to provide a secure basis for accomplishing that goal. First, the whole activity of software development, which constitutes the "minimal meaningful context" (Kuutti and Bannon 1993) of cooperation between systems developers and social scientists, should be taken into consideration. Not only should the immediate objectives of applying social science expertise in systems design be taken into account, but the higher-level goals of, say, the software company, which determine why and how systems developers can be interested in user studies, should also be taken into consideration. Systems developers can only be motivated to change their practices if they can see that contributions from the social sciences can address their higher-level concerns.

A promising approach to doing so seems to be *constructive criticism*, which means critical analysis of existing concepts and techniques from the point of view of how they serve the purposes of software development, as well as suggesting plausible alternatives to or modifications of existing concepts and techniques. Systems developers can hardly be expected to be interested in changing their practices if they do not realize limitations of those practices. On the other hand, even if they understand the limitations, this understanding will have no immediate effect if systems developers cannot see any alternatives they can try. Therefore, constructive criticism implies (1) an attempt to demonstrate that existing concepts and tools for understanding users can be an obstacle to accomplishing the high-level goals of software development by not paying sufficient attention to the social aspects of the use of technology, and (2) providing alternatives to existing practices (new concepts and techniques, as well as modifications of existing ones) that can be understood, assessed, and potentially used by systems developers.

From Tasks to Actions and Beyond

A major challenge for constructive criticism appears to be the lack of a common language social scientists and software developers can speak when discussing issues of mutual interest. Such a conceptual framework, meaningful for both sides, would make it possible to discuss social aspects of the use of technology in the immediate context of software development.

In systems design user studies are typically conducted in the context of usability, which is defined, for instance, as "an overall evaluation of how a system performs in supporting a particular user for a particular task" (Hoffer, George, and Valachich 1996, 879). The use of the word *task* in this definition is not accidental. Currently the notion of task plays a key role in bringing users' and developers' perspectives closer together.

Users' and developers' perspectives on computer technologies are fundamentally different. Users want to achieve meaningful goals, while systems developers are mostly focused on technology per se. Efficient design and use of computer technology require that the differences between users' and developers' perspectives be reconciled to some extent. Users have to formulate their goals according to the opportunities and constraints associated with available technologies, while developers require insight into users' needs to make a system useful and usable. Therefore, a "middle ground" between means and ends—a level of representation of work at which users and developers speak a common language—should somehow be established to ensure mutual understanding. The notion of task is meaningful for both parties. It is not uncommon for users to decompose their work down to the level of specific tasks that can be carried out with the help of a system. As for developers, they can focus on understanding and supporting users' tasks without getting lost in the enormous amount of potentially relevant information about how people use, or might use, computer technology.

Undoubtedly, the focus on tasks has been an important factor contributing to the design of powerful new computer tools in recent years. Task analysis has established itself as a popular practical approach to helping developers provide efficient support for users. However, it is becoming more and more obvious that a heavy focus on tasks is too narrow. It can be a limiting factor that prevents developers from acquiring a deeper understanding of users' needs and that negatively influences the further development of information technology.

Of course, task analysis is not a monolithic approach but rather a generic name for a wide variety of tools and methods. Accordingly, the notion of task has a broad meaning within this approach. However, a closer look at how this term is actually used in specific techniques, like GOMS or KAT (e.g., Dix et al. 1993), reveals some common interpretations of "task" within the task-analysis approach: typically tasks are routine, carried out individually, and have predefined goals. There is no doubt that they constitute a significant part of human-computer interaction and have to be properly understood and supported. It would be a mistake, however, to think that such tasks are the only aspect of the human use of computer technology that need to be supported. Computer use cannot be reduced to just an additive sum of routine tasks.

Empirical evidence and theoretical arguments within the area of CSCW, for instance, call for a major revision of the underlying assumptions of task analysis. Nonetheless, as mentioned above, the notion of task typical of most task-analysis techniques does adequately describe some important aspects of human-computer interaction. Therefore, this notion cannot just be rejected, but must be put into a wider conceptual framework. Reflections on limitations of the notion of task can result in the development of a broader concept that could be meaningful in the context of systems design and, at the same time, subsume social aspects of the use of technology. A possible framework for such conceptual development appears to be activity theory.

Like most versions of task analysis, activity theory construes computer use in terms of hierarchically organized processes oriented toward certain ends. However, functional subordination of goal-oriented processes is not, according to activity theory, the only organizing principle of human activity. First, there are qualitatively different layers of human interaction with the world: activities, actions, and operations. Second, since people at any given moment in time are driven by different, potentially conflicting motives, actions are poly-motivated—that is, they belong to several hierarchical activity structures simultaneously. Third, actions are often distributed between several individuals, so that each person contributes to the collective effort but action as a whole is carried out by the group. Fourth, human actions undergo continuous developmental transformations. Finally, human actions are mediated by socially developed artifacts (Leontiev 1978; Kaptelinin, Nardi, and Macaulay 1999).

From the perspective of activity theory, tasks correspond to lower-level actions. They constitute a significant part of the everyday use of computer technology, but they are usually embedded into higher-level actions that require the definition or redefinition of goals and strategies, are influenced by constraints imposed by other objectives, and are performed in cooperation with other people. It would be fair to mention that in task analysis there is a common distinction between high-level and low-level tasks (e.g., Shneiderman 1998). High-level tasks are defined as those that require problem solving, while low-level tasks, which typically are dealt with within task analysis, are routine ones. Perhaps one way to go about extending the unit of analysis of users would be to convince system developers that they should focus more on supporting high-level tasks, which correspond to higher-level actions, according to activity theory. Those actions are directed toward some meaningful goals that are not directly related to the use of information technologies. They are socially determined in a number of respects. First, one has to take into consideration the social context of work or other types of activities in order to understand how the goals of higher-level actions are being set. The goals can be the result of job assignments, negotiations, competition, or some other social arrangements. Second, methods of accomplishing goals are learned and practiced in a social context through formal learning, casual conversations, occasional help from colleagues, and so on. Finally, social interactions as a part of collective activity, division of labor, and use of shared resources are common features of actions, too.

In my opinion, it is possible to provide rather convincing arguments for systems developers that the current focus on low-level tasks prevents them from developing more successful products—that is, more successful according to their own criteria. For instance, a study of how Macintosh users build and maintain their workspaces revealed a lack of support for users' higher-level actions. In particular, users had problems with arranging resources necessary to complete a project if several applications and types of data (files, e-mail messages, information on the Web) had to somehow be integrated to finish the project. It turned out that the standard Macintosh features—the Desktop, aliases, and labels—did not provide enough support. Other problems included keeping separate private and public information, setting up and cleaning up project-specific workspaces, and so on (Kaptelinin 1996).

It appears that constructive criticisms of the notion of task can be formulated so that they can be meaningful for systems developers. For instance, the fact that some important components of interactive environments, such as the Desktop, are not being used as intended by those who introduced those components, and others, such as labels, are hardly used at all, can be easily attributed to a narrow focus on users' activities. On the other hand, an attempt to focus on larger-scale units of analysis will eventually bring a set of concerns that may require concepts, methods, and tools developed in the social sciences to be assimilated gradually into the practice of software development. The limitations of the concept of task mean that tasks should be analyzed as embedded in higher-level units of activity. Individual and collective activities are, in turn, embedded in larger-scale social context and take place in certain social settings. More specific conceptions of how the idea of embedded activity contexts can be used in design and evaluation of software could be developed, in my opinion, within the framework of concrete discussions between social scientists and software practitioners.

Conclusions

In this chapter I call for redefining the approach underlying the current attempts to provide a more substantial contribution of the social sciences to the practice of software development. The history of such attempts suggests that it is perhaps time to reflect on how two distinct practices—those of systems developers and social science researchers—can mutually influence each other. There are a number of possible ways of implementing this general approach. In this chapter I discuss one of them, namely, building a common conceptual ground, which is needed to focus on issues and problems that would be meaningful for both social scientists and software practitioners. A critical analysis of the notion of "task" as it is used in software development is considered a promising way for social scientists to influence software practice. In this chapter I propose activity theory as a possible theoretical framework for establishing a common conceptual system of reference that can help to bridge the gap between social science research and software development practice.

There are many possible ways of looking at the main topic of the present book—that is, establishing productive cooperation between the social sciences and software practice.

A general claim made in the chapter is that a prerequisite for establishing the above-mentioned cooperation is an understanding of software practice as a separate type of activity with its own actors, motives, goals, and developments. This claim seems applicable not only to constructive criticism, but to many other approaches to changing software practice as well. In this chapter I have presented a brief outline of issues that, in my view, are central for understanding the activity of software development and for using this knowledge as a foundation for further cooperation. This outline needs to be elaborated into a set of more specific concepts, models, and guidelines in order to be useful in a practical sense.

First, the activity system of software development in companies requires a much more detailed analysis. The complexity and diversity of software practices should not be underestimated. There are substantial differences between large, well-established companies and new start-ups, between companies, or divisions of the same company, that are located in different countries, and so forth.

Second, the chapter just mentions the need to reflect on the practices of the social sciences and make them an explicit object of analysis. The social sciences are a mixture of diverse practices, and social scientists might be interested in cooperation with software developers for many reasons. This important issue, in my opinion, deserves special attention.

Third, the chapter oversimplifies when it reduces the relationship between social thinking and software practice to an interaction between two parties: social scientists and software developers in companies. The reality is undoubtedly more complicated. Research and teaching in university computer science departments is often influenced by social science approaches. Many people with a background in the social sciences are employed by high-tech companies and are directly involved in software development projects. Software development takes place not only in companies but also in academic settings. A computer science researcher can create a computer game that conquers the world, and an undergraduate student can develop an operating system that becomes a successful competitor to the one promoted by a software empire. It is likely that products like Tetris or Linux will continue to appear in the future.

Therefore, the area of interaction between social thinking and software practice is populated by many actors with many different interests, agendas, priorities, histories, routines, and preferences. It is essential to make this reality an object of a close empirical study. Such studies appear to be both challenging and potentially rewarding.

Notes

I would like to thank Marina Jirotka, Hans-Erik Nissen, and Chris Westrup for their valuable comments on earlier drafts of this chapter.

1. It should be noted that the "Software Engineering Code of Ethics and Professional Practice" developed by the major software engineering associations—the Association for Computing Machinery (ACM) and the Institute of Electrical and Electronics Engineering (IEEE) Computer Society—emphasizes that above all "software engineers shall act consistently with the public interest" (see http://www.acm.org/serving/se/code.htm).

2. In general, interest in these issues can be traced back at least to the late 1940s, as pointed out by Nissen (chapter 4, this volume).

References

Beyer, H., and K. Holtzblatt. 1998. *Contextual Design: Defining Customer-Centered Systems*. San Francisco: Morgan Kaufmann.

Bødker, S. 1991. Through the Interface: A Human Activity Approach to User Interface Design. Hillsdale, N.J.: Erlbaum.

Bowker, G. C., S. L. Star, W. Turner, and L. Gasser, eds. 1997. *Social Science, Technical Systems, and Cooperative Work: Beyond the Great Divide*. London: Erlbaum.

Button, G., and P. Dourish. 1996. Technomethodology: Paradoxes and possibilities. In *Proceedings CHI'96 Conference on Human Factors in Computing Systems (Vancouver, April 13–18, 1996)*. New York: ACM Press.

Carmel, E., R. D. Whitaker, and J. F. George. 1993. PD and joint application design: A transatlantic comparison. *Communications of the ACM*, 36(6), 40–48.

Carroll, J., ed. 1991. *Designing Interactions: Psychology at the User Interface*. Cambridge, England: Cambridge University Press.

Cole, M. 1996. *Cultural Psychology: A Once and Future Discipline*. Cambridge, England: Cambridge University Press.

Cooper, G., and J. Bowers. 1995. Representing the user: Notes on the disciplinary rhetoric of human-computer interaction. In P. J. Thomas, ed., *The Social and Interactional Dimensions of Human-Computer Interfaces*. Cambridge, England: Cambridge University Press.

Cooper, G., C. Hine, J. Rachet, and S. Woolgar. 1995. Ethnography and human-computer interaction. In P. J. Thomas, ed., *The Social and Interactional Dimensions of Human-Computer Interfaces*. Cambridge, England: Cambridge University Press.

Dahlbom, B., and L. Mathiassen. 1993. *Computers in Context: The Philosophy and Practice of Systems Design*. Oxford: Blackwell.

Dix, A., J. Finlay, G. Abowd, and R. Beale. 1993. *Human-Computer Interaction*. London: Prentice Hall.

Ehn, P. 1988. Work-Oriented Design of Computer Artifacts. Stockholm: Arbetslivscentrum. Engeström, Y. 1990. *Twelve Studies in Activity Theory*. Helsinki: Orienta-Konsultit Oy.

Hoffer, J. A., J. F. George, and J. S. Valachich. 1996. *Modern Systems Analysis and Design*. Reading, Mass.: Benjamin Cummings.

Hutchins, E. 1995. *Cognition in the Wild*. Cambridge, Mass.: MIT Press.

Johnson-Laird, P. 1989. *The Computer and the Mind: An Introduction to Cognitive Science*. Cambridge, Mass.: Harvard University Press.

Kaptelinin, V. 1996. Creating computer-based work environments: An empirical study of Macintosh users. *Proceedings of the ACM SIGCPR/SIGMIS'96 Conference* (Denver, Colorado, April 11–13, 1996). New York: ACM Press.

Kaptelinin, V., B. Nardi, and C. Macaulay. 1999. The Activity Checklist: A tool for representing the "space" of context. *Interactions*, 6(4), 27–39.

Kensing, F., J. Simonsen, and K. Bødker. 1998. MUST—A method for participatory design. *Human-Computer Interaction*, 13(2), 167–198.

Kuutti, K., and L. Bannon. 1993. Searching for unity among diversity: Exploring the interface concept. In *Proceedings INTERCHI'93 Conference on Human Factors in Computing Systems* (Amsterdam, April 24–29, 1993). New York: ACM Press.

Lancaster University and Manchester University, eds. 1994. *Field Studies and CSCW*. COMIC Esprit Basic Research Project 6225, Deliverable D2.2. Lancaster University.

Leontiev, A. N. 1978. *Activity, Consciousness, Personality*. Englewood Cliffs, N.J.: Prentice Hall.

Leontiev, A. N. 1981. *Problems of the Development of Mind*. Moscow: Progress Publishers.

Minsky, M. 1988. *The Society of Mind*. New York: Simon and Schuster.

Nardi, B. 1996. Studying context: A comparison of activity theory, situated action models, and distributed cognition. In B. Nardi, ed., *Context and Consciousness: Activity Theory and Human-Computer Interaction*. Cambridge, Mass.: MIT Press.

Nardi, B., ed. 1996. *Context and Consciousness: Activity Theory and Human-Computer Interaction*. Cambridge, Mass.: MIT Press.

Nardi, B., and V. O'Day. 1999. *Information Ecologies: Using Technology with Heart*. Cambridge, Mass.: MIT Press.

Nyce, J. M., and J. Löwgren. 1995. Towards foundational analysis in human-computer interaction. In P. J. Thomas, ed., *The Social and Interactional Dimensions of Human-Computer Interfaces*. Cambridge, England: Cambridge University Press.

Rogers, Y. 1997. Reconfiguring the social scientist: Shifting from telling designers what to do to getting more involved. In G. C. Bowker, S. L. Star, W. Turner, and L. Gasser, eds., *Social Science, Technical Systems, and Cooperative Work: Beyond the Great Divide*. London: Erlbaum.

Sachs, P. 1995. Transforming work: Collaboration, learning, and design. *Communications of the ACM* 38(9), 36–44.

Shneiderman, B. 1998. *Designing the User Interface: Strategies for Effective Human-Computer Interaction*. 3rd ed. Reading, Mass.: Addison-Wesley.

Strauss, A. 1995. Research issues and an interactionist theory of action. *Mind, Culture, and Activity* 2(1), 18–28.

Suchman, L. 1987. *Plans and Situated Actions*. Cambridge, England: Cambridge University Press.

Suchman, L. 1995. Making work visible. *Communications of the ACM* 38(9), 56–64.

Thomas, P. J. 1995. Introduction: The social and interactional dimensions of human-computer interfaces. In P. J. Thomas, ed. *The Social and Interactional Dimensions of Human-Computer Interfaces*. Cambridge, England: Cambridge University Press.

Vygotsky, L. 1978. *Mind and Society*. Cambridge, England: Cambridge University Press.

Wertsch, J., ed. 1981. *The Concept of Activity in Soviet Psychology*. Armonk, N.Y.: M. E. Sharpe.

4

Challenging Traditions of Inquiry in Software Practice

Hans-Erik Nissen

If software producers/designers acquired social thinking, their software practices would change and result in software products improved from human and societal points of view. This implicit conjecture seems to lie behind recent attempts to add some methods of inquiry borrowed from, for example, ethnography.

Here I will argue for a somewhat different approach. Fundamental presuppositions implicit in current traditions of practical software use and development should be explicitly addressed and challenged.

The redesign of work situations and organizational settings in parallel with technical change dates back at least to the early years of the Tavistock Institute, formed in 1947. In the early 1970s Enid Mumford introduced sociotechnical ideas in the context of developing and implementing computer support. Attempts at participatory design also date back to the 1970s (Whitaker, Essler, and Östberg 1991). Another attempt at bringing social thinking into technical systems design goes back to the systems department at the University of Lancaster. Its influence on software development dates back to when Checkland (1981) presented his Soft Systems Methodology. Studies of software systems failures still indicate that these seldom have their roots in technical shortcomings. Instead they have their origins in social phenomena such as:

- Power struggles and conflicts
- Ignoring of the fundamental need for informal communication in parallel with formalized communication
- Ignoring the amounts of individual and organizational learning involved

• Not understanding the need to make embedded decision rules and their limitations visible

The limited impact, so far, of social thinking on software practice could be explained by the failure of earlier attempts to build on properly constructed, analytically and empirically strong theory and method from the social sciences. (See Nyce and Löwgren 1995; Nyce and Bader, chapter 2, this volume.) According to Kaptelinin (chapter 3, this volume), social scientists have to understand that their insights will only be heeded if they are a good fit with the goals, concerns, values, and priorities of software practitioners. Software practitioners will certainly have their own objectives. They will want to work on the technical frontlines as professionals. However, in most cases their employers will strongly influence the goals and values applied in practice. If software scientists adhere to the advice given by Kaptelinin (chapter 3, this volume), this will limit the kind of constructive criticism of software practices he later urges social scientists to voice.

Here I will focus on the issue of whose values get the most weight in software development: the producers' or the consumers'. Producers usually claim they see the consumer as sovereign. However, a different picture emerges if we look at the practice of having consumers sign requirement specifications they cannot possible understand the consequences of. Most disclaimers of license agreements for software contain a sentence like "The software is provided for use 'as is' without warranty of any kind." No car buyer would accept such a clause. Not surprisingly, cases are reported where a large software investment ends in no software ever being used. This indicates a value balance in use in favor of the software producers. I do not suggest tilting the balance the other way. An even balance would be ideal.

On both sides, much seems taken for granted. This is mediated from generation to generation, on both the producer and the consumer side. In this chapter I will address inquiries by researchers and practitioners into the use, maintenance, and development of computer-supported data processing. Software systems I presume as intentionally developed in order to add value to work tasks or to the everyday-life situations of people mainly outside the group that developed the systems. In this chapter I intend to give reflective practitioners, on both the consumer and the producer side, some ideas on how to question what they have so far taken for granted. This target audience includes the practitioners of tomorrow—that is, students.

In the second section, I will discuss what may lie behind the unequal weight given the values of software producers and the people backing them financially versus the values of consumers and others affected indirectly. To make sense, particularly in discussing abstract concepts, people talk and write about them metaphorically. As Lakoff and Johnson (1980) show, metaphors play a useful role in human communication. However, any metaphor highlights some features of a phenomenon and hides others. In the third section I will critically discuss some metaphors connected with computer use that potentially influence social practice.

To understand whose values get the greatest weight in software development, the factors guiding research and development in the area need some reflection. This goal has motivated my inclusion of the section titled "Two Different Research Traditions." Even though I address this section to researchers, it also applies, with appropriate modification, to practitioners developing software.

Research programs and software development projects aiming at deeper social thinking in software practice will call for collaboration of researchers and developers with different backgrounds. Gaining insight into each other's concepts and terminology takes time and effort; thus I present suggestions on how to improve mutual understanding. The chapter also discusses some implications for software practice. It ends with a brief concluding section.

Background of the Imbalance in Values

Software enterprises need to make a profit to survive. To include human and societal considerations in software calls for adequate resources. Such considerations only will be included if they promise competitive advantages that pay off relatively quickly. Consumer demands for low-radiation screens and the integration of ergonomic considerations into hardware indicate a way of counteracting the current imbalance in values.

A lack of pull from the consumer side will give even the best social thinking by software designers a limited chance of influencing practice. Consumers' pull by itself will not suffice to bring software products into being that have been improved from a human and societal standpoint. It will also take further attempts along the lines suggested by other chapters in this volume to let social thinking influence software practice. The push and the pull have to form an ongoing dialectic.

Having followed the software industry since the early 1960s, I ask myself, How has this industry managed to be technology driven for more than forty years and still succeeds in operating this way? A widespread belief in the unquestionable superiority of new technology provides one explanation. In the particular case of information technology, hardly any earlier images or metaphors of its products and what they could offer existed. The industry itself invented these metaphors largely with the funding of research and sales promotion in mind. People in general, including most managers, did not understand this new technology. Hence, they did not challenge it.

Potential Effects of Metaphors

Software thinking—and the professional language accompanying it—offers a suitable tool for communication among software professionals. At the same time its idiosyncrasies prevent outsiders from understanding it. Professionals communicating with laypeople often get their intentions across most effectively by using metaphors.

Frequently used metaphors become incorporated in everyday language. They thus gain influence both on the worldview of many citizens and on their self-image—for instance, as indicated by the potential side effects of the first three metaphors in table 4.1. As citizens we often act according to our beliefs even if these remain unconscious. When metaphors become part of everyday language, the images used begin to be taken for granted. Lakoff and Johnson (1980) have described the influence on action of metaphors used in everyday language. This suggests a chain of events coupling software thinking with social practice. In using the phrase "social practice" here, I want to call attention to what

Table 4.1
Some metaphors and their potential side effects

Metaphor	Highlights	Potential side effects
Software as an intelligent agent	Software products functioning as if they acted autonomously.	People feeling inferior to software products and their designers. Overrating what software products offer.
Human mind: a computer	Some aspects of how one half of the human cortex might function.	May lower the self-esteem of people, who mostly do not act based on calculations and formal, logical reasoning.
Conduit metaphor	Technical transmission of signals over channels.	Hides the great need of mutual learning in establishing human communication. May induce feelings of their fault in users, when they do not understand computer output.
Knowledge management	Handling of data taken as "established facts" and retrieving these.	Hides who declares something an "established fact." Hides the amount of work and experiential learning needed to establish new grounds for acting.

people do in work and life induced by their primary and secondary socialization.

Software thinkers often use the metaphor of computer artifacts as replacements for people in performing some particular class of operations. Business managers like the idea of automation—replacing people with technical devices. Metaphors of an agent much like a human being have become more and more common when describing the execution of a software product. Salespeople sometimes even talk about intelligent agents. Agent/actor metaphors seem to me to overstate what software products can offer and understate what people do in everyday life and work. Still, expectations people have of software products may be influenced by such metaphors. Some expectations have a fair chance of being fulfilled. They build on well-grounded parts of analogues—for example, comparing a software product to an extremely insecure person always sticking to the rules he or she has been taught. Other expectations, like giving the impression that a computer artifact could judge a situation as an experienced person would be able to, cannot be fulfilled.

Many researchers in artificial intelligence and cognitive science use computer metaphors of human thinking when partially explaining some limited human capability. Restricted to the small community of these researchers, such metaphors cause little harm. However, used in everyday language, they may influence people's self-image. I classify the first two metaphors in table 4.1 as mechanistic models of human beings. They mediate a tradition of humans as machines dating much further back than modern computers.

The two metaphors mentioned belong to what Lakoff and Johnson (1980, 25–29) have called *ontological metaphors*. Another metaphor exists that strongly influences how people think about the use of communication technologies, including computers. Reddy (1979), a linguist, named it the *conduit metaphor*. In one of its forms the metaphor describes human communication as if

> (1) thoughts and feelings are ejected by speaking or writing into an external "idea space"; (2) thoughts and feelings are reified in this external space, so that they exist independent of any need for living human beings to think or feel them; (3) these reified thoughts and feelings may, or may not, find their way back into the heads of living humans. (Reddy, 1979, 291)

The conduit metaphor quietly confuses signals and concepts. Reddy (1979) traces how this confusion forced Claude Shannon and Warren Weaver (1949) to frame information theory under the metaphor's biasing influence. Whitaker (1992, 52–55) presents a brief but deeper account of the conduit metaphor in the context of information systems research. The subject of information highways illustrates a recent variation on the conduit metaphor. Another recent variation takes the form of talking about knowledge management. The conduit metaphor induces beliefs in thought and feelings existing independently of any living human being. Knowledge management induces beliefs in knowledge without a community of knowers. Discarding the conduit metaphor means, for example, reflecting on the fact that the Internet does not simply transport packages of indisputable "facts" and "knowledge."

In table 4.1 I present some highlights and potential side effects of the four metaphors. The side effects shown are, of course, not an exhaustive list. But even these side effects are enough to cause alarm, for two reasons. First, in a historical period of unequal distribution of power and rapid technological change, many people feel inferior and insecure. Trying to act as a responsible researcher, I want to offset these feelings, particularly with respect to information and communication technology. Second, some of the side effects mask features of software use that ought to be brought into the open and be critically assessed. Critical assessments, by many people who feel that they have the right and the competence to challenge technical development based on their own values and experience, will be needed to challenge the qualitative direction taken by new software. Reflective software professionals should welcome such challenges to their roles.[1]

The first step, then, is to become aware of the risks that metaphors from software thinking entail. To get many people to challenge current features of software development calls for teamwork in research and software development. Team members will bring with them different traditions of inquiry; they will have to learn how to join forces in spite of their different backgrounds. This learning process could converge more rapidly if they knew more about various research traditions. In the next section I will briefly introduce two different research traditions.

Two Different Research Traditions

Researchers in computer science have typically drawn on traditions from mathematics, logic, and the sciences. Some researchers in the social sciences have tried to emulate research traditions of the sciences. Others have instead argued that fruitful social research should follow entirely different research traditions. The classification of organizational theories by Burell and Morgan (1979) documents this. I will follow Radnitzky (1970) here, for two reasons. First, challenging software practice and its limited theoretical base presupposes an awareness of its current research traditions. This requires going outside the mainstream of research traditions applied in computer science. (See Nyce and Bader, chapter 2, this volume.) More guidelines for inquiry will be needed, to open horizons for studying the integration of traditions and for critical assessment of and emancipation from them. Second, other traditions introduced will not be presented as substitutes for methods of inquiry successfully used in mathematics and the natural sciences. The aim of introducing them should be to enable deeper inquiry in fields where an object of study can incorporate an investigator's causal explanations into his or her self-understanding and thereby become capable of changing or modifying future conduct. (See Radnitzky 1970, xxxv.) Radnitzky's presentation of research traditions and their research guidelines meets these two criteria.

Radnitzky distinguishes Anglo-Saxon traditions, which he calls *logical/empirical* (LE), and Continental ones, which he calls *hermeneutic/dialectical* (HD). Table 4.2 shows that the two traditions differ considerably in what they emphasize. In some respects they even advocate opposing views. It will help if researchers from different traditions who

Table 4.2
Logical/empirical and hermeneutic/dialectical research traditions compared

Feature	Logical/empirical	Hermeneutic/dialectical
View of "reality"	One observer independent	Many coexistent "realities" dependent on observers
Theory of truth	Correspondence theories*	Coherence theories
Historical context of data collected	Irrelevant	Relevant
Causal connections	Linear chains or trees	Mutual, interlocked influences
Values guiding research	Only science-immanent ones	Both science-immanent ones and external values
Separability of theory from practice	Strictly separable	Theory and practice dialectically related
Research interest	Technical research interests, potentially emancipatory	Mainly hermeneutic and emancipatory interests, can provide social techniques
Main language features	Extensional and denotational	Intentional and connotational

* American pragmatists, whom Radnitzky (1970) gives reasons to classify as mainly applying LE traditions, do not use correspondence theories of truth. Their truth criterion could briefly be stated as "What difference would it make if this were true?" This also enables them to pursue emancipatory research interests and not technical ones alone.

want to cooperate understand each other's traditions. This does not necessarily mean converting to the other traditions. Software practitioners can read this section as an illustration of difficulties in encountering people from a "different culture."

Drawing on Habermas, but also adding some insights of his own, Radnitzky (1970, Vol. II, 5–14) identifies the following five research-guiding interests:

- Technical (work, in practice also guided by economic considerations)
- Hermeneutic, mediating tradition(s)
- Emancipatory
- Improving the world picture
- Improving reflection on existential themes

As indicated above, the two research traditions should be perceived as supplementary. Apel (1967, 56–57) argues that theories and methods of inquiry formed only within HD traditions will not suffice in social science studies. As an explanation he points to the fact that as humans we do not fully understand each other and ourselves. Apel starts from the development of knowledge and self-understanding in an ideal-typical psychoanalytic situation. Radnitzky (1970) presents the essence of Apel's idea as follows:

> We shall consider a psychoanalytic situation where the analysand wishes to carry out a personal analysis in cooperation with the analyst to learn more about his operant motivation and also to increase his psychological possibilities of carrying out his conscious intentions. The *global or final interest* motivating the whole enterprise, on the part of the analysand is ... the *hermeneutic one combined with the emancipatory one*. Having agreed upon the global program, *resource-gathering* may begin. The *dialogue* between analysand and analyst supplies material.... At this stage, among the resources of the analyst, the prenotions which he has qua member of the "same" speech community as the analysand are of particular importance.... It is required that analysand and analyst speak the "same language"—to ensure that they have sufficient shared common life experience.... At this *hermeneutic level* or phase the analyst may achieve *Verstehen* directly, i.e., it is attainable by the good-reason-assay utilizing the aforesaid prenotions. (Radnitzky 1970, Vol. II, 43)

Sometimes analysts can no longer make sense of what their analysand says or does. They reach a crisis in their co-understanding. The psychoanalytic analyst then can draw on another resource, not shared with the analysand: psychoanalytic theory. This theory offers both systematized experience and a professional language, which comprises a causal language. In that language the analyst can think and speak of "motives" as causal factors. This may enable the analyst to explain the speech and other behavior of the analysand. However, he or she does not use such an explanation to manipulate the analysand. The analyst goes back to the dialogue situation and presents theory-based insights in a way reasonably understandable within the life history of the analysand. In other words, the analyst returns to the agreed-on global program of the consultation. This program calls for the analysand to learn more about his or her operant motivation and to increase the psychological likelihood of carrying out his or her conscious intentions.

Apel (1967) and Radnitzky (1970, Vol. II, 45) call turns in social science research that use natural science methods of inquiry and theorizing "quasi-naturalistic turns." These "quasi-naturalistic turns" vastly increase the resources of psychoanalysts and of other specialists—even when attempting to contribute to a research-guiding interest of mediating traditions or an emancipatory research-guiding interest.

Different traditions in undertaking inquiries can legitimately be employed and combined. Decisions on whose and which research interests are to take the leading role and whose and which interests have to take the role of constraints should guide choices and combinations of methods. This will facilitate joint investigations by teams of people with widely differing professional backgrounds.

Another obstacle to mutual understanding is the fact that different team members will probably enter collaboration with different terminology. Behind these terminological differences will lie different distinctions deemed important. In the next section, I call attention to distinctions of this kind and to the importance of not blocking fruitful collaboration by allowing one set of distinctions to prevail.

How to Promote Mutual Understanding

Consumers of computer artifacts, including researchers trying to improve consumers' bargaining position as well as software practitioners, need to achieve better mutual understanding. Here I take consumers in the broad sense of both direct and indirect consumers. For instance, I include not only doctors and nurses in hospitals as consumers of software products, but also their patients.

Lévi-Strauss (1966, 2), based on numerous, concrete examples, shows how distinctions used in different cultures and subcultures depend on practical concerns and theoretical interests. This lends support to an experience-based conjecture of mine. When members of both cultures believe their distinctions are both necessary and sufficient, mutual understanding can be hard to achieve.

Specialists often need to focus narrowly on issues in discussions among themselves. But this entails the risk of ignoring distinctions unimportant in those contexts but crucial in other contexts. If so, the narrowly focused specialist may not perceive a problem that in fact exists. On the other hand, there are people who perceive a solution where none currently exists. The tendency of consumers to put unrealistic demands on computer artifacts represents one possible example. Kaptelinin (chapter 3, this volume) indicates this by stating that users need to formulate their goals according to the features and limitations of the available technologies. However, consumers could also impose constraints on new technology before it even becomes worth the effort to consider acquiring this technology.

Software "producers" often distinguish some people simply as "users" and as different from themselves. Those called "users" do not generally take pride in using software produced by somebody else. In the context of work they probably look on themselves as professional nurses, carpenters, lathe operators, clerks, lawyers, medical doctors, and so on. As citizens they may look on themselves as mothers, fathers, grandparents, members of churches and sports clubs, and so forth. The software producers pride themselves on being benefactors of "users." Such a classification may look innocent. However, this attitude could be seen as patronizing, if the relatively few producers believe they are more important than the many users. People other than software producers may impose still other classifications on those affected by computer artifacts. If so, software practitioners should be attentive and try to understand the scope, aims, and advantages of these alternative classification systems.

Floyd (chapter 1, this volume) distinguishes between the concepts of "action" and "operation." She reserves the former concept exclusively for humans. She links operations with repetitive human action occurring in a specific domain. An observer can describe and document a description of an operation—that is, a common pattern discerned in a number of similar, routine actions. Such a description exists as an entity separated from the series of actions observed. It, or rather an ordered set of such descriptions, could be given as a prescription to a human actor to enact it. Alternatively, the operation can become transformed into a computer program, which when executed performs the operation. Reserving the concept of action exclusively for humans offers one way of distinguishing between people and computer artifacts as agents.

Other software practitioners may choose to ignore or may never acknowledge any difference between people and computer artifacts as agents. These apparent contradictory positions by two groups of software practitioners could be resolved by another distinction. This is the distinction between living beings and artifacts made by Maturana and Varela (1980). A living being, called an *autopoietic machine*, has itself as its overarching product of functioning—that is, it functions primarily to stay alive. They distinguish living beings from what they call *allopoietic machines*. The latter have as the product of their functioning something different from themselves, such as a car. Living beings can become perturbed by independent events. However, their actions are not controlled by such events. They undergo internal changes, which compensate for the perturbations. In other words, they have the capacity to act creatively in a situation in which an observer would expect them to act according to a pattern observed earlier in similar situations.

When observing people in routine work tasks the description may look like a description of an allopoietic machine. The distinction just suggested offers a warning against jumping to the conclusion that people in the workplace are nothing but allopoietic machines. Such a conclusion can damage their self-image and lower their self-esteem.

In the mathematical theory of communication they outline, Shannon and Weaver (1949) distinguish senders from receivers of messages transmitted over noisy channels. These terms are also often applied to human communication by which people intend to inform themselves or others of something. Transposed into this latter context, the distinction presupposes the conduit metaphor. An alternative distinction, which does not entail this metaphor and is consistent with a perception of people as creative, can be found in Maturana ([1970] 1980, 32). In the context of human communication he introduces a distinction between "orienter" and "orientee." The former intends to orient or reorient the latter. A reorientation of an orientee can be triggered, but not controlled, by a message. Moreover, the reorientation is independent of what the message "represents" for the orienter.

The last distinction is closely related to a distinction between two features of language use indicated in table 4.2. There I included a distinction between "denotational" and "connotational" features of language. Maturana ([1970] 1980, 32) investigated the consequences of choosing one or the other as the most important feature in language use:

> So long as language is considered to be denotative it will be necessary to look at it as a means for the transmission of information.... However, when it is recognized that language is connotative and not denotative, and that its function is to orient the orientee within his cognitive domain without regard for the cognitive domain of the orienter, it becomes apparent that there is no transmission of information through language.... The listener creates information by reducing his uncertainty through his interactions in his cognitive domain. Consensus arises only through cooperative interactions in which the resulting behavior of each organism becomes subservient to the maintenance of both. An observer beholding a communicative interaction between two organisms who have already developed a consensual linguistic domain, can describe the interaction as denotative.

In the quotation, the word *organism* should be taken to refer to people. The denotational function of language in the context of information systems development and use is generally taken for granted. I use the phrase "information system" to refer to information processing and management processes comprising both social and technical elements, as Korpela et al. do in chapter 14. The quotation underlines the fact that the denotational function of language presupposes much prior interaction and mutual learning. This often seems grossly underestimated when software systems are incorporated in information systems.

In this section I have covered one way of promoting mutual understanding between professionals trained in different traditions. I have shown how different concepts, based on distinctions important in some contexts but not all, and the terms used for them could be discussed in a constructive way. In the next section I will discuss some implications of these points for software practice.

Implications for Software Practice

Selection mechanisms play a fundamental role in evolution. In the brief history of evolving software practices, technical and economic mechanisms of selection have prevailed. Recognizing this, it should not come as a surprise that human and societal points of view have exerted only a limited influence on software practice so far. Against this background, I have suggested a complementary approach that will introduce and strengthen the human and societal mechanisms of selection.

Reflecting on Metaphors and Traditions of Inquiry

Many people who are directly or indirectly affected by the use of software believe they lack the competence to challenge software because they cannot design or redesign it themselves. Here metaphors created by software practitioners enter the scene, since these metaphors have influenced the self-image and self-esteem of laypeople. Ethically responsible software practitioners should sensitize themselves to the possible side effects of the metaphors they use in encounters with laypeople and meet them as professionals in their own work tasks and lives. Metaphors will still be useful in such encounters. However, they have to be chosen with care.

As illustrated by the conduit metaphor, software practitioners should also make sure that they are not misled by their own metaphors. The metaphorical use of "knowledge management," reifying what people know into separable, salable goods, may also mislead both professionals and laypeople. Korpela et al. (chapter 14, this volume) imagine information systems development (ISD) as introducing and making useful software products in organizations. During the planning of ISD, the first two metaphors can result in underestimating the time and resources needed. In interviews designed to elicit "requirements specifications" they may undermine professionals' chances of grasping complex work situations. (See Nyce and Bader, chapter 2, this volume.)

Generating a strong mechanism for software selection by increasing the self-confidence of consumers will take time. In the meantime, another selection mechanism should be made more effective. It involves effective collaboration with professionals and researchers from disciplines other than software and computer science.

Collaborating with researchers from other disciplines or investigators with different professional training can help software practitioners become familiar with new perspectives and ways of doing things. This will foster communication and otherwise bridge the diverse backgrounds of these groups. It might even inspire software practitioners to reflect on work practices they had been taking for granted and raise questions they had not thought of. I have already briefly discussed alternative forms of inquiry in the section "Two Different Research Traditions." In what follows I will subsume software researchers and commercial practitioners under the phrase "software practitioners." I also provide some material that directly addresses the concerns of researchers.

Software practitioners should learn to ask the following questions: Whose interests should prevail in an investigation or a development project? Who else's interests might conflict with the dominant ones? I do not recommend that software practitioners generally try to resolve conflicts they spot. However, they will improve their chances of making useful and used contributions if they learn to recognize conflict as an issue seldom resolved by new, formal models and networked data processing.

An additional question—Who could act more appropriately based on these new data?—in turns leads to questions like these: Will the individuals who are intended to act more appropriately based on the new data have the means and power to do so? Will they have the competence to do so, or would that demand more learning on their part?

Some research on the implementation and use of new information technology artifacts may help managers provide better leadership so that their subordinates are more productive. Such research is guided by a technical research interest. Other researchers may try to shift the balance of power to allow the values of other groups effectively to influence software development. In their studies they have to follow hermeneutic and emancipatory research interests. However, technical research interests may also guide parts of these latter studies. This might be the case if people, using some computer program, were to place a high priority on their own ability to change the online help of the program. This means different research interests can guide one research program. When this is the case, priorities between the different research-guiding interests have to be established and explicitly documented.

Software practitioners will meet people with whom they only share a basic language and some general experience. In their encounters they have the same kinds of difficulties understanding their informants that a psychoanalyst encounters with an analysand. (The challenge in the latter encounter has briefly been discussed in the section titled "Two Different Research Traditions.") A difference from psychoanalytic therapies is that they will meet different stakeholders with conflicting interests in software use. Hence the experiences of therapists offering modern, brief family therapy would present more parallels to reflect on.

The professional knowledge of software practitioners will normally be incomprehensible to their clients. Likewise, software practitioners will often find the professional knowledge and life experience of their clients difficult to grasp. Like therapists, they should train themselves to become sensitive to the fact that they and their clients will often not understand each other. Describing concrete use cases and rapid prototyping can start to provide shared experience between the two groups. (A use-case model uses *actors* and *use cases* to define what exists outside of a data processing system (actors) and what should be performed by the system (use cases) (Jacobson et al. 1993, 127). Rapid prototyping is achieved by building small-scale inexpensive software artifacts with the goal of evaluating some aspects of a proposed data processing system. More on prototyping can be found in Naumann and Jenkins 1982.) Recent attempts to import ethnographic methods indicate a need to do more to make people from "different cultures" coproduce qualitatively improved software. (See Nyce and Bader, chapter 2, this volume.)

Another lesson to learn from therapists pertains to the question of what primary research-guiding interest to pursue. In the example of a psychoanalytic situation discussed in the section titled "Two Different Research Traditions," the primary research-guiding interest was emancipatory. In the case of ethnographic studies, the primary research-guiding interest is to mediate between the traditions of radically different cultures. Advocates of new technologies often espouse as their primary interest an emancipatory one—making life and work easier for people. Studying their priorities in use will mostly show they emphasize short-range, technical-economic goals.

Reflecting on Improved Understanding with Other Professionals

In collaborating with specialists from other areas, software practitioners often encounter terminological difficulties that hinder mutual understanding. Differences in the kinds of distinctions specialists make frequently lie behind these barriers. I have already touched on some of these differences in the section on promoting mutual understanding; in the following paragraphs, I return to the problem and discuss some of its implications.

Software producers often subsume people using their products under the label "users." However, people's self-image is rarely based on whether they use software products or not. Instead they tend to see themselves as professionals in their own right and as members of particular groups. Specialists from various disciplines use whatever classification systems they find helpful. Human communication—including the choice of metaphor and terminological distinctions—always also informs the participants of how they mutually perceive their personal and professional relationships (see Watzlawick, Helmick Bevin, and Jackson 1967, chap. 2). As part of their job, many software practitioners interact extensively with others. Training in becoming more sensitive to the way others perceive their mutual relationship could make this interaction more effective. The training should involve support from psychologists or others specializing in relationship issues.

Earlier I discussed making or ignoring a distinction between human beings and computer artifacts. Software practitioners should reflect on the consequences of failing to recognize this distinction. This failure can lead people to feel as if they are nothing but machines controlled externally. This in turn can lower people's self-esteem—particularly the self-esteem of those with low self-confidence in the first place. Another consequence can appear in the context of developing large business and citizen support systems. Integrating such systems for automatic functioning without any human intervention may appear to pose a major technical challenge. Only a few of the situations such a system has to handle can be foreseen at the time of its design. Knowing this, one can expect the system to be far from robust. An alternative would be to design a system in which some integrating links were people. Human beings, with their creative capacities, offer flexibility several orders of magnitude larger than computer artifacts do. This, of course, presupposes that people are encouraged to use their flexibility and are not trained to behave like puppets on a string. Most people will exhibit comparative advantages in the realm of flexibility in relation to computer artifacts for many years to come. All in all, it looks as if many software practitioners are still adhering to traditions of good design developed in the days of batch processing on mainframes, not recognizing design options opened by interactivity.

My next example of differences in distinctions was that between sender and receiver on the one hand and orienter and orientee on the other. The former perspective is dominant among software practitioners. It is adequate when reflecting on data transmission but becomes misleading when applied to human communication. Here the second distinction is more adequate. The distinction between two features of language use helps to explain why distinguishing orienters and orientees is more appropriate in the context of human communication.

Software practitioners are well aware of the denotational features and largely ignore the connotational features of language. Concepts employed in software products must have unambiguous interpretations in very limited contexts, such as computer programs, database schemas, and so on. Hence in software development, the denotational features of language should predominate. In the use of software products, the denotative meaning of the terms chosen by software producers should not be taken as self-evident to everybody else.

As mentioned in the section "How to Promote Mutual Understanding," what an outside observer may classify as a denotational feature of human communication has to be preceded by a long period of interaction and learning to achieve mutual understanding. This should make software practitioners aware of the burden of learning they force on people presumed to benefit from the use of a new or modified computer artifact. This learning comprises more than technical training in how to handle a computer artifact, which so far has been the only kind of learning generally recognized when implementing a new artifact. The time and effort needed for these learning tasks should be calculated as costs of investment in new or changed software support beforehand. If this makes some projects look unprofitable that otherwise looked like profitable investments, so much the better. Some research on which to base estimates of learning time and resources would be helpful in making realistic total cost estimates before deciding on a software development and implementation project.

Conclusions

Software and hardware development has not just been technology driven in the past forty years. The industry has also profited, and still does, from a seller's market. This neither will nor—for ethical reasons—should go on forever. A proactive strategy for software practitioners would be to invite more genuine human and societal challenges.

In some niches like computer support for disabled people, this is already the rule. Still, much more remains to be done to give equal weight to consumers' and producers' values in software development in general. Software practitioners who want to invite new challenges have the above material and references to reflect on. As noted earlier, a goal of this chapter is also to provide useful resources for teachers of future software practitioners. These teachers might reflect on to what extent a law school that only educates judges and district attorneys but not defense lawyers represents an adequate model for teaching ISD. Moreover, ISD teachers should reflect on whether the ideal of professionalism they transmit to their students provides insight into the limitations of what they know and of the values they choose to pursue (Ulrich 2000).

Individual software practitioners are seldom free to choose which interests to pursue in their work. However, becoming aware of conflicting interests behind a software development task may still help them in two ways. First, they may recognize that hidden conflicts of interest cannot be resolved by new or changed software alone. Grasping this at an early stage is likely to enhance their chances of professional success by helping them avoid "impossible" tasks. Second, software practitioners who want to act ethically must reflect on whose interests they support.

Note

1. It falls outside the scope of this chapter to go into how to empower laypeople to criticize professionals and to make the latter change their views of their own professionalism. However, Ulrich's (2000) "Critical Systemic Thinking" furnishes both a theoretical ground and practical advice on new ways of helping laypeople interact with professionals on an equal basis. This supports the feasibility of my suggestion to create a pull from the consumer side with respect to software products.

References

Apel, K.-O. 1967. *Philosophy of language and the Geisteswissenschaften.* Dordrecht: Reidel. (First published in German in 1965.)

Burell, G., and G. Morgan. 1979. *Sociological paradigms and organisational analysis: Elements of the sociology of corporate life.* London: Heinemann.

Checkland, P. 1981. *Systems thinking, systems practice.* Chichester, England: Wiley.

Jacobson, I., M. Christenson, P. Jonsson, and G. Övergaard. 1993. *Object-oriented software engineering: A use case driven approach.* 4th ed. Workingham, England: Addison-Wesley.

Lakoff, G., and M. Johnson. 1980. *Metaphors we live by.* Chicago: University of Chicago Press.

Lévi-Strauss, C. 1966. *The savage mind.* Chicago: University of Chicago Press. (First published in French in 1962.)

Maturana, H. R., and F. J. Varela. 1980. *Autopoiesis and cognition: The realization of the living.* Dordrecht: Reidel.

Maturana, H. R. [1970] 1980. Biology of cognition. In H. R. Maturana and F. J. Varela, *Autopoiesis and cognition: The realization of the living.* Dordrecht: Reidel.

Naumann, J., and A. M. Jenkins. 1982. Prototyping: The new paradigm for systems development. *MIS Quarterly* 6(3).

Nyce, J., and Löwgren, J. 1995. Toward foundational analysis in human-computer interaction. In P. J. Thomas (ed.), *The social and interactional dimensions of human-computer interfaces.* Cambridge, England: Cambridge University Press.

Radnitzky, G. 1970. *Contemporary schools of metascience*, Vol. I: *Anglo-Saxon schools of metascience*; Vol. II: *Continental schools of metascience*. Göteborg, Sweden: Akademiförlaget. Second: revised edition in one volume.

Reddy, M. 1979. The conduit metaphor. In A. Ortony, ed., *Metaphor and thought*, 284–324. Cambridge, England: Cambridge University Press.

Shannon, C., and W. Weaver. 1949. *The mathematical theory of communication*. Urbana: University of Illinois Press.

Ulrich, W. 2000. Reflective Practice in the Civil Society: The contribution of critically systemic thinking. *Reflective Practice* 1(2): 247–268. Abingdon, UK: CARFAX PUBLISHING, Taylor & Francis Group.

Watzlawick, P., J. Helmick Bevin, and Don D. Jackson. 1967. *Pragmatics of human communication: A study of interactional patterns, pathologies, and paradoxes*. New York: Norton.

Whitaker, R. 1992. *Venues for Contexture: A critical analysis and enactive reformulation of Group Decision Support Systems*. Doctoral dissertation, Research Reports in Information Processing and Computer Science, no. UMADP-RRIPCS 15.92. Umeå University, Sweden.

Whitaker, R., U. Essler, and O. Östberg. 1991. *Participatory business modeling*. Luleå University, Luleå, Sweden.

II

Informing

Chris Westrup

How is social thinking to be expressed in software development? This question raises a number of issues pertinent to the chapters in this section. First, it draws our attention to what social thinking might be. It is a contention of the authors in this section that social thinking does not occur in a vacuum but rather is an accomplishment intimately related to the activities in which it is expressed. Put negatively, it means that we cannot distill social thinking from its context of use. Social thinking appears to reside in the practices brought to bear by social scientists, systems developers, and researchers in the activities of systems development. Thus, social thinking needs to be considered in terms of practices, techniques, and methodologies that are being utilized or will be utilized in software production and use. Social thinking is itself a situated activity. This leads our inquiry away from theory and toward engagement with approaches, practices, and techniques used to render social life more transparent.

A second issue is one of description versus prescription. Inquiry can be restricted to an appraisal of approaches drawn from social thinking, the appraisal in itself informed by social theory. Empirical examples of the use of techniques coming from the social sciences can be explored and contrasted. The use of social thinking in one's own work practices and interaction can be reflected on and the ways in which social thinking *should* be used in software practice can be laid down. The authors in this section gravitate toward all except the last alternative. Indeed, it emerges from this section that prescription is not a viable way forward for seeking to align social thinking and software production. What seems central is that any form of appropriation of software thinking needs to retain a sense of critical and reflective appraisal. Software developers may seek to mine social thinking for social products to be added to software development methodologies, but such an approach is likely to lead, sooner or later, to usages of social theory that may be opposed to the original intentions in the social sciences. If no quick answer is seen as appropriate, how can social thinking be expressed in software development?

The title of this section is "Informing." Not only does this convey the sense of being aware of social thinking to guide software development, it also can be read as "in-forming": social thinking forms the software production that occurs. Therefore, even with no explicit use of social thinking, software production remains in-formed by a variety of assumptions and beliefs about the workplace. Much of this appears to be based on functionalist views of the organization of work. Another issue is drawing attention to existing processes of sociality within the development process and then, through this, in seeking to articulate different ways of developing systems. In-forming is also seen to reside in the social science–based representations of the workplace. Different formulations of social thinking draw out and formulate aspects of working life—for example, an awareness of the detail of interaction in the workplace or an awareness of the issue of power relations. Thus social thinking is to be found in both articulated and usually unarticulated formulations in the production of software.

But what of software production itself? In this section of the book the focus is not on that aspect though, of course, it must enter into all aspects of the work found in this section. Perhaps it is useful to introduce the issue of scale. Research-based interventions in software development are, by necessity, small scale, but they take place in a vast world of software production. Reformulating social thinking to inform software production has to start in research-based, often resource-intensive, usually complex workplace settings. In these studies, researchers are able (however circumscribed) to formulate social thinking in ways that inform the production of software for these environments. However, there is a problematic of scale. Insights that are learned and discussed here hopefully should be made more widely available. The vehicle of a book such as this is one way of doing this. Arguably, though, we soon run into an issue of scale. Software production is becoming an increasing commodified activity, and even large-scale systems are encapsulated into packages, as the rapid implementation of enterprise resource planning systems shows. How can the insights formulated by an awareness of social thinking be brought to bear on these large-scale software practices? Here, we face a dilemma. Typically, to seek to influence software practice, best practice is codified in techniques or methodologies that can be taught or used as resources from computer-based systems. However, this form of rule-based approach is already seen as inappropriate for informing software production for the simple reason that the complexities of the social science approach are likely to be lost, leading to the unsuitable use of approaches as techniques. On the other hand, can the vast numbers of software developers be taught the details of approaches drawn from the social sciences? This too seems unattainable. Then are we left with a position where expert mediation is required in software development? Should each project have its own resident ethnographer or whatever to ensure that approaches are used in an appropriate way? Here is the dilemma. If we followed this route, we could end up with software developers becoming even further removed from the work setting. They might be restricted to viewing selected video clips or discussing the details with the resident ethnographer who is the expert in these matters.

Among these issues, the contributors in this section show how progress is being made through the use of social thinking to enrich our understandings of the scope of software development. They illustrate the positive contribution of an awareness of social actions and activity in leading to more satisfying systems to support working life.

There are four chapters in this section. The first, by Chris Westrup, seeks to identify ways in which one technique, ethnography, has been used in software development and to argue from that example, how all approaches drawn from the social sciences need to be placed in the contexts of their use. He uses a distinction drawn from Bauman between legislative reasoning and interpretative reasons to explore these notions. The second chapter, by Marina Jirotka and Paul Luff, considers approaches to representing and modeling collaborative practices and suggests some of the sensitivities required of such approaches to conveying the outcomes of workplace studies for system design. In the third chapter, Geraldine Fitzpatrick relates her experiences developing and using a conceptual framework, called the *Locales Framework*, and reflects on whether it was able to serve as a shared abstraction to help make social thinking more accessible to software practitioners. She concludes by considering the general question of whether it is shared abstractions we need or shared people. The last chapter in this section, by Eevi E. Beck, explores the limitations of classifications drawn from the social sciences and elsewhere. She reflects on how any classification produces and is defined by what is made invisible—"what doesn't fit" the residual category. In analysis of fieldwork, the focus of researchers commonly rests on the appropriate use (or construction) of classifications. However, what is left out of and by them can be a useful resource to make an analysis more independent of previous conceptualizations. This may be particularly important in systems development that teaches an ideal of methods based on strict classifications and subdivisions.

5

On Retrieving Skilled Practices: The Contribution of Ethnography to Software Development

Chris Westrup

In discussing software development, it is easy to become immersed in one form of debate. For computer scientists the arguments often center on how software development should be done and, in a quest for relevance, on how good forms of software development may be transferred to others. Within this grouping there are ongoing debates as to how the work practices of groups should be represented either by using more formal models or by other means (see Bannon 1995). But, for many in the business world, the quest is for cheap, common, easy-to-maintain hardware/software platforms that will enable simple interconnection with other systems through the Internet and now mobile forms of communication. Already, lines of tension are fairly obvious. Businesses are busy pursuing with limited success the chimera of simple yet adaptable, secure yet interconnected, cheap yet sophisticated, information systems (for example, see Bergman, King, and Lyytinen, chapter 17, this volume). On the other hand, computer science is busy trying to identify and promulgate techniques of best practice, which may affect business systems (for example, see Binder, chapter 21, this volume). One way to perhaps establish more relevance for computer science is to seek to know more clearly the sites in which computer systems will operate. A way of doing this is to deploy techniques from the social sciences to discover what is going on in organizations.

Several chapters in this book discuss the uses of ethnography as a technique (see Fitzpatrick, chapter 7; Jirotka and Luff, chapter 6; Nyce and Bader, chapter 2; Rönkkö, chapter 11). In this chapter I aim to provide a commentary on the turn to ethnography as a technique in information systems development and research. In particular, the chapter seeks to consider important issues in the use of ethnography, and hopefully to arouse interest and debate on these issues when ethnography is invoked in the arena of information systems development.

The first part of the chapter gives an example of how ethnography has been seen and used in information systems research. In the second section the distinction made by Bauman (1987) between social science used for legislation and for interpretation of social phenomena is introduced to clarify some of the issues at stake in the future use of ethnography in the information systems arena.

Ethnographic Analysis

Ethnography has become increasingly important in discussions of information systems development and has been widely used in the area of CSCW (ACM 1995; Greenbaum and Kyng 1991; Harvey and Myers 1995; Randall, Hughes, and Shapiro 1991, 1994; Sommerville et al. 1993; Suchman 1987, 1995).[1] Ethnography (including ethnomethodology) has also been utilized increasingly often as a means of researching the development and use of information technology (see Button 1993; Lee, Liebenau, and DeGross 1997; Sharrock and Anderson 1993).

In other areas a key reason proposed for using ethnographic approaches is to provide greater depth of understanding of the social.[2] However, within social science what ethnography actually *is* remains a source of disagreement. For example, is it a technique for eliciting cultural knowledge, a detailed investigation of patterns of social interaction, or even a holistic analysis of societies? (Hammersley and Atkinson 1983). Perhaps the most widespread approach is that of cultural interpretation, an approach most commonly associated with Geertz (1973) (see also Hess 1992). In this approach, the ethnographer produces an account of the cultural practices of a specific community using extensive participant observation to develop the account. This leads to the crafting of a "thick description" of the practices of those communities.

The call for and use of ethnography in the development of information systems is associated with Suchman (1987), though others had also been working along these lines for some time (see Wynn 1979; Zuboff 1988). Suchman grounds her argument for the use of ethnography in the recognition that work practice is a social activity based on a foundation of meaningful interaction (see Suchman and Trigg 1991). Ethnography is portrayed as a technique that enables the organization to be recognized and represented as more complex and situated than prior techniques, including those of interviewing, were capable of doing.

One of the more interesting early deployments of ethnography was the work done by a team in Lancaster comprising both computer scientists and ethnographers who worked together in the analysis of an air traffic control system (Randall, Hughes, and Shapiro 1991, 1994; Randall et al. 1999; Sommerville et al. 1993). Their accounts are intriguing because they represent a collaboration built up over a number of years. Their work has, at times, led to articles being written for different audiences, including social scientists as well as those researching issues in requirements engineering and practicing requirements analysts. I will look at the early aspirations of this work in some detail as an example of how ethnography has been deployed in practice and the issues it raises.

Randall, Hughes, and Shapiro (1991) suggest that a move is being made toward a "domain oriented" aspect of systems development. They view this move, somewhat tentatively, as a paradigm shift in development that recognizes previously conceptualized functions as "borne by human agents embedded in complex social and interactional settings" (p. 4). They argue that systems fail because "they were not based on a proper ethnography of the activities to be supported in the first place" (p. 21). They go on to suggest that "an ethnographic approach will produce a much clearer view of the requirements for a system and a much better means of anticipating the dynamic effects on work organisation" (p. 21).

Randall, Hughes, and Shapiro argue for the ethnographer to act as a mediator between the social and developers. The ethnographer has greater access to the social and is able to represent it as a "low-level abstraction" so that systems designers will know what problems they face and where the complexities in the social lie. The ethnographer is able to fulfill this role because an "ethnographic record" has been produced that can be "interrogated" (Randall, Hughes, and Shapiro 1991: 23). This role appears to be unidirectional; ethnographers can speak for the social but do not attempt to speak for developers.[3]

Similarly, in 1994, Randall and associates are upbeat on the contribution of ethnography to systems development:

> The problem of sociology in the context of system design is providing adequate accounts of the "real world" characterisation of work, and it is in this respect that ethnography comes into its own.... A second but related point has to do with ethnography's potential for uncovering the tacit knowledge and understanding embedded in activity.... A third, and perhaps least well articulated, view of the ethnographer's role stems from the *neutrality* of the ethnographer *vis à vis* the wider organisational context.... The sheer width and depth of perception that should evolve from extensive ethnography opens up a space for a sophisticated understanding of *real organisational* life and its interaction with technical artefacts. (Randall, Hughes, and Shapiro 1994: 256–257; emphasis added)

The role of the ethnographer is articulated as being able to determine what the "real world" is and to produce accounts of this world. An additional nuance comes from the apparent neutrality of the ethnographer, which resides in his or her disinterestedness and distance from the rest of the organization. For Randall and his colleagues at this time, the problem was not ethnography or ethnographic technique; rather it resided in how to translate their findings into a form usable for software designers. As they put it, "in essence, the problem is one of translating the rich, textured, and highly detailed description of sociality that is associated with ethnographic enquiry into a form usable by systems designers" (Randall, Hughes, and Shapiro 1994: 246).

The main problem is seen as being the translation from the ethnographic record to an inscription usable by designers, rather than the translation of the social work setting to an ethnographic record. Indeed, they argue that one of the features of ethnography is that it can draw attention away from "abstracted versions of work" that are common in systems design. I, on the other hand, would like to draw attention to the role of ethnography in producing *abstracted versions* of work and then return to the difficulties that ethnography has in producing inscriptions usable in systems design.

Despite the comments just quoted from Randall, Hughes, and Shapiro, arguments as to the neutrality of the ethnographer are looking increasingly shaky. First, there has been concerted criticism, in particular within anthropology, centering on the rhetorical devices used to produce an account of the social (see Clifford, 1986; Clifford and Marcus, 1986). One of the main arguments is that ethnography fails to give details of its own construction and presents its record as if the ethnographer was simply engaged in "reading culture." Instead, Clifford (1986) argues that the production of ethnography is intensely dialogical but that later this is written out of the account in most ethnographies—hence the subtitle of his article, "Partial Truths." Such comments return attention to the means by which the social setting is translated into an ethnographic record.[4] A second argument, drawn from Latour (1990), has also been leveled at ethnographic practice. Dauber (1995) argues that ethnography draws its strength from recording (inscribing) "disparate elements" into standard forms that may be cross-referenced and manipulated to produce a center of calculation that appears to produce an authoritative account of a particular culture. What is at stake is how the notation and account of ethnographers is seen as authoritative. Aspects of this authority derive from the almost circular argument that ethnographers through the production of the ethnographic record can provide a detailed and unbiased account of the nature of the social.

Let us now return to the issue, raised by Randall, Hughes, and Shapiro, as to how the record produced by ethnographers is to be translated into a usable form for systems developers. To do this, I will now turn to the account of the same project furnished by the computer scientists involved for an audience of other computer scientists (Sommerville et al. 1993). Sommerville et al. point out that organizations are not structured according to formal documented standards but that a "working division of labour" is present. The inability to recognize this can lead to systems that "do not meet the real needs of users" (Sommerville et al. 1993: 165). Nor can this arrangement be obtained by user participation because users find it difficult to articulate their "informal and dynamic" working practices.[5] Instead they propose that ethnography can identify this "working division of labour." Sommerville et al. (1993: 167) characterize the results of ethnographic observation as giving "essentially background information which has provided a deeper understanding of the application domain."

One of the key concerns of Sommerville and his colleagues (1993: 170) was how the results of ethnography were to be handled: "Clearly, however, the ethnographic record must be structured in some way so that it can be usefully used by engineers who did not actually participate in the studies of work. Furthermore, if ethnography is to be useful, there must be forward and backward traceability from the ethnographic record to a more structured formulation of the systems requirements."

In other words, what the developers wanted was twofold: first, inscriptions—on paper or in a digital form—that could mobilized as a record of the social setting and, second, for those inscriptions to be capable of manipulation to allow cross-referencing between them. In the case of air traffic control, the developers designed a tool to enable this to be done. For this tool to work, the activities of ethnographers had to be disciplined both in terms of how long they were allowed to spend on site and in terms of their acquiescence to entering their ethnographic record onto the design tool known as the Designer's Notepad (DNP). As Sommerville et al. (1993: 171) explain:

> We [the systems developers] have adopted a working practice whereby the ethnographer does not work on site for long, uninterrupted periods but returns regularly to report on the progress of the work. Interim records can be entered into the Designer's Notepad. Entering these into the DNP focuses the ethnographer's attention on the records and often suggests useful structuring which can take place. The records then become immediately available to the software requirements engineers who are using the tool concurrently to develop a more structured requirements specification.

An interesting feature of this collaboration is the division of work between developers and ethnographers. Sommerville et al. (1993: 172) address this by suggesting that a poor ethnographer "will not understand" a system as well as a good requirements engineer but "a requirements engineer whose concerns are primarily technical rather than human may make elementary errors which would have been avoided with the use of ethnography."

This statement sets out the role of the designer in which the requirements engineer can speak for the information technology and the ethnographic inscription rather than the ethnographer being able to represent the social setting. This move to referring to the ethnography, the inscription, as the source for legitimate information on the social setting appears significant. Only when an ethnographic record can be produced is it capable of representing the "organization" and, as we have seen, this record has had to be put in a certain "usable" format. On the other hand, the requirements engineer is modest; she or he speaks for the information technology, and the sociality to be found in developing systems is downplayed.

What these experiences show is that there is a tendency for ethnographers in the information systems arena to promote their understandings of the social setting as naturalistic, portraying what is there. They tend to overlook the issues of how they obtain their ethnographic accounts and, perhaps even more crucially, *why* they are there in the first place. Instead, the argument is focused on how to make ethnographic accounts of more practical use to software developers. These issues are of wider importance in the search for approaches in the social sciences that inform software practice. Ethnography is but one approach drawn from the social sciences, and applying ethnography raises questions common to the deployment of any approach from another disciplinary arena.

Strategies for the Social Sciences

One way to explore these issues is to go to a wider perspective on the roles of intellectuals in society—a topic considered by Bauman in his book *Legislators and Interpreters* (1987).

Bauman makes a distinction between two types of reason—legislative and interpretative. Legislative reason is tightly bound up with modernity; it is a search for truth through the adoption of sound methods of inquiry. The veracity of what is discovered is legitimated by the methods used. Using correct methods will enable knowledge to be obtained that will be more reliable than opinions and beliefs. Once that knowledge has been collected, then, it is possible to apply it and legislate to others what should be done. This approach is what Rorty has termed *foundational philosophy*, but Bauman (1992: 121) also links this stance to the rise of the nation-state and the need for legislative power backed by legislative reason. He goes on to argue that the foundational fathers of sociology—Durkheim, Marx, and Weber—all denigrated the lay knowledge of individuals and proclaimed the correctness of the methods to be used by social scientists in identifying accurate knowledge about society.

Much of systems development theory (and practice) shares similar ground. Though many different approaches can be identified, most are based on the articulation of clear methods of development, which are to be carried out by systems developers to obtain validated knowledge about the organization. Once this has been collected, it is assumed that this knowledge should be used to design (legislate) the optimal system for the application setting. The argument set against this strategy by those advocating ethnography is twofold. First, the knowledge collected by such methods is unreliable; it makes assumptions about how work is performed in the application setting without being capable of "unearthing the underlying work practices" (Suchman 1995: 56). Furthermore, it is argued that the representation of work in terms of defined procedures, tasks, and operations can obscure the evidence that the efficiency of work is detemined instead by the capabilities of people working in these contexts (Sachs 1995: 38). Second, it is argued that there are serious failings in the installed systems developed according to the tenets of conventional systems development methodologies (Anderson 1996: 3). This is exemplified by the productivity paradox of Straussman and others where installed systems do not appear to have increased organizational productivity. However, both of these arguments could be used to propose ethnography as either an alternative or a complementary approach, but still based on a strategy of legislation. Ethnography would then be distinguished as a method that collects superior evidence on how work is performed and that would enable more efficient systems to be designed and implemented. Ethnographers would be the "experts" to be referred to by systems developers whenever tricky issues are recognized as being present in the work setting. This is very much the position found in the ethnographic work in software development described above.

However, ethnographers could also argue that their approach should be aligned with Bauman's second strategy of interpretative reason. Rather than seeking to dominate through the collection and possession of secure knowledge, interpretative reason accepts that knowledge is both provisional and plural. Knowledge is viewed as situated, socially conditioned, and socially sustained. Interpretative reason seeks to understand other knowledges through dialogue. Information is obtained from others, which leads to understanding, but this process is open ended. At each point, understanding is taken as provisional, and it is expected that reformulating that understanding in conversation will lead to a revised, but still provisional, understanding. Bauman (1992: 133) argues that just as the strategy of legislative reason can be equated with a project of modernism, interpretative reason can be linked to the postmodern condition, which, for sociology, "refrains from the task of 'correcting' common sense."

For ethnographers of work, this injunction to accept and understand the commonsense knowledge of those in the work environment strikes a common chord. The call for dialogue between those ethnographers would seek to understand and ethnographers themselves has also been advocated. For example, Suchman (1995: 63) proposes that the products of ethnographers of work "might become a basis for dialogue" between ethnographers and the subjects of their study. Thus we come to a quandary at the heart of the ethnography of work: Can it be both a strategy of legislative reason and of interpretative reason, or is a choice between the two needed?

Let us pursue what a process of dialogue aimed at mutual understanding might entail. First, it is obvious that to enter dialogue is not necessarily to seek mutual understanding. We may be simply seeking to extract something from the other or to make a point in an argument, or we may be aimlessly chatting. So just as strategies of legislative reason approach a position of an ideal type, much dialogue may have little to do with a strategy of interpretative reason. Though Bauman is at pains not to narrow the interpretative strategy to any one position, it is useful to consider Gadamer's (1975) argument on the place of philosophical hermeneutics to identify some of the issues involved in dialogue and its role in ethnography.

For Gadamer, understanding is a reaching of agreement about something between two individuals. To reach such an understanding requires an acknowledgment of the partiality of an individual's existing knowledge and recognition of the prejudices in one's own position. All objects, he argues, are interpreted as *something* in relation to our prior experience; in other words, we project our experience onto the conditions we encounter. Gadamer views this process of interpretation not simply as a conscious activity, but as strongly connected to historical conditions or tradition, which we embody particularly in our use of language. In this sense, interpretation is not simply a matter of epistemology—the process of knowing—but is linked to ontology—the (conditioned) nature of those who are interpreting. Put simply, all understanding is prejudiced, and one task of interpretation is to recognize the partiality of one's understanding and to be open to a plurality of other understandings. Gadamer's position is centered on dialogue between individuals, a conscious harking back to Greek Socratic inquiry, coupled with a realization that individuals are themselves conditioned by their experiences, their language, their traditions.

If someone practicing ethnography calls for dialogue, what might this entail for Gadamer? Dialogue oriented toward mutual understanding would appear to be founded on individuals talking face to face with an openness for each to reconsider their position and the meanings they attribute. The outcomes of such dialogue will always be provisional: it is assumed that there will not be a complete meeting of the minds, but that each understanding will open up new avenues of inquiry that, at the same time, close down other approaches. How true to the practices of ethnography could this be?[6]

For systems development, the ethnography of work seeks to uncover the work practices of those in the application area. Ethnographers will conduct, one on one, dialogues with individuals, and they will seek to understand the knowledges of those working in that environment. They may even recognize the provisional nature of the understandings they reach. Thus, there are several similarities between the practice of an ethnographer and the strictures of philosophical hermeneutics.[7] Three important differences can be identified. First, the mutual nature of understanding need not be a feature of ethnography. In classical ethnography, à la Malinowski, there were few moves to accommodate an understanding of Malinowski (the ethnographer) for the Trobriand Islanders he studied so extensively. Similarly, the ethnographer of work may not consider disclosure on her behalf as important to the process of understanding. Second, the purposes of dialogue may be more equivocal. Is the purpose of such a dialogue to promote mutual understanding, or to collect a more satisfactory account of working practice? From a functionalist perspective of systems development the latter is seen as critical, but it may be argued that the only path to successful development is through the former. Third, Gadamer focuses on the relationship between two individuals. The capability of achieving a process of mutual understanding with larger numbers is not considered, but it appears that such an increase in scale would lead to a dilution of the quality of that understanding and again raise the difficulty of mutual understanding.

Bauman's argument for an interpretative sociology goes further than taking the common sense of others seriously. He proposes that such a sociology should seek "to clarify" the conditions under which knowledge, including sociological knowledge, is formed and sustained (Bauman 1992: 133). Here, Bauman is drawing attention to the importance of reflexivity in sociological (and ethnographic) practice, something that ethnographers of work have been considering (Button and Dourish 1996; Suchman 1995). Equally important, he seeks to identify the conditions under which this knowledge is formed and focuses attention on the mechanisms of ethnographic practice.

What this could be seen to boil down to, is that the use of ethnography needs careful attention to the conditions in which the ethnography is constructed. Ethnography may retrieve the skilled practices of others, but to what use will that knowledge be put?

Discussion

The identification and representation of the complexity of the social that ethnography provides is undoubtedly an important and worthwhile contribution to the theory and practice of information systems development. But this technique is not a simple panacea. A fundamental difficulty is that on the one hand ethnography identifies this complexity and contextual detail while, on the other, the same techniques construct inscriptions on paper, in computerized form (or on video), which become mobile and decontextualised from the sites of their production. This feature ethnography shares with other information systems development techniques: it produces an abstracted representation of the workplace that can be viewed and discussed by others without the involvement of those who work there.

This raises an ethical issue. What are the effects of ethnographers in their involvement in organizations, and what are the consequences of their work? For social anthropology, which we could describe as the disciplinary home of ethnography, these issues have recently been seen as very important. In the United Kingdom, the Association of Social Anthropologists of the Commonwealth has issued a set of ethical guidelines for good research practice (ASA 1999), which set out the relations and responsibilities of the social anthropologist toward what they call "research participants," toward sponsors, funders, and employers, toward colleagues and the discipline, and toward their own and host governments. In detail the guidelines lay out a series of principles that should be observed wherever possible to protect research participants and honor their trust. One section details the participants' rights with respect to data and publications, which recommends that participants retain the copyright to interview material. Within the information systems arena, these issues have barely been raised.

The issue of trust, which informs how ethnographic work is carried out, needs to be understood carefully. Attempts to make the work practices of others transparent are not innocent. Representation leads to intervention, and it is but a small step for attempts to be made to automate the skilled practices uncovered by ethnography rather than to support them. Perhaps we will find two formulations of ethnography being practiced in systems development. One will remain small scale, research intensive, time consuming, and directed at complex work settings. Here we will find that interpretive-based ethnographies will predominate because the intention is to understand these environments and build specifically developed information systems to support them. The second is one characterized by functionalist preoccupations: the ethnographies seek to uncover the characteristics of certain work domains and then incorporate them into better mass-produced software products. This is the world of Microsoft products (Cusamano and Selby 1996: 226) that seeks to create more accurate representations of the workplace to produce commodity software products. Though the later approach may appear to produce more sensitive products for consumption, it has to be recognized that the developers of software, aided by ethnographies, actually engage in little interaction with those who will use the systems.

Is it then the fate of techniques drawn from the social sciences to become used in very different ways in software development? A prime purpose of this chapter is to try to show that deploying approaches from another disciplinary arena is not simply a matter of taking on a new technique. Indeed the very process of borrowing from elsewhere may lead to an approach in one disciplinary arena embedded in a series of debates and caveats being translated into a technique in another arena. In the field of CSCW at least, there has been continuing appraisal of the status of ethnographic work (for example, see Plowman, Rogers, and Ramage 1995). But when it comes to more wide scale use of ethnography in commercial settings or by those trained in computer science, there is a continuing danger that ethnography might be seen as just another form of expert intervention.

Ethnography has been presented as a way of decoding the social setting—a strategy that is one of providing the legitimate representation of the setting and that is a short step away from using computer systems to legislate what should be done. Taken differently, ethnography is an approach that can provide multiple outcomes and that should not be used as more than a basis for subsequent discussion. It appears that ethnography will be practiced in a variety of ways in software development (just as it has been in the social sciences); much of this is a positive development. However, it seems crucial for the contested roots of the ethnographic approach to remain visible. Rather than ethnography or any other technique derived from the social sciences simply being appropriated without discussion, it would be more useful if software developers understood the approach, its strengths and its problematics. How, is a question that needs careful attention, especially by those who teach computer science.

In short, what the story of the deployment of ethnography may teach us is that computer science in software development is not a question of techniques—it is a skilled practice that constructs artifacts shaping working lives. Rather than seeing social science as having to be imported into software development, it has been there all the time! Software developers are engaged in creating systems that are models of what they believe the working environment is (or should) be. What this book hopefully shows us is that processes of dialogue and critical investigation are always necessary to build competence and trust in the techniques used for software development.

Notes

I would like to thank Brian Bloomfield, Geoff Walsham, and Hugh Willmott for comments on a previous version of this chapter. I would also like to thank Eevi Beck, Geraldine Fitzpatrick, and Marina Jirotka for their useful comments.

1. See also the Web site in ISWorld on Qualitative Methods (www.auckland.ac.nz/msis/isworld/)

2. Dauber (1995: 75) shows this claim has been central to ethnography and goes back to Malinowski, whom he quotes as follows: "It is a very far cry from the famous answer given long ago by a representative authority who, asked, what are the manners and customs of the natives, answered, 'Customs none, manners beastly,' to the position of the modern Ethnographer." Dauber characterizes this position as the ethnographer as hero.

3. This is in contrast to some more open-ended ethnographic work, which looks at the work of designers (see Sharrock and Anderson 1993). In other words, it appears that the deployment of ethnography in requirements analysis tends to reinforce a boundary between developers and "the social" in a feature reminiscent of critiques of ethnography as constituting a boundary between us (as readers) and them (the subjects of the account) (see Clifford 1986).

4. Various methodological devices have been proposed to make this process visible such as writing verbatim accounts from informants, discussions on the construction of the ethnography, and so on (see Hess 1992). How "successful" these can be I will not discuss here (see Latour 1988; Woolgar 1988).

5. Sommerville et al. (1993) use the analogy of the difficulty in obtaining knowledge from experts for the development of expert systems.

6. This might appear to call for an ethnography of the ethnography of work but, for the arguments being raised here, this could never completely resolve this question.

7. Strictly speaking, philosophical hermeneutics is not just another method that must be followed; rather it has been articulated to clarify what the details of mutual understanding are.

References

ACM. 1995. Special issue on "Requirements Gathering: The Human Factor." *Communications of the ACM* 38(5).

Anderson, R. 1996. *Work, Ethnography and System Design*. Technical Report EPC-1996-103 Cambridge EuroPARC. http://www.xrce.xerox.com/publis/camtrs/html/anderson.htm

ASA. 1999. *Ethical Guidelines for Good Research Practice*. Association of Social Anthropologists of the Commonwealth. http://www.asa.anthropology.ac.uk/ethics2.html

Bannon, L. 1995. The politics of design: Representing work. *Communications of the ACM* 38(9): 66–68.

Bauman, Z. 1987. *Legislators and Interpreters: On Modernity, Post-modernity and Intellectuals*. Cambridge, England: Polity Press.

Bauman, Z. 1992. *Intimations of Postmodernity*. London: Routledge.

Button, G. 1993. Preface. In G. Button, ed., *Technology in Working Order: Studies of Work, Interaction, and Technology*, xi–xii. London: Routledge.

Button, G., and P. Dourish. 1996. Technomethodology: Paradoxes and possibilities. *Proceedings of the CHI'96 Conference*. New York: ACM Press.

Clifford, J. 1986. Introduction: Partial truths. In J. Clifford and G. Marcus, eds., *Writing Culture*, 1–26. Berkeley: University of California Press.

Clifford, J., and G. Marcus, eds. 1986. *Writing Culture*. Berkeley: University of California Press.

Cusamano, M., and R. Selby. 1996. *Microsoft Secrets*. London: HarperCollins-Business.

Dauber, K. 1995. Bureaucratizing the ethnographer's magic. *Current Anthropology* 36(1): 75–95.

Gadamer, H.-G. 1975. *Truth and Method*. New York: Seabury Press.

Geertz, C. 1973. *The Interpretation of Cultures*. New York: Basic Books.

Greenbaum, J., and M. Kyng, eds. 1991. *Design at Work: Co-operative Design of Computer Systems*. London: Erlbaum.

Hammersley, M., and P. Atkinson. 1983. *Ethnography: Principles in Practice*. London: Routledge.

Harvey, L., and M. Myers. 1995. Scholarship and practice: The contribution of ethnographic research methods to bridging the gap. *Information Technology and People* 8(3): 13–27.

Hess, D. 1992. Introduction: The new ethnography and the anthropology of science and technology. In D. Hess and L. Layne, eds., *Knowledge and Society: The Anthropology of Science and Technology* 9: 1–26.

Jirotka, M., and J. Goguen, eds. 1994. *Requirements Engineering: Social and Technical Issues.* London: Academic Press.

Latour, B. 1988. The politics of explanation: An alternative. In S. Woolgar, ed., *Knowledge and Reflexivity: New Frontiers in the Sociology of Knowledge*, 155–176. London: Sage.

Latour, B. 1990. Drawing things together. In M. Lynch and S. Woolgar, eds., *Representation in Scientific Practice*, 19–68. Cambridge, MA: MIT Press.

Lee, A., J. Liebenau, and J. DeGross, eds. 1997. *Information Systems and Qualitative Research.* London: Chapman & Hall.

Plowman, L., Y. Rogers, and M. Ramage. 1995, September. What are workplace studies for? *Proceedings of ECSCW'95.* Stockholm.

Randall, D., J. Hughes, J. O'Brien, T. Rodden, M. Rouncefield, I. Sommerfield, and P. Tolmie. 1999. Banking on an old technology: Understanding the organisational context of legacy issues. *Communications of the ACM* 42: 1–27.

Randall, D., J. Hughes, and D. Shapiro. 1991, July. Systems development—The fourth dimension perspectives on the social organisation of work. Paper presented at the SPRU CICT Conference, Sussex University.

Randall, D., J. Hughes, and D. Shapiro. 1994. Steps towards a partnership: Ethnography and system design. In M. Jirotka and J. Goguen, eds., *Requirements Engineering: Social and Technical Issues*, 241–258. London: Academic Press.

Sharrock, W., and B. Anderson. 1993. Working towards agreement. In G. Button, ed., *Technology in Working Order: Studies of Work, Interaction, and Technology*, 149–161. London: Routledge.

Sommerville, I., T. Rodden, P. Sawyer, R. Bentley, and M. Twindale. 1993. Integrating ethnography into the requirements engineering process. *Proceedings of International Symposium on Requirements Engineering*, 165–173. Los Alamitos, CA: IEEE CS Press.

Suchman, L. 1987. *Plans and Situated Actions.* Cambridge, England: Cambridge University Press.

Suchman, L. 1995, September 20. Working relations of technology: Production and use. Paper presented at the ESRC Seminar on Technology as Skilled Practice, Manchester University.

Suchman, L., and R. Trigg. 1991. Understanding practice: Video as a medium for reflection and design. In J. Greenbaum and M. Kyng, eds., *Design at Work: Co-operative Design of Computer Systems*, 65–90. Hillsdale, NJ: Erlbaum.

Woolgar, S., ed. 1988. *Knowledge and Reflexivity: New Frontiers in the Sociology of Knowledge.* London: Sage.

Wynn, E. 1979. *Office Conversation as an Information Medium.* Unpublished doctoral dissertation, University of California, Berkeley.

Zuboff, S. 1988. *In the Age of the Smart Machine.* Oxford: Heinemann.

6

Representing and Modeling Collaborative Practices for Systems Development

Marina Jirotka and Paul Luff

Over the last decade a body of ethnographic studies known as *workplace studies* has emerged that have focused on uncovering the details of work practices and collaborative activities in a variety of settings. These studies, though social scientific in nature, have either directly or indirectly been of interest to developers of technology in the domains in question, or to those designing more general kinds of systems. It therefore has been a concern of both computer and social scientists how best to relate naturalistic studies of work practice and interaction to those involved in the software design process. In this chapter, we consider one of the proposed ways in which findings from studies of workplace and organizational activities can be transformed so they are relevant for systems developers—through modeling.

Modeling is a common technique in engineering in general and in computer system development in particular. Whether it is undertaken formally or informally, it has the merit of focusing on critical aspects of a design problem, of clarifying complex mechanisms and processes, and of communicating particular issues, problems, and solutions between members of a design team. It is also seen as a useful way of providing a more systematic method of transforming an analysis of a current problem or activity into a specification of a solution and then into the actual design of a solution. We explore these objectives with respect to the issues arising when analyses of collaborative activities need to be transformed into the design of computer systems to support cooperative work, particularly with respect to determining the requirements for such systems. In examining how to model the details revealed by analyses of collaborative work and interaction, we briefly look at several recent proposals for modeling social and organizational activities. We then consider a notation, *communicating sequential processes* (CSP) (Hoare 1985), that has been developed to reason about parallel and concurrent activities. With reference to a workplace study undertaken in a financial trading floor, we consider the appropriateness of this notation for presenting an analysis of situated, sequential activities. We discuss the issues that such an investigative exercise raises, both for computer scientists concerned with requirements engineering and for social scientists involved in workplace studies.

Workplace Studies and the Systems Development Process

A wide variety of naturalistic studies of settings have been collected together under the term *workplace studies* (e.g., Engeström and Middleton 1996; Heath, Knoblauch, and Luff 2000; Luff, Hindmarsh, and Heath 2000; Plowman, Rogers, and Ramage 1995). What these have in common is a concern for detailing how work and interaction are accomplished in a wide range of everyday work settings, including such disparate domains as hospitals, construction sites, the shop floors of the printing industry, the bridges of ships, software engineering, medical interactions, architecture and design practices, control rooms of transport systems and NASA mission control (e.g., Button and Sharrock 1997; Filippi and Theureau 1993; Heath and Luff 1996b; Hutchins 1995; Luff and Heath 1998; Rogers 1992; Watts et al. 1996). These workplace studies draw from a variety of analytic orientations, including activity theory, distributed cognition, course-of-action analysis, and symbolic interactionism. But it is perhaps those drawing from the ethnomethodological orientation that are both most prevalent and have been considered most extensively for their consequences for computer system and design, particularly in the field of computer-supported cooperative work (CSCW). Utilizing insights from the work of Harold Garfinkel and Harvey Sacks (e.g., Garfinkel 1967; Sacks 1992), these studies seek to reveal the practices and procedures that participants themselves use to organize their activities in a setting and focus on the ways in which workplace activities are produced in real-time, everyday interaction. Such studies utilize fieldwork, sometimes supplemented by video recordings of naturally occurring events, in order to examine the details of activities in interaction, and the ways participants make use of artifacts, like documents and computer technologies in the course of their work. Thus, rich and detailed analyses have been undertaken concerning the use of documents and technologies within the work of air traffic controllers (Hughes et al. 1988); the ways monitors and screens are utilized as public resources in airport control rooms (Goodwin and Goodwin 1996; Suchman 1993); how software engineering practices shape and are shaped by procedures and formalisms (Button and Sharrock 1994, 2000); the interactional production of deals in financial trading rooms (Heath et al. 1994–95); and the practices surrounding the uses of paper documents and computer systems in general medical practice (Greatbatch et al. 1993).

Although these exercises raise important issues within the social sciences, they also have been of interest to developers of novel technologies. Indeed, many have been undertaken with respect to some technological development or in collaboration with, or part of some program of research by, one of the major computer system research laboratories or one of the national or international technological research funding bodies. Consequently, developers have frequently been involved in drawing out implications for the design of technologies from the studies. These may be for particular systems in the specific domains of the study or more generic technologies. So, the analyses developed by these studies have been drawn on when considering such diverse technologies as media spaces (Gaver et al. 1993); collaborative virtual environments (Hindmarsh et al. 1998); mobile systems (Luff and Heath 1998); workflow systems (Bowers and Button 1995); and networked document production systems (Harper 1998). It is therefore not surprising that in the course of these efforts the researchers, both social scientists and systems developers, have reflected on the relationship of naturalistic studies and the design process and sought to unpack many of the analytic, methodological, and practical issues emerging from such exercises (e.g., Harper 2000; Heath and Luff 2000; Jirotka and Goguen 1994; Jirotka and Wallen 2000; Sommerville et al. 1993). In particular, researchers have frequently considered how methods and findings from the social sciences might most usefully become part of the tools available to the software design community. Researchers have outlined how such studies might influence various aspects of the development process—such as requirements, by providing unique insights into work to be supported or transformed; or design, by determining particular and relevant features of proposed systems; or for enhancing the conceptual apparatus software engineers can draw on, providing alternative and richer ways of thinking about the nature of information, communication, and cooperative work.

Various problems have been raised with respect to undertaking such analyses and representing the findings for use in design. Practical issues have been debated about the level of skill needed by analysts to undertake these types of studies. Also, such studies may take a long time and the results may be too unstructured to fit the organizational constraints of many software development processes. Such problems are not unique to the proposal of drawing on workplace studies for design. They have been raised when other novel methods and approaches have been suggested to support the software development process, whether these be alternative requirements methods, formal specification, or the use of sophisticated development tools. Similarly, the difficulties of transforming analyses of current conduct into prescriptive technological solutions mirror the difficulties that methods analyzing individual and psychological aspects of human behavior entail. It is not unusual that analyses of human conduct would be incommensurate with the demands of engineers seeking predictions concerning the consequences of their proposed solutions. This is also true when considering how to transform findings from more conventional approaches such as task analysis or user-centered system design into recommendations for system development. Moreover, more foundational issues deriving from these studies may need to be addressed. In particular, these issues concern how to analyze activities surrounding the use of artifacts as diverse as documents and computer systems, how to develop analyses of such activities with respect to interactional activities including talk and visual conduct, and how to analyze conduct mediated by and through novel communication and collaboration spaces and devices.

Though there may be a gulf dividing the practices of social scientists from the requirements of software developers, this may not preclude the development of social scientific approaches that can be utilized to advance practical outcomes for software development. Software engineers increasingly recognize that they need to be sensitive to the social and organizational context in which their systems are to be deployed, in general, and to particular work and interactional practices. The potential of considering social practices has gained influence within software development, even into systems engineering, to the extent that proposals have been put forward to "industrialize" ethnography and to suggest ways in which naturalistic studies can be integrated into the design process. For example, some researchers have focused on improving the communication between ethnographers and software designers and have suggested ways of making the process more systematic, for example in terms of a "question-and-answer" approach, where a set of issues are developed for the ethnographers to explore with respect to explicit design concerns (Randall, Hughes, and Shapiro 1994). "Quick and dirty" approaches have also been suggested that attempt to "fit" the ethnographic orientation into the practical time constraints of software development projects. These approaches also provide guidelines for conducting such studies and for structuring observations in such a way that may be relevant for design (Hughes et al. 1997, 1996). More recently, Pycock et al. (1998) consider how virtual environments can be utilized to envision future work practices and processes, drawing on previous ethnographic studies. Though such tools may be useful for presenting ethnographic observations, a critical issue for research lies in determining ways of transforming the ethnographic material so that it remains sensitive to the practices of designers themselves and thus can be readily used by them in the design process, while also preserving the richness of the ethnographic account. With respect to this, one particular software engineering activity has been the focus of much interest. Throughout the development process, software engineers are encouraged to develop models of particular processes, mechanisms, and solutions. These models are not only seen as an aid to communication between designers and others involved in the process, but also for clarification, so that particular issues can be focused on, abstracted, and unpacked. Even if software and system developers do not explicitly adopt or use a formal or structural approach to systems design, they frequently find the need to focus on aspects of a problem, develop solutions that are generic to more than one case, and utilize notations to communicate issues and potential solutions to others (Booch 1991).

Given the complex details revealed in workplace and other related studies, it is therefore not surprising that some researchers have proposed modeling aspects of the social and organizational context in which technologies are to be deployed. Such suggestions have parallels with proposals developed from other orientations that explore the "social" and organizational context of technologies (e.g., Eason 1989; Stamper 1994). They offer one approach for systems engineers to investigate issues of consequence to the specification and design of technology. Perhaps underlying this interest is a concern to provide ways of systematically progressing between the phases of systems development, particularly from domain analysis, through to requirements analysis and specification and thence to system specification and design. A universal modeling language or representation scheme could not only be used unambiguously to convey critical requirements, but also may form the foundation for some processing later, either to develop predictions of outcomes of technological interventions or to develop specifications or even systems. Modeling may therefore bridge stages in the design process whether this is a conventional serial process, a prototyping approach, or some more radical development process. Even if this is not automated, modeling languages and representations offer the potential of expressing clearly and unambiguously issues for others at later times in the development cycle.

Modeling Organizational Activities and Social Interaction

It is often claimed that modeling is attractive to all engineering disciplines because the building of models appeals to the principles of decomposition, abstraction, and hierarchy—features that are perceived to be critical for the design of large and complex systems (see Booch 1991). Because software systems are inherently complex, models of different kinds represent ways that analysts can reason about structures, make trade-offs, and overall give some projection for implementation. In practice, software engineers may draw on a range of modeling techniques;

however there are still only a few studies that have looked at the actual use of these techniques in design. Those that have been carried out imply that modeling techniques are used in different ways from those developers initially intended (Bellotti 1988; Button and Sharrock 1994). Nonetheless, modeling, whether adopted as part of some formal process or an informal activity, does seem to be an intrinsic part of the practices of software development.

In the earliest phases of systems development, those phases characterized as requirements engineering, modeling has been considered a way of understanding and communicating aspects of the physical and social world for the purposes of clarifying what is required from a new system (Myopoulos 1992). The models produced as part of a requirements exercise are perceived to allow analysts to investigate, represent, and communicate various aspects of the technical system. These might include hard process problems, particular system and domain issues, or particular communication patterns, and may assist analysts in determining the system's capabilities and assessing trade-offs when requirements conflict. Similar to the expectations in design, models are undertaken in requirements in the hope that analysts will be able to reason about aspects of the desired computer system in such a way that they may be able to predict systems behavior. However, because models are not only utilized to communicate information to software designers and testers, but also to customers, managers, and users who may not be familiar with the various techniques and notations, they should be clear and relatively easy to understand.

A key concern in requirements has been analyzing social, collaborative, and organizational behavior and developing an understanding of how such information can be made to fit into the process. Thus, research has focused on the problem of communicating this type of information to designers or on how to integrate an understanding of these aspects when making trade-offs between different and possibly conflicting requirements. The techniques for modeling aspects of the social and/or the technical system under investigation in the requirements exercise have fundamentally emerged from the methods utilized in the software development process itself. Therefore, in their efforts to make social and organizational practices available to systems designers, many analysts have attempted to use existing techniques that have been developed specifically for modeling particular aspects of computer systems behavior. We investigate the appropriateness of this practice here, particularly with regard to modeling aspects of social interaction and collaborative work, where critical resources for producing and recognizing activities might be lost in the representations that may not adequately describe them.

Various forms of modeling techniques are available to the requirements analyst in such endeavors. For example, Choobineh et al. (1988) suggest that a model can be developed from various documents, such as forms, that are used in the problem domain. The technique, used primarily in data-intensive applications for database design, views the form as a data model itself where not just the items on the form are analyzed, but also the instructions for completing them. Underlying this approach is an assumption that the structure of forms can provide the basis for the structural components of a functional model because forms provide suitable input to describe the data layout of a system at a high level of abstraction (Chen 1976). A claim supported by Loucopoulos and Karakostas (1995, 41), who state that a form "is a formal model and thus, less ambiguous and inconsistent than equivalent knowledge expressed in natural language."

In assuming that forms are "easy to read and understand" (Choobineh et al. 1988, 242), the technique focuses on the form as a static representation of communication. It considers how the form is designed to be filled in rather than the ways it is used and made sense of by participants. Indeed, when considered in more detail, it may not be straightforward to read and understand a form. Participants may make sense of particular items with respect to other entries and may take for granted items and entries that are elided (see Heath 1982). Making sense of forms relies on a set of interpretative practices and organizational competencies both by the reader and the writer, so that entries are understood with respect to the circumstances of how they were written or how they should be read.

Though particular documents may be critical to the success of social and organizational activities, the tendency to link form filling, or any documentary activity, with a set of explicit and formulizable rules may cause crucial aspects of communication and work activities to be overlooked. Excessive emphasis on these rules and procedures can result in technology that is too rigid and inflexible when put into use.[1]

Other researchers have explicitly considered how to draw from ethnographic workplace studies that reveal the informal, implicit, and tacit aspects of collaborative work in order to develop models to communicate the details of both. Their concern is how to make accessible the complexity and richness of the analysis in a form appropriate for systems developers. For example, Viller and Sommerville (1999) have undertaken a modeling exercise based on an earlier framework developed through a collaboration between social scientists and computer scientists (Hughes et al. 1997, 1995) and utilized an established system design notation, the universal modeling language (UML). They focus their exercise on one characteristic revealed in fieldwork and delineated in the framework: that of "awareness of work." Such an explicit modeling exercise is seen as a recognition that "the design process must not only build up an understanding of the social aspects of the system but also be able to record them in such a way that they can be communicated to other stakeholders and ultimately feed into design itself" (Viller and Sommerville 1999, 12). The use of UML, then, is justified by the fact that it conforms to designers' current work practices, rather than, for example, requiring them to learn new methods or techniques. Their model of "awareness of work" using UML focuses on the interrelationships between, and properties of, personnel and objects, in order for "awareness" of another's activities to be accomplished. For example, the awareness of a particular location of a form indicating the activities that have and are to be performed on it is modeled in terms of a set of objects and relationships. However, characterizing "awareness" in terms of such a semiformal model may misrepresent the very features the model is meant to communicate. Awareness is not a discrete activity tied to particular objects and individuals, but rather a gloss for a disparate set of emerging collaborative practices (see Goodwin and Goodwin 1996; Heath and Luff 1996a). Such models may convey the *knowledge that* an activity is accomplished but neglect the *knowledge how* it is accomplished (see Ryle 1949). The model could neglect what it is endeavoring to convey: the situated and contingent features of everyday work.[2]

The potential for modeling situated action is a central concern for Goguen (1994). Drawing on a fundamental organizing feature of computer science, he outlines a mathematical theory of abstract data types to model the structure of situated activity, utilizing the concept of a situated abstract data type to look at aspects of formal and situated action in naturally occurring activities. He develops a formal model that endeavors to represent how various abstract constructs are oriented toward everyday conduct. It may be argued that he takes a particularly constrained conception of situated and contingent action "in context." This contrasts with analyses such as those by Suchman (1987) or Heath and Luff (2000), which focus on the local and interactional context of the accomplishment of actions and activities. In these analyses the production and intelligibility of an activity is situated with respect to the immediately prior actions of coparticipants. Thus, the context is continually being shaped with respect to the prior actions of others and renewed through the ongoing activity.[3]

Modeling activities revealed by naturalistic analyses, such as those undertaken in workplace studies, may be fraught with difficulties. Recent attempts have sought to provide frameworks for describing, representing, and communicating the social and the organizational aspects of work, the contingent and the tacit, and the collaborative and the situated. By their very nature these are hard to delineate, formalize, and represent. The kinds of activities to be conveyed are produced through informal, interpretative, and interactional practices. It is perhaps not surprising that diagrammatic and formal notations do not seem appropriate to present the complexity revealed through detailed analyses. Nevertheless, these models do not necessarily have to provide complete, or unambiguous, models of workplace activities. The motivations of their designers lie in developing ways to communicate issues of concern—"hard problems," as they have been called—to others in the design process or in raising issues for possible design of solutions. In the following section we consider a notation that has been developed to talk about concurrent and sequential activities: CSP (Hoare 1985). Drawing on this notation, we consider how the notion of situated action may be characterized, what aspects may be modeled, and how they may be communicated to others in the design process.

Modeling Collaboration: An Exercise

CSP, developed by Hoare (1985), is a notation for describing concurrent systems—that is, systems where more than one process occurs at a time. The notation allows the development of, and reasoning about, processes that interact with each other and the environment. CSP also allows for various mathematical models and reasoning methods that provide analysts with resources to reason about possible states and the consequences of various combinations of states occurring. It takes as critical the notion of a process whose behavior is described by a sequence of events it might "use." A process may be put in parallel or interleaved with other processes so that various combinations of events can evolve. Thus, CSP is concerned with sequentiality as well as with parallel and interleaved activities. Given the previous discussion, CSP could also provide a way of elucidating particular aspects of situated social and organizational activities neglected by previous approaches. In the following discussion, we consider this notation with respect to the previous analyses we have undertaken in a particular setting, in this case a financial trading floor (Heath et al. 1994–95; Jirotka, Luff, and Heath 1993). We do not attempt to build a complete model of a workplace setting in CSP. Instead, we wish to investigate the issues that emerge when considering modeling sociointeractional resources using a notation for sequential activities. In this exercise, we will use simple illustrative examples of fundamental concepts in CSP such as interleaving and parallelism.[4]

Communicating Sequential Processes

The development of CSP involved a movement away from considering computer processes as linear and distinct from the environment around them, to systems where events can happen in parallel and interact with other events (Hoare 1985). So, in a concurrent system, the various components are "in (more or less) independent states [and] it is necessary to understand which combination of states can arise and the consequences of each" (Roscoe 1998, 2). This is perhaps most apparent when considering computer communication and distributed systems where various processes occur in separate places. In these cases it is important to model concurrent processes so that consistency between them and the potential communication breakdown can be reasoned about.[5]

Because CSP allows reasoning about processes that interact with each other and their environment, the most fundamental object in CSP is a *communication event*. Communication in CSP has been defined as "a transaction or synchronization between two or more processes rather than as necessarily being the transmission of data one way" (Roscoe 1998, 8–9). Thus, communication events are considered events or actions that can describe patterns of behavior regarding objects in the world. The set of events viewed as relevant in the description of an object is termed its *alphabet*. In CSP a process is the behavior pattern of an object described by the set of events selected in its alphabet. Thus we could define "agreeing a deal" in a trading room in terms of two independent processes: one for "agreeing a price" (PRICE) and one for "agreeing the amount" (AMOUNT) of stock to be bought or sold.

$$\mathrm{PRICE} = \mathit{agreePrice} \rightarrow \mathit{agreeDeal} \rightarrow \mathrm{STOP}$$

$$\mathrm{AMOUNT} = \mathit{agreeAmount} \rightarrow \mathit{agreeDeal} \rightarrow \mathrm{STOP}$$

Here *agreePrice* and *agreeDeal* are events in the alphabet of the PRICE process, and *agreeAmount* and *agreeDeal* are in the alphabet of AMOUNT.

Processes can participate in events in sequence (e.g., *agreePrice* and then *agreeDeal*) and can then be put together in parallel (denoted by the operator ||). When two processes are brought together to run concurrently, events that are in both their alphabets require the simultaneous participation of both processes. However, each process can also evolve its own events independently. So, if we now put PRICE and AMOUNT in parallel

$$\mathrm{PRICE} \parallel \mathrm{AMOUNT}$$

we can see that the two processes are synchronized around *agreeDeal*. Because these processes have been put in parallel, we cannot *agreeDeal* until we *agreePrice* and *agreeAmount*.

We can further extend the complexity by defining a dealing process in terms of PRICE, AMOUNT, and other processes as:

$$\mathrm{DEAL} = \mathrm{PRICE} \parallel \mathrm{AMOUNT} \parallel \mathrm{STOCK} \parallel \mathrm{BUY} \parallel \mathrm{SELL} \parallel \text{etc.}$$

where each of the processes PRICE, AMOUNT, STOCK, BUY, and SELL may be synchronized around *agreeDeal.* However, it is not specified in what order they are accomplished.

Processes may be described as a single stream of behavior, but they may also be influenced by their interactions with the environment in which they are placed. Thus, CSP provides ways of describing processes that offer a choice of actions to their environment (denoted by the operator |). For example, a price fluctuation in the stock market could be described in terms of a simple choice of moving up then down, or down then up. This may be defined as

$$\text{PRICEFLUCT} = (up \rightarrow down \rightarrow \text{STOP} \mid down \rightarrow up \rightarrow \text{STOP})$$

where the process can do the events *up* then *down* or *down* then *up* in either order.

There may also be situations where it is useful to join processes with the same alphabet to run concurrently but without interacting or synchronizing with each other. CSP also offers the ability to provide parallel composition through interleaving (denoted by the operator |||). Here, the processes run independently of each other. If one of the processes cannot participate in the action, the other one must do. However, if both processes could be engaged, the choice between them is nondeterministic. We could then describe two (or more) deals happening at the same time using interleaving

$$\text{DEAL}_1 \mid\mid\mid \text{DEAL}_2$$

where each of these deals is independent of the other and it is not specified which deal will be accomplished.

An Instance from the Trading Floor

Having provided a few basic examples of the fundamental concepts and operators in CSP, we will explore how these might be utilized to represent some of the interactional resources detailed in a workplace study. As an illustrative example we draw from a particular instance considered in an earlier analysis of the financial trading floor (Luff and Jirotka 1998). In this instance, Derek, a salesman in stocks and shares, shouts across the desk to two stockbrokers who trade together (Tim and Paul) for the current prices on "BATS" (the abbreviation for British American Tobacco shares).[6]

Transcript 1

Derek: What are BATS
(1.0)
Paul: ┌That's us
Tim: └BATS
(0.6)
Derek: BATS
(0.4)
Paul: That's us
(5.3) *((Derek comes round and looks at the screens))*
Tim: What have you got in mind sir
(1.0)
Derek: I want to sell a hundred
(0.7)
I want to sell fifty Orange D'you do Orange?

Derek does not get a direct response to his question about the price of BATS. Instead, two traders, Tim and Paul, reply simultaneously with "That's us" and "BATS." Derek then comes around to stand behind Tim and Paul and repeats the name of the share, to which Paul replies again: "That's us." After Tim has asked Derek what he has "in mind," Derek replies he wants "to sell a hundred" and then adds that he also wants to sell "fifty Orange" (telecommunications shares). Thus, Derek, Tim, and Paul move into trading in two stocks, British American Tobacco (BATS) and Orange Telecommunications (Orange). After a little discussion over the prices, when Tim actually begins to reject the deal, they agree to a trade for both the stocks.

Transcript 2

Derek: (Give) me a half penny in one of them
(0.3)
Tim: No (I ┌ts)
Paul: *((To Derek))* └ I'll give you three and a half for the Orange
(0.4)

Derek: That's fair enough
(0.3)
Derek: Three and a half for the Orange
(0.3)
Derek: Three and a half for the BATS
((Tim turns to look at Paul, Paul looks at Tim))
Derek: Thank you

What is interesting about this instance is the ways it is ambivalent to whom Derek's initial request to sell is made. It could be to Tim or Paul, or to both. Although Tim and Paul deal in a common list of shares, they each keep individual accounts, or "books." So, despite collaborating over many deals, they can also trade separately. It is only after Tim's rejection of Derek's suggestion that Paul identifies himself as an alternative buyer. Indeed, up to this moment Paul's participation appears to emphasize the joint nature of his dealing with Tim, repeating "that's us" in reply to Derek's initial request. Even when the trade is agreed on with Derek, it is unclear how the deal will be recorded (booked):

Transcript 3

Paul: Which one are you booking Tim
(0.6)
Tim: Eh (1.5) I'll buy the hundred BATS
(0.3) *((Both start writing in their tickets))*
Paul: All right. (0.5) I'll buy the fifty Orange. (1.0) We're short of ( ) (.) hundred an (.) I know they're high but we're short of a hundred and fifty Vodafone. If we can use th-these fifty (.) Orange to bash em down at some point doesn't matter does it

Such openness and ambivalence are not uncommon in trading, and it would seem important for such aspects to be made clear to anyone developing technologies in the domain.[7]

If we consider some aspects of dealing such as this we could gloss the activities of a trader in a particular stock as a process such as the following:

$$\begin{aligned} SB_{\text{stock}} = {} & \mathit{initiateDeal}_{\text{stock}} \rightarrow \mathit{agreeAmount}_{\text{stock}} \rightarrow \mathit{agreePrice}_{\text{stock}} \\ & \rightarrow \mathit{agreeDeal}_{\text{stock}} \rightarrow \mathit{recordDeal}_{\text{stock, dealer}} \rightarrow \text{STOP} \end{aligned}$$

That is, the process involves a sequence of activities from initiating a deal, agreeing on a price and amount (the critical components that are varied), agreeing to deal at that amount, and then recording the deal. In the example above, Tim, Paul, and the salesman share all the above events except that they record their deals independently.[8] Thus, the activities of the salesman could be glossed as

$$SB_{stock} = initiateDeal_{stock} \rightarrow agreeAmount_{stock} \rightarrow agreePrice_{stock} \rightarrow agreeDeal_{stock} \rightarrow recordSale_{stock} \rightarrow STOP$$

The collaboration between the stockbroker and the salesman could be considered by putting the two processes together in parallel:[9]

$$SB_{stock} \parallel SB_{stock}$$

In the above example, the simultaneous dealing in Orange and BATS may be viewed as independent in the same way that, for example, agreeing on the price of BATS is independent of agreeing on the amount of BATS. In CSP terms,

$$SB_{BATS} \; ||| \; SB_{Orange}$$

The salesman, Derek, knows he has been dealing with two stockbrokers, but he may not be able to tell, and may not care, which of the following four possible sequences of events will complete the process when the record of events, or in CSP terms, traces are examined.[10] These are

$$\langle recordDeal_{BATS, Tim}, recordDeal_{Orange, Tim} \rangle$$

$$\langle recordDeal_{BATS, Tim}, recordDeal_{Orange, Paul} \rangle$$

$$\langle recordDeal_{BATS, Paul}, recordDeal_{Orange, Paul} \rangle$$

$$\langle recordDeal_{BATS, Paul}, recordDeal_{Orange, Tim} \rangle$$

This may not be important to the salesman, because he merely records the local institution as the counterparty to the deal, but as we noted earlier it does not appear clear to the stockbrokers which way to resolve the private activity of recording the deals. This ambivalence is reflected in the nondeterminism arising from CSP's conception of interleaving.[11]

We might also consider the completion of the trade. In this fragment the utterance "Thank you" by Derek not only closes the interaction, but also agrees the deal. Only then can it be concluded as completed. The utterance can be seen to be accomplishing a "double duty," as discussed in some studies in conversational analysis (e.g., Turner 1976). Such double-duty activities could be reflected in CSP by characterizing the closing as an event shared between various processes: the closing "participating" in an "interaction process" (representing the closing of the interaction) and "deal process" (representing the agreement on the deal). These processes could evolve in different ways: an activity like "thank you" both completing the interaction and agreeing to the deal.

The ability for processes to evolve in different ways would allow us to distinguish interactionally between the participation statuses of the participants, for example when considering utterances like outlouds (Heath et al. 1994–95; Jirotka, Luff, and Heath 1993). Such utterances are broadcast not requiring particular responses from particular individuals, being potentially of interest to all the participants within hearing range (as may be the case in Derek's initial "What are BATS"). This could be reflected in CSP, all deal processes having a chance to evolve if an outloud occurs; all having the opportunity to recognize the relevance of the outloud to them and initiate a trading process in a particular stock, but not necessarily. This suggests ways of considering the public and private nature of activities in the workplace. Events in common to the alphabets of more than one process can be shared, and thus be made public. Where processes do not share events, those events can be hidden from other processes, and therefore be private. More important, the different ways activities are made public can be reflected in the ways different processes evolve. The distinction between the public and private nature of activities in the workplace depends on how activities are produced for others, how they are recognized by others, and how they may produce different trajectories of actions for other people. CSP provides the mechanisms for describing collaboration and the coordination that allows us to determine not just that an activity has occurred, but that it has been deemed relevant by other participants, who may then undertake possibly different next activities.

There is therefore a possibility of distinguishing how activities are made public in collaborative settings and the different ways that those activities engender action by coparticipants. Hence, with respect to issues associated with "awareness" considered earlier, it could be possible to reflect the ways participants configure awareness for others and how those activities are rendered sequentially relevant by other coparticipants.

Though the examples given here are brief and merely illustrate some characteristics of CSP, they do suggest that the notation provides resources for reflecting on how the ordering of activities undertaken by individuals can be left open and flexible while at times they can be coordinated with the actions of others. In other investigative exercises we have also considered the extent to which the notation could provide resources for conveying the ways in which the activities of coparticipants are interrelated. Examples include how visible actions produced by a participant, but not explicitly directed at another, can be utilized by others; how a single action can accomplish multiple interactional activities; and how activities emerge and are closed through collaboration (Jirotka 2001). CSP's consideration of parallel and interleaved processes, private and public events, and the potential for outcomes to be nondeterministic provides critical resources for reflecting the contingent, situated, and sequential nature of collaborative activities.

Discussion

When considering recent efforts to model social and organizational activities, it appears that the notations adopted may not have been the most appropriate for modeling the contingent nature of workplace conduct. The notations seemed best suited for focusing on activities undertaken by individuals, certain aspects of which remained stable and are clearly delineated from others. This seems in marked contrast to the workplace activities that these notations were trying to convey and that are revealed by social science studies. These studies suggest how activities emerge and change, with features that may be left ambiguous for practical purposes. It seems important to convey these flexible and open, contingent and situated practices to designers if the technologies they develop are to be sensitive to the settings in which they are deployed.

The notations adopted may indeed obscure the very phenomena they are intending to convey. Attempting to model communicative action in terms of single channels or relationships between coparticipants, as between "speaker" and "hearer" or "writer" and "reader," for example, may hide from view the interactive and collaborative production of the interaction, from moment to moment. Considering "awareness" as a simple property, a relationship—or as a simple activity between individuals and objects—glosses the very practices, complex and heterogeneous, through which participants collaborate and interact.

With its concern with concurrent activities, CSP does appear to offer resources for conveying critical features of collaborative and interactional workplace activities. Of course, this is not to say that it is not possible to convey these features in other notations. Complex models of collaborative work could be developed using object-oriented and algebraic notations, but when considering those approaches it is important to examine the motivations behind the modeling exercise in the first place.

If the modeling exercise is merely intended to convey information to system developers, it is unclear why a formal (or semiformal) notation is necessary, particularly because natural language is quite an effective way of revealing the ambiguous, complex, and rich nature of everyday conduct. Even if there are pragmatic reasons for adopting a particular notation or if it results in parsimonious descriptions, its use may not ensure that the most appropriate aspects of "hard problems" are conveyed. Indeed, it may be that if the objective of the model is to be a communication tool, other resources may be appropriate for this. An analysis of requirements supported by instances from audiovisual recordings captured in the field may both serve to highlight critical issues of relevance to design and also provide ways of conveying the complexity and richness of the work practices under consideration (Jirotka, Luff, and Heath 1993).

Hence, modeling should provide more than a mere communication device; hopefully, for example, it will provide some resources for considering the implications of a particular domain or requirements analysis within the systems development process. One shortcoming of utilizing semiformal notations is that they provide few resources for considering the consequences of the model developed. If the requirements engineer wishes to explore systematically the interrelationships between the components of the model, this either has to be accomplished through detailed inspection or by building appropriate tools for analysis.

Nor is this process necessarily straightforward with formal notations. It is possible using a variety of formal notations to define data types and operators that represent certain aspects of naturally occurring conduct, and these notations can be utilized to outline particular objects, activities, and their interrelationships of interest. Such notations could provide representations of fine details of interaction and collaboration (Jirotka 2001). However, the structure of the modeling notation will not necessarily resonate with the purposes to which it is put. To be able to reason about the model, it is necessary to allow computation to be accomplished on what has been defined, effectively outlining a "program" that "runs" the model in order to explore the consequences of what has been defined. With some algebraic notations it may not be clear how such a program should proceed, or whether the notation supports the relevant kind of processing. CSP not only appears to provide an appropriate structure for reflecting concurrent and collaborative activities, but also a means of interpreting them. Since this approach is primarily concerned with the representation of concurrent activities, embedded within CSP are a range of resources for describing coordinated action. Moreover, the traces inherent in CSP, briefly considered here, are not merely records of the process, but resources for reasoning about the processes defined. The multiple traces produced when executing a CSP model allow for the exploration of the consequences of different definitions of processes.

The capacity to reason with a model suggests a way the modeling activity could provide more than a means of communicating between ethnographers and designers. Undoubtedly there are problems with trying to manage complex descriptions of workplace activities for the purposes of design, particularly given the different analytic resources and practical motivations of the different parties (see Randall, Hughes, and Shapiro 1994). It may be that tools and techniques to "bridge the gap" may indeed assist the communication of analyses of complex activities for the purposes of design, but it would be a shame if in doing so, these approaches obscured the very thing they were intended to convey.

Considering the problem of the relationship between the work of social scientists and computer system developers as one of communication may also overlook the possibility for greater collaboration between the two disciplines. If a modeling technique could facilitate the consideration of particular aspects of the setting, without undue work being necessary to define additional notation and tools, it may be that the modeling exercise would not just be a resource for communication to others in the development process or for providing a conduit to an eventual design. Modeling could be a way to explore the consequences of an emerging analysis so that through it particular aspects could be considered in more detail in the fieldwork. A preliminary analysis of the collaborative conduct of participants, how they are aware of each other's activities, how a particular tool or artifact figures in an activity, or how an activity is initiated, left open, or closed, as examples, could provide the resources for an initial model, which when analyzed could raise issues for further investigation and analysis.

The provision of additional and relevant resources for the earlier phases of the design process may also mean less emphasis is placed on prototyping as the critical means through which social science work can be interwoven with design activities. Appropriate modeling exercises could provide a way for the concerns of developers to inform the emergence of a requirements analysis rather than at a later stage when an initial prototype has been designed and the systems development trajectory is already underway.

Summary

Whether undertaken using a formal, semiformal, or diagrammatic notation, as part of a systematic design phase or as an informal exercise on behalf of a systems designer, modeling is a recurrent activity undertaken by software engineers. It is used as a way to help clarify and communicate issues for the design and specification of technical systems. Modeling would also appear to be one way of bridging the gap between those analyzing through social science studies the nature of workplace activities and those trying to develop appropriate and relevant technologies for such domains. Because the studies of social and organizational conduct tend to be rich and detailed, models of various kinds could provide a way of communicating these details to system developers in the early stages of systems design. Unfortunately, the social science studies have revealed the open, ambiguous, tacit, and interactional nature of social and collaborative activities, which perhaps inevitably prove difficult to model in formal and semiformal notations. Moreover, modeling organizational activities may be particularly problematic when the frameworks used to model them are too rigid and inflexible to account for the emergent and situated nature of social and organizational conduct.

It may therefore be worth reconsidering the role of, and the resources for, modeling when seeking to utilize studies of social practice for systems design. For example, there may be alternative ways of clarifying, communicating, and presenting ethnographic analyses for requirements and design. The analyses themselves, particularly when supported by suitable materials, such as video recordings, may be the most suitable way of communicating what is necessary for different participants at different times in the development process. Modeling, however, may be more critical if, given appropriate tools and notations, it supports the analysis of requirements, raising critical issues not just for design but for social scientific inquiry. This would require a more fine-grained collaboration between social and computer scientists, where the problems are not considered merely in terms of how best to convey information from the former to the latter, or indeed how an understanding of everyday work and interaction can inform systems design. The collaborative effort would also focus on how the requirements for developing technology can support the investigation of social interaction and work practice.

Notes

The authors would like to thank Lincoln Wallen for his contribution to issues discussed in this chapter. We would also like to thank the participants in the field study for all their kind patience while we were undertaking the research. We are grateful, too, for the insightful comments by Geraldine Fitzpatrick, Eevi Beck, and Chris Westrup on an earlier version of this chapter.

1. A case in point involves particular computer systems designed to support medical record keeping by primary-care practitioners (Heath and Luff 1996b). The system was developed that mirrored the information entered on paper forms.

However, in focusing on the "formal" categories that need to be recorded and ignoring the tacit ways medical records are written and read, the resulting system required users to enter information in ways that have none of the subtlety of the paper record. For example, particular items on the computer system have to be entered that were previously elided, particular entries have to be made explicit whose ambivalence could previously be "understood" by any competent practitioner, and pairs or sets of items that were previously "read" and "understood" together are now separated in different screens of the system. It is therefore not surprising that practitioners continued to use the paper records alongside the newly developed computer system.

2. This could again lead to undesirable consequences when the requirements are transformed into design. It could be possible to unduly develop systems that focus on providing information to make colleagues aware "of" particular activities and events and neglecting "how" this needs to be accomplished in a domain. It could be seen that various "awareness servers" focus on the information that needs to be presented to others, rather than on the ways this provision can be made apparent and relevant (Fuchs, Pankoke-Babatz, and Prinz 1995; Hayashi et al. 1999). In a similar vein, the development of media spaces and some collaborative virtual environments have focused on providing additional resources concerning coparticipants rather than on how these resources can be better integrated into the everyday practices and interaction of the users.

3. There may be a danger in any formal analysis of focusing on aspects that resonate with the modeling notation used. In trying to model collaborative or organizational activities in terms of data types, for example, there may be a tendency to focus on the objects, rules, and so on in question rather than on the situated practices through which these objects and rules are made appropriate and relevant to coparticipants. In a different way than the form-analysis approach discussed above, it may be that the resulting model unduly focuses on those objects and "abstractions" rather than on the collaborative and interactional practices through which these are produced and rendered intelligible.

4. There have been a number of previous efforts to model and represent sequential and interactional resources for system design and specification (e.g., Cawsey 1990; Finkelstein and Fuks 1990; Frohlich and Luff 1990; Gilbert, Wooffitt, and Fraser 1990). These authors have been particularly interested in modeling sequential features revealed by analyses of naturally occurring turns of talk (i.e., through conversation analysis (Sacks, Schegloff, and Jefferson 1974)). These efforts have typically used conventional declarative, and linear, formalisms. Further details on this and other modeling exercises can be found in Jirotka (forthcoming).

5. Perhaps the most familiar example is when considering deadlock, where no particular component of a system can make progress because it is waiting for communication from other processes. Livelock is a complementary problem, where a process continues indefinitely because it cannot be interrupted by any external communication. CSP provides a notation so that such issues can be examined and reasoned about.

6. The fragments of talk in this section are transcribed according to the orthography developed by Jefferson (1972) and utilized in the contributions to works such as *Structures of Social Action* (see Atkinson and Heritage 1984). Lengths of pauses are given in seconds in brackets. A pause of 0.1 seconds is represented as (.).

7. This is particularly the case if the intended system is to be used by dealers as they are dealing (e.g., computerized trade input systems or voice recognition systems) (see Jirotka, Luff, and Heath 1993). In such cases it would be important to indicate when a deal (and its details) can be considered noticeably complete and by whom it was accomplished. The technology might not be sensitive to the openness and flexibility of dealing if it required users to complete and "fix" deals at inappropriate times and places.

8. The recording of stockbrokers and sales personnel needs to be seen as two independent activities, because this provides for some cross-checking for the trading room about what was agreed to in the deal.

9. Note that the only difference between these two processes is that in each process there is a private event to record the deal (i.e., not in the alphabet of the other process). This does suggest a way of characterizing the difference between public and private activities, a recurrent issue in workplace studies (Goodwin and Goodwin 1996; Heath et al. 1994–95; Heath and Luff 1996a).

10. One of the ways of considering the effects of processes is to outline a "trace" of the process. Traces are an inherent aspect of CSP and critical when reasoning about concurrent processes. In this case, an example of a trace of events from the interleaving of processes for trading in BATS and Orange that the salesman and stockbrokers participated in could be:

$\langle \mathit{initiateDeal}_{\mathrm{BATS}}, \mathit{agreeAmount}_{\mathrm{BATS}}, \mathit{initiateDeal}_{\mathrm{Orange}}, \mathit{agreeAmount}_{\mathrm{Orange}}, \mathit{agreePrice}_{\mathrm{Orange}}, \mathit{agreePrice}_{\mathrm{BATS}}, \mathit{agreeDeal}_{\mathrm{BATS}}, \mathit{agreeDeal}_{\mathrm{Orange}} \ldots \rangle$

11. Note that this is only one of the ways in which dealing in the above instance is ambivalent. It is not made explicit by the stockbrokers that in offering to trade in Orange, they (or rather Paul) will also trade in BATS. However, this is taken to be the case by Derek and is not rendered problematic by the stockbrokers. It would be important in a requirements analysis to reflect this ambivalence, because it is only at the conclusion of interaction that the deal is "agreed" to. This may be particularly consequential if developers were considering deal recording systems. Similarly, the model would need to reflect that dealers can agree on price and amount in either order, explicitly or implicitly. Again, this is consequential for development of technologies such as voice recognition systems, which aim to record the details of trades from explicit features in the talk (see Jirotka, Luff, and Heath 1993).

References

Atkinson, J. M., and J. C. Heritage, eds. 1984. *Structures of Social Action: Studies in Conversation Analysis*. Cambridge, England: Cambridge University Press.

Bellotti, V. 1988. Implications of Current Design Practice for the Use of HCI Techniques. In *People and Computers IV: Proceedings of the Fourth Conference of the BCS Specialist Group*, edited by D. M. Jones and R. Winder. Cambridge, England: Cambridge University Press.

Booch, G. 1991. *Software Engineering Economics*. Englewood Cliffs, NJ: Prentice Hall.

Bowers, J., and G. Button. 1995. Workflow from Within and Without: Technology and Cooperative Work on the Print Industry Shop Floor. Paper read at ECSCW'95, 10–14 September, in Stockholm.

Button, G., and W. Sharrock. 1994. Occasioned Practices in the Work of Software Engineers. In *Requirements Engineering: Social and Technical Issues*, edited by M. Jirotka and J. Goguen. London: Academic Press.

Button, G., and W. Sharrock. 1997. The Production of Order and the Order of Production. Paper read at ECSCW '97, in Lancaster.

Button, G., and W. Sharrock. 2000. Design by Problem Solving. In *Workplace Studies: Recovering Work Practice and Informing System Design*, edited by P. Luff, J. Hindmarsh, and C. Heath. Cambridge, England: Cambridge University Press.

Cawsey, A. 1990. A Computational Model of Explanatory Discourse: Local Interactions in a Plan-Based Explanation. In *Computers and Conversation*, edited by P. Luff, G. N. Gilbert, and D. M. Frohlich. London: Academic Press.

Chen, P. 1976. The entity-relationship model: Toward a unified view of data. *ACM Transactions on Database Systems* 1(1): 9–36.

Choobineh, J., M. Manniho, J. Nunamaker, and B. Konsynsky. 1988. An Expert Database System Based on Analysis of Forms. *IEEE Transactions on Software Engineering* 14(2): 242–253.

Eason, K. D. 1989. Tools for Participation: How Managers and Users Can Influence Design. In *Participation in Systems Development*, edited by K. Knight. London: Kegan Paul.

Engeström, Y., and D. Middleton, eds. 1996. *Cognition and Communication at Work*. Cambridge, England: Cambridge University Press.

Filippi, G., and J. Theureau. 1993. Analysing Cooperative Work in an Urban Traffic Control Room for the Design of a Coordination Support System. Paper read at ECSCW '93, 13–17 September, in Milan, Italy.

Finkelstein, A., and H. Fuks. 1990. Conversation Analysis and Specification. In *Computers and Conversation*, edited by P. Luff, G. N. Gilbert, and D. M. Frohlich. London: Academic Press.

Frohlich, D. M., and P. Luff. 1990. Applying the Technology of Conversation to the Technology for Conversation. In *Computers and Conversation*, edited by P. Luff, G. N. Gilbert, and D. M. Frohlich. London: Academic Press.

Fuchs, L., U. Pankoke-Babatz, and W. Prinz. 1995. Supporting Cooperative Awareness with Local Event Mechanisms: The GroupDesk System. Paper read at ECSCW'95, 10–14 September, at Stockholm.

Garfinkel, H. 1967. *Studies in Ethnomethodology.* Englewood Cliffs, NJ: Prentice Hall.

Gaver, W. W., A. Sellen, C. C. Heath, and P. Luff. 1993. One Is Not Enough: Multiple Views in a Media Space. Paper read at INTERCHI '93, April 24–29, in Amsterdam.

Gilbert, G. N., R. Wooffitt, and N. Fraser. 1990. Organising Computer Talk. In *Computers and Conversation*, edited by P. Luff, G. N. Gilbert, and D. M. Frohlich. London: Academic Press.

Goguen, J. A. 1994. Requirements Engineering as the Reconciliation of Social and Technical Issues. In *Requirements Engineering: Social and Technical Issues*, edited by M. Jirotka and J. Goguen. London: Academic Press.

Goodwin, C., and M. H. Goodwin. 1996. Seeing as a Situated Activity: Formulating Plans. In *Cognition and Communication at Work*, edited by Y. Engeström and D. Middleton. Cambridge, England: Cambridge University Press.

Greatbatch, D., P. Luff, C. C. Heath, and P. Campion. 1993. Interpersonal Communication and Human-Computer Interaction: An Examination of the Use of Computers in Medical Consultations. *Interacting with Computers* 5(2): 193–216.

Harper, R. H. R. 1998. *Inside the IMF: An Ethnography of Documents, Technology and Organisational Action.* London: Academic Press.

Harper, R. H. R. 2000. Analysing Work Practice and the Potential Role of New Technology at the International Monetary Fund: Some Remarks on the Role of Ethnomethodology. In *Workplace Studies: Recovering Work Practice and Informing System Design*, edited by P. Luff, J. Hindmarsh, and C. C. Heath. Cambridge, England: Cambridge University Press.

Hayashi, K., T. Hazama, T. Nomura, T. Yamada, and S. Gudmundson. 1999. Activity Awareness: Framework for Sharing Knowledge of People, Projects and Places. Paper read at Sixth European Conference on Computer Supported Cooperative Work (ECSCW '99), 12–16 September, in Copenhagen.

Heath, C. C. 1982. Preserving the Consultation: Medical Record Cards and Professional Conduct. *Sociology of Health and Illness* 4(1): 56–74.

Heath, C. C., M. Jirotka, P. Luff, and J. Hindmarsh. 1994–95. Unpacking Collaboration: The Interactional Organisation of Trading in a City Dealing Room. *CSCW* 3(2): 147–165.

Heath, C. C., H. Knoblauch, and P. Luff. 2000. Technology and Social Interaction: The Emergence of "Workplace Studies." *British Journal of Sociology* 51(2): 299–320.

Heath, C. C., and P. Luff. 1996a. Convergent Activities: Line Control and Passenger Information on London Underground. In *Cognition and Communication at Work*, edited by Y. Engeström and D. Middleton. Cambridge, England: Cambridge University Press.

Heath, C. C., and P. Luff. 1996b. Documents and Professional Practice: "Bad" Organisational Reasons for "Good" Clinical Records. Paper read at CSCW '96, November 16–20, in Boston.

Heath, C. C., and P. K. Luff. 2000. *Technology in Action.* Cambridge, England: Cambridge University Press.

Hindmarsh, J., M. Fraser, C. C. Heath, S. Benford, and C. Greenhalgh. 1998. Fragmented Interaction: Establishing Mutual Orientation in Virtual Environments. Paper read at CSCW'98, in Seattle.

Hoare, C. A. R. 1985. *Communicating Sequential Processes.* Englewood Cliffs, NJ: Prentice Hall.

Hughes, J., J. O'Brien, T. Rodden, and M. Rouncefield. 1997. Designing with Ethnography: A Presentation Framework for Design. Paper read at Symposium on Designing Interactive Systems (DIS '97), in Amsterdam.

Hughes, J., J. O'Brien, T. Rodden, M. Rouncefield, and I. Sommerville. 1995. Presenting Ethnography in the Requirements Process. Paper read at Second IEEE International Symposium on Requirements Engineering, at the University of York.

Hughes, J., J. O'Brien, M. Rouncefield, and T. Rodden. 1996. "They're supposed to be fixing it": Requirements and System Re-design. In *CSCW Requirements and Evaluation*, edited by P. Thomas. London: Springer-Verlag.

Hughes, J. A., D. Z. Shapiro, W. W. Sharrock, R. A. Anderson, R. R. Harper, and S. C. Gibbons. 1988. *The Automation of Air Traffic Control.* Department of Sociology, Lancaster University.

Hutchins, E. L. 1995. *Cognition in the Wild.* Cambridge, MA: MIT Press.

Jefferson, G. 1972. Side Sequences. In *Studies in Social Interaction*, edited by D. Sudnow, 294–338. New York: Free Press.

Jirotka, M. 2001. An Investigation into Contextual Approaches to Requirements Capture. Doctoral dissertation, Computing Laboratory, University of Oxford.

Jirotka, M., and J. Goguen, eds. 1994. *Requirements Engineering: Social and Technical Issues.* London: Academic Press.

Jirotka, M., P. Luff, and C. Heath. 1993. Requirements for Technology in Complex Environments: Tasks and Interaction in a City Dealing Room. *SIGOIS Bulletin (Special Issue): Do Users Get What They Want? (DUG '93)* 14 (2 December): 17–23.

Jirotka, M., and L. Wallen. 2000. Analysing the Workplace and User Requirements: Challenges for the Development of Methods for Requirements Engineering. In *Workplace Studies: Recovering Work Practice and Informing System Design*, edited by P. Luff, J. Hindmarsh, and C. Heath. Cambridge, England: Cambridge University Press.

Loucopoulos, P., and V. Karakostas. 1995. *System Requirements Engineering.* Maidenhead, England: McGraw-Hill.

Luff, P., and C. C. Heath. 1998. Mobility in Collaboration. Paper read at CSCW'98, November 14–18, in Seattle.

Luff, P., J. Hindmarsh, and C. Heath, eds. 2000. *Workplace Studies: Recovering Work Practice and Informing System Design*. Cambridge, England: Cambridge University Press.

Luff, P., and M. Jirotka. 1998. Interactional Resources for the Support of Collaborative Activities: Common Problems for the Design of Technologies to Support Groups and Communities. In *Community Computing and Support Systems: Social Interaction in Networked Communities*, edited by T. Ishida. Lecture Notes in Computer Science 1519. Berlin: Springer Verlag.

Myopoulos, J. 1992. Conceptual Modelling and Telos. In *Conceptual Modelling, Databases, and CASE: An Integrated View of Information Systems Development*, edited by P. Looucopoulos and R. Zicari. New York: Wiley.

Plowman, L., Y. Rogers, and M. Ramage. 1995. What Are Workplace Studies For? Paper read at ECSCW'95, 10–14 September, in Stockholm.

Pycock, J., K. Palfreyman, J. Allanson, and G. Button. 1998. Representing Fieldwork and Articulating Requirements through Virtual Reality. Paper read at CSCW '98, in Seattle.

Randall, D., J. Hughes, and D. Shapiro. 1994. Steps towards a Partnership: Ethnography and System Design. In *Requirements Engineering: Social and Technical Issues*, edited by M. Jirotka and J. Goguen. London: Academic Press.

Rogers, Y. 1992. Ghosts in the Network: Distributed Troubleshooting in a Shared Working Environment. Paper read at CSCW '92, October 31–November 4, in Toronto.

Roscoe, A. W. 1998. *The Theory and Practice of Concurrency*. Englewood Cliffs, NJ: Prentice Hall.

Ryle, G. 1949. *The Concept of Mind*. London: Penguin.

Sacks, H. 1992. *Lectures in Conversation*. 2 vols. Oxford: Blackwell.

Sacks, H., E. A. Schegloff, and G. Jefferson. 1974. A Simplest Systematics for the Organisation of Turn-Taking for Conversation. *Language* 50(4): 696–735.

Sommerville, I., T. Rodden, P. Sawyer, R. Bentley, and M. Twidale. 1993. Incorporating Ethnography into Requirements Engineering. Paper read at RE'93: International Symposium on Requirements Engineering, January 4–6, in San Diego.

Stamper, R. 1994. Social Norms in Requirements Analysis: An Outline of MEASUR. In *Requirements Engineering: Social and Technical Issues*, edited by M. Jirotka and J. Goguen. London: Academic Press.

Suchman, L. 1987. *Plans and Situated Actions: The Problem of Human-Machine Communication*. Cambridge, England: Cambridge University Press.

Suchman, L. 1993. Technologies of Accountability: On Lizards and Aeroplanes. In *Technology in Working Order*, edited by G. Button. London: Routledge.

Turner, R. 1976. Utterance Positioning as an Interactional Resource. *Semiotica* 17(3): 233–254.

Viller, S., and I. Sommerville. 1999. Coherence: An Approach to Representing Ethnographic Analyses in System Design. *Human-Computer Interaction* 14(1–2): 9–42.

Watts, J. C., D. D. Woods, J. M. Corban, E. S. Patterson, R. L. Kerr, and L. C. Hicks. 1996. Voice Loops as Cooperative Aids in Space Shuttle Mission Control. Paper read at CSCW '96, in Cambridge, MA.

7

The Locales Framework: Making Social Thinking Accessible for Software Practitioners

Geraldine Fitzpatrick

I was involved in a research group[1] that was building a collaboration environment called wOrlds (Fitzpatrick, Kaplan, and Tolone 1995) to support people working together across space and time. The wOrlds system was supposed to overcome some of the problems with previous workflow-type approaches that had led one user to comment, "Your system has been designed to be idiotproof, the trouble is we're not idiots" (Wastell, White, and Kawalek 1994, 35). Given Suchman's (1987) description of the situated nature of work and the role of plans in work, it was easy to understand this rejection.

In the wOrlds system, we tried to account for this social thinking about the situated contingent nature of work practices by providing shared spaces where work could happen dynamically, rather than a priori workflow prescriptions. When it came to a prototype implementation with a group of systems engineers, however, it quickly became obvious that the wOrlds system would also likely be rejected but for different reasons—we had adopted too much of the metaphor of the spaces in which they worked instead of understanding how people used the spaces to get their work done (Fitzpatrick, Kaplan, and Mansfield 1996). Even though we claimed to be motivated by considerations of the social realm of work, we still "got it wrong." In getting it wrong, we also learned more about the problem of designing interactive systems.

This chapter is a reflection on the next phase in our thinking about how to incorporate social thinking into our own software practices for collaborative systems design. The focus of this next phase was the development of the Locales Framework as a set of concepts based on a notion of *place* as the primary unit of analysis and design. It was conjectured that the framework could be used as a shared abstraction to mediate both understanding the nature of work and designing systems to support this work (Fitzpatrick 1998).

The main point of this discussion is not so much to expound the details of the Locales Framework but to characterize the nature of one particular endeavor to build socially situated software, and to reflect on the Locales Framework as an instance of the iteration in learning more about the problem of design itself. In so doing, the chapter is itself an example of one of the main points argued here, namely that the incorporation of social thinking into software practice is a wicked problem that can only be understood incrementally as solutions are tried and reflected on.

To argue the case, this chapter is structured as follows. In the following section, I characterize why we need social thinking in software practice by defining the problem space as "wicked." I go on to describe our own iteration through a problem-solution space that led us to think about a shared abstraction and a metaphor of place as an appropriate response to the difficulties we had encountered. I then outline the Locales Framework as an instance of a shared abstraction for understanding and designing application software for the support of collaboration, defining locale as the unit of analysis, and outlining the five framework aspects. Finally I reflect on our experiences in using the framework as a way of incorporating social thinking into software practice for collaborative systems. I also reflect more generally on the role of such abstractions.

Why We Need "Social Thinking" in Software Practice

In their book *Computer Science: A Modern Introduction* (1988, first published 1982), Goldschlager and Lister characterize the computer revolution as the "augmentation of man's *mental* powers [where] the pressing of a button can cause a machine to perform intricate calculations, to make complex decisions, or to store and retrieve vast quantities of information" (p. 1). The algorithm—"a sequence of steps which if faithfully performed will result in the task, or *process*, being carried out" (p. 2)—is the pivotal construct that typifies traditional software practice. Requirements analysis and design techniques are largely drawn from mathematical and engineering traditions and are predicated on being able to fully specify the problem at hand and develop a specification for a system to address the problem.

In the years since, especially with the growth of the Internet, this "computer revolution" has become a "communication revolution" and software applications are impacting the social space of work and interaction more directly. It is becoming increasingly accepted that traditional requirements-gathering techniques are no longer adequate to account for the complex dynamic nature of this social world. While the algorithm is still important in the actual coding of systems, the emphasis in requirements gathering shifts to also understanding the social, organizational, and interactional contexts in which the system will be used. This moves software practice into a different problem space. The nature of this problem space, and the ways of grappling with it, started to make more sense for me after I came across the notion of "wicked problems."

Wicked Problems, New Challenges for Software Practice

The term *wicked problem* was coined by Rittel and Webber (1973) to talk about dilemmas in social policy planning but also captured much of our own experience with software practice in computer-supported cooperative work (CSCW). A wicked problem is usually situated in the social realm, where "the aim is not to find the truth, but to improve some characteristics of the world where people live" (p. 167)—our motivation in undertaking CSCW research was to help improve the way in which people can work and interact together through the use of computer-based support. A wicked problem can never be definitively formulated and the problem is only understood progressively as solutions are developed—we had learned a lot about the problem of supporting people working together through developing the wOrlds system. Further, every instance of a general wicked problem is essentially unique: the situatedness of action. As such, there are no right or wrong solutions, only better or worse ones. Nor are there "one size fits all" solutions. In addition, the processes for addressing the problem-solution space are inherently iterative and "satisficing" (Simon 1960).

This definition of wicked problems helped us to reframe some of the general challenges for software practice. First, we need new ways of thinking about software practice that take account of the intertwined problem-solution space and the iterative processes needed to learn more about the problem and come up with better solutions. Second, software needs to be more flexible and evolvable if we take seriously the problem-solution iterations (discussion of which is beyond the scope of this chapter). Third, and my focus here, we need new concepts, methods, and techniques to understand and account for the social realm in which wicked problems are situated.

Many others were already trying to address variations of these challenges within their own disciplines, as were many in the CSCW community. The story that I go on with here is an instance of our own iteration through the problem-solution space of trying to bring social thinking to the design of collaborative systems to support people working together.

Toward the Locales Framework

Through work reported in the CSCW literature, our group was already aware of some of the general problems in trying to bring social thinking to software practice. In particular, some projects that brought together ethnographers and computer scientists—for example, Bentley et al. (1992)—illustrated the valuable insights possible through ethnographic study of the day-to-day practices of people whose work was to be supported. These projects also highlighted the general difficulties in moving from study insights to design.

Against this background, we were also starting to learn how to incorporate social thinking into our own practice. As stated previously, we learned of the limitations of prescriptive solutions for the support of work from experiences with workflow systems and from Suchman's (1987) discussions of the roles of plans in work practice. This led us to the wOrlds system (Fitzpatrick, Kaplan, and Tolone 1995). We did not make any a priori assumptions about how work should happen in wOrlds, but instead provided shared spaces as settings for situated action to unfold.

We were also convinced that the social science approaches were more appropriate than traditional requirements techniques for uncovering and understanding situated work practices in complex domains. Having undertaken a course in this area, I then carried out an ethnographic-based study of a group of systems engineers with a view to understanding their needs so that we could tailor wOrlds for their use. From this we learned two further lessons firsthand.

The exact details of the wOrlds system, the study, and the lessons learned are not directly relevant here. What is relevant is how these lessons motivated the next iteration through the problem-solution space toward the Locales Framework.

Motivating a Metaphor of Place

The first lesson was to do with the mismatch between the containment model of shared space inadvertently embodied in wOrlds and the ways the engineers worked. Many features of wOrlds, such as bounded spaces, were simulated from the physical domain, supposedly to enable people to work in "familiar" ways. The systems engineers, on the other hand, were already exploiting features of their computing environment to work in novel ways that neither wOrlds nor their physical spaces could support.

As with many other systems based on a spatial metaphor, a wOrlds room can be characterized by notions of group related to a bounded space, where you are either in or out, and see everything or nothing. The systems engineers' work on the other hand can be better characterized by "individuals in multiple groups" who make use of a variety of physical and virtual spaces as places of work, and where notions of relationships around centers are more relevant than containment by boundaries. (More detailed discussions can be found in Fitzpatrick, Kaplan, and Mansfield 1996 and Fitzpatrick 1998.)

On seeing this mismatch between the instantiation of a spatial metaphor in wOrlds, and the rich ways the systems engineers used their virtual and physical spaces, I started to think about place instead of space as a guiding design principle—where place arises in the lived relationship between people and the spaces they use. Conincidentally others were also moving toward this notion of place rather than space (Harrison and Dourish 1996).

Motivating a Shared Abstraction Approach

The second lesson, similar to the experiences of many others in the CSCW community (Plowman, Rogers, and Ramage 1995), was that gathering, interpreting, and translating qualitative data for the purposes of systems design was difficult. Even though I came from a computing background and undertook the study with design in mind, it was still difficult to describe the work domain in a way that made sense to other technologists and that pointed to the appropriate forms of support that would work for the engineers' situation.

Reflecting more generally, CSCW is a multidisciplinary community; those concerned with understanding and those concerned with designing tend to come from different backgrounds, neither of which fully prepares their proponents to work at the conjunction of the two areas.

On the one hand, as systems designers, we are not traditionally trained to undertake qualitative studies or to make sense of sociological accounts of work. While we might want to support the "social" insights that emerge from others' workplace studies, it can be difficult to translate these insights into the substance of design[2] (e.g., see Kaplan et al. 1997).

On the other hand, social science traditions used within CSCW, be they ethnomethodology, distributed cognition, activity theory, and so on, were never intended to address the demands of systems design. Plowman, Rogers, and Ramage (1995), for example, talk about the lack of a translation process whereby accounts of the social organization of work can be translated into design information.

A fundamental source of many of the tensions between understanding and designing could be the role of abstractions or models in the different worldviews. Button and Dourish (1996) suggest that computer scientists view abstractions as *generative* in that they give rise to, as well as characterize, system action, whereas ethnomethodologists (and perhaps other social scientists) view abstractions as *analytic* explanations of social action.

Solutions had thus far tended to be driven more from the social sciences—for hybrid forms of social science (Shapiro 1994) and for more pragmatic ethnographic processes (Hughes et al. 1994).

Not wanting to engage in a discussion of the generative/analytic duality of abstractions, but having experienced the issues firsthand, I started to think about whether an abstraction shared by both "understanders" and designers could be a possible solution. The challenge was to create an abstraction that accounted for and was grounded in the sociality of work and allowed for the uniqueness of each workplace setting (the wickedness of the problem domain), while also accounting for the pragmatic needs of design and systems building.

The Locales Framework came to be this shared abstraction based on a metaphor of place.

Locales Framework

The Locales Framework, then, grew out of our own experiences and the experiences of the broader CSCW community with understanding and designing. Underpinning the evolution of the framework was the work of a prominent American sociologist, Anselm Strauss (1993), and his theory of action. As a non–social scientist, I found that Strauss's work gave a coherent conceptual map against which to make sense of many of the ad hoc insights emerging from the workplace studies being reported in the literature.[3]

The central concepts of the theory that I drew on include social worlds, action, interaction, and trajectory. A *social world* is the fundamental building block of collective action (Clarke 1991). Members of a social world are bonded by a common, sometimes implicit, goal and perform *actions* toward the collective purpose. Actions are always embedded in *interactions*, which are continually permuting. Social worlds need "*sites and means*" to facilitate their shared interactions. An *interaction trajectory* captures the issues about how courses of action evolve over time.

Locale as the Unit of Analysis and Design

The primary unit of analysis and design in the Locales Framework is "*locale*." Locale does not exist a priori as does a space or room. Rather, a locale is the place constituted in the ongoing *relationship* between people in a particular social world and the "site and means" they use to meet their interactional needs—that is, the space together with the resources available there. As such, the framework is based on a metaphor of *place* as the lived interaction with space and resources.

In contrast to metaphors of space, which embody principles of boundaries and containment (e.g., see Roseman and Greenberg 1996), a metaphor of place embodies principle of *centers* giving rise to relationships (Fitzpatrick 2000). The shared purpose of the social world, for example, provides a center around which the people, spaces, and resources make sense. With the notion of centers come other notions, for instance, of relationships around the center, of distances from the center potentially definable along multiple different dimensions, and of dynamically varying relationships of centers to one another.

It is because locale arises in the relationship between a social world and its use of space as place, that it is potentially suitable as a shared abstraction for both understanding and designing, albeit used with slightly different emphases for each.

For understanding, the emphasis is put on people and their actions/interactions—that is, on their appropriation and evolution of "site and means" as place for the practical accomplishment of work. This allows for the complex, dynamic, and situated "interactional" aspects of work to be accounted for but not in isolation from where and how those interactions happen.

For designing, the emphasis is put on the "site and means" used by members of the social world to meet their needs, and on how better "sites and means" or affordances could be designed for meeting interactional needs. This allows for the pragmatic needs of design, focusing on the more stable "environmental" aspects enabling interaction but not in isolation from their use.

Locales Framework Aspects

In its current state, the Locales Framework is composed of five aspects. Each of these aspects characterizes the nature of work from a different perspective.

Locale Foundations We first identify the group or social world of concern, looking at features such as the shared goal, how membership is defined, what the internal structures within the group are, and so on. We then identify their *locale* as constituted by the spaces, objects, tools, and resources they use to support their interactions. Locale is the foundation for the rest of the framework in so far as the features identified here facilitate or constrain the life of the social world, as uncovered by the remaining aspects.

Civic Structures This is the broader environment in which the social world and its locales exist. Depending on what is relevant, the environment could be physical, spatial, geographic, organizational, informational, professional, legislative, and so on. We can also consider the external influences on a locale, locale life-cycle processes, how locales are structured and related, and how interaction between locales is supported.

Individual Views This accounts for the fact that groups are made up of idiosyncratic individuals who each belong to multiple social worlds simultaneously. Different members can hold different views over the one locale. Individuals also manage and negotiate different locale views simultaneously over the multiple locales in which they participate at dynamically varying levels of intensity.

Interaction Trajectory This accounts for the social world and locale "in action" over time: past, present, and future; cycles, rhythms, and phases; the performance of work and the articulation of work; routines, contingencies, and breakdowns; information flows; workflows; and so on.

Mutuality Mutuality is the very glue of collaborative activity—how *presence* is enabled in a locale and how *awareness* of that presence is supported. Mutuality enables the "w" questions to be answered—for example, who, what, when, where, why, and (almost a "w") how.

These aspects are explored in detail in Fitzpatrick 1998. The motivations for choosing these aspects are described, and for each aspect, various properties are identified, together with various dimensions along which the properties could be characterized. As an example, a property of interest for a social world might be "role." Roles could be characterized along dimensions such as the following: fixed—fluid; formally defined—informal; imposed—socially agreed on; assigned—self-selected; generic—specific. Questions can also be asked about how the roles arise and evolve, how they are related, how they are known about, and so on.

While we draw out the five aspects explicitly as if separate orthogonal entities, they are in fact highly interdependent and overlapping. The point of the aspects is to suggest different perspectives on the same phenomenon, bringing aspects to the fore that can otherwise be forgotten. Some aspects might be more relevant or important for a particular situation or design focus than others. Further, even if the design focus is on a particular artifact, for example, the framework can provide a background against which the artifact could be viewed in a fish-eye effect. In these ways, we hope to gain a more holistic view of the domain of interest.

Using the Locales Framework

Using the Locales Framework for design generally involves a two-phase approach, as outlined in the following. This two-phase approach would then be iterative, in the fashion of all wicked problems, as the implementation of solutions sheds more light on the nature of the problems, leading to better solutions, and so on.

Phase 1—Understanding the Current Locales The aim of the first phase is to understand the locales of interest in their current state from the perspective of the interactional needs of a social world. This could involve using the framework to structure and make sense of existing ethnographic (or other) data. Alternatively, it could involve going into the domain and directly engaging in the data-gathering process.

For designers who do not have a social science background, the framework could be used as a sensitizing device to help motivate initial questions and observations. For designers who do have a social science background, the framework could be used to help structure data in a form relevant to the purposes of design. For users engaged in the design process, the framework could be used to initiate a conversation to articulate their locales of work and how these are used in their work.

For all these "understanding" purposes, it was hoped that the framework would be sufficiently rich to guide the designer to look for the facilitating and constraining features in the practical accomplishment of work. At the same time, it was hoped that the framework would be general enough so as not to prescribe or circumscribe all that is of interest so that the uniqueness of each situation could still emerge in the account of the workplace.

Phase 2—Evolving New Locales The aim of the second phase is to explore possibilities for how existing locale(s) could be enhanced to better support the activities that take place there, or for how new locales could be evolved.

This moves the focus beyond the emergent situated nature of work per se to the features and mechanisms of the spaces and resources of the locale that support, or have the potential to support, that work. It does this, though, in a way that is driven by interactional needs, understanding the broader context in which that interaction happens, not by a priori assumptions of technological solutions or by idealized abstractions of action.

The design options for meeting those needs can then be explored. The types of questions that would drive this process would be domain specific; however, examples of typical questions might include the following: What interactional needs does the social world have that are poorly or inadequately supported in their current locale(s)? How can the existing locale(s) of a social world be augmented or enhanced to better support mutuality, or individual views, or civic structures, or interaction trajectory? Can technology enable new ways of working? Can new social worlds be facilitated if computer-based spaces and resources were provided to be used as locale?

Hence, the second phase is about exploiting the strengths of any available medium, physical or computational, and the synergy among them, to better meet the social-world needs identified in the first phase.[4]

In Summary

The Locales Framework was proposed as a set of concepts for describing what is as well as envisioning what could be. While it relies on qualitative methods, it has been specifically motivated by the needs of systems design. While it is moving toward systems design, design decisions are grounded in an understanding of the group's needs. Hence, the framework tries to embrace both social and technical concerns and mediate both.

It needs to be interpreted and used by designers as a tool, not a recipe. It can be a sensitizing device, giving "social thinking" pointers or heuristics for key elements of a collaborative work environment. It can also help focus on the use of space and its affordances for support of interaction, space and its affordances being the very concerns of software practice. At the same time it is sufficiently high level, open, and incomplete so as not to prescribe or circumscribe all that is of interest. Hence, the framework is a shared abstraction in the sense of being a common background or starting point against which domain-specific concepts and abstractions can be drawn, and design solutions can be explored.

Does the framework capture the "right" aspects or the only possible aspects for the support of collaborative work? Surely not. As with all wicked problems, a robust dialogue between exploration of abstract frameworks and their use in practice is essential if either is to be advanced. Hence, this is an early working framework that will be evolved with use for the purposes of both analyzing work domains and designing, building, and deploying systems for collaboration support within those domains. In the following section, I begin some of this reflective dialogue.

Reflections

The reflections presented here are based on my own and other colleagues' experiences in using the Locales Framework. These include the following: a study of a telehealth environment, with insights feeding into the design of new facilities for support of remote consultation (Kaplan and Fitzpatrick 1997); a study of a group of distributed researchers (Fitzpatrick, Kaplan, and Parsowith 1998); a study and facilitated workshop with a government department, with a focus on its information and communication flows; a heuristic evaluation of two groupware systems (Greenberg et al. 2000); the design of a generic collaborative toolkit embodying some of the principles from the Locales Framework (Mansfield et al. 1997); and various workshops describing the framework to people from industry.

On the Framework

Our experiences do suggest that the framework concepts have been able to provide a starting point for thinking about the broader contexts in which our applications will be embedded. In hindsight, this has proved most useful for software engineers who do not have a social science background and who do not want to, or know how to, engage with the intricacies of social theories—the framework can offer more than traditional software requirements techniques alone for bringing social thinking into software practice.

The framework is not an algorithmic solution, for CSCW concerns at least. As expected, this has proved to be both a strength and a weakness.

Its strength is that, in presenting such a broad brush of concepts, it can provide enough structure to support the beginnings of understanding while still allowing for the uniqueness of each workplace to demand appropriate attention. The workaday world is rich and complex, and by definition, such concepts will always be incomplete and inadequate. Because every instance of a wicked problem is unique, every situation will have unique issues, concerns, needs, and so on. Regarding this uniqueness and complexity, the aspects are not simple distinct areas to be worked through in order as a simplifying formula. They are interlinked, and their articulation is highly incremental and evolutionary, providing a multifaceted lens to help interpret and structure the complexity from different angles, but only as deemed appropriate. Ultimately, it is about letting the situation itself guide and inform what are the important issues and if or how the framework can be most usefully applied. As discussed by Beck (chapter 8, this volume), what does not fit can be a valuable analytic resource.

Having said this, the framework, especially as laid out with characterizing properties and dimensions for each aspect, can usefully serve as a set of heuristics or a sensitizing checklist. A danger, however, is that some people might think these can be applied in a mechanistic cookbook fashion as if sufficient for "social thinking." Obviously this would trivialize the domain under consideration and ignore the practical accomplishment of both the work we seek to support and the work required for understnading and designing.

Its weakness, therefore, is that, not being an algorithmic solution, there is considerable effort required to creatively and intelligently interpret, evolve, extend, or even discard (aspects of) the Locales Framework for the situation at hand; hence people are integral to the process. For the more "traditional" computer scientists I have worked with, this has proved problematic, explained perhaps by the more structured mathematical/engineering bias in their education. It could just be the case that some computer scientists will never want to use any such framework themselves, preferring instead that others engage in the understanding work.

It could also be the case that the processes for actually using the framework have not been explained clearly enough. Articulation of the framework to date has concentrated on laying out the various aspects and associated concepts, not on explaining how to apply them. To facilitate wider use, the processes for working with the framework should be made more visible and accessible. Hopefully this effort will become easier as we build up a corpus of studies and experiences.

A further weakness of the framework can be seen with regard to design. While it has been very useful for motivating design decisions at a higher conceptual level, it has not been as useful for informing the substance of design for specific solutions; the designer is still left to translate the motivations into actual systems. While this is better than ad hoc "implications for design" included at the end of many workplace studies, there is still a long way to go.

A design strength, on the other hand, is that use of the framework did prove useful for promoting design decisions that took account of the broader context of work. With locale as the unit of presentation in the design motivation, together with the different framework perspectives, we are able to tell a more complete story of what could be. For example, the design suggestions for the group of distributed researchers not only touched on new technologies to augment the existing locale, but also new ways of using their existing physical spaces and furnishings and technologies, as well as pointing to critical interorganizational issues.

In using the framework, the question of how to design better locales, or what even constitutes a better locale, becomes highlighted as a significant issue. At the moment, this is largely left to the intuition and skill of the designer. In one sense, this is not a problem since design is a creative process. The difficulty is related more to the relative newness of CSCW design as a field, and more generally to the newness of software practice around interactive systems. Other creative design disciplines such as architecture have rich, well-established traditions to draw upon.[5] Such design knowledge about socially situated systems is only beginning to evolve. Are there principled approaches that could suggest what constitutes a better locale design?

On the Relationship to Other Social Thinking Approaches

The Locales Framework is obviously not the only approach for dealing with wicked problems and for bringing social thinking into software practice. The participatory design community has a long tradition of engaging with users in a "contextual approach to design of computer artifacts" (Kyng 1998). The MUST method developed by Bødker, Kensing, and Simonsen (chapter 13, this volume) and Soft Systems Methodology (Checkland 1981) are other similarly motivated approaches.

Other conceptual frameworks have also been developed. Hughes et al. (1997), for example, proposed a number of viewpoints for presenting ethnographic data to designers. Coming more from an HCI/user-centered design background, Beyer and Holtzblatt (1998) have developed various work models for providing a structured representation of user work practices. Interestingly, there is considerable overlap in the representational concepts of both these approaches and the Locales Framework aspects despite being developed relatively simultaneously and independently.

Perhaps the closest approach to the Locales Framework is activity theory. At some levels, activity theory can serve many of the same functions as the Locales Framework: a unit of analysis that encompasses both the social and the technical; a focus on the broader context, not just on technology or artifacts in isolation; enabling description of what is as well as envisioning what could be; and so on.

On the other hand, the complexity and plurality of expressions of activity theory can make it difficult to come to grips with—at least that has been my experience. For the purposes of design, it is very much a theory under evolution. The efforts reflected in the work of people such as Bødker (1991), Engeström (1991), Kaptelinin (chapter 3, this volume), and Kuutti (1992) are important contributions to helping make activity theory more accessible to software practitioners.

Perhaps the key difference between the Locales Framework approach and these other approaches is its purposeful focus on providing an open, evolvable framework of concepts that can be relevant for both understanding the social situation and for relating software development to it. In this way, the Locales Framework is not just a tool for potentially making social thinking accessible for software practitioners, but it also attempts to "mediate joint practice"[6] through the development of shared abstractions.

On the Primacy of Abstractions or People

On a final reflective note, the previous discussions about the open, evolvable nature of the Locales Framework, and about the critical role of people in interpreting and using the framework, beg the question of what role the shared abstractions really do play in mediating joint practice.

In attempting to account for the uniqueness of each situation and not wanting to provide a solution that prescribes or circumscribes all that is of interest, researchers have deliberately characterized the concepts in very open ways. But do the concepts then end up so high level and open as to be of limited value for both understanding and designing?

To what extent does the assumption that a toolkit such as the Locales Framework could be useful for software practitioners ignore the invisible work in the skilled practical accomplishment of social thinking (Forsythe 1999)?

How does the framework become a shared abstraction in the first place? Is it an idealized expectation? Sharing does not happen by decree but by active engagement and negotiation, but by whom and how? What is actually shared? These processes have not been explicitly addressed to date.

To what extent does the articulation of a framework such as the Locales Framework, and the assumption about it being shared, inadvertently give primacy to the conceptual tool and not the people in the process? Are the successful outcomes due more to the people involved and their sensitivities and creativity rather than to the framework itself? Is this also the case for the other complementary approaches just noted?

Instead of looking for shared abstractions, is it "shared people" we need, people who can engage with both the understanding of social needs and the practice of software design, who can be edge dwellers of both communities, and who can facilitate and mediate the right sorts of dialogue? How would we define or legitimize the role of such people in software practice?

These are open questions for me. I started this chapter by saying that it would be a reflection of the next phase of our own journey in trying to incorporate social thinking into our software practices to create collaboration systems that would actually be useful. I have gone on to describe the Locales Framework as if it were the product of this phase. Maybe instead what I have been describing is part of my own process toward becoming a "shared person," an edge dweller—itself an ongoing process of "doing" social thinking in software practice. Since this is a wicked problem, we will only learn more about these questions as we try different solutions.

Notes

Eevi Beck, Victor Kaptelinin, Chris Westrup, and Yvonne Dittrich have given invaluable feedback on earlier drafts of this chapter—thank you. Simon Kaplan and Tim Mansfield have been closely involved in the evolution of the work presented here. I am grateful for their insights, challenging discussions, and contributions. I also acknowledge the contributions of the rest of the wOrlds research group at UIUC and the DSTC. The work reported in this chapter has been funded in part by the Co-operative Research Centre Program through the Department of Industry, Science & Resources of the Commonwealth Government of Australia.

1. The wOrlds group, led by Simon Kaplan, was located first at the University of Illinois at Urbana-Champaign in the United States, and was reestablished at the Distributed Systems Technology Centre in Australia in 1995. In Illinois, the group members included Bill Tolone, Doug Bogia, Ted Phelps, Mark Fitzpatrick, and Annette Feng. In Australia, members included Ted Phelps, Mark Fitzpatrick, and Tim Mansfield.

2. Some innovative programs are now being developed—for example, at University of Karlskrona/Ronneby and the Information Environments program at the University of Queensland—that are attempting to educate people with a mix of social and technical skills.

3. While this theory played a critical role in the evolution of the framework, it is not needed in the application of the framework. Ultimately the framework perspectives can be motivated, used, and populated independent of Strauss's theory.

4. Note the focus here is not on how to recreate physical domains in the virtual realm, nor on how to make virtual interactions "just like" face-to-face interactions.

5. For example, most "good" homes are designed with basic components of kitchen, bathroom, living room, and bedroom. The creativity is in the detail of the components, how they are related together, and how the facade of the home is presented.

6. I am grateful to Yvonne Dittrich for highlighting this point for me (personal communication, November 2000).

References

Bentley, R., J. Hughes, D. Randall, and T. Rodden. 1992. Ethnographically-Informed Systems Design for Air Traffic Control. In *Proceedings of the Conference on Computer Supported Cooperative Work*, 123–129. Toronto: ACM Press.

Beyer, H., and K. Holtzblatt. 1998. *Contextual Design: Defining Customer-Centered Systems*. San Francisco: Morgan Kaufmann.

Bødker, S. 1991. *Through the Interface—A Human Activity Approach to User Interface Design*. Hillsdale, NJ: Erlbaum.

Button, G., and P. Dourish. 1996. Technomethodology: Paradoxes and Possibilities. In *Proceedings of the Conference on Computer Human Interaction*, 19–26. Vancouver: ACM Press.

Checkland, P. 1981. *Systems Thinking, Systems Practice*. Chichester, England: Wiley.

Clarke, A. 1991. Social Worlds/Arenas Theory as Organizational Theory. In D. Maines, ed., *Social Organization and Social Process: Essays in Honor of Anselm Strauss*, 119–158. New York: Adeline de Gruyter.

Engeström, Y. 1991. Developmental Work Research: Reconstructing Expertise Through Expansive Learning. In M. J. Nurminen and G. R. S. Weir, eds., *Human Jobs and Computer Interfaces*. Amsterdam: Elsevier Science Publishers.

Fitzpatrick, G. 1998. The Locales Framework: Understanding and Designing for Cooperative Work. Doctoral dissertation, University of Queensland, Brisbane.

Fitzpatrick, G. 2000. Centres, Peripheries, and Electronic Communication: Changing Work Practice Boundaries. *Scandinavian Journal of Information Systems* 12: 115–148.

Fitzpatrick, G., S. Kaplan, and T. Mansfield. 1996. Physical Spaces, Virtual Places, and Social Worlds: A Study of Work in the Virtual. In *Proceedings of the Conference on Computer Supported Cooperative Work*, 334–343. Boston: ACM Press.

Fitzpatrick, G., S. Kaplan, and S. Parsowith. 1998. Experience in Building a Cooperative Distributed Organisation: Lessons for Cooperative Buildings. In *Cooperative Buildings: Integrating Information, Organization and Architecture*, 66–79. LNCS 1370. Heidelberg: Springer.

Fitzpatrick, G., S. Kaplan, and B. Tolone. 1995. Work, Locales and Distributed Social Worlds. In *Proceedings of the European Conference on Computer-Supported Cooperative Work*, Stockholm: Kluwer.

Forsythe, D. E. 1999. "It's Just a Matter of Common Sense": Ethnography as Invisible Work. *Computer Supported Cooperative Work* 8: 127–145.

Goldschlager, L., and A. Lister. 1988. *Computer Science: A Modern Introduction*. London: Prentice Hall International.

Greenberg, S., G. Fitzpatrick, C. Gutwin, and S. Kaplan. 2000. Adapting the Locales Framework for Heuristic Evaluation of Groupware. *Australian Journal of Information Systems* 7: 102–108.

Harrison, S., and P. Dourish. 1996. Re-Place-ing Space: The Roles of Place and Space in Collaborative Systems. In *Proceedings of the Conference on Computer Supported Cooperative Work*, 67–76. Boston: ACM Press.

Hughes, J., V. King, T. Rodden, and H. Andersen. 1994. Moving Out from the Control Room: Ethnography in Systems Design. In *Proceedings of the Conference on Computer Supported Cooperative Work*, 429–439. Chapel Hill, NC: ACM Press.

Hughes, J., J. O'Brien, T. Rodden, M. Rouncefield, and S. Blythin. 1997. Designing with Ethnography: A Presentation Framework for Design. In *Proceedings of the Conference on Designing Interactive Systems*, 147–158. Amsterdam: ACM Press.

Kaplan, S., and G. Fitzpatrick. 1997. Designing Support for Remote Intensive-Care Telehealth Using the Locales Framework. In *Proceedings of Designing Interactive Systems*, 173–184. Amsterdam: ACM Press.

Kaplan, S., G. Fitzpatrick, T. Mansfield, and B. Tolone. 1997. MUDdling Through. In *Proceedings of the Thirtieth Hawaii International Conference on Systems Sciences*, 359–548. Honolulu: IEEE Compute Society Press.

Kuutti, K. 1992. Identifying Potential CSCW Applications by Means of Activity Theory Concepts: A Case Example. In *Proceedings of the Conference on Computer Supported Cooperative Work*, 233–240. Toronto: ACM Press.

Kyng, M. 1998. Users and Computers: A Contextual Approach to Design of Computer Artifacts. *Scandinavian Journal of Information Systems* 10: 7–44.

Mansfield, T., S. Kaplan, G. Fitzpatrick, T. Phelps, M. Fitzpatrick, and R. Taylor. 1997. Evolving Orbit: A Progress Report on Building Locales. In *Proceedings of Conference on Supporting Group Work*, 241–250. Phoenix: ACM Press.

Plowman, L., Y. Rogers, and M. Ramage. 1995. What Are Workplace Studies For? In *Proceedings of the Fourth European Conference on Computer-Supported Cooperative Work*, 309–324. Stockholm: Kluwer.

Rittel, H., and M. Webber. 1973. Dilemmas in a General Theory of Planning. *Policy Studies* 4(1): 155–169.

Roseman, M., and S. Greenberg. 1996. TeamRooms: Network Places for Collaboration. In *Proceedings of the Conference on Computer Supported Cooperative Work*, 325–333. Boston: ACM Press.

Shapiro, D. 1994. The Limits of Ethnography: Combining Social Sciences for CSCW. In *Proceedings of the Conference on Computer Supported Cooperative Work*, 417–439. Chapel Hill, NC: ACM Press.

Simon, H. 1960. *The New Science of Management Decision*. New York: Harper and Row.

Strauss, A. 1993. *Continual Permutations of Action*. New York: Aldine de Gruyter.

Suchman, L. A. 1987. *Plans and Situated Actions: The Problem of Human-Machine Communication*. New York: Cambridge University Press.

Wastell, D. G., P. White, and P. Kawalek. 1994. A Methodology for Business Process Redesign: Experience and Issues. *Journal of Strategic Information Systems* 3(1): 23–40.

8

What Doesn't Fit: The "Residual Category" as Analytic Resource

Eevi E. Beck

How do you keep foregrounded the ironic and iffy things you're doing and still do them seriously[?]

—Donna Haraway 1990

We often see multiplicity and heterogeneity as accidents or exceptions. The marginal person, who is for example of mixed race, is seen as the troubled outsider; just as the thing that doesn't fit into one category or another gets put into a "residual category." ... [This] habit perpetuates a cruel pluralistic ignorance. None of us are pure. None of us are even average. And all things inhabit someone's residual category in some category system.

—Leigh Star 1994

This is a chapter on doing research—on the theory and practice of method.

At the seminar that inspired this book, Jim Nyce suggested "the residual category" as a discussion topic. I borrow the notion of "what doesn't fit" and ask how this can be used as a resource in analysis of empirical situations (field notes, interviews, and so on). In the methods literature I have come across few cases where such a take on analysis is mentioned at all, let alone discussed. I will do so here, also including the messy business of our emotions, tactics, and so on as researchers. I wish to support a claim that paying attention to what doesn't fit can be one useful resource (of many) in reflections on empirical and theoretical knowledges. I do not wish to propose a new term, or method—these are not what is important—but to point to some analytic practices that may appear in many guises: paying attention to exceptions, the odd case, "what doesn't fit" previous conceptions. The purpose is to help broaden the set of practices seen as part of empirical analysis. In the process I provide examples of practical applications in analyses, and an idiosyncratic review of some relevant theory.

Categories Residual and Otherwise

The "residual" is what is left over (e.g., what is stuck to the sides of a vessel when most of the contents have come out); what is left when the main part has been accounted for. Categorization (sorting phenomena into prelabeled groups) is a practical achievement—and a major problem in standardization, when categories are meant to last across situations. The residual is what cannot be adequately categorized (falls outside the box, or "illegally" belongs to two places).

"What is left out" of categories has been little theorized in computing (but see Bowker and Star 1999; Star 1991, 1995; Suchman 1993). Yet the issue is particularly important to computer science research: we design systems that often purport to cover "all" (in some area) and that, even when they do not, introduce or reify categorizations. Computer scientists have good reason to be interested in theoretical and practical problems around categorization.

Consider attempts to bring "context" to the attention of systems developers. Social scientists have made great efforts to persuade computer scientists that in our technical designs, we need to take into account the context for the use of the (future) technology. Many have taken onboard part or all of the argument—there is even a debate on "how far to go." Still, what this is to mean remains elusive even for some who accept the general argument. I once saw a talk by a computer scientist who used one of our most common schematics—a diagram with several labeled boxes with arrows between them, some pointing directly or via others to a process (central box) and others pointing out of it. One input box was labeled "context." To me, this visual representation of "context-in-a-box" epitomized a number of conversations with fellow researchers about "how to include context": many are looking for a set answer.

But "context" fades as you examine it and it becomes clear how difficult it is to give the term a meaning beyond "what we are not looking at right now." "Context" is constructed by "noncontext" (focus), and vice versa.

In a similar way, all categorizations depend on dichotomy; a category is constituted by what is not included. Categorizations only work by contrast: what is in and what is out; what is in this and what in that category. The difficulty arises when a category system (a categorization) is thought to cover all instances, all possibilities—or, indeed, when categories are thought to be distinct, or lasting. In a closed system where the analyst sets up (defines, enumerates, imagines) all permissible (or projected) instances, such as values of a variable in a program, no problem may be evident. But for example in systems analysis, computer scientists are to use a number of analytic tools that we may not think of as "formalized"—such as structured diagrams, entity-relationship modeling, or dataflow diagrams—through which in effect the analyst is to play God and set, if "only" by imagination, the complete landscape, the total set of permissible inputs and outputs. As previous requirements engineering methods are found inadequate, new approaches have been introduced (Dittrich, chapter 12, this volume).

Analytic Resources

Analysis is a contestable term. It is shorthand for the work of trying to understand a situation. My usage in this chapter follows from my wish to speak to computing science: I mean to invoke, in a community I believe to be familiar with the term, a sense of the familiar. In computing science, "analysis" is a safely established notion in discussions of method. This is the term whose connotations I seek to infiltrate; I seek to strengthen a particular layer of the term's meaning. *Resources*, on the other hand, is a suitably vague term for anything that specific persons in specific settings may find helpful for doing what they do.

In my experience, researchers and practitioners who have learned "as we go" have often picked up the "how" of empirical investigations—or as much of it as we care to be interested in—but not so much the importance of self-reflection: the "why." I believe the latter is essential for our ability to continue developing methods suitable for our work. Dittrich (chapter 12, this volume) and Korpela et al. (chapter 14, this volume) develop arguments for computing researchers to turn our techniques onto ourselves. At the moment I wish to delve deeper into the "how," to a place where part of the answer becomes a matter of self-reflection/self-observation.

How do researchers who study the worlds of work (and home, and so on) come up with "findings"? Why do some statements, certain occurrences, emerge as worth writing about out of the infinitude of impressions, field notes, interview responses, documentation, audio or video recordings, and so on, that field study usually generates? This is a crucial question—to practitioners, admirers, and dependants (users) of science alike—yet it does not receive the attention it deserves. The question is important in two ways: First, it is relevant for those wishing to learn, or develop, practical abilities in this area—as a fairly straightforward "how" question. Many and diverse skills are used during these gradual processes, and although there are no correct answers, skill and technique can to some extent be taught (the rest is personal experience). Second, how is it, in practice, that certain events become "scientific fact"? In this case, the question is an epistemological "why" that can be extended in a number of philosophical-cultural-political directions (as Donna Haraway (1997) and others have done).

Of particular interest to me here is what we do but do not talk about—things we practice but do not teach but that nevertheless could be an indispensable part of doing what we do (i.e., stopping doing them could materially change what we do and what we produce as "results"). In this chapter I point to a collection of practices that I believe are part of many researchers' analytic "toolkit" but that are rarely discussed.[1] This can be seen as a partial answer to both senses of the question above of how we end up with "findings."

What Doesn't Fit: Practices of Seeing

I once had the pleasure of cosupervising a master's student with Markku Nurminen. At one point where I felt we were a little stuck, he asked the student: "Did you see anything that surprised you?" At its simplest, that is what this chapter is about. However, we can—and, I claim, should—take this further. Such processes may at times include honoring—but not blindly following—vague impressions, niggling feelings that something "isn't quite it," and other indications that can be hard to verbalize, let alone admit into one's publicly displayed repertoire of analytic resources.

To keep our feet on the ground, I provide some examples from the published literature in this section. Here I am interested in the ways the authors in their analyses made active use of experiences that "didn't fit" what they were expecting.

In her doctoral dissertation in sociology that critically examines the role of taboo in rendering caregiving work largely unacknowledged, Lise Widding Isaksen (1994, 14–15) writes of her emerging relationship to her topic: "Collecting empirical material on taboo aspects of caregiving was not my explicit purpose.... What I had really wanted originally was to examine whether or not my hypothesis that informal caregiving had considerable welfare consequences for family women was empirically valid."

Isaksen's methods discussion is original, interesting, and at times provocative in demonstrating her wrestling with the subject matter she sees emerging. She provides an example of an interview experience that vividly recounts reactions that eventually led to this shift. The interviews she was conducting at the time were not meant to touch issues of bodily excretions; they were only intended to deal with the circumstances that had led the informant family to apply for room at an institution. But interviewees would indirectly speak of the incontinence aspects of looking after their relative. So difficulties surrounding incontinence was not new to Isaksen as a topic of conversation. Nevertheless, witnessing it was different.

In the mid-1980s, she was interviewing an informant in his home while he was doing the daily tasks of looking after his wife with senile dementia and growing incontinence:

> In my field book, where I noted down interviews and observations, I only wrote what Alfred had answered to my questions. When I nevertheless still have a vivid memory of the interview this many years later, it is due to the unusual combination of smells and tasks that constituted the context for the conversation. I found it unpleasant to witness the wife's visit to the toilet. I reacted to the door being left open, and to smells from frying fish and from the wife's business at the WC being mixed. Seeing the big pan full of soiled bedlinen ... in ... the kitchen ..., made me shiver. (Isaksen 1994, 12)

Meeting the home life of this family had a double edge for her: such category-crossing double uses of space were not meant to happen (neither the physical mixing of smells that "belong to" separate spaces, nor the conceptual mixing of food and excrement). And she, an outsider, was not meant to know it firsthand.

Isaksen struggled with one more layer of taboos: an epistemological one. Reflecting on her own "correct" reaction, she continues: "Instead of writing down what happened during the interview and my reactions to it I defined my own unease as distinctly emotional and without scientific relevance" (pp. 12–13).

She found: "As member of a culture in which the body's emptying functions are not appropriate to talk about, the thought of such functions has more often filled me with disgust than with scientific curiosity. However, gradually it became clear to me that I could not progress in my work on the uniqueness of care work without including its bodily dimensions" (p. 10).

Isaksen's case is fascinating as a clear example of "following the actors": by opening her eyes to her own reactions (and those of her colleagues) she was able to see what was in front of her. The shift necessitated including herself as a (re-)actor in the situation, rather than as (a sympathetic, but nevertheless an) observer.

Leigh Star (1991, 34–39) writes of how her allergy to onions doesn't fit what's expected at restaurants, causing, among other things, a 45-minute delay at a fast-food chain. Using this as a point of departure in the paper, she raises a number of complexities surrounding standardization and humans as members of multiple social worlds. This is another paper that has attracted considerable interest among fellow researchers as bringing to the attention of a certain research community perspectives on heterogeneities and standardization.

Star's interest in invisible work and in categorizations, especially in their boundaries, has resulted in a book, together with Geof Bowker, on classification, its ambiguities, its practices, its politics (Bowker and Star 1999). In their introduction, they write of their practicing residual categories:

> Our computer desktops are no less cluttered [than our desktops]. Here the electronic equivalent of "not yet ready to throw out" is also well represented. A

quick scan ... reveals eight residual categories ...: "fun," "take back to office," "remember to look up," "misc.," "misc. correspondence," "general web information," "teaching stuff to do," and "to do." We doubt if this is an unusual degree of disarray or an overly prolific use of the "none of the above" category so common to standardized tests and surveys. (Bowker and Star 1999, 2)

The examples above are particularly interesting for demonstrating the use of personal experiences as a springboard for one's academic thinking. I believe this is not unusual as a practice; however, acknowledging so in writing breaks taboos about "scienticity," and few authors do so.

Kristen Nygaard is famed for co-inventing object-oriented programming and for starting off what became known internationally as the Scandinavian approach—now participatory design—through a now-famous project. Both had the purpose of strengthening the workers' hand in shaping computing technology with which they were to be working. The current volume is based on a seminar in 1999 that was preceded, in 1988, by a seminar on "Software Development and Reality Construction," in which Nygaard participated. His contribution to the book that followed (Nygaard 1992) describes how the ground was laid for this to become more than just another research project (a steering committee had already accepted a research plan):

During the summer 1971 I felt more and more uneasy about this plan, but I could not spot what was wrong. Gradually it dawned upon me that our strategy would produce some reports about systems, and two researchers who had knowledge on behalf of the union members....

The reorientation was painful, but eventually we chose to tell the steering committee that we had to completely change the project plan. I hope that similar choices will not turn up too often in the future. The key decision was the acceptance of the following statement:

"In most research projects the results of the project may be said to be what is written in the project reports. In this project another definition will be applied: We will regard as results actions carried out by the trade unions, at the local and national levels, as a part of or triggered off by the project."

... The immediate consequence was that the local unions got a new and pivotal role. (Nygaard 1992, 56; original emphasis)

Nygaard recounts here the triumph and discomfort of turning around, of letting go the previous idea of what the project would be like and taking on a new one. The "new and pivotal role" for the trade unions was what later became the major inspiration from this project to many others. As recounted by Nygaard, then, and retold by me, this reorientation was the crucial point that "Changed History." And this could suffice for the current chapter. But this—like the other stories in my chapter—was an after-the-fact view, perhaps a particularly striking one. The importance of this otherwise mundane event (mundane because project descriptions are changed or ignored all the time) is constructed from the privilege of hindsight, of success. But note the hint at pain—twice stated—that birthed Nygaard's turnaround and the reorientation itself. What was that about?

My own empirical studies of coauthoring (Beck 1994) produced the following example. In a pilot study, one interviewee would not provide a simple answer to an introductory question: How large was the group she had been in? Her response was a story of coauthors coming and going, of people taking responsibility for a while and then drifting away. I could not make her agree to a single number. Reflecting later on how wrong it felt to try to, caused my first questioning of own methods. What I initially had seen as a natural but odd case that I needed to discount to arrive at "what designers would need" (i.e., a conception of typical group size), became the start of a small exploration into the variability of group sizes. Although I never made this a major focus, this revealed inappropriate conceptions in my area of designing for a unitary "group."

Practices of seeing what doesn't fit, then, range from the mundane to the grand. It is deeply situated, practical, ambiguous, messy. It can painfully jar with expectations, including those of our peers. Isaksen struggled with the practical-epistemological taboos of academic peers: "During the work with understanding how the appearance into visibility of "the disgusting body" can initiate complex social mechanisms, I presented various drafts to colleagues at home and abroad. The most common reaction was people feeling embarrassed, being provoked, and/or turning their heads away … even when presented in the abstract language of science" (Isaksen 1994, 10; original emphasis).

And Nygaard's in many respects paradigmatic project did not become so for that which political or scientific "rational logic" could not capture. His main experience has been deleted from the legend:

> The Iron and Metal Project was carried out by approximately 120 persons.... [117] were local shop stewards and union members. To work in such a project demands a different kind of self-discipline and understanding of your own role than traditional projects. To make this well understood in academia is next to impossible. One has to be exposed to it through own participation. The cooperation in the Iron and Metal Project certainly is one of the most valuable and significant experiences of my work. (Nygaard 1992, 59)

What Doesn't Fit: Theories of Looking

This section is anomalous to this chapter, just as the chapter is anomalous to practice: How can you (attempt to) name—let alone theorize—what has been forgotten, ignored? The main answer lies, I think, in our practices. But considerations at more theoretical levels do exist that can inspire reflection and practice. (For lack of a better description, I am calling a theory or theories not the research practices that might be given such a label or any results of them, but the manifestly existing body of ideas, concepts, and so on about such practices.)

Several methods that were previously thought the realm only of "social scientists" (whoever they may be) but that have demonstrated their direct relevance to and have gained acceptance in computing, have strong roots in hermeneutics. Hermeneutics theorizes interpretation, and includes the perspective that no one can fully understand another person's understanding. This has a number of consequences, including, according to the philosopher Charles Taylor ([1971] 1998), the impossibility of a verifiable science of humans. Hermeneutics and related approaches have been extremely influential in a number of academic disciplines and have been applied in a variety of ways of relevance to the present discussion. My brief comments here in no way do justice to it, or to its influences. Taylor argues that the human sciences are hermeneutic in nature, thus (among other things) necessitating an element of reflection in its practitioners that requires openness, thus self-reflection. Gadamer is known, among other things, for advocating asking questions of and entering into dialogue with classic texts. As read by Susan V. Scott (2000), Gadamer's thesis as relevant to the present chapter has three major aspects. First, human agents encountering a phenomenon start by building an interpretation of it. Second, "all interpretations are based upon an individual's past experience, perception of the present and projection of the future; these form prejudice, which Gadamer regards as pre-learning rather than an innately negative form of bias." Third, only parts of our experiences can be captured by scientific method.

According to these philosophers, then, any understanding by or of humans is interpretation, which further means that bias or prejudice—personal, "cultural," and so on—is inseparable from the process. By simple extension, all aspects of the (human) work of conceptualizing and implementing computing systems are likewise so. The ramifications of seriously taking this perspective into the core of computing are dazzling. To conduct and interpret such analyses requires competencies that differ significantly from what many computer scientists (practitioners, students, researchers, educators) were taught. The reorientation can evoke major struggles over fundamental questions of meaning.

Aspects of such struggles are treated extensively in the present volume. Relevant contributions include Yvonne Dittrich's review of changes in perspectives on software engineering and discussion of what ethnography may contribute (chapter 12); Geraldine Fitzpatrick's process of developing a bridging framework (chapter 7); Chris Westrup's discussion of legislation versus interpretation (chapter 5); and Marina Jirotka and Paul Luff's elicitation of struggles over modeling (chapter 6).[2]

Ethnographic approaches that have been used in conjunction with systems development include grounded theory and ethnomethodological ethnography. In chapter 5, Westrup brings hermeneutic (interpretive) perspectives on the relationship between ethnography and systems development. My present interest is in aspects that seem to allow for, point to, and make use of, more of "what doesn't fit" than in many other approaches.

Grounded theory (developed by Anselm Stauss and Barney Glaser; for an introduction, see Strauss 1989) includes practices where the researcher time and again returns to the data and/or the situation under study (e.g., work at a hospital ward). Concepts (preliminary categories with names) are formed to capture what the analyst has noticed, and at one point these are challenged, examined more deeply, by more or less systematically contrasting the category label with other senses of the term in different contexts. Techniques are proposed to help the analyst consider a wide range of perspectives on the proposed concept. This includes regular meetings of analysts (students, others) for mutual discussion of each person's ongoing empirical work (Strauss 1989). An important purpose of the meetings is to encourage sensitivity to experiences that are not readily explainable or understandable to the analyst, including, for example, personal reactions or feelings (Star, personal communication, 1996). In grounded theory, this is considered a powerful resource for deepening and widening the analysis.

Ethnomethodology, however, questions and possibly rejects theory building. As an approach to field study it is radically open to questioning all assumptions about "how things work." A key insight is the impossibility of enumerating the complete meaning of, for instance, a conversation. Background assumptions cannot be exhaustively listed, because they get constructed as the question is invoked. Trying to make explicit constructs what you are looking at/for: at some point you have to give up and appeal to a shared understanding. Context is necessarily indexical.[3] For the current discussion, this raises the parallel problem: when you try to elicit "background" it unfolds, extending further and further, because looking (naming) constructs further background. So looking at, boxing off, naming, a residual category constructs new ones, ad infinitum.

Star's writings build on grounded theory. Major themes include boundaries and their costs—their establishment, maintenance, and transgression. Several points are directly relevant here. Star's writings provide a rich source for discussions around issues of categorization, of the marginal, and of the establishment and crossing of boundaries. The quotation from Star introducing this chapter is from an argument about analysts' poor history of dealing with multiplicity beyond attempting to reduce it to homogeneity (Star 1994:5). She has called for a Sociology of the Invisible. Invisible work is made so by being, by and large, ignored, unacknowledged, by anyone beyond those doing it. In high-profile jobs, too, parts of the work may be more or less visible. For example, together with Karen Ruhleder, Star conducted a study of an international network of scientists who were to start using a "collaboratory" system for collaborating with their peers (Star and Ruhleder 1996). They detail the practical problems for some of these scientists in actually beginning to use the system. Such problems can constitute considerable obstacles in the practical experience of implementing network and other new systems, yet they go largely unacknowledged in the computing research community.

Computer scientists interested in the processes and problems that systems analysis originally purported to solve could do well to examine empirically based theoretical insights into categorization. The main empirical study in Bowker and Star 1999 is of a large internationally maintained list, the International Classification of Diseases (ICD). Since it is a list of causes of death, one might expect a well-constrained domain. However, Bowker and Star recount negotiations, political concerns, ethical issues, history, and so on that affect the shaping and continual review of the list. It turns out not to be possible to cover all possibilities in this (serious attempt at a complete) category system. The need to make residual categories and manage their use is fascinating reading. Bowker and Star theorize their emergence and purposes. Their notion of "distribution of ambiguity" names one of the ICD(-committee)'s evolving practices for managing residual categories and their effects on the statistics.

Many issues raised in this chapter have been subject to explorations, both practical and theoretical, among feminist philosophers of science, including sociologist Leigh Star, cited above, and biologist and historian of consciousness Donna Haraway (e.g., Haraway 1997).

Mathematical biologist Evelyn Fox Keller has studied the life and career of biologist Barbara McClintock. McClintock won the Nobel Prize for discovering genetic transposition. She studied genes in corn and noticed some kernels with an odd color at one point. She was sufficiently intrigued to want an explanation—and discovered that parts of chromosomes can swap places. In Keller's interpretation, the discovery was only possible because of McClintock's worldview, making her open to seeing as a positive challenge something that was not explainable by current theories. Hence Keller's point that preconceptions (about what kinds of phenomena/theories will count as satisfactory explanations) shape science (Keller 1985).

Discussion

As Dittrich recounts in chapter 12, we computer scientists are increasingly becoming aware of the need to reflect on our own investigations into the environments of future systems, whether they are called *case studies*, *requirements analysis*, *fieldwork*, or anything else. The reorientation has, however, brought challenges. Not only are we inviting ourselves to look at situations that previously were considered outside our realm, but few have training that supports doing so, or learning how to. Unambiguously defined properties that are the ideal and possible to achieve in (parts of) a computer program have little relevance for the messy business of trying to understand something of the lived, experienced world. Yet computer scientists use such conceptual frameworks as tools. "Social thinking" related to "software practice" to me points to this paradox. My chapter is an attempt at encouraging certain ideas about how to conduct such empirical investigations—that is, a specific incarnation of what might be described as "social thinking" in the midst of software practice (systems analysis, requirements engineering). I hope the chapter can, first, bring to a new audience—especially computer science students—the idea that "what doesn't fit" can be a useful resource in the work of understanding computer-use situations. Second, hopefully the chapter can contribute to reflection on existing practice and thereby to developing this reflection further.

In the practical examples I may have cast the researcher who paid the right attention to her feelings, intuition, and so on in the hero's role. This has at least three fallacies. First, the experience may at the time bear little resemblance to the heroic, as vividly shown by Isaksen, but also in Nygaard's allusions to pain. Recounting happenings and (re-)actions in stories or as "results" necessarily provides a simplistic view of the processes even to those who experienced them. Am I supporting the notion that this can be conveyed, told, rationalized, nourished, planned for? Second, others are rarely given a glimpse of the processes that lead to the later stories. I am therefore in danger of holding up as an ideal for action something almost wholly unrelated to real action in the situation. Third, several of the researchers in the examples ended up proposing new concepts or new categories. Does this mean that better categorizations are the answer—we can "cover all" if the categorization is good enough? I do not believe so. Any person, and any community of researchers, has a partial perspective. Seeing this enhances our understanding. Contributing some concepts that enlarge this understanding is likewise beneficial. Most important, however: the examples are meant to reveal new approaches and new conceptions that go beyond the original categorizations, showing the latter to be inadequate, thus opening rather than closing off categorizations. This is the transforming potential. We need not get away from all categorizations—but trying to do so may bring its own rewards.

Still, I am offering examples in order to say something stronger than that "it can be done." Some landmark pieces of research became so when researchers dared to see what was in front of them and take appropriate steps, although there was no precedent for their actions. With the examples, I hope to appease any fear of this unknown territory that may arise. I also wish to stretch the established limits of "methods" discussions through arguing for including in the researcher's display of methodology more of her or his own reactions as a resource. To support adventurous voyagers, I emphasize the successes of McClintock and Nygaard, thus appealing to our hunger for peer recognition.[4]

As discussed earlier, theories exist that can be made relevant to this undertaking. Hermeneutic and related theories remind us of the necessarily interpretational process of understanding others; ethnomethodological analyses call our attention to ways this interpretation is organized in (inter-)action. Feminist attention to means and consequences of interpretation where ideology states there are none continues to be invaluable. Grounded theory and (some) feminist methodological approaches take such lessons into the practice of method (drawing out personal reactions as an explicit part of research), a beautiful spin-off being theorizing of the work of construction and upkeep of categorizations as well as being blighted by them into invisibility. All in all, these are diverse and strong indications of the impossibility of capturing everything in any categorization of the importance of paying attention to the differences between categorizations and the phenomena being categorized. I have proposed "what doesn't fit" as an informal label that might invoke this curiosity about difference while conducting (or theorizing about) empirical work. For a science whose material and method involve the transformation of abstractions into categorizations, this questioning must be important.

Regardless of the success of this specific attempt, the discussion in this chapter is important for a number of reasons. First, it is useful: as demonstrated by the examples above, analytic attention to aspects that "didn't fit" has produced results not otherwise obtained. Answers (or more detailed questioning) have in many cases arisen to questions that could not otherwise have been asked (because they were not part of the researcher's horizon of possibilities). Second, this approach is already being practiced. If it is reasonably common, it is beneficial to a methodological discourse to make this explicit. If it is not a common practice, it may be interesting to ask why not. Third, discussion of the issues addressed in this chapter is of interest for epistemological reasons: it makes explicit a little more of the process of analysis. Fourth (the personal side of the third point), the approach sketched here can benefit researchers. Legitimizing the conscious attention to and use of some of the reactions, feelings, and so on that arise during analysis provides for a more "whole" experience through reducing the need to act as if the intellect were the only faculty that entered into analysis.

The process of opening up what gets "put away," pushed to the sides, is the business of looking at what challenges and even negates what we thought we knew. This is why it is such a powerful perspective to return to while conducting "analysis" of empirical situations. It requires, however, being open to having our beliefs challenged when we take on the role of analysts. Keller's (1985: 167) reminder is useful that even within science, what counts as knowledge is not uniform across cultures of research. In the quotation that introduces this chapter, Haraway put succinctly a parallel question about scientific knowledge and how to act, as a scientist, on this and related insights about the (messy) practices of scientists (in Penley and Ross 1990). Haraway confronts researchers with the question of how to be honest about our practices without losing their meaning. In my reading, she is ultimately concerned with how to improve science by incorporating into its practices some of the questioning, and into image(s) of its practices, the results, of critical studies of science.

If we are convinced that events and data that "don't fit" are worth looking into, how do we do this? Invoking what is vaguely referred to as "intuition" does not bring us much further than the possibility that the question cannot be answered (some might argue this is good). We can sensitize ourselves. Bowker and Star argue for computer scientists to expose ourselves to a wide range of perspectives on life and work, especially from sources with a different worldview than that usually perpetuated in computer science. Poetry may be one such form of expression; feminist critique another (Bowker and Star 1999, 302).

My conviction is that another key is accepting what "troubles" you, living with it as part of you, looking at it from different angles. Here I imagine a good mix of self-reflection and analytic attention (as well as patience) as an ideal: being willing and able to live with the disturbances; to look at them, see them, for as long as it takes—then expect more disturbances. Shifting the "grounds" can help: something in the background may provide a more convincing answer. By definition, a need to change viewpoints can be hard to detect, and impossible to reason your way to. Yet my point is not to champion the following of whims, but daring a closer look at "whims" that refuse to go away. This is what I mean by taking own reactions seriously.

"What doesn't fit" can hardly be described, yet I have tried to do so academically. This could be taken as a proposal for a technique that can be applied. It is not. The basic problem—but also the beauty—is that the practices I am pointing toward are elusive, ambiguous, insufficient, insecure, and above all, deeply personal. Further, Star (1995:6) reminds us that trying to make visible what was previously hidden is complex, and brings with it potential dangers. These are not the usual claims for a method of or approach to analysis in computing. Awareness of these practices and of their value can, however, be raised, shared, taught (and named, discussed). For analysts, paying attention to our own reactions has a number of benefits and can be a powerful resource. It raises a host of questions and is not easy to confront or to carry out. To publicly admit to such work practices is rare but has started gaining a foothold among practitioners of science. This strategy can be fraught with dangers—

including the greatest of them all, loss of respect among peers for not being a "serious" scientist. Moreover, shy creatures, these practices could be damaged by attempts at naming (as in the present chapter): some practices thrive in darkness, in the shadows cast by the brightly lit stage props of "scienticity." But I would rather have those well-worn screens reveal their holes so that we can see what else is there, because I think such scrutiny makes for a more robust science and more whole scientist.

So despite everything, I wish to encourage approaches that legitimize paying attention to our hearts, and have tried to make that aspect of research visible by writing about it. The paradox of the title of this chapter is that however many categories we create, however much we make explicit, there will always be a "residual." This should keep us from ever thinking we have covered everything—and that is the point. Feeling "troubled" can be uncomfortable. But if you find you are in this situation, try to listen carefully.

Notes

For inspiration, I would like to acknowledge the participants at the Dagstuhl seminar (especially Christiane Floyd, Kalle Lyytinen, Jim Nyce), and Leigh Star. For helpful comments: Yvonne Dittrich, Laurence Habib, Viktor Kaptelinin, Ralf Klischewski, Svein Myreng, Knut Rolland, Chris Westrup, Margunn Aanestad. For funding: the Norwegian Research Council.

1. ... and thus, in a nice symmetry, the setting as well as the substance of the practices I am writing about entail pointing out something that doesn't fit established norms for what we should focus our own or others' scientific attention on. My implicit claim that such practices may be common is tenuous.

2. Some readers might find the theoretical background of my position more understandable by reading some of these other contributions.

3. "A representation is indexical when its truth depends on the occasions of its use" (Agre 1997, 230). In other words, "context" is wholly situation dependent and cannot be defined except in relation to specific circumstances. This seems hard to reconcile with a computing science that has become used to defining "objects" in the "world" according to the needs of programming. Agre (1997) discusses sources of such difficulties in relation to artificial intelligence (and proposes computational alternatives; for computing and indexicality in particular see pp. 230–234). To me, the "context-in-a-box" episode discussed toward the beginning of this chapter is an illustration of the generality of this difficulty.

4. This hunger—haunting, insatiable—is to me a feature of life in academia that is necessary to keep our structures of competition going. I will go as far as to assert that what keeps us and our colleagues—friends as well as foes—insatiable is the "sugar" that, as in the song, "keeps the world goin' round." (Sugar: not good for you, but the highs are enjoyable and get you hooked so that you do not or will not notice your dependency, the lows generate hunger for more; political pressures to keep things as they are seem perpetually stronger than efforts to Summon Truth.) I would love to see an ethnomethodological inquiry into our practices of co-constructing the need for peer recognition.

References

Agre, P. E. 1997. *Computation and human experience.* Cambridge, England: Cambridge University Press.

Beck, E. E. 1994. *Practices of collaboration in writing and their support.* CSRP 340, School of Cognitive and Computing Sciences, University of Sussex.

Bowker, G. C., and S. L. Star. 1999. *Sorting things out: Classification and its consequences.* Cambridge, MA: MIT Press.

Haraway, D. 1997. *Modest_Witness@Second_Millennium. FemaleManã_Meets_OncoMouseÔ.* New York: Routledge.

Isaksen, L. Widding. 1994. *Den tabubelagte kroppen: kropp, kjønn og tabuer i dagens omsorgsarbeid* [The taboo ridden body: Body, gender and taboo in today's care work]. Doctoral dissertation, Department of Sociology, University of Bergen, Norway.

Keller, E. F. 1985. *Reflections on gender and science.* New Haven, CT: Yale University Press.

Nygaard, K. 1992. How many choices do we make? How many are difficult? In C. Floyd, H. Züllighoven, R. Budde, and R. Keil-Slawik, eds., *Software development and reality construction.* Berlin: Springer-Verlag.

Penley, C., and A. Ross. 1990. Cyborgs at large: Interview with Donna Haraway. *Social Text* 25/26: 8–23.

Scott, S. V. 2000. Lived methodology: A situated discussion of "truth and method" in interpretive information systems research. Department of Information Systems, London School of Economics and Political Science, Working Paper 91 (Series ISSN1472-9601).

Star, S. L. 1991. Power, technology and the phenomenology of conventions: On being allergic to onions, in J. Law, ed., *A sociology of monsters: Essays on power, technology and domination,* 26–56. London: Routledge.

Star, S. L. 1994. *Misplaced concretism and concrete situations: Feminism, method and information technology.* Gender-Nature-Culture Feminist Network, Working paper 11, Department of Feminist Studies, University of Odense, Denmark.

Star, S. L. 1995. Introduction. In S. L. Star, ed., *The cultures of computing*, 1–28. Oxford: Blackwell.

Star, S. L., and K. Ruhleder. 1996. Steps toward an ecology of infrastructure: Design and access for large information spaces. *Information Systems Research* 7(1): 111–134.

Strauss, A. L. 1989. *Qualitative analysis for social scientists*. Cambridge, England: Cambridge University Press.

Suchman, L. 1993. Do categories have politics? In *Proceedings of the Third European Conference on Computer-Supported Cooperative Work* (Milan, Italy, September 13–17), 1–14. Dordrecht: Kluwer.

Taylor, C. [1971] 1998. Interpretation and the Sciences of Man. *Review of Metaphysics* 25(1): 3–51. Sections I and IV, reprinted in E. D. Klemke, R. Hollinger, D. W. Rudge, with A. D. Kline, eds., *Introductory readings in the philosophy of science*, 3rd ed. Amherst, MA: Prometheus Books.

III

Grounding

Yvonne Dittrich

Relating social thinking and software practice in order to develop usable and useful computer applications is one of the main motivations for this book. The concepts, methods, and tools to do so have to be grounded in a realistic picture not only of the practices of software use but also of the practices of software development.

Approaches and schools focusing on the design of usable and useful applications, like participatory design, the Scandinavian approach of information systems development, or computer supported cooperative work, are mainly concerned with understanding the use context and developing design proposals. As important as the understanding of the use context and the involvement of users are, leaving out the development practice can lead to a lack of familiarity with the developed methods and tools by the practitioners who are supposed to apply them. And how can we expect methods to be applicable if they are not developed based on a thorough understanding of the practice they are meant to support?

Empirical research on software development has long been dominated by quantitative, measurement-oriented approaches. The goal is the improvement of technical qualities, like reliability and correctness, for example, or control of the software development process in terms of lead time and costs. Empirical research that relates software development practices, methods, and use qualities, can help to integrate use orientation throughout the development process in a practical way.

The contributions in this section open up a discussion of software development practice in which rigorous project models, quantitative success criteria, and competition are often part of the situation. Compared to other software qualities, usability and usefulness are problematic to measure. Use qualities emerge from the relation between the product and its use context; they not only depend on observable attributes of the software itself. Success regarding use qualities is therefore not as easy to argue as regarding lead time, number of errors detected during use, or performance, for example.

Methods of promoting usability and usefulness are often constructive measures, oriented toward providing conditions during software development that make a usable outcome possible or more probable. Participatory design, for instance, promotes communication about future technology and its use between users and developers and encourages a process of mutual learning. Evolutionary development promotes close feedback loops, to test the design ideas and correct them at an early stage.

Introducing these methods implies a major change of software development practices for most companies. A grounded understanding of software development practices will contribute to improving software engineering methods, whether they are meant to promote use orientation or not. Social science approaches, especially qualitative ones, promise to facilitate a broader understanding of the software development processes. But empirical research in software engineering goes beyond applying social science methods in yet another area of social life. These methods have to be adapted if used in a context oriented toward change and improvement. Both software engineering researchers and practitioners are interested in making things better.

The chapters in this part of the book take steps in that direction. The authors explore how software practitioners and researchers can make use of social thinking for developing and adapting software development methods.

In chapter 9, Urs Andelfinger develops a conceptual framework to understand the social and organizational background of software development projects regarding the context of development as well as the context of use. The framework can be used by researchers to analyze projects. But it is especially meant as a tool to map out the background of a project and to provide orientation for practitioners themselves.

Chapter 10, by Jacob Nørbjerg and Philip Kraft, provides a set of examples showing how the organization of software development influences the conditions for use orientation as well as the use qualities of its outcomes. They argue for taking the social context of software development into account when striving for use qualities.

Kari Rönkkö's contribution in chapter 11 provides an ethnomethodologically informed case study about requirements handling during the design of an integrated method and tool development project. It can be read as an example of the research argued for by Nørbjerg and Kraft. Rönkkö also uses the example to discuss the relationship of social science method oriented toward understanding the sociality of (software development) work and the change orientation inherent in software engineering research.

Chapter 12, by Yvonne Dittrich, outlines a framework for how to conceptualize and perform empirical research in software engineering. Cooperative method development makes it possible to utilize the results of qualitative as well as quantitative empirical methods for method development together with their users, the involved practitioners. This allows an exploration of methods promoting use orientation under industrial conditions.

9

On the Intertwining of Social and Technical Factors in Software Development Projects

Urs Andelfinger

In software development projects, social and technical factors are closely related. Tom deMarco (1997), for example, points out in a novel about project management that ambiguous requirements specifications may be a sign of unresolved conflict among different systems stakeholders. The point here is that the reason for ambiguity in a specification is not attributed to a bad specification technique or immature methodology, but to what, for the moment, we will call "the social."

The insight into the important role and influence of the social on software projects is certainly familiar to every professional software project manager. But it is difficult to find coherent frameworks that help in better understanding the obvious intertwining of technical and social factors in real software development projects (Minnemann 1991). Even software engineering as the academic discipline of how software development should be conducted does not have a generally accepted, coherent conceptual foundation of what it means to deal with the social aspects of real software projects—for example, when it comes to perceiving and settling conflict between different stakeholders. This stands in sharp contrast to the wealth of concepts, methodologies, and techniques that software engineering offers on the technical side of software development projects.

Of course, this shortcoming is partially understandable because of the specific academic scope and values of software engineering. Software engineering is oriented toward generative abstractions and technical constructions on the way to the software *product*, and its values stand for the well-known prescriptive attitude of engineering disciplines in general. The social features of software projects are often better accessible through analytic abstractions and through understanding of the software development process. These tasks normally belong to the disciplinary realm of the social sciences and are outside the scope of a traditional engineering perspective.

Succeeding in software projects requires both: understanding *and* constructing. The thesis is that bridging this gap can be facilitated by providing an adequate conceptual framework and by deliberately intertwining different rationales and academic disciplines. In the following sections this topic will be addressed in more detail. I will focus on a project management perspective where "the social" refers mainly to the organization and management of the software production per se. The emphasis is on informing software project managers about the inherent intertwining of the social and technical aspects of daily project life. Further research will be needed to extend this notion of "the social" toward aspects of, for example, user involvement, participatory design, and usability.

Two Ways of Looking at Programming

This section contrasts two perspectives on programming. I will intentionally use a simplified and to some extent overemphasized description. This will help later in establishing a better understanding of what the specific characteristics of the technical and the social in software projects are and of how they are intertwined.

The first perspective on programming is represented by the academic discipline of software engineering. The origin of software engineering was the 1968 NATO conference "Study Group on Computer Science" in Garmisch Partenkirchen. The conference participants agreed on the newly coined term *software engineering* of F. L. Bauer in order to overcome what was meant by the newly discovered phenomenon of the "software crisis": "The whole trouble comes from the fact that there is so much tinkering with software. It is not made in a clean fabrication process, which it should be. What we need, is *software engineering*" (Bauer 1993, 259).

A lot of progress toward more reliable and more usable software systems has effectively been made following the "fabrication process perspective" of software engineering. But as Parnas and Clements (1985, 82) pointed out, the rationalistic attitude of pure software engineering is not sufficient for real-life software development projects: "We will never find a process that allows us to design software in a perfectly rational way." And McDermid (1991) explicitly defines software engineering as a comprehensive endeavor of science *and* art that clearly goes beyond a clean fabrication process.

These insights into the wicked nature of software development in practice fundamentally challenge the pure software engineering perspective of programming. A wider perspective on programming is necessary to take the social context of software and its development into account. Programming is essentially a comprehensive human activity and has ends that reach beyond the technical. This does not devalue software engineering, but it shifts the focus away from a clean fabrication-process perspective toward a perhaps more adequate conception of what software projects are about.

An essential contribution toward an understanding of programming as human activity was developed by Peter Naur. He proposed to understand programming mainly as theory building about "the manner in which the problems at hand are solved by program execution" (Naur 1985, 253). Compared to the task of theory building, he claims that all documentation and implementation activities are secondary. With his concept of theory building, Naur refers to the whole software development process, not just to what usually is called programming or coding.

There is some criticism of Naur's theory-building view concerning the idea that each programmer has to build an individual theory (Bertelsen and Bødker, chapter 19, this volume). What software projects need is in fact an adaptation of the theory-building view that allows for collaborative theory building—that is, between users, designers, software engineers, and management. And the theory building should not be confined to functional theory building only. What is needed in software projects is an interdisciplinary sort of *extended* theory building. For example, it might be helpful to also develop an understanding of how the economic interests of the project are linked and mapped to the technical software artifact per se. Despite the critique of Naur's theory-building view, his basic idea seems quite adequate as a first step toward successfully extending the fabrication-oriented software engineering perspective to the needs of real-life software projects.

Another important contribution to the understanding of programming as human activity has been proposed by Nygaard (1986). He describes a whole set of core concepts that aim at understanding program development essentially as a social activity. To this end, he introduces and distinguishes concepts such as individual and collective perspectives, process and structure, and he differentiates several stakeholders—that is, users, managers, designers, programmers, and operators. Nygaard's concepts inform us in a sound way about "the social" in terms of interest groups, of conflict versus harmony, and of other important phenomena that we experience in real-life software practice. The technical implementation thus becomes a means for nontechnical ends and purposes.

To summarize, the software engineering perspective (in its simplified purity) may well be useful to precisely design, implement, and test code. However, software projects reach beyond. Getting a meaningful and usable software product requires an understanding of the use and development context. Software project managers also have to cope with and mediate between the different perspectives and interests of various stakeholders. These tasks may be supported by various forms of collaborative and interdisciplinary extended theory building. Consequently, the programming-as-human-activity perspective developed here does not ignore the necessity of technical implementation activities, but embeds them in a broader context. In the next section I will further investigate the relationship between these two perspectives on programming.

Understanding Software Projects: The Conceptual Framework

According to the software engineering perspective, software development projects are normally supposed to follow some sort of what is commonly called a *life cycle*. Life cycles exist in various forms, for example as linear waterfall models as well as various forms of spiral models that are more appropriate for the evolutionary and incremental nature of software projects. Although these models are different in detail, we can abstract some common generic cornerstones on a very simplified level. The cornerstones are considered the starting points and the corresponding results of some specific activities that take place in between. They should be understood as conceptual entities and epistemological aids to inform and structure software-project practice. I do not claim any ontological or exhaustive status for them.

At the outset, software projects normally start from a rather fuzzy cornerstone, namely the *setting of use* for the software product to be developed. One of the main challenges to reach the next cornerstone is to decontextualize and to transform the tasks at hand into computable problems. This cornerstone is therefore reached when *a requirements specification* and *state of shared understanding* of what exactly has to be developed is established. This may also be conceived of as *functional* theory building.

Based on the achieved problem understanding and requirements specification, the *technical implementation* is reached through coding activities that have to follow some standardized and measurable procedures as preconditions for provable and correct software. ("Correct" in this context means with respect to the requirements specification document; with respect to the setting of use, I prefer to say: software is valid.) Eventually, the software product is introduced into its setting of use and the life cycle can start anew.

Of course, to accomplish these tasks, *resources* have to be allocated to the project, which encompass technical and engineering methods as well as staffing, project management know-how, and funding. The conception of software projects that follow an instantiation of the described general life-cycle pattern is widely accepted as one of the core concepts of software engineering. Because this perspective is so widespread and because it covers the most prominent characteristic of software projects, namely their product orientation, I suggest calling this arena the *foreground* of software projects. The foreground is thus roughly determined by the three cornerstones of the life cycle, namely, the setting of use, requirements specification, and technical implementation, and the activities that take place in between them. The resources are conceived of in this perspective as being the means of getting the product done.

When contrasting this product-oriented view on software projects with practical project experience, one discovers that important aspects are missing that are needed to adequately understand what software projects are about.

In real-life projects, we have to cope with *actors* and *stakeholders*. Also, software projects normally have technical as well as economic and social *objectives:* they are supposed to meet some stakeholders' *interests* and they should be useful, meaningful, and usable. Last but not least, software projects are always embedded in a *development context*, which comprises, for example, the general organizational culture and the politics that are inevitably linked with all software projects. To accomplish these tasks, specific resources are needed: different forms of formal and informal communication, various forms of discourse, negotiations and the like, power and funding being two very effective means of coordination.

It is in this setting that the nontechnical and social issues of the software development projects are tackled: determining the scope and setting the purpose and meaning of the project, getting the management decision about the project, and so on. Compared to the rather evident product-oriented foreground of software projects, these aspects here are typically more fuzzy, hidden, and to a great extent implicit. Therefore, I suggest calling this setting the *background* of software projects. The notion of background does not at all mean that it is less important than the foreground of the projects. It simply alludes to the fact that it is normally more implicitly dealt with in software projects, and some of its main aspects are only partially accessible for explicit analysis. Instead, the background can be characterized by attributes like situatedness and context dependency, or validity instead of correctness, which may imply that different perspectives might exist at the same time. Other challenges of the background are dealing with a fuzzy and always-changing development context, to acknowledge that politics and power are immanent and to accept that residual categories remain because real-life problems are wicked problems.

The interesting question now is how the foreground and background of software projects are intertwined or otherwise related. Donald Schön's concept of *reflective practice* can be used to provide a framework for understanding this interrelationship (Schön 1983). The basic idea of reflective practice is that sound professional activity is not solely about problem solving, but that all professional problem solving also requires and implies some sort of concurrent problem understanding or problem framing. Conversely, valid problem framing requires and implies some effort of problem solving where the results are systematically fed back to the problem-framing activities. Reflective practice can therefore be considered a two-sided concept that is at the same time analytic and generative.

The idea of reflective practice can now be applied to software development projects. Reflective practice may occur on the technical level of the foreground in software projects. There it focuses on the functional side of the project and is related to the functional theory building. It can roughly be conceptualized as a deliberate and permanent iteration of technical problem-solving and problem-framing activities. This insight is already generally accepted by software engineering through iterative and evolutionary development processes.

But the main power of the notion of reflective practice lies in its potential to intertwine the technical aspects of the foreground with the wicked set of economic interests, organizational constraints, and multiple social perspectives of the project's background. The main challenge for this kind of reflective practice lies in its interdisciplinary nature, which means essentially that concepts and modes of thinking originally stemming from different disciplinary arenas have to be combined into a comprehensive set of mutually connected concepts.

At this point, reflective practice goes clearly beyond a clean fabrication process. It is no longer only a concept of permanent oscillation between analytic and generative activities with a technical focus. It is also a permanent oscillation between different disciplinary attitudes and ways of thinking by which ultimately the (technical) foreground and the (social) background of software projects become intimately intertwined. As a result, the technical work of the foreground in software projects gets done *and* gets its meaning and validity. In other words, the technically focused activities of a "normal" development process are inscribed into a broader range of activities that equally cover technical and social factors, whereby meaning and validity are given to what is produced on the technical level.

Of course, this is an analytic and very rough description of the nature of reflective practice in software projects. To sum up, the notion of reflective practice extends the software engineering perspective on software projects by the following:

- Disciplinary enrichment—that is, by including a multiperspective and multidisciplinary approach (technical, social, organizational, and economic perspectives are together taken into account)
- Methodological enrichment—that is, by including various forms of explicit and implicit, formal and informal activities, negotiations, and technical work, be it on an individual or on a group level, that help accomplish the product-oriented tasks *and* the concurrent problem-framing processes
- Process enrichment—that is, by integrating a deliberate principle of iterating between the problem-solving and the problem-framing activities

Figure 9.1 illustrates the intertwining of the technical and the social in software projects that were introduced earlier. Basically, the intertwining of the technically oriented foreground with the more socially oriented background is achieved by reflective practice based on various kinds of resources. Reflective practice produces some technical product, but it also allows for relating the technical work to its background, to give it meaning and to satisfy the background's interests. It is important to understand the framework as an epistemological aid for better understanding software projects and informing project practitioners, but it does not pretend any ontological or exhaustive status. The claim of the framework compared to real project work is thus similar to Suchman's notion of plans compared to situated action (Suchman 1987). Plans are conceived as a valuable resource for purposeful human activity, but as ultimately subsidiary to situated action itself.

Case Study: Developing a Mechatronics Software

In this section the conceptual framework is illustrated by a case study. The following description is far from complete. It is intentionally reduced to a few of the project's main characteristics to illustrate the essence of the framework.

The general context of the case study is a large, globally operating automotive supplier. One branch of the company is in charge of delivering motor control systems, which are also called motronic systems. An example of a motronic systems is the ignition control composed of hard-

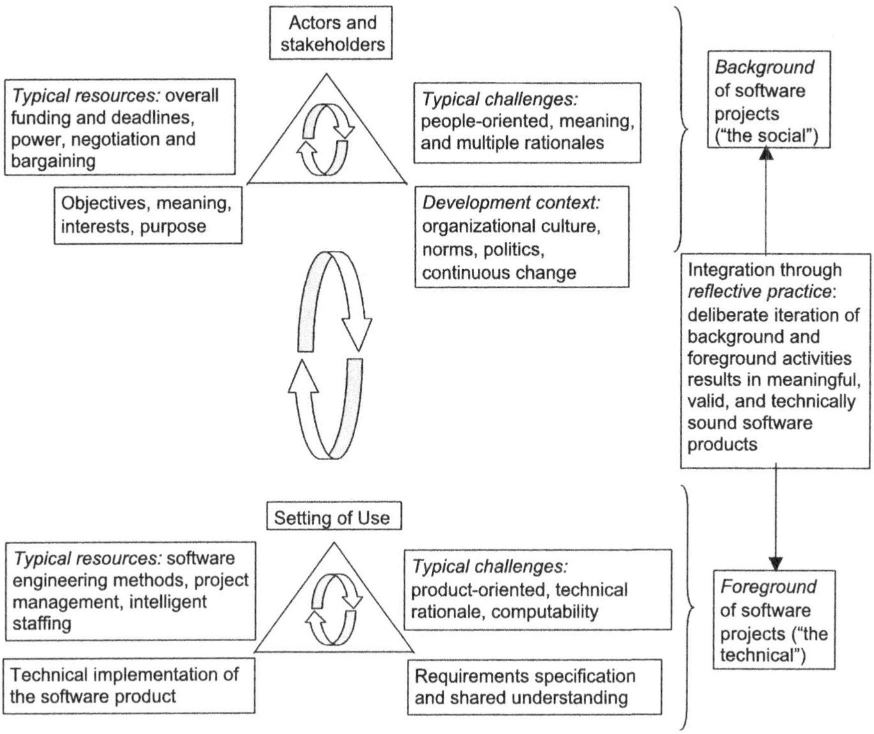

Figure 9.1
Framework of the intertwining of social and technical factors in software development projects

ware devices and software that together help minimize the air pollution of the engine. Motronic systems are thus sophisticated mechatronic devices, and the motronic software plays a central role with regard to functionality and to reliability of the overall system. The motronic software has to meet a complex set of requirements. The most prominent are zero-defect, real-time constraints and memory efficiency.

There is also a close dependency between the international car industry and new generations of motronic devices. When a new car model is scheduled by one of the leading global car manufacturers, this event is transformed to a corresponding motronic development project at the automotive supplier. Consequently, the concrete trigger for launching the project that served as a basis for the case study was the announcement of a new car model by one of the supplier's largest clients. This was the opportunity to also improve the economic situation of the whole department and to implement some new functional requirements and enhanced environmental protection regulations in the new motronic device.

The increasing demand for often-similar motronic development projects then led some of the supplier's managers to launch a department-wide strategic software innovation initiative. I focus in the following on the introduction of the platform approach and on the CASE approach.

Instead of coding every generation or every customization of motronic devices anew, the innovation initiative demanded that a platform approach should be followed in every new motronic software project. Ideas of object orientation should be used because they promised increased reuse of software objects for every new version or new generation of the motor control systems. To comply with this requirement, there was an initial platform project launched that was the first to jump from coding in assembler to code in C++ in the motronic department. Only after the platform modules had been finished was it planned to spread and reuse the modules in customer-specific development projects.

Besides the platform approach itself, a major innovation for the project team was the change from so-called pair programming to code generation by means of a self-made CASE tool. In earlier projects, each module was implemented by a pair—consisting of a functional designer and a programmer—in an evolutionary and iterative way. Pairwise programming combined the experience from the application side and from the coding side in order to meet the overall quality requirements like functional zero defect and maximum memory efficiency. This proved to be an efficient way to cope with the inherent complexity of motronic software and to achieve high-quality functional theory building. The shift toward CASE-driven implementation was mainly due to management's strong belief in the general superiority of a clean fabrication process. They hoped for substantial cost-reduction potential by code generation and fewer coding errors compared to pairwise programming.

Among the most important stakeholders in the setting of the case study were the project manager, the software engineering manager, and the product manager.

The project manager was very experienced and had already developed several motronic devices. From his standpoint, the platform project was a logical next step in his career path.

The software engineering manager had brought up the CASE idea, and he saw a good opportunity for his career path to bring this innovation succesfully into the development practice. The CASE shift was facilitated by the (unintentionally unrealistic) assumption that explicit and formalized functional specifications are already produced in the actual development process. The only step that seemed missing was that the functional specifications needed to be translated into the CASE formalism. Based on these formal specifications, the code-generation feature of the CASE tool seemed promising for the software engineering manager. The job that should be left for the programmers was to automatically generate code out of the specifications and to optimize it manually toward memory efficiency and real-time constraints.

The product manager played probably the most important role among the three main stakeholders. On the one hand, he pushed the new generation of motronic systems for economic reasons, which gave his arguments considerable weight. On the other hand, he represented in some way the customers of the new software. The software project's time constraints were, for example, mainly derived from the car manufacturer's schedules for their new cars and were brought into the project via the product manager.

The set of facets described up to now is roughly what constitutes the *background* of the case study. In the following I briefly sketch the corresponding *foreground*. The whole framework is illustrated in figure 9.2.

The project team started with about twenty programmers, three chief programmers, and the project manager. The project size rose quickly—and after four months it reached about 100 programmers, who were partly organized along functional platform modules and partly already along the different car platforms the software was supposed to run on. The project size remained stable for almost a year. The platform team was then split up and shifted toward the client-specific teams, where more and more client-specific customization had to be carried out.

Of the three main stakeholders, only the project manager was really also acting in the foreground of the project. The software engineering

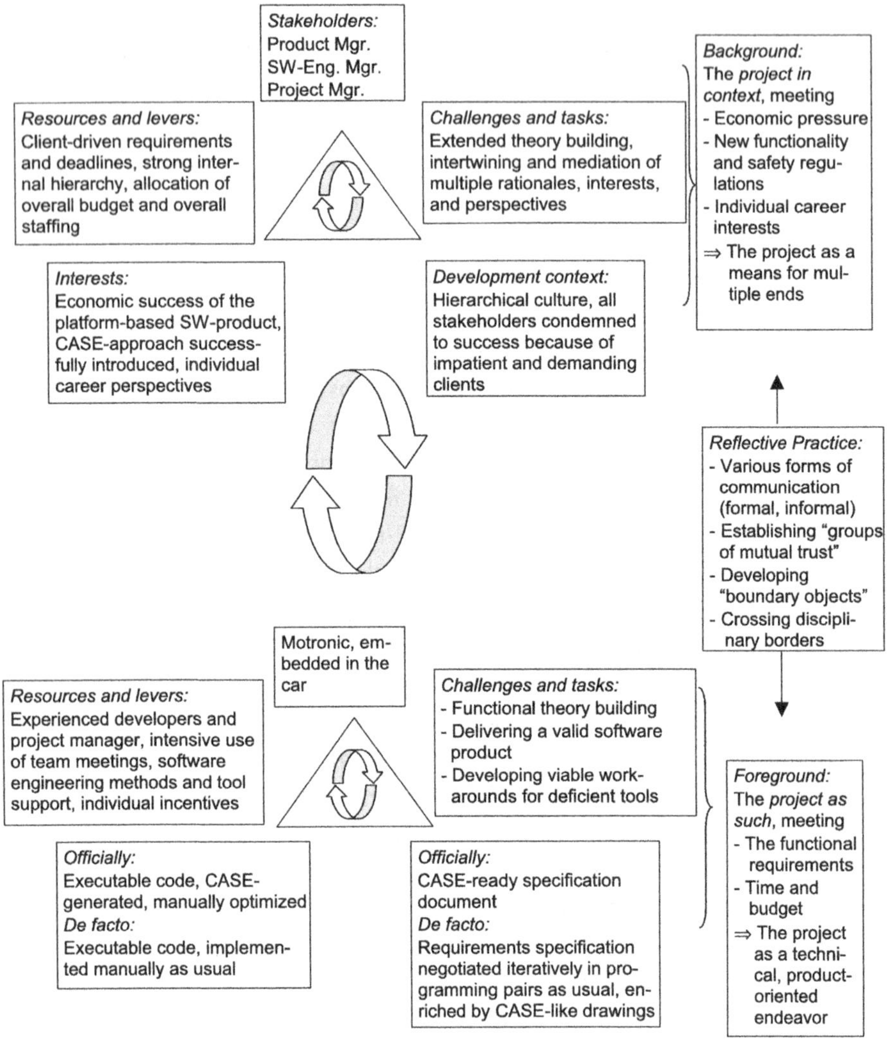

Figure 9.2
The conceptual framework applied to the mechatronics project

manager and the product manager were positioned higher up in the hierarchy of managers. Their position alone was sufficient for the project to be obliged to go the CASE way and to meet the client's deadlines despite the huge technological challenges that had to be met in the foreground.

Interestingly, the priorities of the product manager were practically taken for granted in the foreground of the project. They were omnipresent but almost never explicitly mentioned. Everybody just knew about the key role of the economic-success criteria in the platform project, regardless of any other potential argument from, for example, the technical perspective. So it was mainly the CASE shift and the new functional features and higher safety requirements that were explicitly brought into and dealt with in the foreground. It was the task of the software developers (in cooperation with the functional designers) to implement these requirements in the software product. In the following I will concentrate on the impacts of the CASE introduction.

The CASE introduction popped up at the beginning via a changed workflow: instead of pairwise programming there was a new division of labor introduced between functional designers and programmers. Now they had to communicate by means of formal functional specification documents instead of working in pairs with a high degree of interactive and incremental code development. From the standpoint of the clients (the car manufacturers), the new development process was not especially important. What counted most for them was the delivery of reliable software on time. But for the software engineering manager it was of great importance that the platform project serve as a successful proof-of-concept for his CASE approach.

In the programming practice the CASE tool was soon revealed as functionally deficient and the new division of labor had not been sufficiently prepared and trained for. Obviously, it was not an adequate substitute for the former collaborative functional theory-building process. The situation for the project manager was consequently quite messy: he had to work around the CASE tool in order to meet the deadlines for the promised software, while at the same time saving his and the software engineering manager's face. This was the moment where reflective practice came into play, helping integrate the foreground and background of the project.

Quickly, a proven technical workaround was found, which had to be supported on the communication level by intelligently chosen *boundary objects* (Star 1989). Boundary objects are a particularly efficient means of coordinating collaborative work situations because they allow different stakeholders to agree on the common essence of a concept, while allowing for further individual interpretation, completion, and modification.

The politically correct wording of the newly invented boundary object was "we are following an instantiation of the CASE approach," which essentially meant: we use the CASE tool as a drawing tool, but we code in pairs approximately as we did before. The creation of the boundary object may be considered a form of extended theory building, whereby the technical and the social in the case study became intertwined. The boundary object thus served the upper manager's individual stakes and allowed the project manager to deliver the product essentially on time.

For the current project the informal bypass to reestablish the old working conditions was unofficially accepted. On a concurrent track of activities, the project manager established informal relationships with the software engineering manager and the product manager. These negotiations eventually ended with the promise that in future projects, the old division of labor (pairwise programming) would officially be reintroduced to compensate for the functional deficiency of the CASE tool.

This short description has illustrated the use of the conceptual framework in practice. There is no question that software projects have to deliver a software product, and the project described above effectively did so in the end. But what at first glance looks like a "project as such" is nearly always a "project in context," related to a wider background. To have a tool to grasp this context helps the actors orient their action in regard to the background as well as to the foregrond. In the next section I will elaborate on this idea.

Toward Software Practice: Enhancing Software Engineering

The framework and the case study offer a conceptual foundation for how to envision what software projects are about. Certainly, their most obvious task is to deliver a software product. But the "project as such" is embedded in a larger context, which can partially be captured in terms of attributes like meaning, situatedness, multiple rationales, power, and politics. The arena of real-world software projects therefore reaches beyond the clean fabrication process that software engineering is striving for. If we fail to acknowledge the specific challenge of software projects, which consists in the permanent intertwining of the project's technical foreground with its background context, we might end up at the extreme with two risks:

- Either we get a product without meaning or without validity. This danger turns up in phenomena like shelfware and is the essence of the so-called software crisis. This risk is inherent in a one-sided software engineering approach.
- Or we end up with theoretical insights, meaning, and understanding without getting a product, because we are biased toward the reflective attitude prevailing in many of the social sciences.

So, software projects need the deliberate intertwining of social and technical competencies and the oscillation between different academic disciplines and professional practices. Software projects are at the same time about a product *and* about meaning, about reflection *and* about design. This is what I would like to call *software practice*. Software practice takes seriously the social and organizational embedding of real-life software projects. It can thus be considered as embedding software engineering in a broader frame and as informing software engineering by social thinking, though it is not intended to be an alternative to software engineering.

Consequently, the conceptual framework relies in the foreground on software engineering, but extends it by including a project's intrinsic background. Its purpose is not to criticize the complexity of real-life project contexts, but it is a means of informing the project manager in his or her daily practice that *is* just wicked and messy. Nor is it meant as a formal methodology or as an exhaustive ontology for software projects, but it has to be instantiated and adapted in every situation accordingly. To this end it offers a conceptual foundation for a more adequate problem framing and it offers more levers to intervene in software projects than a clean-fabrication-process perspective that is the guiding principle of (traditional) software engineering. Even if some of the constraints cannot be changed in the current project, chances are great that by applying reflective practice, subsequent projects can work under improved conditions and more pitfalls can be avoided.

Project managers are well off when they know about the inherently wicked nature and the interdisciplinary challenges of software practice. The framework serves in this context as a first blueprint to better conceptualize this complexity. Project managers are even better off if they dispose of nontechnical know-how and interdisciplinary capabilities to adequately intertwine the foreground with the background by means of reflective practice. For example, the reflective practice in the case study required—besides technical competencies—that the project manager establish a lot of communicative relations and develop generally accepted boundary objects in order to satisfy, as much as possible, the different views on the "project as such." A prerequisite for being able to do so is extended theory building. Extended theory building means developing an interdisciplinary understanding of how, for instance, the economic rationale and the functional requirements are linked to and satisfied by the technological solution in the foreground. This task in turn can be supported by establishing formal and informal "groups of mutual trust." They allow for communication processes to intertwine the different perspectives without the distortion of phenomena such as power and hierarchical relations.

To summarize, the conceptual framework contributes to an understanding of software practice as follows:

- It offers a conceptual foundation for our perspective on software practice as an intertwined sociotechnical endeavor (though quite analytic and of course very simplified). Thus, it makes conceptually understandable the links between the technical and the social in software practice that for example deMarco (1997) alluded to in his statement about inconsistent requirements that are interpreted as unsettled conflict among different stakeholders.
- It suggests that software projects are about creating a technical product *and* about creating meaning and shared understanding. Therefore, it analyzes the final software product as the result of an ongoing intertwining

of social and technical factors during the development process, which is different from just being the product of a clean fabrication process. It should be understood as an epistemological support for understanding and informing software practice. It is by no means exhaustive and does not raise any ontological claims.

• It sharpens the disciplinary scope of software *engineering* versus complementary disciplinary competencies that are additionally needed for succeeding in software *practice*. In particular, it offers a rationale for why communicative methods and social skills are as crucial as software engineering skills in software practice and it provides hints on when and how to apply each of them. In this sense it does not make software engineering obsolete but gives it a broader frame, which may help to get valid software that meets both technical and social criteria. Thus the framework may enhance software engineering education toward the goal of sound qualifications for software practice while preserving the disciplinary locale of software engineering per se.

Directions for Further Research

The conceptual framework developed in the preceding sections suggests that software practice is at the same time about producing a technical result and about creating meaning and satisfying the interests of involved stakeholders. Therefore, I have stressed the importance of envisioning the necessary mediation between the product-oriented foreground and the corresponding social background of software projects as *reflective practice*. Several issues offer themselves for further investigation:

• We are all witnessing the rapid growth and acceptance of the World Wide Web and of Internet-based applications. This has many implications for software development and use. One essential consequence is that software projects are increasingly developing software for which the use context is widely unpredictable. This raises many questions on how we organize for embedding sufficient meaning and for getting sufficient background in the software product so that it can be used in valid ways in very different situations. Some ideas are presented in other contributions to this book (e.g., Eriksén, chapter 20; Fitzpatrick, chapter 7).

Important research questions that arise include the following: How can we preserve and incorporate sufficient topical content (which seems a prerequisite for valid software development and use) into the software product in the presence of the increasingly multitopical context of software use? How much topical content is "sufficient"? How can our concepts of background and of reflective practice contribute to these challenges?

• The framework suggests a conceptual foundation for integrating what we call in simplified terms the technical and the social in software projects—while preserving their individual rationales and characteristics. The underlying premise is that the deliberate combination of different disciplines and rationales effectively supports the necessary intertwining of the technical and the social in sound software practice.

Further investigation is needed as to whether this premise should eventually result in the creation of new disciplinary locales for software practice. This might include questions if and to what extent the rationale for each single discipline would be altered by such a move—for example, the social sciences would become more instrumental, which could cause them to lose some of their inherent analytic qualities.

Alternatively, it might be investigated whether it is advantageous to preserve different disciplinary approaches in order to maintain an inherent tension and oscillation between reflection-oriented and produc-t(ion)-oriented rationales. There is some evidence that it might even be dangerous to integrate everything into one common disciplinary platform (Nissen, chapter 4, this volume). But keeping different disciplinary platforms for the inherently interdisciplinary concept of software practice may impede its acceptance—at least in academia.

The specified directions for further research can be investigated from a practical or from a reflection-oriented standpoint. However, the conceptual framework of software practice has made us cautious about the pitfalls of this distinction. Therefore, the framework can also be considered an appropriate blueprint for bringing out the relevant research issues in terms of reflective software research. This may eventually contribute to software research that withstands day-to-day tests and to software practice that leads to improved conceptual understanding and academic mastery.

References

Bauer, F. L. 1993. Software-Engineering—wie es begann. *Informatik Spektrum* 16: 259–260.

deMarco, T. 1997. *The Deadline: A Novel About Project Management.* New York: Dorset House Publishing.

McDermid, J. A., ed. 1991. *Software Engineer's Reference Book.* London: Butterworth Heinemann.

Minneman, S. L. 1991. *The Social Construction of a Technical Reality: Empirical Studies of Group Engineering Design Practice.* Xerox PARC SSL-91-22. Palo Alto, CA: Xerox Corporation.

Naur, P. 1985. Programming as Theory Building. *Microprocessing and Microprogramming* 15: 253–261.

Nygaard, K. 1986. Program Development as a Social Activity. In H.-J. Kugler, ed., *Information Processing '86: Proceedings of the IFIP Tenth World Computer Congress,* 189–198. Amsterdam: North-Holland.

Parnas, D. L., and P. C. Clements. 1985. A Rational Design Process: How and Why to Fake It. In *Proceedings of the International Joint Conference on Theory and Practice of Software Development,* 81–100. Berlin: Springer.

Schön, D. L. 1983. *The Reflective Practitioner: How Professionals Think in Action.* New York: Basic Books.

Star, S. L. 1989. The Structure of Ill-Structured Solutions. In M. Huhns and L. Gasser, eds., *Distributed Artificial Intelligence,* 37–54. London: Pitman.

Suchman, L. 1987. *Plans and Situated Actions: The Problem of Human-Machine Communication.* Cambridge, England: Cambridge University Press.

10

Software Practice Is Social Practice

Jacob Nørbjerg and Philip Kraft

Like the other contributors to this book, we are concerned with two broad issues: (1) How do we determine what software or information technology (IT) system would be useful or appropriate in a particular workplace or other setting, and (2) how do we organize the making of such software systems?

In this chapter we examine the assumption that producing competent IT-based systems is chiefly either a technical task or a matter of adequately "surfacing" user requirements. We examine how informal organizational issues interact with the formal specification and construction process to affect the way software systems are actually made. We maintain that the software development process and its result are determined not only by the quality of the requirements definition process or the systematic application of best software engineering practices, but also by the formal and informal relations between user and developer organizations, management structures and work practices in software development, and so on; in short, by the organizational context of software work.

User Practice and Software Practice

Research into software development tends to address the above questions as if they were separate issues. For example, management information systems (MIS), computer-supported cooperative work (CSCW), and participatory design (PD) researchers are quite good at studying the social organization of workplaces for which the software is being made.

In the hands of skillful practitioners, MIS can facilitate the product-specification phase of software and systems design (Kendall and Kendall 1995; Mathiassen et al. 2000). MIS researchers, however, are not particularly concerned with the details of the software/system design process. They are even less concerned with the details of the actual process of making software or IT systems—for example, constructing dataflow diagrams and software systems or writing code. In contrast, software engineering (SE) and related research tend to ignore both what is being made—the final product—and how it is likely to be used. Instead, SE concentrates on uncovering universal "best practices" in software design and production programming. Because they are by definition universal, "best practices" are to be applied regardless of the nature of the software, the IT system, or the situation of the users.

There is, however, relatively little research on the social and organizational context of software development. Such research, we believe, is even more important if we wish to produce more user-friendly or user-oriented systems, as discussed in this book. In the next section we outline a framework for the study of software production in context. Then follow examples to illustrate how specific software and management practices at different levels, from the local team to emerging globally organized software production chains, affect the software production process and its outcome. We also discuss the impact of recent attempts to organize and manage software production through the application of so-called software process maturity models.

The "Social" of Software Practice

Figure 10.1 illustrates a simple framework to describe the activities and organizational relations in the production of software. The figure shows information systems development as a sequence of distinct steps or activities:

1. Analyze a work situation and/or an organization and develop a vision of a new situation, including a new or changed computer or software product. The description of the new computer or software product is part of the vision.

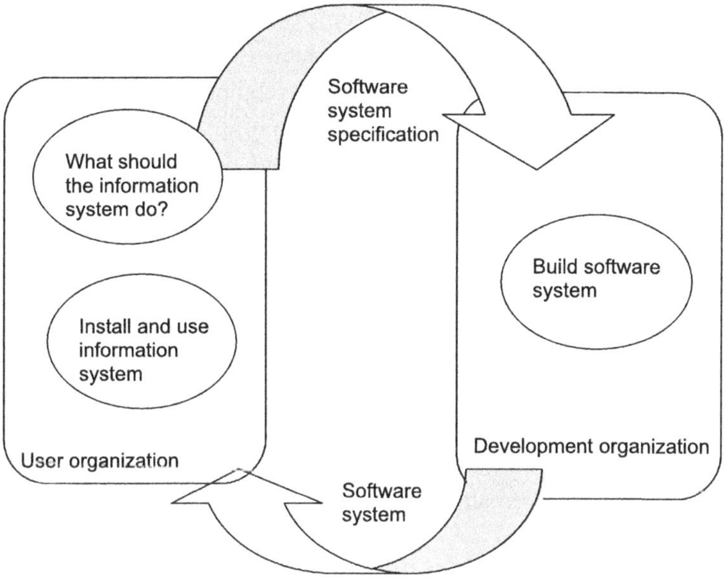

Figure 10.1
A simple model of information systems development

2. Construct the computer or software product described in the previous step. This activity is usually divided into several substeps, such as requirements specification, systems design, programming, testing, integration, and so on.
3. Introduce/implement the computer or software product together with other changes needed to implement the vision; make appropriate modifications based on field experience.

We realize that the model does not fully illustrate the complex, intertwined, and iterative nature of "real" systems development. It does, however, illustrate the conventional approach to information systems development, one that involves distinct activities carried out by different people who work in different organizations, and do so under constantly changing conditions. The model, further, serves to caution us as we seek to understand how software is made. The development and implementation of a complex technology such as an IT-based system are shaped only in part by deliberate managerial decisions, by carefully structured organizations, by formal divisions of labor, and by clear-cut economic incentives and limitations (see Bansler and Havn 1991; Franz and Robey 1984; Knights and Murray 1994). There is a complex relationship between technology and work—none more so than in IT work. The specificity of the software or system being created will invoke informal, sometimes illicit, workplace relations, call forth "hidden" employee skills and experience, and rely on fortuitous "accidents," in ways that cannot be anticipated or even described by traditional managerial methods (see Cusumano and Selby 1998). Thus, it is not sufficient to describe how an idea for a software system is formally transformed into a product—that is, to list the rules and divisions of labor that characterize the software production process. We also need to examine how the organization of the production process and the situation of the user(s) can affect the nature of the software product itself.

Social Thinking vis-à-vis Software Practice

Different research traditions have grown around the information systems development process in figure 10.1, each tradition raising different questions about how software is made. MIS research has concentrated on specification methods: How do we determine what a software product should do and how it will work? PD and CSCW research are extensions of this approach, having taken the radical step, at least among science and engineering disciplines, of asking potential IT users what they would like in a new software system and how they would like it to work. Software engineering, on the other hand, has concerned itself with questions such as the following: Can we create better/faster/more accurate design and production tools? What are the most appropriate data and process algorithms for this category of problem? What are the most cost-efficient and time-efficient ways to organize production planning and management?

The different research traditions draw on different reference disciplines and produce different kinds of results. MIS, particularly the "younger" PD and CSCW research traditions, draw heavily on organization theory and other social science disciplines. It has produced much valuable insight into the complex relationships between human work, technology, and organizational change. SE research, on the other hand, is more firmly grounded in traditional technical and engineering research. It focuses chiefly on development tools and techniques, as well as on normative guidelines for the organization and management of software development projects.

Predictably, these different research approaches have led to a bifurcation in the perspective on the making of software and IT systems. MIS, CSCW, and PD are generally limited to specifying "customer requirements" and to designing "user-friendly" interfaces. In contrast to these "soft" exercises (which are often perceived as part of personnel management or marketing), software engineering focuses on the "hard"—that is, engineering and technical—issues of measurement, process control, and eliminating faults in the design and production of code. Combined, the two distinct approaches reduce the making of software to parallel but largely unconnected activities: (1) a purely technical if complex production process (nominally) based on (2) rather less precise and change-prone user preferences.

Apart from the transmission of functional and user specifications to the software design and production workers, there is no regular connection between MIS and SE workers. In other words, once detailed (or at least technically feasible) descriptions of a software product are submitted by MIS and applications specialists, the actual construction of that product proceeds as a technical exercise in selecting the "right" development, production, and management tools.

This is a much too simplified reduction of the actual process of software development. It neither accurately represents what goes on in the software design and production processes nor is it of much use in organizing and managing a real project. We note, for example, the following important, and extremely common, situations in real-world software production processes that are not covered by this simple view of the process:

- Activities are not necessarily sequential. In practice if not in theory, specification does not always precede production; the idea of what should be included in the final product and how this should be done frequently develop and change in the course of the production process.
- Informal cooperation is widespread. The work of conceiving, making, and implementing a system usually takes place in different organizational

entities (possibly but not necessarily in the same firm) and involves (mostly) different kinds of workers. Sometimes, these (different) people will talk with each other—even when they are not supposed to. These informal and sometimes illicit conversations contribute in crucial ways to the software design and production processes, although they exist nowhere on formal organization/workflow charts.

• The external contexts of software design and production are more or less ignored. "Virtual" worksites are treated the same way as worksites down the hall. The political and cultural relations between these workplaces are at least as important as the technical infrastructure that permits data to flow between them.

In short, the software product is the outcome of a social process involving many people in informal as well as formal relationships. In the following paragraphs we will give examples of how this process and its results depend on the details of organizational structure, management practices, and organizational power and control.

Software Practice in Context

For all the interest in and importance of software work, in the fifty years since the emergence of computer programming as a distinct occupation there has been remarkably little research on how software is actually made. Most research, as we have noted, has been instrumental—that is, managers and engineers have tried to figure out what software to make and how to provide the appropriate tools for the job. Social scientists have studied software and IT work because it is an emerging and dynamic area, closely connected to larger changes in management and organizational practices (see Braverman 1974; Beirne, Ramsay, and Panteli 1998; Knights and Murray 1994; Kraft 1976; Kraft and Dubnoff 1986; Sharpe 2001). Some CSCW, software engineering, and other researchers have also studied software work practices, often with an eye to developing methods and techniques that better "fit" the actual needs and practices of software development (Bansler and Bødker 1993; Curtis, Krasner, and Iscoe 1988; Nørbjerg 1994). Generally, however, most research has been reasonably free of the details of software production work.

In this section we offer a brief examination of the work of making software systems. We illustrate through admittedly arbitrary examples how the social and political contexts (broadly defined) of software workplaces, the nature of the product, the kinds of tools, and the situation of users interact to organize and shape the software production process. The examples illustrate cooperation and coordination problems at the team level, issues in global software production, and what we believe to be important implications of new managerial trends in software production.

Formal and Informal Practices

Software development work is usually distributed across several categories of software workers. A common distinction is the one between the analyst and the programmer. The analyst is responsible for the analysis of the user's or customer's needs, and for translating these needs into a specification or description of the new software product. The specification serves as a contract between the software producer and the customer, but it is also used as a "blueprint" for the technical implementation carried out by the programmer.

This work arrangement originates in managerial desires to minimize labor costs and to closely monitor the labor process itself. Although such an arrangement lends itself to neat organizational charts, it is in practice often accompanied by communication and coordination problems that lead to buggy systems or systems that do not live up to the analysts' or users' expectations. The problems are usually attributed to faulty or incomplete requirement specifications. Hence the search for analysis and documentation tools and techniques that ensure completeness, consistency, and unambiguity in the requirements documents.

The communication problems and misunderstandings, however, are not purely technical. Often they are found in the work organization itself and in the nature of the software product, as the following examples illustrate. (The examples are from Nørbjerg 1994, 1995; Kraft 1981.)

Depending on Informal Practice The first setting is a development team in a regional telephone company's information systems (IS) department. The team was developing a new IS to manage the company's telephone cables, switches, and connections. The software development team consisted of an analyst and two programmers. A manager and two clerks from the company's cable management department were associated with the project as user representatives. The specifications (screen designs and functional descriptions) were produced by the analyst and the user representatives and subsequently handed over to the programmers.

One of the programmers worked on a data-entry screen to register data about connections between telephone lines and signal amplifiers. The programmer's first solution was technically correct, but it required considerable redundant data entry because he had misunderstood how cables and amplifiers are physically connected. The misunderstanding was discovered and corrected when the analyst made an informal demonstration of the implementation for the user representatives.

On another occasion the same programmer worked on a part of the system intended to register data about cable and switch reconfigurations in exchange offices. He realized that the specifications failed to cover all possible reconfigurations and worked out an alternative design to cover the missing cases. The changes were approved by the analyst and implemented.

The interesting question is what causes these kinds of communications problems. A straightforward answer is that the cause lies with the quality of the specifications: successful communication between analyst and programmers depends on consistent, complete, unambiguous, and fault-free specifications that the programmer can translate directly into running code. The specifications in the above cases obviously failed to meet these criteria, and it is therefore easy to blame the analyst for doing sloppy work.

Further analysis of the case reveals that this is too simple an explanation. When asked about the quality of his specifications, the analyst replied that he knew they were too "user oriented" (i.e., failed to give the programmer precise instructions), but he was not able to make them more "programmer oriented" because this would require current knowledge about the tools utilized and general development environment prevalent in the company. But, working as an analyst, he did not have time to keep up with the rapid technical changes in the programming environment: "I haven't programmed for three years [and] I am unfamiliar with how we program here [and] with the development environment as such."

Thus we see that the specific organization of work, which makes it the responsibility of the analyst to produce specifications, at the same time reduces his ability to do so satisfactorily. The resulting communication problems and misunderstandings could have resulted in a system other than the intended system.

Turning to the programmer, we also see how the traditional division of labor created problems, but that in this case local (informal) modifications to the work organization helped solve the problems. The programmer is, in the traditional work arrangement, a "techie" who is not supposed to concern himself with the application domain of systems. His job is to "simply" produce programs according to specifications. The programmer, however, had attended a course in "cable management" arranged by the user manager. This helped him discover some of the analyst's mistakes, although, as we have seen, his application-domain knowledge was not perfect or complete, leading to "imperfect" solutions in some cases.

Finally, looking at the whole development project, we see how the close organizational relations and informal ties between users, analyst, and programmers supported early discovery and correction of errors and misunderstandings.

Struggling with Formal Practice Another example illustrates a similar situation, but one with a different context and different outcomes.[1] A production programmer in a military electronics company was responsible for writing a module to transmit data to another program module, which in turn would format the data for specialized user displays. The division of labor was highly detailed and extremely hierarchical: the software that sent the data and the software that reformatted the data for display were the responsibilities of two other programmers at different geographic sites. Further, each of the programmers was directed to use only approved off-the-shelf tools for constructing their modules; they were not permitted to deviate from the rules governing their use. Finally, none of the programmers were given any information about the nature of the data, where the data came from, where they were going (apart from the preceding and subsequent steps in the production process), or even the larger purpose of the system as a whole. This extreme division of labor was not the outcome of military-mandated security precautions, but was rather a reflection of the highly fragmented and rigidly hierarchical organization of the parent corporation.

The programmer's interface module constantly failed during tests, no matter what the programmer or her manager tried. Informal suggestions from software colleagues were no help. Finally, the programmer asked her manager what the system was supposed to do. He did not know. His manager did not know. When the programmer's manager made informal inquiries at a still higher level, the immediate response was, in effect, "this is none of your business and is in any case irrelevant to the proper performance of the programmer's job." Only when the project failed to meet the deadline did senior managers relent. The interface programmer, with reluctant approval from senior project managers, was then able to talk with some of the group managers. She learned the software was part of a system that simulated the computer operations of laser-guided cannons. Her module in particular simulated the monitoring of the state of cannon cartridges. Although this was a real-time analogue process, she had been given specifications that implied data flows at constant rates. Other details omitted from the specifications were that the data had originated in English measurement units, while the displays were given in metric units. Finally, further investigation revealed the conversion algorithm built into the mandated programming modules was faulty: it was converting English-to-metric in a 1:1 ratio. "It was a joke, I couldn't believe it," said the programmer. "It was the most basic sort of mistake imaginable, but I practically had to get Pentagon clearance to ask the simplest questions."

Thus, we see how the general pattern of division of labor in software development results in coordination and communication problems. This may ultimately lead to quality problems or unintended changes to the software product. Software workers frequently build and maintain informal relations with other software workers and with users to overcome these problems, as we saw in the first example above (see also Curtis, Krasner, and Iscoe, 1988). However, as the second example shows, organizational boundaries and rigid managerial practices may hinder this informal interaction.

Globalization of Software Practice

Research on multinational software production chains (O'Riain 2001; Sharpe 2001) underlines the continuing centrality of the product, geographic place, and informal work relations in the making of software and software-based systems. Sharpe's typology of software products based on their use (systems through integrated applications suites to end-user modifications) forces us to address the international division of labor as the outcome of political and economic processes as well as technical ones. Production programming takes place in Ireland and India not just because Irish and Indian programmers are cheaper than American or Scandinavian programmers, but because standardization in work practices now permits multinational firms to subcontract many formerly complex tasks to "body shops" regardless of location, seeking out the cheapest and most reliable contractors able to do an adequate job (Sharpe 2001).

However, the solution to the problem of "how do we get the most code for the cheapest labor costs?" has produced another problem, as O'Riain has shown in his case studies of a Silicon Valley company and its Irish contract workers (O'Riain 2001). O'Riain's cases graphically demonstrate how design and development decisions are made "where they shouldn't be" to meet deadline pressures. Deadline pressures are deliberately used by offsite California managers to control largely unsupervised contract workers in Ireland. Tight deadlines produce products when expected and do so in part by creating a temporary camaraderie among the contract workers. But the same pressures also reduce potentially fruitful cross-organizational cooperation, while they encourage other practices home-office managers might not appreciate if they knew what was going on. For example, the Irish contract workers would strip or change requirements or withhold information about design problems when facing a tight deadline. Furthermore, distance, deadline, and cultural differences encourage an "it's us against the home office" mentality, further reducing the likelihood of genuine cooperation between sites and therefore further reducing the likelihood of effective communication. Finally, because the contract work is temporary and short term, the Irish contract workers often refused to share information with each other because such information could become crucial in the competition for securing subsequent contract work. Thus the generation of ideas and techniques based on common workplace experience is in effect sabotaged by the built-in competitive nature of the production programming contract process itself (for another view, see Ullman 1997).

Gaining Control over Software Practice

Software development usually involves different organizational entities (different firms or departments within the same firm). As such, the relationship is dominated by the same power games and political maneuvering as other organizational relations (see Franz and Robey 1984; Knights and Murray 1994). This is, however, usually hidden under a web of formal, contractual relationships and formal communication lines.

Software Process Improvement (SPI)—a fairly recent approach to software production management—can, among other things, be interpreted as an attempt to improve the software development organization's position vis-à-vis the user organization in these maneuvers (Humphrey 1989). SPI is an attempt to improve efficiency and quality in software development through coordinated and carefully planned changes across the software development organization. Elements affected include project and people management, development techniques and tools, organizational structure, quality control and improvement, productivity and quality measurements, and so on.

To prioritize and coordinate this effort, SPI applies the idea of software process maturity (Paulk et al. 1993) as a "measure" of an organization's ability to control its software development. (For definitions of maturity and approaches to the assessment of maturity, see for example Humphrey 1989; Kuvaja et al. 1994; Paulk et al. 1993; Rout 1995.)

An interesting discussion about SPI concerns the effects on the management and control of software workers, because it is easy to imagine scenarios of increased levels of management control as maturity grows. In the present context, however, we will discuss how the SPI movement may affect the relationship between user and developer organizations.

Among the well-defined procedures in the mature software organization are those that regulate relations between users and developers, as for example, change management, planning (and replanning), and estimation procedures. This means that interactions between users and developers, particularly interactions that may result in changes to the development process or the product, are formalized and channeled through specific routes (customer relations offices, change control boards, and so on). The mature software organization will no longer allow the kind of ad hoc interaction and change typical of immature software organizations and (presumably) more or less taken for granted by (immature) user organizations.

This can give the development organization firmer control over the process and the product. Formal and regulated lines of communication will, on the other hand, also reduce opportunities for informal learning and insight that develop continuously in the course of development—opportunities that may be crucial for the success of the development project, as illustrated in the examples above. Furthermore, the reductions in informal developer-user interactions will shut developers off from an important source of information about the application domain and the users' needs (see Beirne, Ramsay, and Panteli 1998; Curtis, Krasner, and Iscoe 1988).

Another example concerns the collection and use of process measurements. Metrics and measurements play an important role in SPI: the more "mature" the organization, the more data about the process are collected and used to plan and monitor projects, as well as to evaluate and improve productivity and quality of the development process and the product.

The data are collected and used primarily for internal managerial purposes, but having (and controlling) statistics about past performance can be an important asset in contract negotiations with users, too. As the instructor at an SPI tutorial put it, "If you have the statistics in place, you can document to the customer that developing this system, to that level of quality, will cost so much and take so much time."

The problem is, of course, that the interpretation of any measurement of software process performance is highly contextual (Sommerville 1996) and subject to organizational politics (Iversen and Mathiassen 2000; Kohoutek 1996). Nevertheless, numbers are imbued with an air of authority and rationality, and since the development organization "controls the numbers," it also controls which numbers to present and their "proper" interpretation.

Discussion

It should come as no surprise that the work of producing software development—like all other work processes—is shaped by a complex mix of the nature of the work product, the tools and techniques to use, formal and informal organizational structures and management practices, organizational politics and power games, as well as the formal procedures and the more-or-less hidden or illicit work practices of the developers. The above examples show us how this "organizational" context of the work of producing software affects not only the way the product is made but also its outcome—the information system—in more-or-less hidden ways:

1. We see how small decisions made "along the way" by different players contribute to the shaping of the production process and the final product. Some of these decisions are subsequently confirmed and documented as illustrated in the first example, while others are deliberately hidden from management, depending on organizational structure and management practices.

2. The success of a software development project, in terms of producing a usable product that meets the users' requirements, will often depend on informal communication links and cooperation between different participants—especially between future users and technical development staff. The informal cooperation may ignore organizational boundaries and formal communication channels. The examples have illustrated how organizational structure and management practices can both facilitate and obstruct this informal interaction. In the telephone company example, managers and users could establish and maintain fruitful cooperation and communication channels, while the programmer working for the military contractor (in the second example) had to overcome considerable management resistance to get access to vital information. The Irish contract workers in O'Riain's study, on the other hand, had neither the time nor the inclination to establish informal links with other parts

of the development project. In fact, their behavior can be interpreted as an attempt to establish and maintain local control over the work process at the (potential) cost of the product's use quality.

3. We saw how the firmer control over development practices, decision processes, and communication embedded in the software-process-improvement paradigm may reduce the opportunities for fruitful informal interaction among software developers and users. But as pointed out above, they can also increase the development organization's control over the development process at the expense of the users' or customers' control. This last point also cautions us against tacitly assuming that a software-producing organization's main interest is to serve users, their parent organization, or society, as Nissen also observes in chapter 4.

Social Theory and Software Practice

The goal of this book is to explore how to "bridge the gap" between the rich and complex world of user work and user organizations and the structured "technical" world of software programmers and programs, hopefully in this way contributing to the production of better (in some sense) software. Social thinking, understood as theories, models, and techniques adapted from the social sciences, is supposed to be a useful means toward meeting this goal. The underlying assumption seems to be that social thinking will make software professionals change their practice and produce better—from a human and societal viewpoint—products (see also Nissen, chapter 4, this volume). Contributions to this book deal, for example, with how techniques from the social sciences can inspire software work practices (Kaptelinin, chapter 3), or how metaphors (Fitzpatrick, chapter 7) or modeling representations (Jirotka and Luff, chapter 6) can help improve communication between developers and users.

While we share a commitment to the book's objectives, it should come as no surprise that we find this instrumental perspective on social theory technique limited and problematic. "Social thinking" techniques are going to be used in a specific organizational context, which, as we have pointed out, will influence the way they are used as well as the results of using them. Nyce and Bader make a similar point regarding the importance of the larger "cultural" context of software development (chapter 2, this volume). Further—as Nissen has pointed out in chapter 4—we, as software development researchers, cannot just assume that (commercial) software-producing organizations share our goals and priorities.

Thus, attempts to improve the work process and results of "software practice" must take the context of that practice into account. We encourage, in other words, a thorough analysis of the organizational context or conditions of "software practice." Such an analysis—probably building on (social science) theories of work and organization—can, among other things, identify potential pitfalls and limitations of the application of "social thinking" to software practice.

Conclusion

Over the years we have learned that "user organizations" and "user work" cannot be understood entirely as rational or technical systems, yet we continue to think of software development as a fundamentally technical and rational process. But software development organizations are organizations too, and software work is work too, and it is time to study software organizations and work in the way we have studied other organizations and other work.

In this chapter we have argued that there is a complex relationship between the organizational context of software development, formal and informal management practices, physical and social organization of the work, developer skills, the nature of the software being produced, and so on, and the actual outcome of software production. Failing to acknowledge this relationship when discussing how to change the software production process may lead to a repetition of past failures: well-intended and detailed methods and guidelines that have little effect on practical software development.

Note

1. The details have been altered to protect the privacy of the software worker employed in a military-related workplace. The changes do not materially affect the situation described.

References

Bansler, J. P., and K. Bødker. 1993. A Reappraisal of Structured Analysis: Design in an Organizational Context. *ACM Transactions on Information Systems* 11(2): 165–193.

Bansler, J. P., and E. Havn. 1991. What Has Computer Interfaces Got to Do with Human Jobs? *Proceedings of the Conference on Human Jobs and Computer Interfaces.* Dordrecht: Kluwer.

Beirne, H., H. Ramsay, and A. Panteli. 1998. Developments in Computing Work: Control and Contradiction in the Software Labor Process. In P. Thompson and C. Warhurst, eds., *Workplaces of the Future*, 142–162. London: Macmillan.

Braverman, H. 1974. *Labour and Monopoly Capital.* New York: Monthly Review Press.

Curtis, B., H. Krasner, and N. Iscoe. 1988. A Field Study of the Software Design Process for Large Systems. *Communications of the ACM* 31(11): 1268–1287.

Cusumano, M. A., and R. W. Selby. 1998. *Microsoft Secrets: How the World's Most Powerful Software Company Creates Technology, Shapes Markets, and Manages People.* New York: Simon & Schuster.

Franz, C. R., and D. Robey. 1984. An Investigation of User-Led System Design: Rational and Political Perspectives. *Communications of the ACM* 27(12): 1202–1207.

Humphrey, W. S. 1989. *Managing the Software Process.* Pittsburgh: Addison-Wesley.

Iversen, J., and L. Mathiassen. 2000. Lessons from Implementing a Software Metrics Program. *Proceedings of the Hawaii International Conference on Systems Sciences* (Wailea, Hawaii, January 4–7). Los Alamitos, CA: IEEE Computer Society.

Kendall, K. E., and J. E. Kendall. 1995. *Systems Analysis and Design.* 3rd ed. Englewood Cliffs, NJ: Prentice Hall.

Knights, D., and F. Murray. 1994. *Managers Divided: Organisation Politics and Information Technology Management.* Chichester, England: Wiley.

Kohoutek, H. J. 1996. Reflections on the Capability and Maturity Models of Engineering Processes. *Quality and Reliability Engineering International* 12(3): 147–155.

Kraft, P. 1976. *Programmers and Managers: The Routinization of Computer Programming in the United States.* New York: Springer.

Kraft, P. 1981. The Production of Skill: Technology and Context in the Workplaces. Paper presented at the annual meeting of the Southern Sociological Society, Louisville, KY.

Kraft, P., and S. Dubnoff. 1986. Job Content, Fragmentation, and Control in Computer Software Work. *Industrial Relations* 25(2): 184–186.

Kuvaja, P., J. Similä, L. Krzanik, A. Bicego, S. Saukkonen, and G. Koch. 1994. *Software Process Assessment and Improvement: The BOOTSTRAP Approach*. Oxford: Blackwell.

Mathiassen, L., A. Munk-Madsen, P. A. Nielsen, and J. Stage. 2000. *Object Oriented Analysis and Design*. Aalborg: Marko APS.

Nørbjerg, J. 1994. *Kvalifikationer og Samarbejde i Systemudvikling* [Skill and Cooperation in Systems Development—in Danish]. Doctoral dissertation. Technical report no. 94/28, Department of Computer Science, University of Copenhagen.

Nørbjerg, J. 1995. How Developers Learn: Skill Distribution and Skill Building in Systems Development. In B. Dahlbom, F. Kämmerer, F. Ljungberg, Y. Stage, and C. Sørensen, eds., *Proceedings of IRIS 18*, Gothenburg Studies in Informatics, Report 7, Gothenburg.

O'Riain, S. 2001. Net-Working for a Living: Irish Software Developers in the Global Workplace. In R. Baldoz, C. Koeber, and P. Kraft, eds., *The Critical Study of Work*. Philadelphia: Temple University Press.

Paulk, M. C., B. Curtis, M. B. Chrissis, and C. V. Weber. 1993. *Capability Maturity Model for Software, Version 1.1*. Technical report no. 93-TR-024, Software Engineering Institute, Pittsburgh.

Rout, T. P. 1995. SPICE: A Framework for Software Process Assessment. *Software Process—Improvement and Practice*, 1 (Pilot Issue): 57–66.

Sharpe, R. 2001. Globalization: The Next Tactic in the 50-year Struggle of Labor and Capital in Software Production. In R. Baldoz, C. Koeber, and P. Kraft, eds., *The Critical Study of Work*. Philadelphia: Temple University Press.

Sommerville, I. 1996. *Software Engineering*. 5th ed. Workingham, England: Addison-Wesley.

Ullman, E. 1997. *Close to the Machine: Technophilia and Its Discontents*. San Francisco: City Lights Books.

11

"Yes—What Does That Mean?" Understanding Distributed Requirements Handling

Kari Rönkkö

"Yes—what does that mean? Who is it written for? Why do they need that? What roughly are its contents, and what do they want it to look like? Key elements are missing there!" These were the reactions of a manager talking about his requirements.

I mumbled something like, "Key elements are missing?"

The manager continued: ". . . and it is difficult to determine who introduced these requirements. It is the customer, but the customer is an unknown quantity."

The organizational model in this project, a document-driven software development approach, succeeded in providing enough guidance for structuring the overall software development process, but it was less successful in facilitating project members' everyday coordination needs in handling the requirements. This chapter is based on a qualitative study of a distributed project within an internationally prominent supplier of equipment for telecommunications systems and related terminals. The chapter deals with two main issues. I show how the central problem of requirements engineering and software development is not completeness, but collaborative theory building and mutual intelligibility. Then I use the study to illustrate how a qualitative approach can help realize these cooperative goals. By addressing these issues, the chapter also contributes to meeting the challenge raised by Nørbjerg and Kraft in chapter 10—the challenge of taking the context of software practice into account, especially the importance of informal cooperation.

The structure of the remainder of the chapter is as follows. First, I discuss contradictory ideas from the field of requirements engineering and software development. Second, the project is presented. Third, I describe the epistemological grounding of the methods used to study the project. Fourth, the project members' struggles with the complex organization of work today are highlighted. Finally, conclusions derived from both the project members' struggles and the application of the qualitative methodology are presented.

Requirements Engineering

Requirements handling is a much-discussed topic. In analyzing the complex ways social and technical factors affect the development of software, Jirotka and Goguen (1994) refer to the problem of requirements as a high-cost feature of the software development process in the latter stages of the development life cycle. They suggest that one possible interpretation for this is insufficient knowledge of the effects of the various available requirements methods used in the development process. They claim that we in fact only have begun to realize how requirements are actually construed and used in large software development projects (Jirotka and Goguen 1994, 2–3).

Within software engineering, the overall approach for handling the role of software requirements and the whole development process could be described as devoted to the idea of rigor and control. Methods have been developed to guide and control software development work. In models of this kind, requirements are the sole starting point for the development process. Developers should be able to handle them without further knowledge of the use context or the history of a project; a formulaic approach to requirements is emphasized. According to McDermid and Rook (1991), no single interpretation of a language exists, pointing to the fact that possible misinterpretation of requirements during software development will always exist. Their contribution to this somewhat obdurate problem remains the proposal to develop an adequate formal language to minimize the misinterpretation possibilities. McDermid (1994) notes that no methods capable of adequately dealing with requirements for sociotechnical systems during software development seem to exist. He also points out that requirements are negotiated, not captured, warning us against the belief that well-defined requirements exist that are waiting to be discovered. He introduces three different approaches in requirements capturing and analysis, naming them orthodoxy, fundamentalism, and heresy.

The *orthodox* approach emphasizes global holistic considerations and a uniform view of requirements. The problem is that the process leading to the creation of specifications starts in the wrong place, with requirements other than the fundamental ones. The requirement initiators are forced to provide more detail than is desirable in order to define requirements. This approach leads to low flexibility in design and implementation, because the overspecification obstructs change. The system presupposed is effectively influencing the design decisions before the determination of individual requirements takes place (McDermid 1994, 25).

The *fundamentalist* approach addresses the issue of overspecification by focusing on a small number of key requirements for a system—so-called cardinal-point requirements. This approach seems to solve some of the problems of the orthodox approach, but it introduces others. The cardinal-point requirements are typically very ad hoc, resulting in disparate and underspecified requirements and often necessitating large amounts of nonobvious problem-domain knowledge in order to be interpreted correctly. There is no guarantee that the requirements are consistent, and problems can arise from underspecification. There is also the risk of not bringing enough problem-domain knowledge into the requirements; systems developers often seem to lack this kind of knowledge in particular (McDermid 1994, 27).

The essence of the *heretical* approach is captured in the idea that it is impractical to produce complete, consistent, and implementable requirements specifications. Potential conflicts always exist that can only be unambiguously identified once there is an overall idea of the design. This view conflicts with ideas such as those represented by the waterfall model, and thus it requires another process model, enabling iterative and evolutionary development work. An advantage of the heretical approach is that conflicts between nonfunctional requirements and fundamental objectives can be recognized, which is not easy in the orthodox or fundamental paradigm. With the heretical strategy, there is more freedom to change requirements and to achieve an implementable compromise. It is easier to validate the design with customers than it is to reach agreements on requirements, since customers agree to what they are actually going to get, not to what an analyst assumes they have required. In the most fundamental heresy, there is no fully elaborated requirements specification and requirements are finalized with the produced design. Ehn (1988) represents the Scandinavian participatory design (PD) approach (Ehn 1988, 35). Since they are critical to existing requirements analysis, especially the orthodox approach, McDermid still acknowledges the requirement approaches as being effective if used under appropriate circumstances. He sees requirements as a problem of appropriate choice and implementation of a normative method (McDermid 1994, 37). Work-related problems are, in this view, still solved through putting trust in rigor and control applied in the use of adequate methods.

Other authors have offered perspectives on requirements handling more closely connected to human and social issues. Concerned with what it means to program, Peter Naur claimed in his article "Programming as Theory Building" as early as 1985 that programmers build theories relating the design documentation and the software itself to its anticipated use. In other words, texts resulting from software development are outside the reach of what can be determined by rules (Naur 1985, 257). In her article "Software Development as Reality Construction" (1992)—influenced by Naur—Christiane Floyd claims that we do not analyze requirements; we construct them from our own perspective. She bases her argument on constructivist thinking. She suggests that methods in use are orientation aids affected by our personal priorities and values and by our interaction with others constructing requirements (Floyd 1992, 95).

During the case study that provides the empirical basis for this chapter, we tried to understand how software developers actually deal with requirements during design and implementation. The following section introduces the project. I then discuss the methodological approach we used in greater detail. After the analysis of the empirical material, I will come back to the issues discussed in the preceding paragraphs.

The Project Studied

How to approach widely distributed software development projects through qualitative methods is a well-known difficulty (Newman 1998, 76–77). One reason is that the project members' roles often change with every project phase—that is, there is no recurrent stability. Another problem pertaining to the distribution of work is how and where to identify what is relevant for the study. An additional problem is how to recognize and make sense of distributed work taking place at different locations at the same time. The project studied was divided into four subprojects distributed over five different locations in Sweden. The subprojects in turn were divided and distributed. Contracted companies were involved in the project. Consequently, it was difficult to define the setting and approach of the study.

The company involved produces advanced products and systems for wired and mobile communications in public and private networks for customers in more than 100 countries and has a long history in the telecommunications field. The project studied was performed in and by a Swedish component of that organization.

The project aimed at developing a graphical programming environment, including training and methods. The environment was supposed to handle the company's existing telecom code used in their telephone exchanges. The high-level programming language supported by the graphical environment is Specification and Description Language (SDL). The main project was named the *SDL-Project*. SDL makes tool-supported code compilation into lower-level languages possible. This means that a SDL description can be translated into an executable application without manual coding, leading to shorter development time and increased quality.[1]

The SDL project included the SDL ToolCore subproject handling development of the code generator together with features of the tool. Also included were the following: a Training Subproject handling and developing SDL training; a Methods Subproject handling the coordination of all SDL methods as well as standard methods; and a SDL Tool Subproject caring for signal handling, configuration management, release handling, function change, test port, and test methods. Two associated projects existed. The main Technical Orderer was located in Germany, and subprojects had Technical Orderers located in Sweden, Germany, the United States, and Spain.

The field material is built up of maintaining and taping project meetings such as system group meetings, Project Leader meetings, steering group meetings, and the execution phase's kick–off day. By hanging around in the local field where the main projects management and the SDL Tool Subproject were located, nontaped interviews were done with code developers, and taped interviews were held with the main Project Manager, four Subproject Managers, the Product Owner, the Configuration Manager, the person responsible for project quality, and the main customer (main Technical Orderer). Because of distance, the interview with the main customer located in Germany took place by telephone. All other project members were interviewed at their local workplaces, with the concrete artifacts they used at work within reach to refer to. As can be seen, the study is somewhat top heavy, with the majority of the members studied being in some kind of management position. To place the study in the organization and get responses on the findings, a steering group was created consisting of two people from the university, the SDL Tool Subproject Manager, the Product Owner, and the Maintenance Project member. In that group, the decision was made to give the study a subproject perspective. The group had regular follow-up meetings where fieldwork and early writing results during the field study were discussed.[2] This chapter is the product of later retrospective reflections on the material.

The next section discusses the methods we used, their epistemological grounding, and the problems perceived when relating them to software engineering.

Methods

The empirical study was conducted during a five-month period through applying a "quick and dirty" (Hughes et al. 1994) ethnomethodologically informed ethnography, supplemented by interviews as a way of uniting perceived field experiences. I use the term *informed* to refer to the approach that Hughes, Randall, and Shapiro (1992) pioneered, as the first serious attempt I am aware of to connect ethnomethodology (EM) with design issues in work practice. Recent reflections concerning the usefulness of EM-informed ethnography can be found in (Harper, Randall, and Rouncefield 2000, 66–71). EM perceives the division of labor between the project members as routinely manifested in their own meaningful orientation to their work. Technology and work are, in this view, treated as technology-in-use, which is perceived as indivisible. EM is a highly descriptive framework with the goal of providing an alternative procedural description of achieved and achievable phenomena without sacrificing the describable, recognizable recurrences of ordinary activities. In this way, the perceived or recognized structure in itself becomes the achieved phenomenon. This perspective may not seem obvious with respect to software engineering research, where developed structures are valued in and of themselves, and where the goal of the research is to develop these new structures in the form of processes, methods, rules, and insights generally applicable to software development work. As a consequence, from an EM point of view, software engineering approaches also tend to obscure, misrepresent, or ignore the existence of a real world of work. Instead the perception of work is derived from the model or structure of work rather than from the activities in the work setting itself. EM-informed ethnography focuses on the activities themselves embedded in the socially organized domains—the locus of decision making—not in the structures developed.

It seems important to specify the epistemological foundation that the ethnography carried out in this project rests on, as a way of integrating other research perspectives (Anderson 1996, 16). With respect to methodological assumptions, I take it for granted that phenomena in the social world are not constituted in such a way that they can be retrieved again by social scientists to enable scientific experiments—in contrast to the situation in the natural or physical sciences. Thus, social scientists' conclusions remain speculative. I also assume that no one scientific method exists, in the sense of "the method," that is better suited to reveal the social organization of the social setting's activities.

From an EM-informed ethnographic viewpoint, a crucial question is whether researchers have spent enough time in the field. Tracing patterns and identifying themes in a rigorously scientific manner is resolved through the use of the *documentary method*[3] (Garfinkel 1996b, chap. 3). The documentary method cannot be evaded; there is no "time out." This method is employed without exception to establish the correspondence between the phenomena actually witnessed and the underlying phenomena studied. Investigators interpret what appears to happen based on documentary evidence from the corpus of their experienced knowledge from within that setting.

It makes a difference what the documentary method is applied to—whether to a description of the phenomena or to already-developed structures. In the latter case, the findings are also influenced by some scientists' views, and by the circumstances occurring when the coded results are worked out—that is, circumstances surrounding the need to use scientific language to furnish a scientific way of to create consensus and action (Garfinkel 1996b, 24).

In both cases, the danger exists that an analysis can be grounded on the perceived coded structures instead of on the actual phenomena. The problem is that the coded results, the secondary scientific constructions, can be taken to be a part of the actual social organization they purport to describe. That leaves us at the point where we started; the crucial point is whether the researchers have spent enough time in the field to grasp what is going on. To be able to interpret the story, it is necessary to have worked up enough feeling for how a "competent member" in that field uses the documentary method.

To show the validity of my use of EM-influenced epistemology, I have to show how I handled this methodological problem. I have to explain my field material and its credibility from my own perspective. I have to show how and where I have spent time in the field (necessary in order to be able to make sense of the members' activities). And I have to keep the EM commitment to show the "raw material" in the resulting text (the justification I have for arguing that any particular thing is "going on" should be evident, because ethnomethodology is highly concerned with the warrantability of data). I address these points in the following section, which presents the results of an EM-informed ethnography. Later I draw conclusions from the material shown.

Most of the "raw" evidential material included in this chapter is drawn from interviews and is not in itself the direct representation of the members' methods in action (which the transcribed meeting would be an example of). The interview material shown is actually retrospective "talk about" the interviewees' methods in use. This conflicts to some extent with the EM idea, though ethnography is anything but a unified method and is perhaps not even a method at all, as Shapiro (1994) has pointed out. Perhaps it is best regarded as an umbrella term for various analytic frameworks; in other words, it is a qualitative methodology. Yet it is important to show the epistemology influencing the ethnography performed, despite the tensions in the use of the approach.

The next section presents part of a discussion from a steering group meeting as well as comments by subproject leaders, ending with suggestions for improving the project.

Requirements in a Distributed Project

The project members had problems getting organizational support in coming to terms with the scope of the requirements they were supposed to implement, despite the company's traditional way of managing projects. Through a document-driven waterfall-like model (or perhaps because of it), some requirements could only be traced with difficulty; others could not be traced at all. The SDL project preceded a reorganization caused by a strategic overall reshuffling of the international firm's line organization. This reorganization resulted in a reduction in scope of some of the subprojects. As a result, and also because of the complexity of the work distributed, it became difficult to adhere to the project's original plans.

Problems Regarding Requirements

This section touches on a range of problems.

Steering Group Meeting At the time of the change from feasibility phase to execution phase (TG2), the different subprojects were not in phase with each other's and the project plan. Some parts of the necessary requirements specifications not yet finished were discussed during a steering group meeting:[4]

Standard Methods Project Leader: At this point I had a question, how shall we describe it? Because the description in the IP, because in the IP we describe, we do not have these requirements so to speak, we will remove a lot of the requirements, the issue will be totally different.

Chair: To reach formalism in the . . .

Standard Methods Project Leader: Yes it has to be described in some way . . .

Chair: Yes.

Standard Methods Project Leader: Shall it be done in the IP or in some other way?

Customer-Organization Representative: Draw it in an updated IP.

Main Technical Orderer: I do not believe we have the competence to exactly describe it . . .

Standard Methods Project Leader: No.

Main Technical Orderer: In order to support the project, we must have a new suggestion on what has to be done, we need new suggestions on that . . .

Chair: In the project we really would want to be able to make the TG decision; can we handle the issue in some way that will not delay that decision any more?

Main Project Leader: The fact that this delays the delivery plan, it is surely affected whatever the case, this is what worries me.

Chair: Not in all.

Main Project Leader: Yes in all, we will have to remove standard methods from delivery five and six, we have an open IP, we also have an open project specification, and an open main project specification.

Chair: Is there no way we can close them, and still have them with us? Not to get stuck in a lot of . . .

Customer-Organization Representative: That is my opinion too, on how to solve this, because this is actually not the only "one" we have; there is the training, we could also include the code generator. In my opinion it would not be wrong to close them, to give TG2 on the prerequisite that actually is the existing situation.

Main Project Leader: Hmm.

Customer-Organization Representative: Then we will have a TG2B later, or whatever you call it.

(Steering group meeting, March 5, 1999)

Despite the fact that the expected foundation for the TG2 decision did not exist, the suggestion from the Customer-Organization Representative was exactly that: to make the TG2 decision. The situation that occurred together with the perception agreed on in the meeting actually became the foundation on which the TG2 decision was made. In this way, the decision reached in this meeting was not about the completeness of any requirements specification, but about collaborative theory building and mutual intelligibility. The result of the discussion was the development of a sustainable arrangement that would allow the project to continue without a rigorous implementation plan and clearly delineated requirements specifying the work to take place.

In the following paragraphs, I will elaborate on the difficulty the project members articulated in coming to terms with their requirements, and will also discuss a related issue: their problems in tracing requirement originators. That brings to the surface the way project members described their requirements-handling work as a collaborative activity. In the first subsection I give two examples of how members perceived their trouble in handling requirements. In the next subsection I sketch solutions proposed by members to the requirements problems. I then conclude the section by discussing what I suggested to help the situation.

ToolCore Subproject Leader Problem How to handle requirements was planned as a straightforward issue. The idea of their model was to deepen the conception of requirements through references in the documentation. On the first level, the requirements were put together to form an overview; on this level, there were a few lines of explanation connected to each requirement and references to other documents. If a reference was pursued, more detailed explanations, its origin, the customer organization, reference names, and other related documents should be found. But when discussing requirements with the project members, it often seemed that there was something about the model that did not make sense: "Yes there is, as I said before there is a reference pointing to another document where it is possible to read more exhaustively, at least sometimes, not every time, sometimes there only exist a few lines of text. This has caused a lot of major problems" (Project Leader, ToolCore Subproject).

ToolCore Subproject Developer Problem When asking a Project Developer in the same subproject how he managed to grasp the requirements he was supposed to implement, he answered: "I don't, I mean I can't understand them only from the text in the requirements specification. What I do is, I contact the technical person that stands behind that specific requirement. The problem with this is that the person's name is never mentioned in the requirements specification, I mean the actual persons that once figured out the requirement" (Developer in the ToolCore subproject). Despite the fact that he was involved as an expert on compiler requirements in the formal project, he could not put his trust in the project's model for handling requirements.

Training Subproject Leader Problem The Training Subproject Leader expressed the same confusion about coming to terms with requirements: "Yes—what does that mean? Who is it written for? Why do they need that? What roughly are its contents, and what do they want it to look like? Key elements are missing there! And it is difficult to determine who has introduced these requirements. It is the customer, but the customer is an unknown quantity."

Developing Solutions to the Requirements Problems The project members deemed the reference-document plan unsatisfactory. When traveling around talking to project members, I stumbled on a number of different ways to solve this conflict, solutions developed independently by the different project members. They actually seemed to be unaware that this was a common problem. These meetings with the project members also showed that, on some occasions when the project members succeeded in locating requirement initiators, they actually did not always have the time to help them: "They perhaps thought that yes, yes, I will look at that problem soon and get back to you later, but they did not always get back to us. This has made things really difficult for us" (ToolCore Subproject Leader).

ToolCore Subproject Leader Solution The ToolCore Subproject Leader developed a sophisticated strategy of turning the problem around, actually making it the requirement-originator organization's problem: "In my subproject, during the autumn in the feasibility, I solved this. I chose to solve this problem as follows: if we did not manage to get a requirement clear, we simply decided to produce a solution. Out of that solution the customer then had to understand how we perceived the requirements."

ToolCore Subproject Developer Solution The code developer from the same subproject presented another solution. On his own initiative, he had established an informal network of contacts including technical persons all over the world, persons involved in the use of the earlier version of the code compiler now being tried out in real work settings:

> I have to do my own research, starting to contact people, asking around to find out where this requirement originated. That means finding the technical individual responsible for every requirement, finding the people who originally wrote down the requirements, and other technical people as well, people who might have an interest in the specific requirements. I start asking around with the help of e-mail and the telephone, asking questions like: What does *x* mean, and why? Then negotiations arise concerning the requirements. It is very seldom that I don't use my contacts; sometimes there are up to six people involved in a discussion concerning the requirement, people from all over the world. It often takes days to get an answer. (Developer in the ToolCore Subproject)

The same technicians who were part of this informal network actively contacted the developer as well. A network of technical engineers had established both the project's formal structure and its model for documentation.

Training Subproject Leader Solution The Training Subproject Leader approached the problem by traveling to his Technical Orderer, and "refused to leave" before they had tracked down and talked to all the requirements initiators together:

> Requirements could come from separate individuals who later on had just disappeared. There is one special requirement there that has lasted a long time despite major protests from both the contractors and me: a requirement about a higher degree of simulation. But there is already a tremendous amount of simulation. There is simulation all the time; you do a little design piece, then you simulate that, almost like doing a compiling test when coding, the same way it is with the high-level specification language. We started to sort out where this requirement came from, and who is taking credit for this. It turned out to be someone from Finland; it was a woman who did this off the top of her head at a meeting. (Training Subproject Leader)

This requirement was eliminated after the conversation with the Finnish requirements initiator. In fact, fifteen of the original twenty-five requirements were removed as a result of spending weeks with tracing and negotiation work.

Proposed Method Changes as a Result of the Study

As a consequence of the study, methodological refinements were proposed. These refinements included additions to the company's requirements reference model: names, references, and contact information regarding the requirements initiators or other individuals who could take responsibility for the requirements should be given together with other details pertaining to the requirements specifications. If requirements sources are unknown, difficult to track down, or not available, that should be noted in the field reserved for contact information.

The company, of course, already provided such information, but not on this level. As could be seen from the examples, the contact information previously available was insufficient. The new system would save many hours' time in future distributed software development projects.

Implementing the solution suggested above is not as easy as it might appear. Crucial investments, responsibilities, and organizational sacrifices have to be taken care of. In a large international company even a small change in the worldwide project management model calls for major effort. Changes of course have to be explained and inserted in existing manuals and training programs, and distributed in the organization. How to change experienced project people who do not use manuals or take part in training programs? Other concerns are that employees now and then change their division and organization, and staff in key positions perhaps do not wish to be, or even have the time to be disturbed. The ToolCore Subproject Leader touched the problematic when saying: "I believe that the individuals who once wrote the requirement had a good grasp at that time, but time passes. And of course they do not always detail the requirement in a large amount of text ... in this case, only four lines. If you go back six months later and ask this person again, then he or she might not even remember; even worse, they might have changed their opinion." A proposed change in methods of the type just outlined would benefit from follow-up research aimed at showing how it adapts to and incorporates ad hoc features not easily described or captured in a method recommendation.

Conclusions

This section ties the findings together.

Is Completeness the Core Problem in Requirements Engineering?

By focusing on the actual *work*, this chapter has highlighted mundane achievements during software requirements handling in a distributed software development project. These are achievements that otherwise risk passing unnoticed during the members' ordinary daily interactions.

In McDermid's (1994) view, the difficulty with requirements handling seems to have to do with finding the right model to control the requirements process. He suggests a hybrid approach: an orthodox model incorporating features from the fundamental approach, as they address different problematic aspects of requirements handling. The present study led to a somewhat different insight into the developers' needs. It seemed as if the most prioritized need was to interact with someone who could take responsibility for being requirements initiator, having adequate authority to negotiate a requirement interpretation. From this standpoint, the complete specification of requirements—which seemed to be the aim of McDermid's (1994) work—would not actually make the difference hoped for. In other words, developing structured processes that lead to a complete requirements specification is perhaps not the core problem to be solved.

Relating Human and Social Issues to Software Engineering through Descriptions

A methodological problem has occurred when relating EM-informed ethnography to software engineering. EM is a truly descriptive epistemological framework, and as such it has nothing to say about design. Software engineering is about improving the software development practice. To make a difference in software engineering, it is necessary to provide design proposals on the perceived problems. Replacing activities in work practice with "structures" or tables conflicts with the EM epistemology. EM-informed ethnography describes the social world as it unfolds, avoiding any transformation of the perceived activities taking place. EM politely refuses to lend itself to any imaginary work, claiming that the "instances" collected from the field speak for themselves and do not need to be organized around a core theory or cognitive model. EM is suspicious of the opposite tendencies—that is, to transform the "raw material" by making it conform to preconceived formats (Lynch and Bogen 1996, 266–267). Without disputing such achievements, EM asks "what more" is there to be discovered that the artificial formats tend to obscure (Garfinkel 1996a, 6).

The conclusions I draw from applying this approach are the following.

First, it is possible to relate human and social issues to software engineering without doing a transformation of the "raw" evidential material.

Second, the raw material gleaned from the field is actually closer to the social phenomena than the interpreted versions are. I do not deny that the raw material has to be interpreted at times, as the discussion of the documentary method earlier revealed. I also do not deny that we need certain formats or frameworks that make it possible to discuss important themes in creative work. But I argue that social practices as they actually occur cannot be discerned or judged through rationalizations built on imaginary work. Garfinkel (1996, 22) has captured the issue metaphorically by saying that it is "very much like complaining that if the walls of a building were gotten out of the way, one could see better what was keeping the roof up."

Third, EM-informed ethnography in itself seems to suit the task of studying an ongoing work practice, but it does not support the envisioning of possible future ways of developing software. It is merely a starting point by making visible the actual activities that have occurred; in other words, it brings to light the work of today that is to be changed.

Fourth, I am not totally convinced that EM-informed ethnography is the best methodological choice when studying distributed software development. The use of the interview material seems to bear this point out. Much of the field material included in this chapter is project members' talk about their own work methods—that is, not the researcher-perceived "methods" in use. Within EM this is referred to as *talkaboutable* or *storyable*.[5] This situation occurred because, as a researcher, I found their talk about their requirements extremely interesting and did not have an opportunity to observe the occasions where they actually did what they talked about in the interviews.

To the extent that the EM descriptive view has been borne out in this chapter in some sense, it has been done in the spirit of regarding the result as "one possible version" of many others (Garfinkel 1996b). I also point to the humble attitude expressed by the founder of EM: "I hope that there is room in this discussion for those studies which take the importance of witnessable recurrent phenomenal fields of detail seriously and as a primary issue, in whatever other respects they may differ" (Garfinkel 1996a, 6).

Notes

I would like to express my appreciation to the other contributors to this section of the book, who have questioned, clarified, and made useful suggestions on various points in the chapter—especially Yvonne Dittrich. Thanks also to Bo Helgeson, Jeanette Blomberg, and Dave Randall, who in their roles as course leaders in the doctoral course "Work Practice and Technology II" provided helpful comments on an early version of the chapter. Thanks as well to the course participants, especially Hans Tap, who critiqued the EM material.

1. This description is borrowed from the company's own Web site.

2. The field material discussed in this chapter is to some extent part of my master's thesis in an interdisciplinary program combining human work science and computer science. The reflections in the chapter are part of my Ph.D. studies.

3. Garfinkel (1996a, 78) has said that "the method consists of treating an actual appearance as 'the document of,' as 'pointing to,' as 'standing on behalf of' a presupposed underlying pattern. Not only is the underlying pattern derived from its individual documentary evidences, but the individual documentary evidences,

in their turn, are interpreted on the basis of 'what is known' about the underlying pattern. Each is used to elaborate the other." To decide a correct correspondence is a question of producing through interpretive work a correspondence that members of a community of cobelievers would agree on—that is, on "common sense knowledge of social structures" (Garfinkel 1996a, 96, 76).

4. The transcription is of "spoken language," a form of expression that often is fragmented and locally dependent. It is the usual way to transcribe speech within Interaction Analysis.

5. Lynch and Bogen (1996, 281) note that "strange as it may sound, one must establish a right to have seen something and to have seen it *that* way (as storyable)." What the members talked about in the taped conversations was the perceived real-world problems that bothered them. This was talk about the actual unfolding-work-practice side of "structures" such as plans and methods.

References

Anderson, R. J. 1996. *Work, Ethnography, and System Design.* Cambridge, England: Rank Xerox Research Centre.

Ehn, P. 1988. *Work Oriented Design of Computer Artifacts.* Stockholm: Arbetslivscentrum.

Floyd, C. 1992. Software Development as Reality Construction. In C. Floyd, H. Züllighoven, R. Budde, and R. Keil-Slawik, eds., *Software Development and Reality Construction.* Berlin: Springer Verlag.

Garfinkel, H. 1996a. Ethnomethodology's Programme. *Social Psychology Quarterly*: 59(1): 5–21.

Garfinkel, H. 1996b. *Studies in Ethnomethodology.* Cambridge, England: Polity Press.

Harper, R., D. Randall, and M. Rouncefield. 2000. *Organisational Change and Retail Finance: An Ethnographic Perspective.* London: Routledge.

Hughes, J. A., V. King, T. Rodden, and H. Andersen. 1994. Moving out of the Control Room: Ethnography in System Design. CSCW '94. *Proceedings of the Conference on Computer Supported Cooperative Work*, 429–438. Chapel Hill: ACM Press.

Hughes, J. A., D. Randall, and D. Shapiro. 1992. Faltering from Ethnography to Design. CSCW '92. *Proceedings of the Conference on Computer Supported Cooperative Work*, 115–122. New York: ACM Press.

Jirotka, M., and J. A. Goguen. 1994. *Requirement Engineering: Social and Technical Issues.* London: Academic Press.

Lynch, M., and D. Bogen. 1996. *The Spectacle of History.* Durham: Duke University Press.

McDermid, J. A. 1994. Requirement Analysis: Orthodoxy, Fundamentalism and Heresy. In M. Jirotka and J. Goguen, eds., *Requirement Engineering: Social and Technical Issues*, 17–40. London: Academic Press.

McDermid, J. A., and P. Rook. 1991. Software Development Process Models. *Software Engineer's Reference Book*, ed. J. A. McDermid. London: Butterworth-Heinemann.

Naur, P. 1985. Programming as Theory Building. *Microprocessing and Microprogramming* 15: 253–261.

Newman, S. 1998. "Here, There, and Nowhere at All: Distribution, Negotiation, and Virtuality in Postmodern Ethnography and Engineering." *Knowledge and Society* 11: 235–267.

Shapiro, D. 1994. The Limits of Ethnography: Combining Social Sciences for CSCW. CSCW '94. *Proceedings of the Conference on Computer Supported Cooperative Work*, 417–428. Chapel Hill: ACM Press.

12

Doing Empirical Research on Software Development: Finding a Path between Understanding, Intervention, and Method Development

Yvonne Dittrich

Empirical research on software engineering is becoming more and more important. Ideally, this research should address real-world problems, and its results should have practical applications. Taking practice seriously would encourage the production of more usable methods supporting software development under realistic conditions.

Many approaches to empirical research on software development exist within the software engineering community and in other scientific disciplines, though they often evolve independently of each other. Because the development of software is undeniably a social activity, the whole spectrum of the social sciences can be mined for research approaches. But what strategies are suitable for research on this kind of social activity, and how do the results inform the development of concepts, methods, and tools? Specific examples of empirical research are used to reflect on these questions in this chapter. Lessons from three different projects provide a foundation for outlining important issues to be considered when going into empirical research in software development. Whose perspective do we adopt when designing our case studies? How do we relate to those we study? How do we formulate our proposals for change? Issues that in other contexts are regarded as ethical questions become methodological issues when empirical research takes place in the context of an engineering discipline. At the end of the chapter, I reflect on the role of empirical research in software engineering from an epistemological point of view.

About the "Why" of Empirical Research: A Historical Introduction

Software engineering has a more specific history than other engineering disciplines. It did not develop out of an established practice seeking abstractions, concepts, and models to support further developments. It was founded because of the lack of such practice. The founding of software engineering as a discipline at the conference in Garmisch-Partenkirchen in 1968 was a conscious effort, reflecting an attempt to scientifically redesign its practice. The problems of software development at that time are often cited: the unsatisfactory quality of existing software from the standpoint of efficiency, safety, and usability, as well as delays in software development projects and sometimes their termination without results. Though there is general agreement regarding the problems leading to the founding effort, the "software crisis," proposed solutions vary. What unifies the different approaches is a common effort to improve—or rather to design—practice with the help of concepts and methods to be developed. This design effort becomes visible in the different metaphors used to describe the software development process. The term *engineering* was deliberately coined to promote the research area (Bauer 1993), *industrial production* was already present at the founding conference as well (McIlroy 1969), and the *design* of software was propagated in the context of software architecture (Floyd 1992, 1994). These "design metaphors" or "*Leitbilder*" (Hellige 1996) have been used to identify research subjects, as criteria for method development, and to promote methods for practitioners.

A design of practice was probably the only way to develop the discipline in the specific historical situation. It led to a problematic relationship between the research on and the practice of software development. A survey of German software development companies indicates that formal methods are rarely applied in industrial practice (Deifel et al. 1999). Robert Glass puts the matter more harshly in his observations on the twenty-fifth anniversary of the discipline published in *IEEE Software*. Through the vehicle of fiction, Glass evaluates today's situation from a vantage point twenty-five years later and claims that the software research now (in 2020) has overcome its crisis. He classifies most of the existing software engineering research as arrogant and narrow: researchers who never worked in practice claiming to know what is good for that practice, advocating their theoretical products without taking the use context seriously, and so on. Similar problems seem to exist for approaches focusing on usability and user-centered design, as a workshop title at the INTERACT'99 conference—"How to Make User Centred Design Usable?"—indicates (Gulliksen, Lantz, and Bovie 1999). Indeed, participatory design (PD), use-oriented design, and findings in areas like human-computer interaction (HCI) and computer-supported cooperative work (CSCW) are rarely referred to outside universities and other research institutions. On the other hand, many software development organizations nowadays use principles and methods similar to the ones developed in PD research, without being aware of the relevant discourse.[1]

Research results are seldom implemented in software development organizations in a canonical form. The way methods and principles are applied depends on other circumstances as well. Technological development, diversification into different application domains, and the organizational and economic context in which software is produced are examples of other factors influencing the selection and adaptation of methods and tools (Floyd 1994). A possible way to understand these processes and their influence on the usability of methods is empirical research on software development.

There is a tradition of empirical research and action research in the areas of information systems, PD, and HCI. This research mainly focuses on the interaction of computer applications and their use context. There is less research looking at software development itself. (For a more thorough overview, see Nørbjerg and Kraft, chapter 10, this volume.) The present chapter is a result of preliminary experiences with such research.

Since software development is undeniably a "social activity" (Nygaard 1986), empirical methods from the social sciences are potentially useful. The first investigation already shows a not-unexpected methodological diversification; different research foci like individuals, groups, and cultures require different approaches, quantitative versus qualitative research has been argued about over decades, and different fundamental theories provide different conceptual frameworks for analysis. What kind of social phenomena are accessible through what kinds of empirical research?

Applying social science methods in software engineering research opens up another question. For the social sciences, the influence of the researcher and the research findings on the research subject(s) on the one hand is a methodological problem that has to be taken into account in the evaluation of the field material, and on the other hand is subject to ethical considerations. Improving the social activity studied is the very purpose of software engineering. How do social science methods that focus on the observation of social practices relate to the development of concepts, methods, and tools? There is an ongoing discussion of the relationship between work-practice studies and the design of computer applications in the CSCW discourse. How do these studies apply to the design of methodological, conceptual, and computer tools for software developers (Singer et al. 1997)? Does the PD tradition in Scandinavia (Floyd et al. 1989) or action research (Mathiassen 1997) provide a better framework for developing methods? Or should we—and can we—treat the organizations hosting our research as laboratories (Basili 1996)? These questions point to the relationship between researchers and research subject(s) and are often regarded as ethical issues. They become methodological problems in the context of an engineering discipline that aims at the improvement of the practice it studies and is not only interested in the understanding of this practice.

Feedback from practice has always had high esteem in software engineering research. As early as twenty years ago, empirical research on software development began to take shape. In the next section, I reflect on existing approaches to this kind of research. In the following sections, I then use some of my own research to discuss the above-mentioned methodological issues. Choices regarding the perspective researchers take, their role in the field, and what motivates change influence the research results and should be considered carefully. The chapter concludes with some reflections on the gains and limitations of empirical research in software engineering.

Empirical Research on Software Development

Empirical arguments—for example, in form of reports of personal experience—have been honored in software engineering research from the beginning, especially if the arguments could be supported by quantitative measurements. Since the early 1980s, more systematic approaches to empirical research on software development have emerged, both as part of software engineering research and as social science research. The different kinds of research discourse have hardly seemed to know each other. The following subsections briefly introduce three rather different types of empirical research on software development.

The Software Engineering Laboratory

Basili proposes that software engineering should follow the model of other physical sciences and develop an experimental paradigm (Basili 1996). Thus, software engineering research should develop models of and methods for software development and analyze and evaluate them. To do so, software engineering researchers need laboratories to test their hypotheses. Because realistic settings are important, research and industry should create such laboratories together. Researchers can develop and evaluate models appropriate for a specific company and help to improve the software development there. Industrial practice provides a realistic set of projects for experimentation.

What such research might look like is described in Basili and Green 1994. As an example, the authors report several experiments with key elements of the Cleanroom development method, replacing testing with reading and peer review. In the first set of experiments, graduate students and personnel at the Software Engineering Laboratory—a cooperative effort between the University of Maryland and the NASA Goddard Space Flight Center—used reading and testing on programs seeded with errors. The different approaches were quantitatively compared. In a second step, some lab groups in a university course were partly assigned to use Cleanroom development, where unit testing was replaced with peer review; other groups used traditional testing methods. Here again the different approaches were evaluated regarding their performance in error detection. The results underscored the superiority of reading and peer review versus testing. So two case studies using NASA projects were designed and evaluated. Emphasis was put on the measurable variables making improvement visible in a quantitative manner. The cooperation between researchers and practitioners seemed to be more a matter of co-operation between researchers and software development management. The subjects were observed and their performance was measured, analyzed, and evaluated. However, they did not seem to participate in the setup of the experiments and the case studies, nor did they appear to take part in the design of the improvement and evaluation criteria.

Reflective Software Development

Lars Mathiassen (1998, 80–81), from Aalborg University in Denmark, describes his research approach to software engineering as follows:

> The problems, challenges, and opportunities involved in systems development practice are considered the starting point for systems development research. Research activities yield experience-based knowledge that leads to new, and hopefully improved, practices. The knowledge that is developed is both interpretive, helping us to understand and make sense of practice, and normative, providing support for performing systems development or improving present practices.

Mathiassen's understanding of systems development practice is based on Schön's concept of the "reflective practitioner" (Schön 1983). Practitioners are active in research as they make their thinking and strategies visible for the researchers and use the researchers' results to support their own reflection-in-action. "'The reflective researcher,'" says Mathiassen (1998, 81), citing Schön, "'cannot maintain distance from, much less superiority to, the experience of practice ... he must somehow gain an inside view of the experience of practice.'"

Research is performed as action research, in this case meaning that researchers take part in industry in software development, software-process improvement, and so on. To understand practice, several forms of representations are introduced that, when used by the practitioners themselves, also provide useful research material (Mathiassen 1997, chaps. 2–4). Formalizations regarding methods and processes are understood as helpful representations as well (Mathiassen 1997, chap. 5).

Action research is complemented by case studies and experiments where necessary and suitable (Mathiassen 1998, 81).

Software Development as Cooperative Work

Because software development is a cooperative effort, software development has become a subject of discussion in CSCW. (Schmidt and Sharrock 1996). Traditionally, empirical research in CSCW has mainly used qualitative methods—for example, ethnography and ethnomethodologically informed ethnography, often combined with PD processes as action research. Key issues include the use of representations and design work as embodied practice (Suchman and Trigg 1993), organizational constraints and their influence on work practice (Button and Sharrock 1994a, 1994b, 1996, 1998), the development of organizational patterns from within the project group (Potts and Catledge 1996; Robertson 1996; Tellioglu and Wagner 1997), and the interaction of work practice and computer-based tools (Grinter 1996, 1998). The focus of this type of research is on understanding the ways the members of a software engineering project achieve the situated design and coordination of their cooperative effort.

Research of this kind is mainly rooted in ethnography. The researcher tries to understand software development as work practice from within. This sometimes leads to what software engineers perceive as the appreciation of a skillfully performed bad practice. The interesting question—what makes a disadvantageous practice less troublesome than changing the habit?—is seldom asked. Few authors use the studies to further develop methods or tools for developers. (See Grinter 1996 and Singer et al. 1997 for exceptions.)

All three approaches are successful from a research point of view. Their findings have been appreciated and discussed in the respective communities. They contribute to a better understanding of software development practice, each from a specific perspective. Thus methods developed by them and the improvements proposed make sense from their respective point of view, and the evaluations justify them. However, they differ fundamentally regarding the choice of empirical methods, the conceptualization of software development, and the kinds of improvements proposed. How can software development practice provide the empirical basis for such widely differing research results?

Three Cases

One of the main arguments against methods promoting use orientation in design and development of software is the impracticability of these methods for commercial software development. A way to address the problem is to "take our own medicine." That is, we should apply the principles of use-oriented design and development to the design and development of software engineering methods: empirical research and cooperation with industry allow us to explore the situational constraints for practitioners. We regard empirical methods as a toolbox to be applied in a situated way, and we are aware of the difficulty in relating empirical findings to change proposals. The participatory attitude prevents us from subscribing to one of the above-mentioned methodological schools. We take the practitioners' own understanding of their work as a starting point for the adaptation and development of methods.

In this section, I present three projects that allowed us to gain experience with the methodological difficulties of such research. Surprisingly, the problems did not arise along traditional lines: quantitative versus qualitative, understanding versus improvement, and so on. Methodological problems seem to play out in a different way in the context of a discipline aiming at and being expected to provide improvement of practice. The following section extends this discussion.

How Can Distributed Software Development Be Observed?

During the spring of 1998 a software engineering course at the University of Kralskrona/Ronneby (now Blekinge Institute of Technology) in Sweden cooperated with a programming project at the University of Oulu in Finland. The goal of both project courses is to simulate realistic industrial software engineering environments. Thus they involve customers outside the university. Moreover, the supervision is organized in terms of role playing, with an experienced project leader—if possible from industry—playing the role of a department head in Ronneby, and an older student learning about project management as a project leader for the team in Oulu. The Ronneby project team in this specific project consisted of fourteen software engineering students working twenty weeks full time for the project plus four students from other programs. The Oulu team consisted of three students. Because of the difference in size and purpose, the relationship between the two projects was designed as a contractor-subcontractor relationship. The customer for the distributed project was a Swedish company; the task was to develop a business simulation program that could be used for the training of management. (See Johansson, Dittrich, and Juustila 1999 for a more detailed description and evaluation.) A teacher observing the projects would have been too intrusive, we assumed, so we looked for students in Ronneby and Oulu who could study the cooperative efforts. Students at both locations observed the project and the cooperation it entailed as an empirical basis for their thesis work (Alriksson and Rönkkö 1998; Petman 1999).

The cooperation turned out not to be good at all. On the Ronneby side, the absence of the Finnish team and their concerns in the project meetings and in the everyday work situation became a remarkable phenomenon in itself. The students therefore focused on observing instances of cooperative design in Ronneby. They recognized that face-to-face communication in meetings and in corridors as well as a mutual awareness achieved through working in the same room were the most important preconditions for cooperative design and implementation (Dittrich and Rönkkö 1999).

During the fieldwork and the analysis of the material, it became clear that only part of what was going on was "observable" in a straightforward sense. The way project members made use of overheard conversations or bits of information from the corridors in their design and implementation was not visible at all. The spreading and updating of a compatible picture of the common product was so embedded in everyday practice that it was hardly recognizable. The observed and analyzed occasions of co-construction were exceptions pointing at what eluded the observers.

The student on the Oulu side had not had as much experience in ethnographic fieldwork as his Ronneby counterparts, and his informants did not work with the project full time. Problems with access to the project room and similar difficulties left him with insufficient observational material. So we decided to focus on an analysis of the interaction documented between the groups by e-mail and in chatrooms, complemented by interviews with the Finnish project members. It was possible to pinpoint different factors influencing the communication, like power relations, cultural issues, and styles of communication (Petman 1999).

Traditional observational techniques could be applied to capture meetings. To understand everyday work practices, interviews and the evaluation of written communication seemed more suitable. Qualitative methods borrowed from ethnography and interaction analysis turned out to be helpful for understanding what was going on from the members' point of view. Quantitative analysis of the e-mail communication collected was tried in one case but did not contribute to an understanding of the communication difficulties.

It turned out to be important that the student observers became part of the project—for example, by using the project room as a workplace themselves. They could put their observations into a larger context, and they were informed when the project changed times or places for meetings. At the end, the student observers gave a presentation of their results for their respective project group. Criticism naturally arose: the fieldworkers and teachers knew about the problems long before the problems showed up in the project group. They should have sounded a warning earlier.

Requirements Handling in a Distributed Software Development Project

The second project took place in cooperation with an international telecommunication company. The project was a combined programming-tool-and-method development project. Subprojects, including a subcontractor outside the company, were distributed all over Sweden. The "Technical Orderers"—the representatives of departments that wanted to use the technology and therefore had the necessary competencies regarding requirements and design—were distributed over several countries. (For more detailed information and an evaluation of the outcome, see Rönkkö, chapter 11, this volume.)

After the fieldwork got off to a difficult start, we decided to set the study up in the organization in a very visible way. We organized the empirical research as far as possible according to the project model of the company. The supervisors within the company and the university took over clearly defined and well-known roles as "Project Leader" and "Product Owner." Because we recognized that the subprojects and their leaders had the most problems regarding coordination over a long distance, we decided to focus on their point of view. Since the study took place in a corporate context, we also decided to adopt their perspective and invite them to take part in the design of the study, as well as in the analysis of the field material. We made that visible for the whole project; we asked the leader of the local subproject to act as a Technical Orderer for the study.

The fieldworker had an office close to the local project members. However, hanging around in the same office area as the project members turned out not to provide enough opportunity to gain an understanding of what was going on. So we decided to interview subproject leaders and project members in the different locations in Sweden. Additionally, other project members were interviewed and several project meetings and telephone conferences were taped.

As the project just moved over to the design phase according to the company's waterfall-like project model, the main problem for the project members was to understand the requirements collected by the Technical Orderers that were handed over from the prestudy phase. To clarify issues that could not be understood from reading the documents, to straighten out ambiguities, and to check whether a design idea would fulfill the requirements, the different project members had different strategies for getting personal feedback from the Technical Orderers all over the world.

None of these strategies was supported by the company's project model. Nevertheless, the project model was appreciated as a common reference point and as a means of coordination between the different sites and across different cultures. The project members seemed to regard their own workarounds as necessary corrections in an incomplete world. They were measures to make the plan work rather than a sign of criticism and ignorance.

Criticizing the process model for not supporting common theory building between domain experts and developers and proposing alternative process models would have been a possible resolution. However, our understanding of the importance of the companywide process model as a common frame of reference and as a means of coordination restrained us from such a proposal. We proposed a rather small change: adding the requirements initiator(s) to each requirement to ease the project members' access to them.

Designing for Design in Use

This project started just recently. Together with two industrial partners —one telecommunications provider, one small software development company—it explores the deployment of a flexible database technology that allows for the change of the data model during use (Diestelkamp 1999). There are different ideas on how such technology could be useful in software development: prototyping database applications, developing business areas, supporting the change of data structures, and so on. The project under discussion involves support for rapidly developing business areas. In addition to concrete design issues regarding functionality and user interfaces that have to be addressed, methodological and organizational questions have to be solved. Issues that can be studied when such technology is introduced include the following: To what extent can users change an application? When does a change become a task for maintenance and further development? How is the distribution of work between users, technical support, and software engineers affected? How can an organization document and keep track of the changes implemented by the users?

The subject of this project—different from both the others—is the introduction of new technology and changes in development methodology and processes. Thus from the beginning we were aware that our role as researchers in the project was not only that of observers. The pure observation in the second project turned out not to be organizationally neutral. An active involvement can be expected to be at least as problematic, though the specific forms of cooperation are yet to be developed.

Regarding the changes in methods and in the process model, we will use the results of our fieldwork as input for what we preliminarily call "cooperative adaptation and development of methods." We plan to evaluate and refine these measures together with the project members. Parallel to the workshops, we plan to observe the project and the implementation of the measures designed in a participatory way.

Regarding methodology, we expect the problematic issue in this project to be how to combine empirical research and intervention. Action research as described in Mathiassen 1998 might provide a framework for understanding and reflecting on the interaction between these approaches. However, how we in our specific situation should interpret the framework is not yet clear. We plan to use the empirical findings both to justify the conclusions we draw in a scientific way and as input for the joint method development. We started out using qualitative methods—interviews, document evaluation, and participatory observation—to understand what goes on in the project and to understand the development culture. However, we expect the way we relate to the project and its members to have as much influence on the research results as any of the methodological decisions.

Choices to Make

Empirical research in software engineering takes place under conditions that differ fundamentally from those in other disciplines. In software engineering, as opposed to the natural sciences, we observe social situations that are not only unique regarding the persons involved, the organizational setting, and the software produced but that also include our fellow humans with expectations, opinions, and interests. Unlike those working in the social sciences, we are called on to think about improvements in the situation beyond just understanding it—in other words, to develop methods that will then be used in the practice we observe. That means that our empirical research not only aims at understanding but also at changing the situation, which is what the people we observe usually expect of us.

Our research takes place in and becomes part of the social setting it tries to understand, whether we take that into account or not. Therefore, issues that in other settings tend to be regarded as ethical questions concerning the implications of research become methodological questions for us. The nature of the relationship between the researchers and the subjects of research decides what we get to see and what our results look like. Traditional methodological questions acquire new dimensions in this context. The questions or choices discussed in the remainder of this chapter are the result of reflecting on the projects described above. At the end I propose a framework for designing empirical research in software engineering as cooperative method development.

Understanding from Within and Looking from Without

With respect to empirical methods, the question we are confronted with is not necessarily whether to apply qualitative or quantitative methods. Software development projects are often one-of-a-kind efforts. They are seldom comparable and are often highly dependent on situational contingencies. Thus every quantitative method is questionable, if it is not related to a set of projects producing the same kind of software in a comparable environment.

The methodological question we are confronted with is whether to try to understand the software development practice from within and relate our conclusions to that perspective or to take an outside perspective on what is relevant. Trying to understand the software development practice from within and taking the concerns of the practitioner involved seriously kept those of us in the other project from naively criticizing the project model and proposing an evolutionary one. A common frame of reference might be worth the effort of working around it if necessary.

Ethnography and ethnomethodology, for example, have the declared purpose of focusing on the practices of certain cultures and communities from within. They aim at understanding a situation from the participants' point of view. However, if we just apply a member's perspective, we cannot contribute much to the situation. Independently of our methodological choices, we have to relate the member's point of view to our background as researchers in order to see areas of possible improvements.

What is Our Relationship to the People We Study?

Doing empirical research in industrial practice puts the researcher in a situation influenced by contradicting interests, hierarchies, and personal antagonisms. In such a situation the observation of how software development takes place can have organizational and personal implications (Suchman 1995). As we learned in the first two cases, the stance we take in relation to the project, its members, and the organizational context will influence what we will be allowed to see.

When it comes to proposing changes, the situation is even more difficult. Do we treat projects and project members as guinea pigs on which to impose our recommendations, or are we all partners in a cooperative effort? Do we invite the developers, project leaders, or management to the discussions about possible improvements? How do we introduce our proposals into the organization? How we resolve these questions will influence the success as well as the evaluation of the proposed changes.

What Do We Base Our Method Development On?

Even within an empirical research paradigm, the basis for developing methods as well as for making proposals for concrete changes can be decided on in different ways. Basili (1996) proposes the development of abstract models as in the physical sciences. Thus the empirical research is designed as laboratory research. The source for the change proposal is the general models; that means theoretically motivated relationships between activity and outcome that have already been experimentally confirmed.

Iversen, Nielsen, and Nørbjerg (1998) report on a project where the fatigue of the practitioners of several model-driven, software-process-improvement efforts led to a different approach. The starting point of the research and later of the improvement project involved the problems recorded by the practitioners themselves. Improvement measures addressed problems of the project leaders and their teams rather than an abstract maturity level.

Even in such a cooperative method-development effort, the researchers' contribution is "biased" by their idea of what software is and how it should be developed. This background and conceptual as well as methodological knowledge represent the researchers' contribution to the cooperation. The cooperative setting, on the other hand, can be used to challenge the theories and models we bring with us and to develop them further.

Toward Cooperative Method Development

If software engineering methods are understood not as a prescription for action, but as resources, as tools for the software developers, the arguments that are valid for use-oriented design and development of software might be applicable here as well. The usefulness of methods might improve if they are designed, implemented, and evaluated in cooperation with the people who want to use them. Methods can be understood as providing support for a certain way of doing software development and not lending themselves easily to others. On the other hand, as detailed and prescriptive as a method might be, it has to be interpreted and adapted by the software developers so as to reflect the circumstances and contingencies of the concrete situation. The actual implementation has to be designed in use. Learning from PD and evolutionary development, method development can be organized in terms of design-implementation-evaluation cycles, providing space for learning among all participants, practitioners as well as researchers.

As in PD, empirical methods can be used to supplement the cooperative effort and to help the researchers acquire an understanding of the practice the other project members are involved in (Kensing, Simonsen, and Bødker 1998; Karasti 2000). Results of the empirical studies can serve as input into the cooperative process.

Such an understanding of cooperative method development could be developed into a framework to conceptualize and organize empirical research in software development together with the practitioners involved.

What Do We Gain?

The chapter started out by exploring the historical background of the rather difficult relationship between software engineering research and software development practices. Empirical research on how software development actually takes place, and efforts to relate method development to this research, represent one way of bringing research and practice closer together. Three different approaches to empirical research were introduced, providing three different ways of tackling the methodological problems of such research. The approaches differ not only regarding the empirical methodology they apply, but also in terms of the conceptualization of software development and the improvements proposed.

In the context of some personal empirical research, methodological issues were raised along a different dimension. The relationship to the people involved, the perspectives we bring to bear in trying to understand the software development practice, and the basis for our proposals for improvements turned out to influence what we were able to see and therefore what kind of results we could produce. The section culminated in a proposal for using PD as a frame of reference for the cooperative development of methods. Looking back at the description of the three different approaches for empirical research on software development, this result puts their diversity in a different light. Each of them constructs the relation to their research subject(s) in a different way. Different answers to the questions posed in the last section result in different methodological choices and in different perspectives on the same phenomenon.

One might say this turns the purpose of empirical research upside down. If the relationship between researcher and researched—and therefore the theoretical framework of the researchers—influences the results, how then can empirical research prove anything? This question is not new; it has been raised in different epistemological discussions for some time. Within the social sciences, the Critical Theory of the Frankfurt School, for example, has addressed that issue (Adorno et al. 1987). In the context of the natural sciences, Paul Feyerabend (1993) argued—and showed for physics and astronomy—that theories provide conceptual frames of reference that are incommensurable with each other. Relevant empirical experiments and observations are identified in relation to these frames of reference. They are therefore not appropriate for evaluating different theories but are useful in elaborating and further developing their respective conceptual framework and theory.

Because software engineering is an engineering discipline whose goal is to develop instruments to support software development, this interaction between researchers and their subject is not a problem but rather the program. Even empirical research aims, in this context, at the improvement, not only at the understanding, of practice. The epistemological problems suggest themselves in unusual forms. We construe our subject through our conceptualizations and the design of the empirical research as well as with the help of methods and tools we develop based on these findings. What we can reach is some kind of constructive proof. From a specific perspective, a certain set of distinctions, categorizations, and concepts apply and help to improve software development practice in a specific way.

Notes

This chapter would not have been possible without the cooperation of the students and practitioners involved in the projects. Eevi Beck, Ralf Klischewski, Jakob Nørbjerg, and Urs Andelfinger contributed important comments. In many useful discussions, Kari Rönkkö, Olle Lindeberg, and Sara Eriksén helped me clarify the ideas that developed into the chapter.

1. I am aware that I am putting software engineering and use-oriented research together here in a controversial way. This appears justified because, in my view, both suffer from a lack of understanding of software development practice. Coming from a use-oriented software engineering background myself, my motivation for carrying out empirical research on software development stemmed from arguments regarding the (nonexistent) usability of these methods.

References

Adorno, T. W., R. Dahrendorf, H. Pilot, H. Albert, J. Habermas, and K. R. Popper. 1987. *Der Positivismusstreit in der deutschen Soziologie.* Darmstadt: Hermann Luchterhand Verlag.

Alriksson, M., and K. Rönkkö. 1998. Softtalk: Communication in Distributed Software Development. Bachelor's thesis, Department of Computer Science and Business Administration, University of Karlskrona Ronneby, Ronneby, Sweden.

Basili, V. 1996. The Role of Experimentation in Software Engineering: Past, Current, and Future. *Proceedings of the ICSE '96*, 442–449. New York: ACM Press.

Basili, V., and S. Green. 1994, July. Software Process Evolution at the SEL. *IEEE Software* 11: 58–66.

Bauer, F. L. 1993. Software Engineering—wie es begann. *Informatik Spektrum* 16: 259–260.

Button, G., and W. Sharrock. 1994a. The Mundane Work of Writing and Reading Computer Programs. In P. ten Have and G. Psathas, eds., *Situated Order: Studies in the Social Organization of Talk and Embodied Activities.* Washington, DC: University Press of America.

Button, G., and W. Sharrock. 1994b. Occasioned Practices in the Work of Software Engineers. In M. Jirotka and J. Goguen, *Requirements Engineering: Social and Technical Issues.* London: Academic Press.

Button, G., and W. Sharrock. 1996. Project Work: The Organization of Collaborative Design and Development in Software Engineering. *Computer Supported Cooperative Work*, special issue on Studies of Cooperative Design, 5: 368–386.

Button, G., and W. Sharrock. 1998. The Organizational Accountability of Technological Work. *Social Studies of Science* 28: 73–102.

Deifel, B., U. Hinkel, B. Paech, P. Scholz, and V. Thurner. 1999. Die Praxis der Softwareentwicklung: Eine Erhebung. *Informatik-Spektrum* 22: 24–36.

Diestelkamp, W. 1999. Promis, a Generic Product Information Database System. In R. Y. Lee, ed., *Proceedings of the ISCA 14th International Conference* (Cancun, Mexico, April 7–9). Raleigh, NC: ISCA.

Dittrich, Y., and K. Rönkkö. 1999. Talking Design. *Proceedings of the IRIS '99*. Technical Report TR-21, Department of Computer Science and Information Systems, University of Jyväskylä, Jyväskylä, Finland.

Feyerabend, P. 1993. *Against Method*. 3rd ed. London: Verso.

Floyd, C. 1992. Software Development as Reality Construction. In C. Floyd, H. Züllighoven, R. Budde, and R. Keil-Slawik, eds., *Software Development and Reality Construction*. Berlin: Springer Verlag.

Floyd, C. 1994. Software-Engineering—und dann? *Informatik Spektrum* 17: 29–37.

Floyd, C., W. M. Mehl, F.-M. Reisin, G. Schmidt, and G. Wolf. 1989. Out of Scandinavia: Alternative Software Design and Development in Scandinavia. *Journal for Human-Computer-Interaction* 4: 253–380.

Glass, R. L. 1994. The Software Research Crisis. *IEEE Software* 11: 42–47.

Grinter, R. E. 1996. Supporting Articulation Work Using Software Configuration Management Systems. *Computer Supported Cooperative Work*, special issue on Studies of Cooperative Design, 5: 447–465.

Grinter, R. E. 1998. Recomposition: Putting It All Back Together Again. *Proceedings of the Computer Supported Cooperative Work CSCW 1998* (Seattle). New York: ACM Press.

Gulliksen, J., A. Lantz, and I. Bovie. 1999. How to Make User Centred Design Usable. (Workshop proposal.) In S. Brewster, A. Cawsey, and G. Cockton, eds., *Human-Computer Interaction: INTERACT '99*, Vol. II. London: Chapman & Hall.

Hellige, H. D. 1996. Technikleitbilder als Analyse-, Bewertungs- und Steuerungsinstrumente: Eine Bestandsaufnahme aus informatik- und computerhistorischer Sicht. In H. D. Hellige, ed., *Technikleitbilder auf dem Pruefstand. Leitbild-Assessment aus Sicht der Informatik- und Computergeschichte*. Berlin: Edition Sigma.

Iversen, J. K., P. A. Nielsen, and J. Nørbjerg. 1998. Problem Diagnosis Software Process Improvement. In T. J. Larsen, L. Levine, and J. I. DeGross, eds., *Information Systems: Current Issues and Future Changes*, 111–130. Laxenburg, Austria: IFIP.

Johansson, C., Y. Dittrich, and A. Juustila. 1999. Software Engineering across Boundaries: Student Project in Distributed Collaboration. *IEEE Transactions on Professional Communication*, 42: 286–296.

Karasti, H. 2000. Co-constructing Shared Understandings of Work Practices for System Design: The Interplay of Views. *Occasional Papers from the Work Practice Laboratory*, vol. 1, no. 1, University of Karlskrona/Ronneby.

Kensing, F., J. Simonsen, and K. Bødker. 1998. MUST—A Method for Participatory Design. *Human-Computer Interaction* 13: 167–198.

Mathiassen, L. 1997. *Reflective Systems Development.* Dr. tech. thesis, Aalborg University. Available at http://www.cs.auc.dk/~larsm/.

Mathiassen, L. 1998. Reflective Systems Development. *Scandinavian Journal of Information Systems*, 10: 67–118.

McIlroy, M. D. 1969. Mass Produced Software Components. In P. Naur and B. Randell, eds., *Software Engineering: Report on a Conference Sponsored by the NATO Science Committee*, Brussels Scientific Affairs Division, NATO, 151–155.

Nygaard, K. 1986. Program Development as a Social Activity. In H. J. Kugler, ed., *Information Processing 86*, 189–198. Amsterdam: North-Holland.

Petman, T. 1999. Communication Matters. Master's thesis, Department of Information Processing Science, University of Oulu, Oulu, Finland.

Potts, C., and L. Catledge. 1996. Collaborative Conceptual Design: A Large Software Project Case Study. *Computer Supported Cooperative Work* 5: 415–445.

Robertson, T. 1996. Embodied Action in Time and Place: The Cooperative Design of a Multimedia, Educational Computer Game. *Computer Supported Cooperative Work* 5: 341–367.

Schmidt, K., and W. Sharrock. (guest editors). 1996. *Computer Supported Cooperative Work*, Special Issue on Studies of Cooperative Design, 5.

Schön, D. A. 1983. *The Reflective Practitioner: How Professionals Think in Action.* New York: Basic Books.

Singer, J., T. C. Lethbridge, N. Vinson, and N. Anquetil. 1997. An Examination of Software Engineering Work Practice. In *Proceedings of CASCON '97* (Toronto).

Suchman, L. 1995. Making Work Visible. *Communications of the ACM* 38: 56–64.

Suchman, L., and R. Trigg. 1993. Artificial Intelligence as Craftwork. In S. Chaiklin and J. Lave, eds., *Understanding Practices: Perspectives on Activity and Context*, 144–178. New York: Cambridge University Press.

Tellioglu, H., and I. Wagner. 1997. Negotiating Boundaries: Configuration Management in Software Development Teams. *Computer Supported Cooperative Work* 6: 251–274.

IV

Organizing

Jesper Simonsen

How is software practice related to organizing issues like organizational change? And how can social science–related research on software practice be organized in order to reveal relevant issues within this practice? These are the questions that this section addresses. The title, "Organizing," can thus refer to both software practice and organizational change—as well as to the organization of the research on software practice. The section argues for the need to relate information systems research and information systems practice by organizing the research as action research in collaboration with information systems practitioners. You will be introduced to different approaches to such research, including activity theory and actor-network theory. In addition, the topic of software practice and organizational change is addressed by behavioral theories of decision making and participatory design techniques. The section is introduced with a study aiming at changing software practices by disseminating a method inspired by the latter two approaches.

The initial chapter in this section—chapter 13, "Changing Work Practices in Design"—is authored by Keld Bødker, Finn Kensing, and Jesper Simonsen. The chapter reports on the final phase of a ten-year research program in which a new method for design in an organizational context has been created. The method has been developed through a combination of theoretical studies and experimental work based on ten different action-research projects in various organizations in Denmark and the United States in cooperation with designers and users from the companies involved. Finally, as reported on in the chapter, the method was used and evaluated by three Danish information technology (IT) organizations. The authors' role in these projects was restricted to method dissemination—analyzing the IT designers' current work practices, proposing changes, teaching, supervision, and coaching—and evaluation of the method in close cooperation with the designers in the three companies. The chapter reflects on experiences gained in relation to the method-dissemination activities—that is, changing work practices of designers doing real-life industrial projects.

In chapter 14, "Information Systems Research and Information Systems Practice in a Network of Activities," Mikko Korpela, Anja Mursu, H. Abimbola Soriyan, and Anne Eerola focus on the relationship between information systems research and information systems practice. They argue that just as practitioners must engage in a collaborative relationship with users to produce appropriate products and services for their clients, so also must researchers engage in a collaborative setting with practitioners. To understand software practice in real life, researchers need ethnographic methods as much as—if not more than—practitioners need ethnographic methods for information systems development. Korpela et al. suggest that research projects should be based on action research, and they give an example from an ongoing project in which they use activity theory as their approach to information systems research.

Chapter 15, "Reaching out for Commitments: Systems Development as Networking," by Ralf Klischewski, uses actor-network theory to conceptualize software practice. In general, the networking approach offers great potential for reflecting on and managing the phenomena related especially to distributed information systems development environments. This approach views software practice as a series of activities aimed at consecutively allocating resources at interrelated places in order to promote the development and use of information systems. Recurrent activities are identified as essential to achieve progress in systems development projects. Such activities are identified by applying concepts and terminology from actor-network theory, and by circulating and (black)boxing commitments from the actors involved. To encourage actors to contribute the required resources at appropriate times and places, the approach is exemplified in a case study of the implementation of an information system supporting the examination administration at a large university.

Chapter 16, by Bettina Törpel, Volker Wulf, and Helge Kahler, involves "Participatory Organizational and Technological Innovation in

Fragmented Work Environments." The authors have tried to impose different participatory design techniques in two projects in networked organizations: one project with interorganizational collaboration between a steel mill and two engineering offices, and another project involving a project-based network of freelancers in the service area. Törpel, Wulf, and Kahler found that the participatory design techniques they proposed did not apply as well as expected in the two projects. They claim that crucial presuppositions embedded in participatory design are not in effect in many (especially small) organizations. As a consequence—and based on their experiences from the two projects—they argue for a reconsideration of some of the central notions in participatory design like "organization," "interests," "design," and "projects."

In chapter 17, Mark Bergman, John Leslie King, and Kalle Lyytinen address the issue of "Large-Scale Requirements Analysis as Heterogeneous Engineering." As a starting point, they criticize traditional theories within requirements engineering that reduce requirements engineering to an activity where a technical solution is documented for a given set of goals. In contrast, they argue that a requirement should specify a set of mappings between problem and solution spaces, which are both socially constructed and negotiated. They propose an alternative concept for requirements engineering—referred to as *functional ecology of requirements*—that is based on behavioral theories of decision making as suggested by organizational scientists like Simon, March, Olson, and Lindblom. This leads to a model where requirements engineering is viewed as a process of relating a current solution space to a problem space—and further, to a future solution space. Under this model, requirements are not waiting to be discovered by an analyst, but rather are systematically constructed through an iterative and evolutionary process of defining and redefining the problem and solution spaces. The resulting requirements specification is hence a product of a coevolutionary process of discovery and decision, in which both the solution space and the problem space are constructed. It remains a social process of negotiation and inquiry that is constrained by bounded rationality and limited organizational resources.

13

Changing Work Practices in Design

Keld Bødker, Finn Kensing, and Jesper Simonsen

This chapter discusses attempts in three information technology (IT) organizations to change work practices in design. The endeavors were related to the introduction of a new method for design in an organizational context, developed by the authors (Kensing, Simonsen, and Bødker 1998a; Bødker, Kensing, and Simonsen 2000). The method has been developed through a combination of theoretical studies and experimental development (Kensing 1999). In the experiments we—as designing researchers—have carried out ten design projects in various organizations in Denmark and the United States in cooperation with designers and users from the companies involved (Bødker and Kensing 1994; Kensing, Simonsen, and Bødker 1998b; Simonsen 1997; Simonsen and Kensing 1997).

We demonstrated that the method and the conceptual framework worked well when we carried out the design projects in cooperation with designers and users from the companies. To put the method to a "reality test," we recently completed projects in three Danish IT organizations. Our role in these projects was restricted to method dissemination—analyzing the IT designers' current work practices, proposing changes, teaching, supervising, and coaching—and evaluation of the method in close cooperation with the designers in the three companies. In this chapter we reflect on our experiences in relation to the method-dissemination activities—that is, the changing work practices of designers doing real-life industrial projects.

The chapter is structured as follows. The first section contains a description of the research approach applied. In the second section, we briefly present the method we have developed and introduced in the three organizations. In the third section, we present the three organizations and the activities performed in each organization. The fourth section concludes the chapter with lessons learned.

Research Approach

The research was carried out in cooperation with three Danish companies—the Radio Station, the University Hospital, and the IT Consulting Company—and sponsored by the National Danish Centre for IT Research. Our responsibility was method-dissemination activities (teaching, supervision, and evaluation), and evaluation of the practices of IT designers in real-life industrial projects. The project was organized as an action-research project with two coordinated agendas:

1. The industrial agenda aimed to increase the method repertoire and the understanding of early design as part of systems development activities. Each company received support to start experimenting with new work practices in design based on an understanding of the current practice in design projects. The researchers facilitated these activities in cooperation with designers from the three companies. Teaching and supervision of relevant issues in new work practices was an integral part of the researchers' responsibilities.

2. The research agenda focused on contributing to the further development of a conceptual framework about and a method for design in an organizational context. More specifically, the research questions of the project were formulated as follows:

- What are the strengths and weaknesses of current approaches to design activities?
- How is the method evaluated by designers in the three companies in relation to other approaches to design in an industrial context?
- What are appropriate ways of introducing the method supporting designers in an industrial context?
- How can the method and the conceptual framework be revised based on experiences and dialogue with the designers involved?

The project was organized as three independent projects, one in each of the three companies. We had deliberately chosen three quite different companies in relation to market situation, products, IT strategy, and so on to facilitate cross-company learning, as well as to test the method in varied settings.

Due to space limitations we will focus on the method-dissemination activities, the most central research question thus being: *What are appropriate ways of introducing the method supporting designers in an industrial context?* The other research questions are also relevant and will be touched on when appropriate. We refer the reader to Kensing 1999 for a review of arguments in relation to the design of the method.

Our approach to method dissemination was based on two basic premises. First, introduction of a new method should be coupled straightforwardly to experienced challenges in design projects. Designers do not just change work practices because of "whims" or "accidentally." They need good reasons for engaging in time-consuming activities like learning a new method in a stressed working situation. So, "challenges" like problems experienced, new technology, a new user domain, or the like, were assumed to be good starting points for introducing a new method. Second, traditional teaching cannot stand alone in method dissemination. There is obviously a need for general presentations and written material to introduce a new method. But designers also often need guidance on how to undertake specific tasks in a project or feedback on material they have produced. Furthermore, we knew that for some designers, being able to work closely with future users—that is, often highly skilled professionals—was new, and so some kind of personal coaching might be necessary.

The MUST Method

The MUST method supports participatory design in an organizational context, this being in-house or contract development (see Grudin 1991). We use the term *design* in the same way architects do—focusing on the analysis of needs and opportunities as well as the design of functionality and form. We acknowledge that in a succeeding development process further design is needed, and that when applying a computer system users might find new ways of utilizing the system or come up with additional demands.

We see a method as a resource for action (Suchman 1987), and as a learning tool that practitioners have to experience and adapt in ways they find suitable to their current project (Mathiassen et al. 1996). In this vein the MUST method is presented as offering four types of resources (Bødker et al. 2000):

- A conceptual framework identifying the basic elements of design in an organizational context
- Four principles to guide the design project
- Four phases designed to organize the design project as a stepwise decision-making process
- A broad set of techniques and representation tools to be used in concrete activities based on the designers' preferences and understanding of the situation in question

We consider the four principles indispensable, because they express the "soul" of the method and guide the design process. These principles are as follows:

1. *A coherent vision.* We see the design activities as a first step in introducing sustainable IT. We deliberately use this ecological concept as a metaphor in an attempt to capture an overall perspective of the use of the method. A design project needs to address and take into account the technical, organizational, and educational issues. A sustainable basis for the organization's decision making, and for the technical and organizational implementation, should also include an evaluation of foreseeable consequences and an estimate of the costs of implementing the design.

2. *Solid user participation.* User participation makes it possible to establish a mutual learning process. The designers need knowledge of the work domains to be supported by IT, and the users need knowledge of the technological options. This is the pragmatic argument for user participation. We also advocate user participation for political reasons—that is, users have a right to influence their work situation, including the IT applications.

3. *Work practice experienced by firsthand encounters.* Designers can get valuable information about a particular domain from reading about the field or from interviews with experienced professionals. But in design we also need to know how work actually gets done, and that requires firsthand encounters—for example, by observation or other ethnographic techniques.
4. *Anchoring.* We use "anchoring" as a metaphor that moves beyond the design-implementation dichotomy. For a vision to materialize, it needs to be deeply rooted in the organization—that is, with management and the steering committee, who decide if it should be implemented; with those who will carry out the technical and organizational implementation—the latter including educational/training activities; and with the users, who will have to live with its consequences.

Design in an organizational context is perceived as an open-ended process. Often, there is no clear statement of problems that all groups can adhere to, there is no clear idea of the kind of IT support needed, or there is no clear idea of how the project should be carried out. To cope with this situation of uncertainty, we propose to organize the design process in a way that supports a stepwise decision-making process in the organization. This is facilitated by identifying a number of documents and prototypes supporting an increasingly focused decision about the kind of technology needed.

Activities in the Three Organizations

In this section we describe the three organizations and the method-dissemination activities carried out in each.

The Radio Station

The Radio Station had embarked on a major project the technological goal of which was to replace the analogue platform for production and broadcasting with digital technology over a couple of years in all its branches.

The MUST group got involved in this due to positive evaluations of earlier projects involving one of the branches, the internal IT department, and researchers from the MUST group (Kensing, Simonsen, and Bødker 1998b; Kensing 1999). For the project reported on here, a senior and a junior researcher together with two graduate students cooperated with one of the first local branches to get the new technology. It happened to be the same branch that had worked with the MUST group before—hereafter referred to as "the branch." An important difference, however, was that this time the primary contact was the business unit, while in earlier projects it had been the IT department. The cooperation with the Radio Station ran over two years. The most intense period was during the five months that the branch carried out the design part of its project. The Radio Station invested two person-years in the cooperation and so did the researchers.

A central project group prepared guidelines for the local projects in each branch. First a design project should be carried out investigating the organizational goals of each branch and their relations to the new technological infrastructure. The central project group would for the projects in each branch review a design report before a realization phase could be embarked on. The divide into design and realization projects and the content of the design part were inspired by the MUST method.

The researchers arranged a two-day workshop on the MUST method for the branch's project group and steering committee. The workshop consisted of lectures on the overall approach and some details about the tools and techniques for project management, which were tried out in group work. The participants from the branch expressed concerns that the method was difficult for them to comprehend. However, they decided to use the method based on the positive evaluation of its use in an earlier project. The researchers were concerned, too, primarily because the branch's project group was comprised of users only. But the researchers agreed to the changing conditions for the test, even though they had IT designers in mind as the primary target group of the method.

The researchers familiarized themselves with the technical and organizational conditions of the project. They read strategic plans about the project and interviewed managers and other individuals considered central to the success of the project. Finally, they observed the various work processes involved in radio production. All these activities are considered important as part of the researchers' preparation for the supervision.

The researchers organized another two-day workshop for the project group, this time focusing on the MUST method's tools and techniques for data collection and analysis: How to carry out interviews and observations? How to deal with the data collected in systematic ways? A major proportion of the MUST method was used by the branch's project group, which every now and then asked the researchers for supervision, or else the researchers intervened themselves when they found it necessary. Also, the chair of the steering committee was supervised on his role as to the overall progression of the project. The researchers kept track of the project through meetings and informal contacts. In addition, they observed the project group (seven times, primarily during meetings) and the steering committee (three times, only during meetings).

The project group of the branch used the following elements of the MUST method:

- The overall layout of the project: a separate design project followed by realization; the suggestions for structuring the design project were followed to a large extent
- A specific technique for project establishment
- Interviews and observations for data collection
- Scenarios and theme-based analyses and presentations
- A high degree of user participation leading to well-anchored visions for change at the branch

Around twenty supervision sessions were held during the five months of the design project. The researchers gave specific advice as to how to carry out various activities as well as feedback on the intermediate and final reports. After the branch had finished its design project and waited to proceed to the technical and organizational implementation, the researchers wrote a report on their evaluation of the test. The report remained for internal use only, but later design projects in other branches have drawn on experiences from the design project of the branch.

The University Hospital

The University Hospital is a large, modern hospital with many specialized hospital wards. In 1990, the hospital's IT department changed its strategy for information systems (IS) development from in-house development to acquisition of (customized) generic systems or development of customized systems by external vendors/software houses. The change had two main justifications. More numerous and more reliable generic systems became available on the market from multiple vendors, and the IT department had difficulty maintaining a staff with core competencies on modern platforms and modern development technologies.

When the project started, the IT department was at the end of a five-year action plan of 100 MDKK (approximately U.S. $15 million). The projects in the action plan ranged from small projects with a budget of 200,000–300,000 DKK and less than one-year development time to large multimillion DKK projects with a development cycle of several years. Thus they had profound experience with IS development in an outsourcing context but needed time and other resources to reflect systematically on their experience to identify areas for improvements. They saw this project as a perfect opportunity to do this. The aim of the project thus was to contribute to improved work practices in IS development. The project group consisted of two IT consultants and two researchers. The total effort amounts to twelve months divided equally between the two groups.

The new project model had meant several changes in relation to competencies compared to the situation in in-house development. Job titles had changed from analysts and programmers to IT consultants. Some of the "old" analysts and programmers had left the IT department, and new staff had been recruited. Still, core competencies were technology related, and the IT consultants openly admitted facing challenges related to the new situation. They often discussed during lunch how they could better learn from each other's experiences, and there was an open attitude about the need to learn from experience and failures.

The project was divided into three main activities, each resulting in a report that was presented and discussed among the department's IT consultants and acted on by management. In the terminology of the hospital, the activities were named "screening," "diagnosis," and "proposals for cure." However—unlike in hospitals—in this project the "patients" had the full freedom to choose the proposals they would continue with.

In the "screening" activity all twenty projects were characterized along a number of key parameters on the basis of a survey questionnaire distributed to all project managers. This gave an overview of the projects, which enabled management to select five projects for further investigation.

In the "diagnosis" activity the five projects were studied in detail. Interviews were carried out with all involved IT consultants, with management of the IT department, as well as with representatives from the user departments, who had taken part in the projects, and with representatives from two suppliers. Furthermore, documents from the projects were studied. The aim of this activity was to find areas where the section, with its background and experience, could improve quality in its work practices through the use of new methods or by the use of new tools. All together the investigation gave voice to seventy-one problems, twelve from the user representatives, seven from the suppliers, and fifty-two from the IT consultants and their superiors. Not all of these are mutually exclusive, and in the report they were grouped into ten problem areas.

For the final "proposals for cure" activity three areas had been chosen as subjects for potential improvements:

- Work practices in preanalysis and specification
- Project models and contractual models
- Roles

A number of proposals, based on literature studies and the MUST method, were presented. First of all, a more elaborate project model was suggested. The elaboration concerned the design activities to be organized to more explicitly support an ongoing decision process, and to involve users more actively in the projects. Next, it was suggested that a broader view of tendering be allowed for. In some projects, a tender could be made very early to include innovative visions from suppliers (with inspiration from architectural competitions and Euromethod; see Euromethod Project 1996). In other projects, a tender could be made on the basis of a more detailed specification. Finally, it was suggested that a project-handbook framework be developed, including a description of the division of labor and responsibilities between roles in the user departments and the IT department.

For reasons outside the scope of the project, it turned out that no new design projects would be started in the project period (because of delivery problems with a new central IT system, the IT department had to restaff all projects to cope with problems due to the change of the millennium). So, despite a positive commitment to the proposals from management and the IT consultants, it was not possible to carry on with implementing and testing the proposals.

The IT Consulting Company

The dissemination project in the IT Consulting Company took place in a department that offers a platform for advanced tax-audit solutions within the compliance area. The customers consist of central tax and audit administrations in a country or state. The generic IT platform offered is highly tailorable, and an engagement with a new customer is introduced by a design project that identifies the customer's needs and the potential with regard to implementing (parts of) the IT solution. The preliminary design project is financed by the IT Consulting Company and carried out by senior consultants from the department. Tender, purchase, development, and implementation processes may later follow the preliminary design.

The cooperation with the IT Consulting Company took place in two phases. The first phase was an initial preparation stage mainly conducted by the researcher. The MUST method was introduced by a series of presentations. In addition, interviewing managers and consultants in the department served to identify different problem issues for which it could be relevant to experiment with the MUST method. Here a primary focus was placed on the method's anchoring principle. The preparation phase resulted in a project charter and a baseline plan for a following project phase. The second phase was a project stage mainly conducted by consultants from the company with the researcher observing, supervising, and reviewing written materials. A design project with a new customer was chosen as the project where the IT Consulting Company would experiment with the method. Specific techniques related to the anchoring principle were practiced and later used at the customer site. The project phase was concluded by an evaluation of the overall experimentation with the method.

During the project, the IT Consulting Company experimented with the following new work practices as suggested by the MUST method:

1. Project establishment with the customer, including the production of a project charter and a baseline plan
2. Tape-recorded interviews and transcriptions of the tapes
3. Affinity diagramming
4. Diagnostic and virtual mapping
5. Review of a baseline with the customer (including top management) presenting preliminary findings and conducting a mapping session
6. Writing scenarios
7. Reporting and presenting the findings for the customer in accordance with the guidelines from the method

The project was evaluated as a success. The customer chose to continue the project with the IT Consulting Company, and the IT Consulting Company decided to implement the MUST method both within the department, where the cooperation took place, and as a part of the company's overall and general model for design and implementation of IT.

Lessons Learned

In the section titled "Research Approach," we described our approach to method dissemination as being based on two fundamental premises:

1. Introduction of a new method should be coupled very straightforwardly with experienced challenges in design projects.
2. Traditional teaching cannot stand alone in method dissemination.

These premises have emerged from earlier projects. As described by Kensing (1999), a combination of lecturing, making room for reflections on current and emerging practices, establishing apprenticeship relations, and supervising technical as well as personal skills have proven instrumental in changing work practices. The central point is to *get beyond detached reflection* in the interaction between a researcher and designers in efforts to change the designers' work practices. A designer who is given a general presentation of, for example, a new technique is left on his or her own when relating it to personal work practices. And a researcher who is told about events and changes in a recent project is left with the question about what *really* happened. So, to get beyond the say/do problem (Blomberg et al. 1993; Goguen and Linde 1993), we advocate that the researcher get involved in the work practices of the designers, which subsequently makes it possible for him or her to reflect on problems in designers' current practices when presenting a new technique or proposing changes in design practice.

Next, we turn to a closer inspection of lessons learned about method-dissemination activities. We do this under three headings, which capture important issues in relation to our central research question: *What are appropriate ways of introducing the method supporting designers in an industrial context?* Along the way we also touch on issues in relation to the other research questions mentioned above. The headings are:

- Commitment to change
- Observation led to a breakthrough in the dialogue
- Accepting the stranger

Commitment to Change

A commitment to change is an important success factor in any change process, and thus also for method dissemination. It is general wisdom that management commitment is pivotal. In the IT Consulting Company, for example, it was the department manager who originally took the initiative. The manager was highly engaged in the project and took part in it as the project manager. In the Radio Station the IT manager took the initiative. When he left, two levels of management in the business unit with whom we worked confirmed the commitment. Both companies had originally taken the initiative to engage in the method-dissemination project by contacting the researchers and requesting our help. In other words, they knew beforehand that they could do things better and had decided to spend resources in trying to improve their design processes.

Experimenting with the new method in the IT Consulting Company took place in a commercial project with an important customer. The project in the Radio Station had the highest management attention since it was a major investment. This encouraged the companies to take a serious and critical approach in learning, using, and evaluating the different activities and techniques from the method.

In the University Hospital, a large number of projects had been carried out following the outsourcing strategy. There was a very positive attitude toward the need for changing work practices in design; the IT consultants openly discussed problems in the projects at lunch and in their weekly meeting. However, they did not have the time and resources to investigate these problems thoroughly for the purpose of identifying similarities across projects. For these reasons, we chose to design the project in two steps. The first step focused on identifying problems, investigating similarities, and proposing improvements. In the second step, the IT department would choose which of the proposals they wanted to carry on with. Unfortunately, for reasons beyond the scope of the project (to be explained below), we never made it as far as the second step.

The very organization of the project into two steps reflects our understanding of another aspect of the importance of commitment to change: changes should address areas needing improvements. To locate these areas, we had to spend time identifying common problems and their nature across the projects. The projects chosen for detailed investigation were carefully selected to reflect the diversity of IT projects at the hospital. And great care was taken to present preliminary findings to the whole group of IT consultants before reporting to management. Such presentations were done at a regular basis throughout the project; it was arranged as a meeting, or a part of their weekly meeting, where our findings documented in a report had been distributed to the participants in advance. The discussion often resulted in changes and additions to our report.

An important message can be drawn from this project: methodological work in an IT department serving business needs always has to respect operational issues. So when in this case the delivery of a central new IT system caused problems, all the attention and energy of the IT department had to be channeled toward this serious situation. And that meant away from our project.

Observation Led to a Breakthrough in the Dialogue

To be able to communicate effectively with designers in industrial companies, researchers benefit from observing the designers while experimenting with the new work practices.

In the project with the IT Consulting Company, the researcher made general presentations of the method before the project with the customer took place. In retrospect, we realized that these presentations were basically an account of abstract knowledge that the designers had to relate to their individual experiences, not shared by the researcher. The researcher could only relate to, and give examples from, his individual experience from projects and situations that the designers had not experienced. We often experienced struggles to understand each other, since both the researcher and the designers were interpreting the abstract method descriptions from different practical and situated experiences. This changed dramatically when a common ground was established. During the project at the customer site, where the researcher participated as an observer, a shared base of experience was developed. This led to a breakthrough in the mutual dialogue: different aspects of the method (and its general guidelines) could now be related to situated project conditions and events that both the researcher and the designers had taken part in. This shared base of experience established possibilities for discussing how the method could be applied in specific situations. Discussing the method based on shared experience also reassured the designers that the researcher was able to understand their conditions and work situations. In other words, this contributed to confidence in the researcher, which is another premise for the designers' commitment to change.

In presentations of the method at seminars in the Radio Station, the senior researcher was able to relate to the earlier project with the branch in which the method was used and from which he had also learned about the production of radio programs. This established some common ground for the communication. However, the researchers did not experience the project group while striving to use the method, except for a few techniques used at project group meetings or during supervision sessions.

Accepting the Stranger

Accepting the stranger is primarily a message for the participating industrial company—but also a lesson that presents food for thought for the researcher. Observing the activities of designers is vital for the researcher in order to be able to communicate his or her knowledge/method to the designers (as discussed above). At the outset, project members from all three companies agreed to this condition. But to some of the participants in the projects this issue became a reason for concern later on.

In the IT Consulting Company, the project members were all senior consultants with well-established work practices that they were highly experienced with. They felt concerned when the researcher, through his observations and "following them around," came close to and became aware of some of these practices. One consultant explained during the project that they in fact had already "written" 80 percent of the final report for the customer even before they had the first visit at the customer site. This was immediately recorded by the researcher, and later it turned out that the consultant had felt very annoyed by this. He was concerned with how the researcher would interpret this "work practice" and how it would be presented to other colleagues and managers. The "80 percent rule" could be explained in a positive way: the consultant was a highly experienced and knowledgeable domain expert, and 80 percent of his findings in general had been experienced before with other customers. But it could also be explained in a less positive manner: the consultant had a tendency to jump to conclusions and recommend IT solutions to a customer based on his knowledge of the company's IT portfolio, rather than on the needs and problems observed at the customer site.

The diagnostic analysis performed at the IT Consulting Company was based on a series of interviews and led to a report pointing out four different problem issues in the company where it could be appropriate to experiment with the method. One of these problem issues entailed an internal conflict within the company. The conflict was rooted in a dilemma of prioritizing the IT platform. On the one hand, they could prioritize the IT solution as a generic system where new releases could be offered to all customers. On the other hand, the individual customer's specific needs could be prioritized in a way that could lead to different tailored systems, hard to maintain through new versions of the generic system modules. The manager was not happy that this conflict was identified in the report and suggested that his employees not read the report—a recommendation that did not align with the dissemination approach.

The concern about accepting the stranger was also important in the University Hospital. The approach was that changes in work practice had to be based on a common understanding of the areas that needed improvement. That clearly involved some kind of evaluation of past and present performance, which implied evaluations of individuals, because the projects were often staffed with few IT consultants. And strangers (university researchers) took part in this evaluation. For a project completely dependent on a constructive dialogue with all involved IT consultants, this dilemma seemed somewhat unresolvable. How did we handle the situation? First, for a considerable part of the project period the researcher spent full days in the IT department, which meant that he took part in lunchtime conversations as well as various meetings, and thus became less of a stranger. Second, we always sent out interview summaries to the persons interviewed to allow them to correct what would become the project's record. Third, again and again we stressed that our objective was to identify general problems, not to expose success stories or failures. And finally, we took great care not to name individuals in the reports or oral presentations. The lesson seems to be that establishing and maintaining a positive attitude toward dissemination projects requires considerable attention to confidentiality and personal-integrity issues.

Summary

In this chapter we have described method-dissemination activities in three IT organizations and reflections on the course and outcome of the activities. The activities were related to introducing a method for design in an organizational context as part of changing work practices in real-life industrial design settings. The reflections were presented as three lessons: "Commitment to Change," "Observation Led to a Breakthrough in the Dialogue," and "Accepting the Stranger."

Under the heading "Commitment to Change," we illustrated the importance of management as well as designers' commitment to the activities. Management commitment was given serious attention. However, in one of the projects we came to realize how upcoming problems in relation to the basic business functions of the IT organization meant that management attention was directed away from our project. Designers' commitment was achieved by a constant focus on presenting and discussing preliminary findings and results with the designers in the respective organizations.

Under the heading "Observation Led to a Breakthrough in the Dialogue," we described how the interaction between researcher and designers changed dramatically when the researcher closely followed designers trying out new work practices in a project. Until then, presentations and discussions had somehow been blocked, since both designers and the researcher were interpreting method descriptions and descriptions of design practice from different practical and situated experiences. The researcher's observation of the designers' work practice established a common ground from which experiments could take off.

Finally, under the heading "Accepting the Stranger," we described our experience engaging in the work practices of designers. As an outsider, the researcher has to constantly strive to find a delicate balance between identifying areas for improvement and not blaming individuals. If individuals are blamed, they draw back and their commitment is lost. Since designers' commitment to dissemination activities, and to changing work practices in design in general, is pivotal, focus on the balance between general problem areas and problems caused by individuals should be maintained throughout the activities.

A basic premise of our approach to method dissemination has been to get beyond detached reflection in the activities between researchers and designers. The actual interactions in the organizations, and their outcomes, have demonstrated that for the kind of method-dissemination activites reported on here, knowledge of actual design practice and joint activities have proven instrumental.

The activities reported on in this chapter were part of a research project with the objective of testing and revising an approach to design in an organizational context developed by the authors over several years. The feedback from the activities described in this chapter, as well as other activities, was incorporated in a revised approach, documented by the authors (Bødker, Kensing, and Simonsen 2000).

Note

The National Danish Centre for IT Research has supported the research reported in this chapter. We also thank the designers and managers of the three organizations involved in the project—the Radio Station, the University Hospital, and the IT Consulting Company—for their support and willingness to take part in the project and their courage in inviting us to engage in changing their work practices. Also thanks to Maria Bergenstjerna, Jarle Brosveet, Helge Kahler, and Torbjörn Nordström for comments on a draft of this chapter. Finally, we wish to thank Dixi L. Henriksen for improving our English.

References

Blomberg, J., J. Giacomi, A. Mosher, and P. Swenton-Hall. 1993. Ethnographic Field Methods and Their Relation to Design. In D. Schuler and A. Namioka, eds., *Participatory Design: Principles and Practices*, 123–155. London: Erlbaum.

Bødker, K., and F. Kensing. 1994, April. Design in an Organizational Context—an Experiment. *Scandinavian Journal of Information Systems* 6(1): 47–68.

Bødker, K., F. Kensing, and J. Simonsen. 2000. Professionel IT-forundersøgelse—grundlaget for bæredygtige IT-anvendelser. Copenhagen: Samfundslitteratur.

Euromethod Project. 1996. Euromethod. Version 1. July 1996. (www.fast.de/Euromethod).

Goguen, J. A., and C. Linde. 1993. Techniques for Requirements Elicitation. *Proceedings of the IEEE International Symposium on Requirements Engineering*, 152–164. Los Alamitos, CA: IEEE Computer Society Press.

Grudin, J. 1991. Interactive Systems: Bridging the Gaps between Developers and Users. *IEEE Computer* 24(4): 59–69.

Kensing, F. 1999. Method Design and Dissemination. In J. Pries-Heje, C. Ciborra, K. Kautz, J. Valor, E. Christiaanse, D. Avison, and C. Heje, eds., *Proceedings of the Seventh European Conference on Information Systems, Copenhagen*, 386–402. Copenhagen: Copenhagen Business School.

Kensing, F., J. Simonsen, and K. Bødker. 1998a. MUST: A Method for Participatory Design. *Human-Computer Interaction* 13(2): 167–198.

Kensing, F., J. Simonsen, and K. Bødker. 1998b. Participatory Design at a Radio Station. *CSCW: The Journal of Collaborative Computing* 7(3–4): 243–271.

Mathiassen, L., A. Munk-Madsen, P. A. Nielsen, and J. Stage. 1996. Method Engineering: Who's the Customer? In J. Brinkkemper, K. Lyytinen, and R. J.

Welke, eds., *Method Engineering: Principles of Method Construction and Tool Support*, 232–245. Proceeedings of the IFIP TC8, WG8.1/8.2 Working Conference on Method Engineering. London: Chapman & Hall.

Simonsen, J. 1997. Linking Design to Business Strategy through Functional Analysis. In R. Galliers, S. Carlson, C. Loebbecke, C. Murphy, H. R. Hansen, and R. O'Callaghan, eds., *Proceedings of the 5th European Conference on Information Systems*, 1314–1327. Cork, Ireland: Cork Publishing Limited.

Simonsen, J., and F. Kensing. 1997. Using Ethnography in Contextual Design. *Communication of the ACM* 40(7): 82–88.

Suchman, L. 1987. Plans and Situated Action: The Problem of Human-Machine Communication. Cambridge, England: Cambridge University Press.

14

Information Systems Research and Information Systems Practice in a Network of Activities

Mikko Korpela, Anja Mursu, H. Abimbola Soriyan, and Anne Eerola

Most of the chapters in this book deal with software practice as the *development* of software products. In the present chapter the emphasis is on the *use* of software products in organizational information systems (IS), and particularly on the *introduction* of software products into organizations, which we understand as information systems development (ISD). The fact that motivates this chapter is the widely acknowledged need for up-to-date empirical research on software/IS development practice (e.g., Russo 2000).

Like other authors (also in this volume), we apply the theoretical framework of *activity theory* (Bertelsen and Bødker 2000; Engeström and Miettinen 1999; Hedegaard, Chaiklin, and Jensen 1999; Kaptelinin, chapter 3, this volume; Kuutti 1999). However, we have developed a more practitioner-oriented notation, which is briefly introduced in the beginning of the chapter. Like Kaptelinin in chapter 3 of the present book, we also use the activity-theoretical framework to discuss the relationship between research and practice. However, Kaptelinin studies the *direct* relationship between social scientists and software developers in joint projects, mainly in the human-computer interface (HCI) and computer-supported cooperative work (CSCW) domains, while we study an *indirect* relationship mediated by IS researchers in the ISD domain. These two chapters thus complement each other.

The present chapter is the third publication in a series analyzing different aspects of ISD from an activity viewpoint. The first paper (Korpela, Soriyan, and Olufokunbi 2000) introduces our theoretical models of work activities and activity networks, and argues that activity analysis can be used as an everyday requirements analysis method by IS practitioners.

The second paper (Korpela, Mursu, and Soriyan 2001) analyzes IS development itself as an activity. The focus of this third publication is on the relationship between IS research and IS practice. Further publications are being prepared on the relationship between software development and ISD, and on the societal and business contexts of activities.

The structure of the chapter is as follows. We first define what we understand by the concepts *information system*, *software system*, and *activity*. In the third section we apply these concepts in describing some elementary relations between information systems *use* and information systems *development*. In the fourth section we argue that analogous relations are required between information systems *development* and information systems *research*. This is the main message of the chapter, which is illustrated in the fifth section by a case from Nigeria. Finally, the relevance of the chapter is assessed and conclusions are drawn.

Definition of the Main Concepts

Our analysis is based on the long Scandinavian tradition of IS research (Iivari and Lyytinen 1998). In IS research, an *information system* is regarded as something fundamentally different from a software package as such. An IS refers to the information processing and management processes within an organization. It includes both technological and social elements, whether as two separate systems or as a social system containing technological elements, depending on the definition (Avison 1997; Davis 2000).

IS as a scientific discipline and professional practice deals with the use of information technology, particularly software systems, in organizations. Therefore IS is an applied social science in the way other organizational and work sciences are. It is a fundamentally different discipline and practice from software engineering, to say nothing of computer science in the narrow sense (Mingers and Stowell 1997, 11–12). However, ISD is closely related to software engineering in the way town planning is related to construction engineering—the former is about how the products of the latter can be used appropriately for collective human purposes. If towns are buildings, parks, and roads in use, then information systems are computers, software, and networks in use.

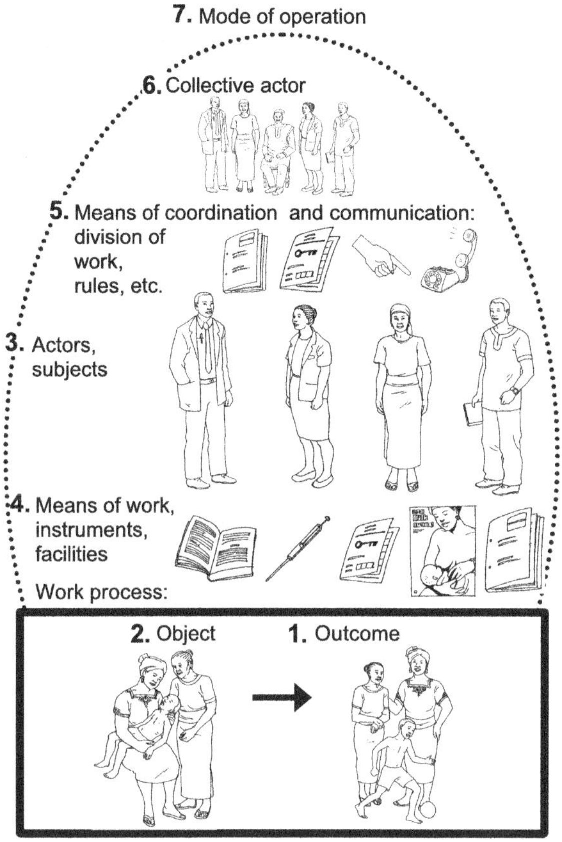

Figure 14.1
The elements of a work activity, using patient care as an example

More specifically, our approach is based on *activity theory*, particularly as it is applied to work development in Finland (Engeström 1987, 1990, 1999; Engeström, Engeström, and Vähäaho 1999). In this approach, the unit of analysis is a work activity, which basically comprises a number of people working on something shared in an organized way—not necessarily at the same time and place—to produce a joint outcome. Figure 14.1 presents our model of a work activity, using a patient-care activity in Nigeria as an example. It is not intended to be a fully covered case.

The model has been discussed in detail elsewhere (Korpela, Soriyan, and Olufokunbi 2000; cf. Engeström 1987, 78). For the purposes of the present chapter it suffices to identify the elements of a work activity:

1. The *outcome* is what defines an activity, its *raison d'être*. The motive of a patient-care activity is to produce health for the people.
2. The *object* is the starting point or raw material, which is transformed into the outcome during the *work process* of the activity. In a curative view, the health problems of the patients are the object of patient care; in a preventive view, potential health risks in the local population can also be seen as an object.
3. Various *actors* are needed to transform the shared object into the outcome. To produce health, physicians and nurses are needed, but so are community health workers and medical records officers.
4. The actors have different *means of work* at their disposal, to act on the object. Physicians can apply their medical knowledge, nurses can use syringes, community health workers can use health-promotion material, and so on. The means can be individual or shared, like a medical record.
5. The actions of the individual actors need to be organized through *means of coordination and communication*. In patient care, the rules defining the division of labor between doctors and nurses are an example of such a means, and a medical record also acts as a coordinative and communicative means.
6. All the actors taken together act as a *collective actor*. In patient care, the outcome is not produced by any individual actor alone, but by the multiprofessional health-care team.
7. Finally, all the elements must fit together in a systemic way, characterized as the *mode of operation* of the activity. For example, a patient-care activity can operate in a hierarchical, physician-dominated mode, or in a more collaborative mode. The latter mode requires different rules, records, and so on than the former.

The next concept that we will need in this chapter is an *activity network*. The elements of an activity (actors, means, object, and so on) are always produced by some other activity. Likewise, the outcome of an activity is usually intended for some other activity, either as a means,

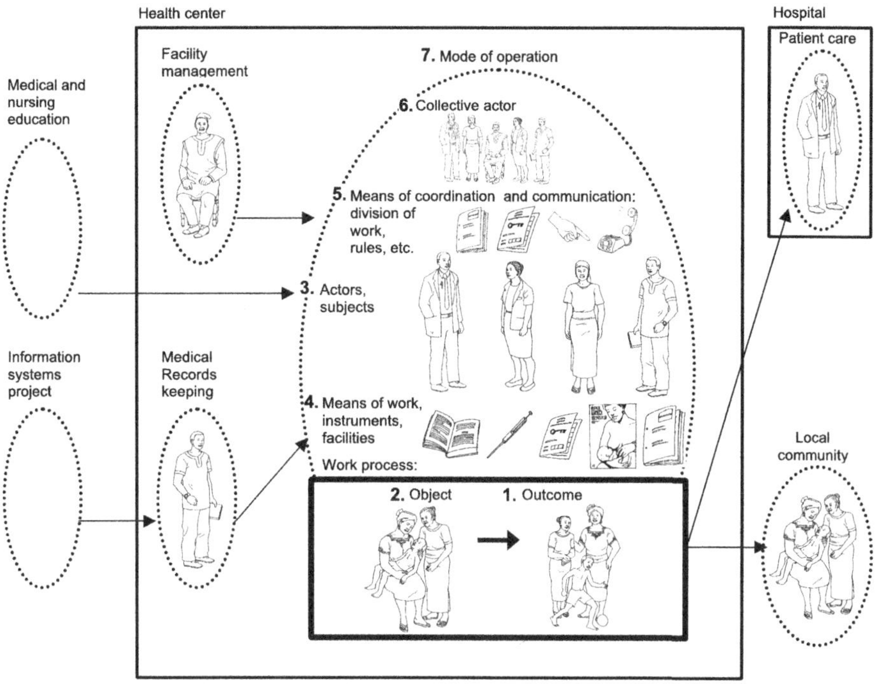

Figure 14.2
Parts of the activity network around patient care, split by organizational boundaries

object, or actor of the latter. Taken together, these production/service relations between activities form complex webs or networks. Within the networks we can identify chains of activities that are required for some ultimate output, like service chains in health care or value chains in business.

In figure 14.2 we have presented some of the network relations around patient care. The outcome, improved health, is intended to serve the local community, but uncured cases from primary health care also form the object of secondary care in hospitals. The medical records are produced by a record-keeping activity, the physicians and nurses by educational activities, some of the rules by the health center's management, and so on. The activities within the same organization are controlled by a shared management activity, while other network relations are split by organizational boundaries. The production/service chains run through multiple tiers of activities; for instance, new computer-based means for the record-keeping activity may be produced by an IS project activity.

Information technology can be used in various roles within activities—either as a *means of working on the object* (e.g., in medical care, a physician may use a clinical decision-support system to diagnose a patient's health problem) or as a *means of coordinating the collective process* (e.g., an appointment-scheduling system in a clinic may be used to organize the workflow of several professionals). All the bits and pieces of information technology being used in a given activity may not necessarily form a *system*—therefore we emphasize that it is the activity that has a systemic nature, not necessarily the "information system" embedded in it (Korpela, Soriyan, and Olufokunbi 2000). The fundamental frame of reference of IS science and practice should be the "collective work setting," not IS per se because the latter is a subordinated category.

Lacking a better term for the "technologically facilitated information processing aspects of a work activity," we continue to use "information system" as a shorthand. However, we use it simply to refer to the use of information technology (manual or computer-based) in a collective work activity, either as means of work or as means of coordination and communication.

Like the relations between actors and objects and the relations between different actors within an activity, the relations between activities are also mediated by means. Here lies the third role in which information technology can be used—as a *means of networking* between activities. The Internet and various interorganizational electronic data interchange systems are prime examples.

Correspondingly, we define ISD as the process by which some collective work activity is facilitated by new information-technological means through analysis, design, implementation, introduction, and sustained support. It should be noted that according to this definition, ISD can include some software development, but it can also be entirely based on previously existing pieces of software. A *software system* is an artifact that can be "embedded" in one or more work activities.

In figure 14.3 we have "zoomed in" into an IS project facilitating medical record keeping by new computer-based means, so that the latter can facilitate patient care, health education, and management by better reports. We leave the detailed discussion of ISD as an activity, however, to another publication (Korpela, Mursu, and Soriyan 2001).

IS Development Facilitating an IS Use Activity

Let us now take a more abstract look at the network of activities around IS development. By definition, the most fundamental purpose of IS development is to facilitate some work activity by means of some software. The software itself, like any other technology, is "sleeping" (Nurminen, Reijonen, and Tuomisto 1994)—that is, it is just a possibility of becoming something useful, until the IS users awaken it to life as a means in their own work activity. The IS development activity thus facilitates or provides means to the IS users' activity (figure 14.4). During the development activity, "sleeping software" becomes a "live information system."

The reason the users need the IS is that they too provide some products or other services to their clients, and the IS is to improve the production of these services, or the services themselves, in some way. In the example in the previous section, the medical records officers (users) need a patient information system in order to provide the doctors and nurses (users' clients) with better information. The doctors and nurses in turn need better information in order to provide health care in a better way, or to provide better health care, to their patients (clients' clients).

The developers thus facilitate the users to facilitate their clients. In the chain of activities, each object activity in turn provides the reason for existence for its facilitator activity (figure 14.4).

These observations are elementary indeed. IS practitioners and theorists have long recognized that IS developers and users need to engage in other kinds of relations as well, if the systems developed are to be useful for the users. The user-centered design tradition in its many manifestations has argued that the developers need to use more-or-less laborious ethnographic methods (Westrup, chapter 5, this volume) in order to try to grasp the essence of the users' work, before they can develop the kind

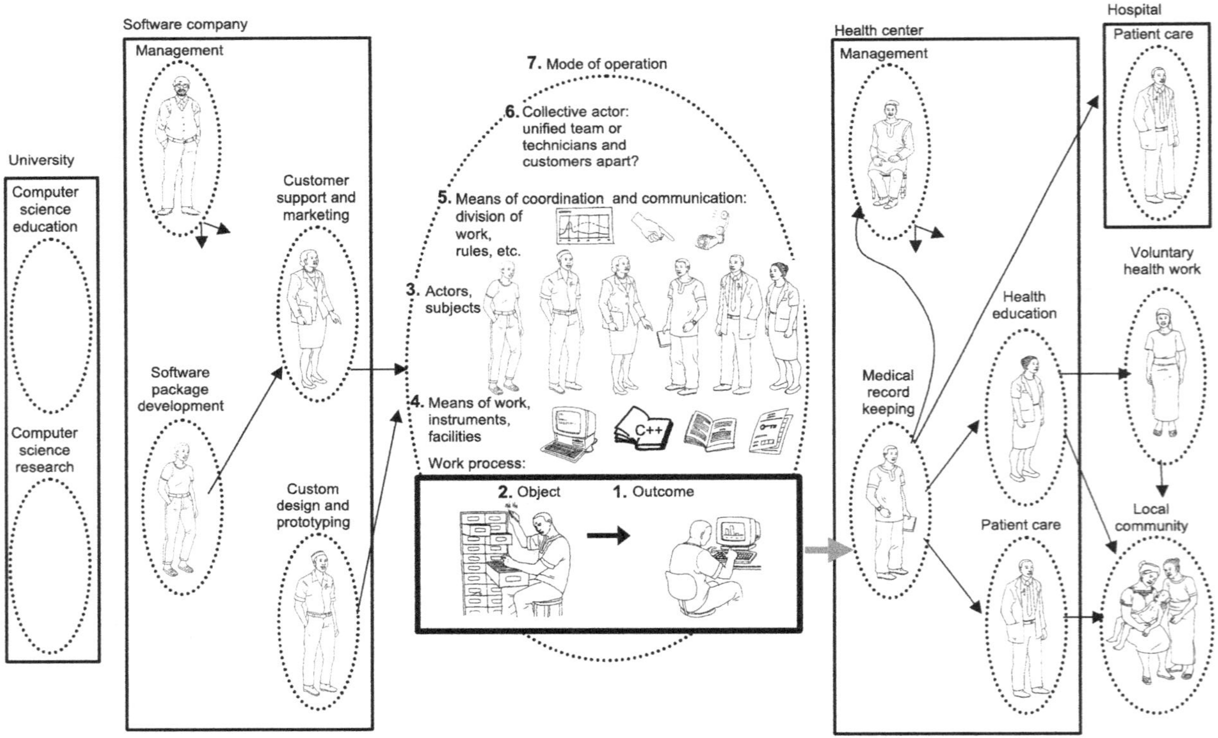

Figure 14.3
An information systems project for a health center as an activity, together with parts of the activity network

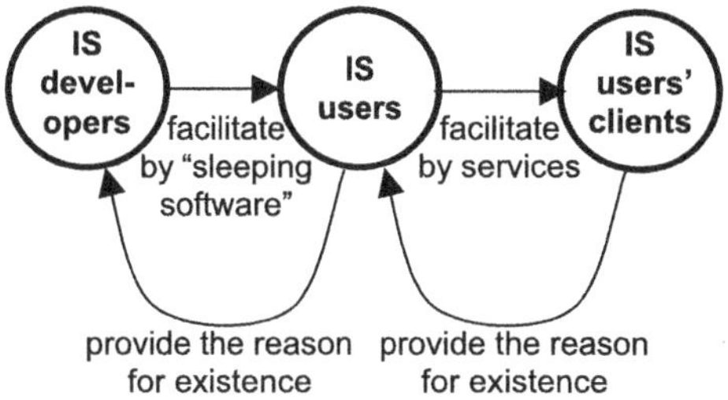

Figure 14.4
Schematic diagram of the elementary relations between IS developers, IS users, and IS beneficiaries

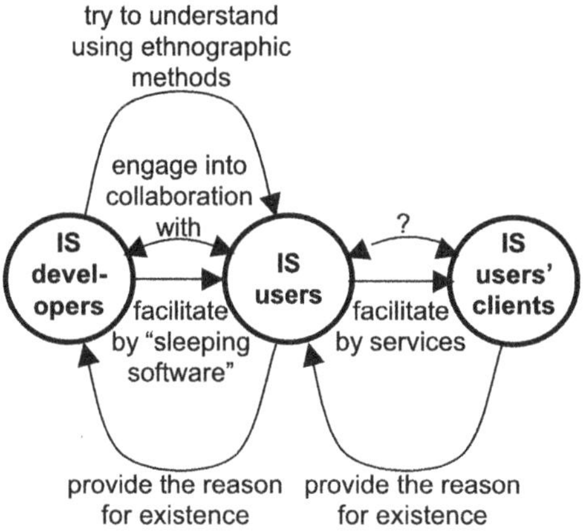

Figure 14.5
Schematic diagram expanded by "user-centered" and "cooperative" development

of means that the users really need (figure 14.5). The cooperative design (Greenbaum and Kyng 1991) and participatory design (Kensing and Blomberg 1998) movements have argued that a one-way relationship is not sufficient, but that the developers and users need to engage in a collaborative relationship, learn from each other, and jointly find out what kind of IS will be appropriate.

The relationship between the IS users' activity and the IS beneficiaries' activity may or may not be analogous to the relationship between the IS developers and the IS users. In many walks of life today, however, there

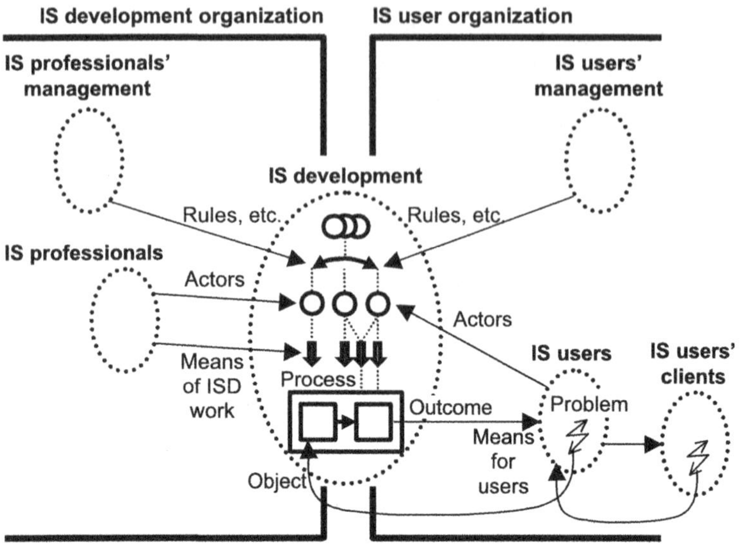

Figure 14.6
The composition of IS development activity (Korpela, Mursu, and Soriyan 2001)

is an expressed need for more mutual relations than before along a service chain. In business this trend is manifested in "network economy" and extranets. In health care also, a more collaborative relationship between professionals and patients or citizens is being demanded. IS practitioners are thus not the only ones searching for ethnographic, participatory, and cooperative methods for their work.

Elsewhere we have presented a more detailed analysis of ISD as an activity (Korpela, Mursu, and Soriyan 2001). We see it as a boundary-crossing temporary activity at the border of two departments, companies, or other organizations (figure 14.6). The starting point is a problem in the users' work process—a need for better facilities. If the users or their management believe the problem can be solved by new IT facilities, they will usually set up a project—that is, an ISD activity, to study and solve the problem. As previously discussed, there is a loop of relations between the IS use and ISD activities—the former provides the object (requirements) for the latter, and receives the outcome of the latter as a new means for itself. Similarly, the IS users need their improved facilities to address problems in their clients' activities. The clients' activity implies what kind of facilities the users will need.

The temporary ISD activity gets its actors from two permanent activities—the users' and the IS practitioners' ordinary activities. The latter actors can be from an in-house department within the user organization, or hired from outside. Even in the case of in-house development, the means of coordination of an ISD activity—project management rules, and so on—also stem to a large degree from two different management activities, presenting different organizational cultures. The various means of work of the ISD activity—methods of requirements analysis and design, and so forth—tend to originate from the IS professionals' side. The process of the ISD activity is often called the "systems development life cycle."

We intentionally emphasized that an ISD activity starts from perceived needs for change on the user side, and is not predetermined to apply any specific kind of technology in solving the users' problem. By this we want to stress that ultimately ISD is about *work development*, or "activity development." The basic task of ISD is to analyze the work activity to be facilitated by the would-be IS, and to figure out how a "problem"—or misfit, tension, defect, contradiction, demand—within it can be soothed by information-technological means.

In practice, of course, there are different kinds of ISD activities:

- At one extreme, "activity seeks software"—the focus is on intentional work development through whatever ready-made technologies may exist that could facilitate the work in question.
- At the other extreme, "software seeks activities"—many ISD projects start because a software company has made a successful deal, and the software package then needs to be "deployed" and "implemented" in the customer organization.
- In a mixed case, in a typical pilot or tailor-made software project, the mode and processes of a work activity are developed in parallel with developing a new software package to support that mode of work.
- In software package development, the use activity and ISD may not be present in reality at all—the software system is developed for an imagined, future ISD activity.

In any case, the software will remain sleeping unless it becomes a new means for the users when developing their work activity.

IS Research Facilitating IS Practice

We have mentioned that the elements of any work activity are produced by some other activity. Where does IS development get its actors, means of work, and means of coordination? Obviously, the actors are "produced" by educational activities—basically by university education in computer science, software engineering, or information systems, followed by on-the-job and continuing education activities. The means of systems development include hardware and software produced by various companies, but the core means are immaterial methods of analysis and design, originating from the theoretical work done in academic institutions. The means of coordination and control in ISD are essentially principles, rules, and methods of project management, which are implemented as corporate standards but are indirectly also based on academic theorizing. Thus if not directly, then indirectly IS research and education are some of the most important contributing activities for ISD.

Just as IS developers facilitate IS users, so do IS researchers facilitate IS practitioners by means of work and means of coordination (figure 14.7). The means are essentially methods of conducting various subtasks of ISD itself and ISD management. The methods can be materialized into tools, and they are often organized into comprehensive methodologies based on a unifying underlying set of principles, approaches, and theories. Like software, theories, methods, and tools are a "sleeping" technology until they are adopted by practicing IS developers in their work activity and transformed into skills.

The analogy between the ISD versus use activities on the one hand and the IS research versus development activities on the other hand can be extended further. Whether researchers realize it or not, IS practice provides the reason for existence for IS research—if IS research does not even indirectly facilitate IS practitioners in facilitating the IS users, then it is irrelevant in the society.

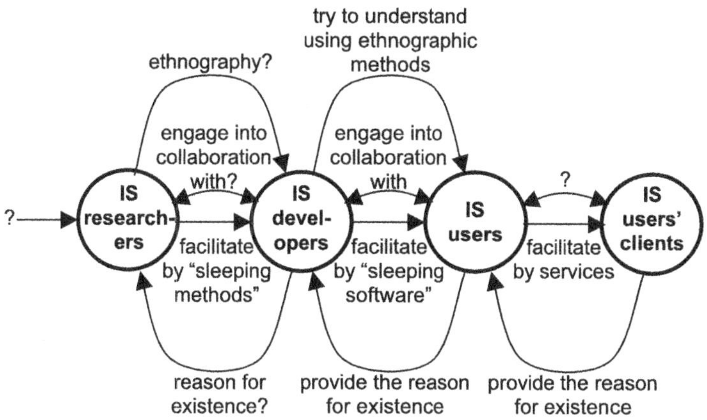

Figure 14.7
The schematic diagram expanded by IS research

Dozens of ISD methodologies have been developed by researchers, but few were ever used in practice. Similarly, many practical ISD projects have failed and the software developed in them was never used. As mentioned in the previous section, the main remedy for failing ISD projects has been to intensify the relationship between developers and users, through "user-centered" or "participatory/cooperative" design. By analogy, the main remedy for failing ISD methodologies should be to intensify the relationship between researchers and practitioners, through "practitioner-centered" or "participatory/cooperative" IS research. In the same way that IS practitioners must engage in a collaborative relationship with the IS users in order to meet their clients' needs, so must IS researchers engage in a collaborative setting with IS practitioners (figure 14.7).

To produce appropriate facilitation addressing the most important needs of the practitioners, researchers and practitioners have to jointly analyze the latter's work activity—that is, ISD practice. To understand ISD practice in real life, IS researchers need ethnographic methods as much if not more than the practitioners need ethnographic methods for ISD. What collaborative analysis and prototyping are for IS developers, *action research* (Avison et al. 1999) is for IS researchers.

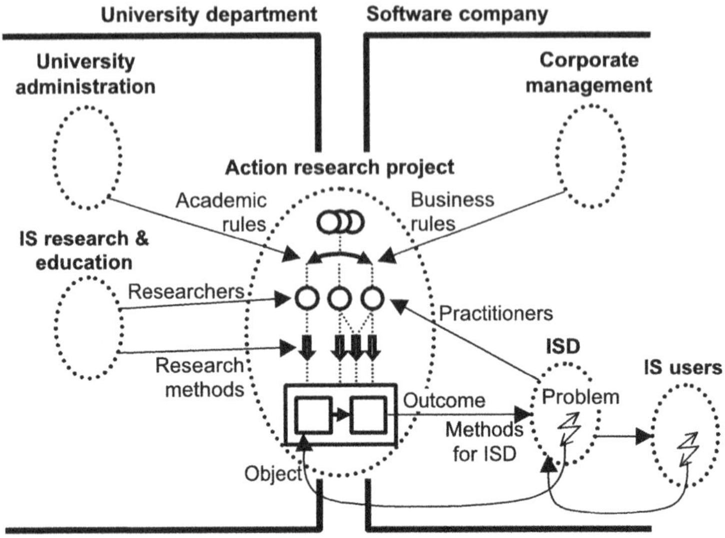

Figure 14.8
An action-research project on ISD as an activity

An action-research project as an activity (figure 14.8) is very similar to a collaborative ISD project (figure 14.6). The project is a temporary activity across the boundary of two organizations, namely, a university department and a software company or the like. The object of the action-research activity is a perceived need for transformation, a "problem," in the ISD practice of the software company in question. Through joint efforts of the practitioners and the researchers, the "problem" is intended to be transformed into a "solution," an outcome that can be adopted by the practitioners as improved methods in their current and future work. Action research resembles piloting in the sense that the current customer's problem is seen as a manifestation of a more general problem common to many customers. The outcome (software system in piloting, research results in action research) is intended to be packaged and applied to a wider market after the initial development.

In action research, the researchers are experts in research methods, while the practitioners are experts in the object—that is, their own work practice. However, if the practitioners are skilled and experienced in analyzing the users' work activity, they should be prepared to turn the same analytic and developmental skill to their own work activity. Therefore, in an action-research project on ISD, the means of work may not be as biased in favor of one group of actors only as they tend to be in ISD projects. A dichotomy is apparent, however, regarding the means of coordination—rules, methods, and techniques of project management—which may be rather different in academic research projects and in practical systems development projects.

Programming and software development in general has been studied to some extent, but unfortunately few comprehensive empirical research projects on ISD practice have been reported recently. It is thus likely that ISD today (Klischewski, chapter 15, this volume; Lyytinen, Rose, and Welke 1998; Russo 2000) is quite different from the model that the IS education in universities is based on. Like the Danish MARS project in the late 1980s and early 1990s (Mathiassen 1997, 1998), the MUST project (Bødker, Kensing, and Simonsen, chapter 13, this volume; Kensing, Simonsen, and Bødker 1998), also in Denmark, is a rare example of a long-term effort to study everyday ISD by action-research methods with the objective of facilitating the practitioners with improved methods. In the next section, we provide another example by presenting a smaller Nigerian undertaking with similar aims.

Case: The INDEHELA-Methods Project in Nigeria

Since 1998 we have been engaged in a research project called *INDEHELA-Methods* (Methods for Informatics Development for Health in Africa) in Nigeria, West Africa (Korpela et al. 2000; Soriyan et al. 2000). It is a joint project by the Obafemi Awolowo University (OAU), Ile-Ife, Nigeria, and the University of Kuopio, Finland. The main objectives of the project are, first, to produce empirical information and understanding of the practice and problems of ISD in Nigeria, and second, to facilitate Nigerian ISD practitioners by improved methods, techniques, practices, and education, according to their needs. The research design has three inputs followed by a constructive phase and dissemination of results (figure 14.9).

The main idea is to identify specific needs for improved methods in the existing practice, and then to use suitable "Northern" methods and

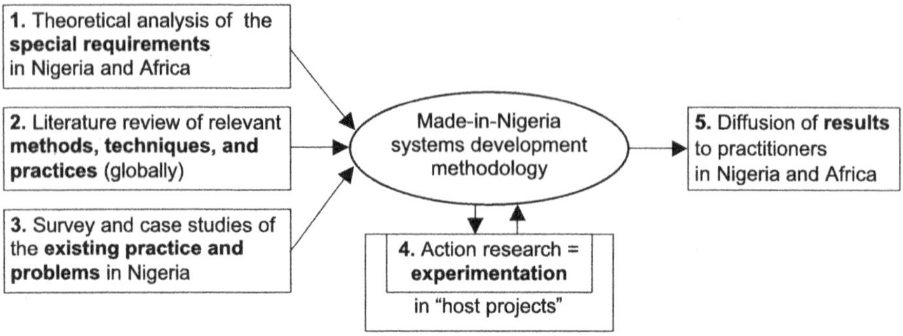

Figure 14.9
The overall research design of the INDEHELA-Methods project (Korpela et al. 2000)

practices as raw material in developing adapted methods and practices that are more appropriate to the requirements of Nigerian software and IS practitioners. Different methodologies are used in different parts of the research design:

- *Theoretical analysis and literature reviews* are used on the one hand in tentatively identifying factors in which Nigeria as a context for ISD might differ from industrialized countries (box 1 in figure 14.9), and on the other hand in identifying potential inputs from industrialized countries (box 2).
- *A quick questionnaire survey* is conducted in as many Nigerian software companies as possible, to get a "landscape view" of the industry as a whole and to identify the most appropriate areas for development, as perceived by the company managers (part of box 3).
- *In-depth case interviews* are conducted in a few different software companies focusing on one or two recent projects of theirs, to get a detailed "profile view" of how software applications and information systems are actually developed in Nigeria (part of box 3).
- *Action research* (box 4) is used in the constructive phase to experiment with potentially more appropriate methods and practices identified through the previous three nonparticipatory parts. New methods and practices are tested and further developed first in a health-care IS project

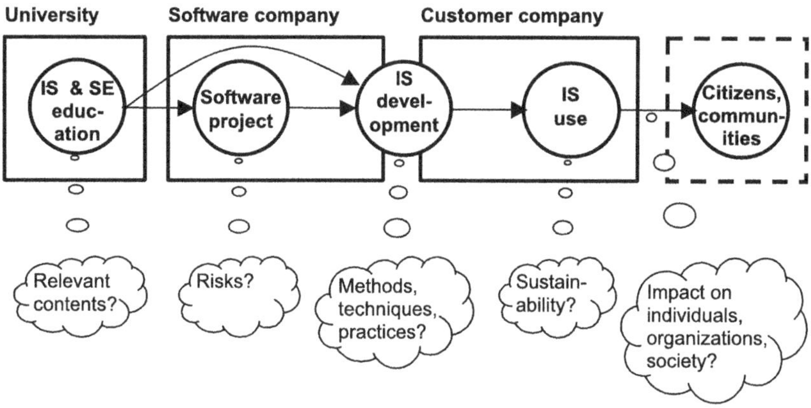

Figure 14.10
The main research questions in the INDEHELA-Methods project (Soriyan et al. 2000)

of the Obafemi Awolowo University itself, then in one or a couple of real-life projects in voluntary software companies.

• *Educational material* is produced as the deliverable outcome of the project, in the form of a draft textbook—*Lecture Notes on Information Systems Development in Africa*—which is used in disseminating the results of the project to students and practitioners.

The project started in 1998 and received funding until the end of 2001. Several research questions have been addressed by different researchers during the project. The research questions deal with different parts of the chain of activities around ISD (figure 14.10). Initially, the empirical research focused on the risk factors in software development projects in Nigeria compared to three other countries where a similar study had been conducted. The scope of this multicountry study soon appeared too limited, however, for our purposes (Mursu et al. 1999).

The main focus of empirical research was then shifted to painting the "landscape view" of software industry in general and the "portrait views" of specific ISD projects, to find out what kind of ISD methods, techniques, and practices are in use in the industry in Nigeria. Thereafter the research focus moved in two further directions—first, to studying which factors affect the long-term sustainability of IS in user organizations, and second, to assessing the relevance of the present university education in comparison to the needs of the service chain. Ultimately the project should discuss the impact of IS on the citizens and communities at the end of the service chain, and through them on the society in general. Regarding all the research questions, the objective is not only to describe how things are, but to proceed into a constructive phase where potential solutions are developed to address the perceived needs for improvement.

In the case studies we have used the activity-theoretical framework as a checklist (Korpela 1999) in discussing the actors, process, and means of the case projects. To avoid the abstractness of the theoretical model, we developed a couple of illustrated diagrams depicting different fictitious projects in a Nigerian setting, like the one outlined in figures 14.1 to 14.3. The fictitious projects were described to the interviewees using the illustrated diagrams as examples of what we are interested in, and the same elements of the real-life case projects were then discussed. The analyses of the real projects are summarized in similar diagrams supported by in-depth details of all the elements and the dynamics during the projects.

The case studies produce a backward-looking static view of projects that have been completed already. The real challenge is to proceed into the developmental phase in which the researchers enter an ongoing project and ask the practitioners to analyze the needs for improvement in their activity and their network.

The research design of the project is outlined here to illustrate one possible way of engaging IS researchers and practitioners in a collaborative development activity. At the time of the current book's publication, the project is ongoing and the main results remain to be published. Readers interested in more details on the research methodology and results are encouraged to contact the authors.

Discussion and Conclusion

In this chapter, we presented a rough overview of the activities and relationships along the IS service chain, focusing on the relationship between IS research and ISD. We kept the discussion on a very general level and did not, for instance, study in detail the way software development and ISD as activities are intermingled in various settings. We concentrated on the main activities along the service chain and ignored all the other activities linked to the main activities in the complex web that one would find in reality. We did not study the elements and relations within the activities in detail, and we merely offered a static snapshot picture instead of a dynamic motion picture of the historical development. Furthermore, we did not discuss the impact of organizational boundaries, financial transactions, gender-based or other cross-sectional divisions, or broader societal preconditions around the activity network.

The scope of scrutiny was intentionally limited to the basic relations, in order to keep the essential issues clear. The essential message is that *IS researchers need to engage in collaboration with IS practitioners*, just as the practitioners have realized that they need to engage in collaboration with the would-be users.

Although we applied the activity-theoretical framework in a very limited way in this chapter, we believe it is an exceptionally useful analytic framework for IS researchers because it combines individual/educational, technological, collective/organizational, dynamic, and networking aspects of real-life work into a comprehensive, systemic, theoretically grounded and sufficiently detailed whole. However, a few areas require further theoretical and methodological development. We have already mentioned the need for a more dynamic, developmental analysis of the tensions and "problems" within the network of activities. Such an analysis, however, should be conducted by the actors themselves in action-research settings.

Another area for major further research is the linkage between software development and ISD. We have suggested elsewhere (Korpela, Soriyan, and Olufokunbi 2000) that the activity-theoretical concept of individual action corresponds to the object-oriented modeling concept of use case, bridging the existing gap between software engineering methods and business or activity development methods (see the discussion of *task* by Kaptelinin in chapter 3). Additional research is needed to investigate this proposal in detail.

The notion of mediated relations between activities—that is, of the means of networking—is a new one and needs to be developed through further theoretical and empirical research. The same applies to the organizational, financial, divisional, and broader societal issues already mentioned (see Walsham 2000).

Much more empirical action research is required in two directions. First, what is ISD really like as a work practice today? Second, what kind of activities are IS education and research, what are their objects, outcomes, actors, means, and developmental "problems," and who facilitates the researchers (the question mark at the left end of figure 14.7—a potential place for social science input)? For the first part, researchers and practitioners need to jointly study and develop ISD practice. For the second part, researchers need to turn their analytic and developmental machinery toward themselves, to self-develop IS research as a collective work activity.

Note

The INDEHELA-Methods project is funded by the Academy of Finland. The figures were drawn by Reetta Korpela.

References

Avison, D. 1997. The "discipline" of Information Systems: Teaching, research and practice. In J. Mingers and F. Stowell, eds., *Information Systems: An Emerging Discipline?*, 113–136. New York: McGraw-Hill.

Avison, D., F. Lau, M. Myers, and P. A. Nielsen. 1999. Action research. *Communications of the ACM* 42: 94–97.

Bertelsen, O. W., and S. Bødker. 2000. Introduction: Information technology in human activity. *Scandinavian Journal of Information Systems* 12: 3–14.

Davis, G. B. 2000. Information systems conceptual foundations: Looking backward and forward. In R. Baskerville, J. Stage, and J. I. DeGross, eds., *Organizational and Social Perspectives on Information Technology*, 61–82. Boston: Kluwer.

Engeström, Y. 1987. *Learning by expanding: An activity-theoretical approach to developmental research*. Helsinki: Orienta-Konsultit.

Engeström, Y. 1990. *Learning, Working and Imagining: Twelve Studies in Activity Theory*. Helsinki: Orienta-Konsultit.

Engeström, Y. 1999. Activity theory and individual and social transformation. In Y. Engeström, R. Miettinen, and R. Punamäki, eds., *Perspectives on Activity Theory*, 19–38. Cambridge, England: Cambridge University Press.

Engeström, Y., R. Engeström, and T. Vähäaho. 1999. When the centre does not hold: The importance of knotworking. In S. Chaiklin, M. Hedegaard, and U. J. Jensen, eds., *Activity Theory and Social Practice: Cultural-Historical Approaches*, 345–374. Aarhus: Aarhus University Press.

Engeström, Y., and R. Miettinen. 1999. Introduction. In Y. Engeström, R. Miettinen, and R. Punamäki, eds., *Perspectives on Activity Theory*, 1–16. Cambridge, England: Cambridge University Press.

Greenbaum, J., and M. Kyng, eds. 1991. *Design at Work: Cooperative Design of Computer Systems*. Hillsdale, NJ: Erlbaum.

Hedegaard, M., S. Chaiklin, and U. J. Jensen. 1999. Activity theory and social practice: An introduction. In S. Chaiklin, M. Hedegaard, and U. J. Jensen, eds., *Activity Theory and Social Practice: Cultural-Historical Approaches*, 12–30. Aarhus: Aarhus University Press.

Iivari, J., and K. Lyytinen. 1998. Research on information systems development in Scandinavia—unity in plurality. *Scandinavian Journal of Information Systems* 10: 135–185.

Kensing, F., and J. Blomberg. 1998. Participatory Design: Issues and concerns. *Computer Supported Cooperative Work* 7: 167–185.

Kensing, F., J. Simonsen, and K. Bødker. 1998. MUST—a method for participatory design. *Human-Computer Interaction* 13: 167–198.

Korpela, M. 1999. Activity analysis and development in a nutshell. Handout, version 2. Available at http://www.uku.fi/atkk/actad/nutshell.html [5 August 1999].

Korpela, M., A. Mursu, and H. A. Soriyan. 2001. Information systems development as an activity. *Computer-Supported Cooperative Work*: Special issue on Activity Theory and Design 11(1–2).

Korpela, M., H. A. Soriyan, and K. C. Olufokunbi. 2000. Activity analysis as a method for information systems development: General introduction and experiments from Nigeria and Finland. *Scandinavian Journal of Information Systems* 12: 191–210.

Korpela, M., H. A. Soriyan, K. C. Olufokunbi, and A. Mursu. 2000. Made-in-Nigeria systems development methodologies: An action research project in the health sector. In C. Avgerou and G. Walsham, eds., *Information Technology in Context: Studies from the Perspective of Developing Countries*, 134–152. London: Ashgate.

Kuutti, K. 1999. Activity theory, transformation of work, and information systems design. In Y. Engeström, R. Miettinen, and R. Punamäki, eds., *Perspectives on Activity Theory*, 360–376. Cambridge, England: Cambridge University Press.

Lyytinen, K., G. Rose, and R. Welke. 1998. The brave new world of development in the internetwork computing architecture (InterNCA): or how distributed computing platforms will change systems development. *Information System Journal* 8: 241–253.

Mathiassen, L. 1997. *Reflective Systems Development.* 2 vols. Dr. tech. thesis, Aalborg University, Aalborg.

Mathiassen, L. 1998. Reflective Systems Development. *Scandinavian Journal of Information Systems* 10: 67–118.

Mingers, J., and F. Stowell, eds. 1997. *Information Systems: An Emerging Discipline?* New York: McGraw-Hill.

Mursu, A., H. A. Soriyan, K. C. Olufokunbi, and M. Korpela. 1999. From software risks to sustainable information systems: Setting the stage for a Delphi study in Nigeria. *Journal of Global Information Technology Management* 2: 57–71.

Nurminen, M. I., P. Reijonen, and A. Tuomisto. 1994. Whose work is software? In G. E. Bradley and H. W. Hendrick, eds., *Human Factors in Organizational Design and Management—IV (ODAM IV)*, 381–386. Amsterdam: Elsevier.

Russo, N. L. 2000. Expanding the horizons of information systems development. In R. Baskerville, J. Stage, and J. I. DeGross, eds., *Organizational and Social Perspectives on Information Technology*, 103–111. Boston: Kluwer.

Soriyan, H. A., A. S. Mursu, A. D. Akinde, and M. J. Korpela. 2001. Information systems development in Nigerian software companies: Research methodology and assessment from the healthcare sector's perspective. *Electronic Journal of Information Systems in Developing Countries* 5. Available at http://www.is.cityu.edu.hk/ejisdc/ejisdc.htm

Walsham, G. 2000. Globalization and IT: Agenda for research. In R. Baskerville, J. Stage, and J. I. DeGross, eds., *Organizational and Social Perspectives on Information Technology*, 195–210. Boston: Kluwer.

15

Reaching out for Commitments: Systems Development as Networking

Ralf Klischewski

The objective of research in the fields of information systems, systems development, organizational informatics, or participatory design is to reflect on the interrelationships between complex social activities and the implementation of information technology (IT) in organizations. The ongoing effort to provide sound theory explaining these interrelationships is impeded not only by incompatibilities in the approaches to scientifically framing "the technical" and "the social," but also by the rapid changes in the kinds of new IT emerging and in its methods of dissemination:

1. *Drawing a line between systems development and systems use has become less appropriate* for the purpose of reflecting on current practice. More and more, systems development includes the customization, deployment, and use of standard products, and systems use more and more requires situated design and creativity (adaptation, configuration, customizing, modeling, interface design, and so on). Thus, the life cycle of a software product consist of consecutive development/use activities.

2. *The goal of systems development and use is to create an infrastructure* serving organizational needs, with both "developers" and "users" contributing to its growth. Organizational units concerned with systems development and use subsequently embark on joint efforts (instead of one unit delivering a ready-to-use product to some other unit(s)).

3. As *computer-based networks extend system boundaries for IT applications*, the various actors using and cooperating via the system are often separated by organizational boundaries, linked by some cooperative arrangement rather than because of a hierarchical power structure. Instead of one social actor being able to exercise power over all the other

actors, *development and use take place in distributed environments* that are neither organized nor controllable as a whole—that is, each organizational unit involved is capable of independent decision making. Thus, communication within the project and with users and/or other stakeholders, sharing views and perspectives, clarifying conflicts, achieving consensus, and adapting to an evolving correspondence between actors—all these measures become more and more critical success factors.

Reframing the Systems Development Process

In practice, much of the work in information systems development is still organized in projects, but, increasingly, the actors involved find themselves in an unstable organizational environment for the time of the project duration. New challenges for project management include coping dynamically with questions such as the following: Who constitutes the project members? What are the project aims and tasks? Who and when to contract with, inside and outside the project, and what for? How to plan and evaluate progress? Scientific observation and reflection always require a framing for the duration of inquiry. Because established frames for process modeling usually assume stable organizational conditions, we need new kinds of research approaches in order to answer the above (and other) questions.

Here, the notion of information systems development (ISD) will comprise all activities involved in getting a computer-based information system in an organization up and running (Kling and Lamb 1999; see also Korpela et al., chapter 14, this volume, for clarification of the term). In the research field addressing ISD the search for adequate framing has led to different assumptions and "schools" subscribing to a certain kind of "great divide" (Bowker et al. 1997) between the social and the technical, each centered around a specific key object of interest: ISD as establishing sociotechnical systems, as a social activity, or as part of organizational change (see Klischewski 2000). To shed light on the dynamic phenomena, research in this field concentrates either on "factors" explaining process variations by studying their associations with independent variables, or on "recipes" linking dependent with independent variables (e.g., Robey and Newman 1996). Process models attempt to relate subsequent events (such as "encounters" linked by three kinds of "episodes"; Newman and

Robey 1992) or to provide a rich picture of the process as a whole (e.g., stage models; Damsgaard and Scheepers 1999).

All these approaches provide a rich framework for inquiry. But they are limited in their ability to explain the development progress, because they (1) focus on a single aspect, which tends to suppress reflection on other driving forces, and (2) assume stability for the frame of inquiry, where shifts—for example, in the system boundaries, the set of actors, or the organization in focus—challenge the validity of the overall picture. A theoretical basis for inquiry in today's ISD therefore should address the issue distribution and dynamics. Of the approaches already introduced in ISD research, actor-network theory (ANT) best fulfills this requirement since it is concerned with explaining the growth of networks, relating various elements without any presuppositions about how to frame the relationship of social actors and IT.

Here, a new approach called "systems development as networking" is suggested to reflect ISD processes. The key research questions is the following: *How do systems developers recruit and mobilize (enough) allies to forge a network that will bring out and support the use of "the system"?* Pursuing this question, it is possible to (1) bypass the "great divide" in such a way that the relationship of humans and IT may remain undefined, (2) integrate the microlevel and the macrolevel of reflecting on systems development processes, and (3) provide new frames for conceptualizing and managing the phenomena related especially to distributed and dynamic development environments.

In the following pages, I explain how ANT can support this kind of research. Based on this theoretical approach, ISD is reconceptualized as networking with (black)boxed commitments. This framing of ISD is applied to a case study of the implementation of computerized support for the examination administration of a large university. Summing up, the potential of approaching "systems development as networking" is pointed out for ISD research and practice.

Actor-Network Theory for ISD Research

Reconstructing the "success" of science and technology as the extension of networks enrolling human and nonhuman resources, Latour suggests it is important to "arrive before the facts and machines are blackboxed or [to] follow the controversies that reopen them" (first "rule of method"; Latour 1987, 258). Being concerned with the practice of science, he intends to completely bypass the subject-object dichotomy that is still the basis of the modernist scientific worldview. Instead, he investigates the relationship between humans and nonhumans and interprets "scientific" approaches as "the gaining of access, through experiments and calculations, to entities that at first do not have the same characteristics as humans do" (Latour 1999, 259).

ANT had its origins in social anthropology and the sociology of science, to "denote an emerging set of ideas about networks of association, in which groups of heterogeneous allies, by virtue of the strengths of their aligned interests, create those black-boxes that eventually come to be seen and accepted as the facts of everyday life" (McMaster, Vidgen, and Wastell 1999, 345). Within ANT (see Law 1997) a "network" is much like a structure, except that there is no assumption that specific links or nodes in the network are guaranteed. Networks may be imagined as scripts, which means that one may read a script from, for instance, a machine that tells or prescribes the roles that it, the machine, expects other elements in the network to play. Building and maintaining networks is an uphill battle; the links and nodes in the network do not last on their own but need constant maintenance work, the support of other links and nodes. Thus, networks are processes or achievements rather than given relations or structures. To become associated with and enrolled in those heterogeneous networks, "actors" (or "actants") may be both human and nonhuman—that is, the various elements of the heterogeneous network are all equally able to act on one another. For ISD research, ANT seems promising since it

- Bypasses the "great divide" of the technical and the social: elements of the network (e.g., social actors or IT devices) do not have to be prescribed as such. Investigation focuses only on the interrelations of the heterogeneous elements enfolding the network without having to subscribe to certain assumptions about the relationship of social actors and IT.
- Makes it possible to integrate the microlevel and macrolevel of reflecting on ISD processes: Latour (1991, 118) argues that "the macro-structure of society is made of the same stuff as the micro-structure" and

therefore the same methodology may be applied. There are objections to this claim (see Walsham 1997), since focusing only on action excludes the influence of persistent institutionalized structures. However, in analyzing ISD processes, the ANT approach offers great potential for integrating reflection on everyday project work and on the whole process life cycle (see below).

During the last decade, the work of Bruno Latour and others that pertains to ANT has inspired a number of researchers to reflect on project experiences and to conceptualize the interrelationship of actors in the sociotechnical contexts of systems development. Framing systems development as networking draws on the following claims relating ISD and ANT as results of past research:

- *ANT as practical research method.* It provides concepts (theory) as ways of viewing elements and suggests tracing these elements in empirical work (methodology). People and artifacts (e.g., organizational members and computer-based systems) may be analyzed with the same conceptual apparatus (Walsham 1997).
- *IT as subject for blackboxing.* Analyzing a case, Vidgen and Master (1996, 250) show how IT implementations "become blackboxes as a result of dissemination through time and space."
- *Translation of success factors.* Gasson (1999, 320, 307) suggests that "the success of a design initiative is dependent upon the 'translation' of the interests of influential actors" and therefore "design goal definition must proceed recursively through the processes of design, which require new approaches to the design and development of organizational information systems."
- *Beyond strong symmetry of humans and nonhumans.* Jones (1999) argues that interpretation is central to the process of information systems design, implementation, and use. Between structuration theory and ANT he calls for a "relaxation of the assumptions of strong symmetry between human and material agency" (p. 299). Since intentionality is a specifically human characteristic, "human agents seek to channel material agency to shape actions of other human agents" (p. 297).
- *Toward process management.* As McMaster, Vidgen, and Wastell (1999, 352) seek to "understand adequately the process through which

stabilized networks form," they suggest two models (courtroom and a parliamentary democracy) of "due process" to enable an ongoing approach emphasizing inclusion and exclusion of humans and nonhumans in ISD.

• *Methods as actants.* Atkinson (2000) employs ANT to explain the use of a given ISD method (i.e., SISTeM) and the resulting interventions in organizational problem situations. He introduces the method as a "mutable mobile" being enacted, enrolled, and translated in actor networks and, at the same time, as an actant contributing to the change of existing networks in organizational work settings.

ISD research related to ANT has provided a rich body of valuable insights. However, ANT is primarily an analytic approach, and the ANT-based framings of ISD elaborated so far are not appropriate for generating methods and guidelines for IS practitioners. To achieve this, we need to focus in more detail on the parts of the network that (1) contribute to the dynamics—that is, to the growth of the network, (2) provide the "glue" for relating the distributed network elements, and (3) can be manipulated by the social actors involved (e.g., system developers). Here, I suggest focusing on the role of commitments, but other aspects (such as the impact of trust) need to be explored as well.

Creating Networks by Boxing and Circulating Commitments

Inspired by the work of Latour and others, the notion of networking is used here to conceptualize systems development "in-the-making." As noted earlier, the key research question is the following: *How do systems developers recruit and mobilize (enough) allies to forge a network that will bring out and support the use of "the system"?* There can be many answers to this question, depending on how the network relations are explored in detail. As one possible answer, the following hypothesis is used to trace project action and provide methodological guidance:

> Systems development, aiming at establishing a system based on computer networks, must also establish a network of commitments by all actors whose consent and effort are necessary to make use of the computer system's potential by putting these commitments in a "(black) box" and circulating them among those actors.

Here, the notion of commitment refers to an agreement that something within an social actor's realm may be moved around, transformed, and allocated at some place for the purpose of systems development and use. "Something" could be physical or abstract objects (software, computer, financial asset), personal opinions expressed in public (judgment, decision, consent), certain tasks to fulfill or activities to do in the future (work effort, availability), professional knowledge (e.g., about work processes), or anything else that might be a resource for effective system use.

To get a computer-based system in an organization up and running, it needs subsequent promotion and support by a number of social actors. Each commitment to promotion and support could be essential and a prerequisite for further steps of development and implementation. Achieving a single commitment (including resolving conflicts) might even require complex social activities. But as soon as it is "there," the following activities just draw on this commitment—that is, further steps in development and implementation align all past commitments to establish the flow and allocation of resources in due time.

In this view, commitments are to reduce complexity and to channel and transform the *input* (the resources committed by a social actor) toward an *output* (the allocation of the resources required for effective use of the computer-based system—for example, exploitable expertise, continuous service, process patterns, application procedures, work organization, system components). To work with commitments in the development process, they must be *boxed*. In another words, a line has to be drawn around them, to take them away from the actor who made the commitment, to circulate them and make them a "function" or eventually a "brick" in building the system. Being boxed, commitments are (immutable) mobile plans for allocating resources.

In principle, the boxes could be anything as long as they are mobile and circulate commitments on allocating resources. Typical examples found in projects are public opinions, common beliefs, role assignments, documents (reports, contracts), budgets, accepted work routines, and a variety of technical devices. These boxes become *black* as soon as they are referred to only in terms of their input and output, as they become part of other boxes, being transformed, without making visible the social process in which they have been established or that could lead to a withdrawal of the commitment. In each situated development and implementation process, a unique wrapping of commitment boxes is needed to create a network relating actors' resources to places and transforming those resources into a function for effective system use.

Whereas *blackbox* and *immutable mobiles* are prominent terms within ANT, *commitment* is not. This notion refers to the intentionality of humans as distinct from nonhumans. This is an a priori assumption for the duration of the inquiry in order to provide an operational framework for ISD research to be able to follow systems developers through their projects. The following case study attempts to point out the role of commitments circulated, their "acting on" other elements in the network—how the machinery (software) calls for commitments, how the social actors call for commitments, how the social actors commit themselves (or not), how the existence (or lack) of commitments affects the development process and transforms the software system, and so on.

Case Study: Computer Support for an Examination Administration

A large German university (not including the university hospital) employs 3,300 people and provides education for about 40,000 enrolled students (1988–1999). The organization is structured into nineteen more-or-less independent departments as well as some functional units (such as the central computing center). In 1996, the university established and institutionalized a task force for its own organizational development (Project University Development or PUD) with one focus on examination administration. There, the need for a computer-based system was triggered by escalating examination requirements due to the modularization of study programs as well as the university management's interest in decentralizing the examination administration (i.e., eliminating central examination offices). The project planning and the effort to enroll a number of actors to support the project started in 1997. The introduction of a computerized information system mainly affects the few dozen persons handling the administration procedures. But with a secure infrastructure, every staff member and student could become a user of the system (to avoid duplicated effort in recording and communicating relevant data).

The author plays an active role in the case reported. For someone who is a teacher, researcher, and IS expert at the same time, there is not always a clear distinction between the roles of an IT user, scientific observer, and member of a development team. In the following discussion, "IS expert team" refers to the author and his colleague as well as to three students who assisted with the development work for a limited time. Further technical development is carried out by the selected software producer and the university's central computing center.

The material presented is based on electronic and printed project documents collected from the very beginning, including meeting invitations, public opinion statements, official meeting notes, as well as internal diary notes from project members. In April 1999 the IS expert team issued a report on the case analysis as a basis for introducing a computerized system to support the examination administration. The report included the stakeholder map shown in figure 15.1 (translated from German) to depict the relevant actors as potential users at that time (who, except for the public, also had access to the report).

Throughout the course of the project several stakeholder maps have been used. Variations of the above include/exclude individuals and professional groups, specific departments, examination offices, works councils, data-protection officer, development actors (software vendors(s), computing center(s) within the university, IS expert team). Since 1997 many commitments (or the lack of them) have influenced the course of the ISD. A number of the commitments have been regarded as essential for the progress of the project (in retrospect we have identified those as milestones; see also the last section). Thus, the table of commitments included as table 15.1 represents one way of telling the project story, including the resources related to the project and the kind of boxing by which the commitments for resources were circulated (see Klischewski 2000 for more details).

Each of these commitments is related to a series of events with certain actors involved, each has been configured differently in a box, and each box has been more or less circulated, used, and translated to advance the project. None of these commitments are independent; all draw on commitments circulated before. To demonstrate the analytic frame in more detail, we reopen the box of the commitment "We run the system!"

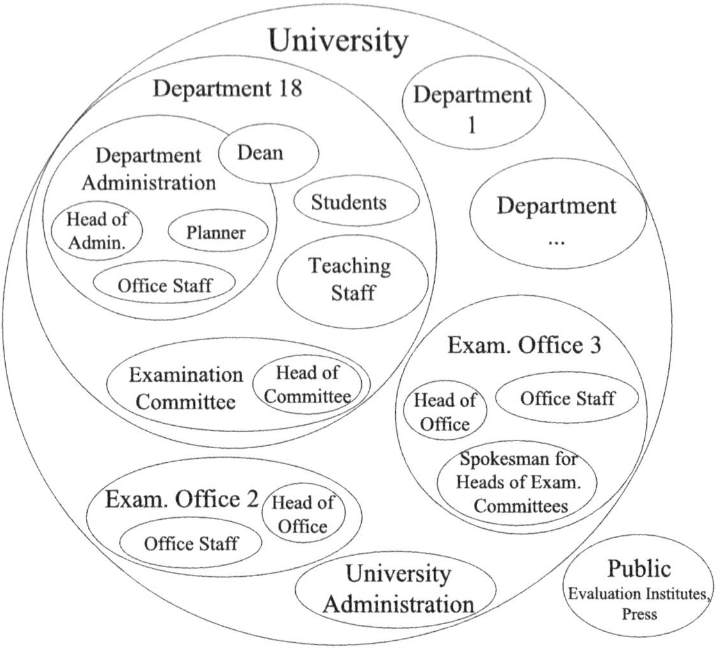

Figure 15.1
Stakeholder map of social actors concerned with the use of an IS for examination administration

(made by the informatics department by the end of 1999) and examine it more thoroughly as an extension of the network "in-the-making" to support the use of the system. The following series of commitments interrelating social actors and resources necessary for the project represents the history of this commitment and, at the same time, the fragile structure supporting it (see figure 15.2).

1. *IS for decentralized examination administration!* In 1997, the manager (not an IS expert) of the *PUD*-subproject (on reorganization of the examination administration) circulated a study of the history and past organizational development of the examination administration at this university that calls for a decentralization policy. Both the informatics and the economics department subscribe to this policy, as they agree to participate in the pilot project (1998). In addition to reflecting the outspoken and circulated opinion, the commitment is further boxed

Table 15.1
Commitments essential for the development project

Commitments essential for development	Boxing for circulation	Resources related
Signing up of IS expert team for systems development (July 1997)	Meeting notes, role: expert, (later: contract/budget)	Work effort, professional expertise, availability
"Buy! Don't make!"—decision of major stakeholders to use an existing software and to call for customization and additional development if necessary (May 1998)	Public opinion, common understanding	Opinion, consent
Agreement of administration staff to share work expertise in detail (Nov. 1998)	Report on workplace analysis	Consent, professional expertise
Cooperation agreement between university and software producer (Feb. 1999)	Tender, contract, software	Consent, financial asset, software
IT experts within the university subscribe to observing privacy regulations (Feb. 1999)	Public opinion, system specification	Consent, professional expertise
Administration and pilot departments agree to formal involvement of the works councils and their participation on a regular basis (Oct. 1999)	Public opinion, contract	Consent, work effort
Departments (informatics and economics), PUD, university administration, and central computing center agree on cooperation during implementation (Nov. 1999)	Signed document ("goal agreement")	Roles, responsibilities
Departmental staff shifts daily agenda to concentrate on system introduction (Nov. 1999)	Roles, tasks, schedules	Work effort, availability, professional expertise
"We run the system!"—the commitment of the informatics department for server hosting (Dec. 1999)	Running system, assignment, role	Professional expertise, work effort, availability, IT devices

Table 15.1 (continued)

Commitments essential for development	Boxing for circulation	Resources related
Decision to put the system in productive mode (i.e., some portions of examination administration now rely on the established computer support) (March 2000)	Formal decision, roles, tasks, schedules	Consent, work effort, availability, professional knowledge

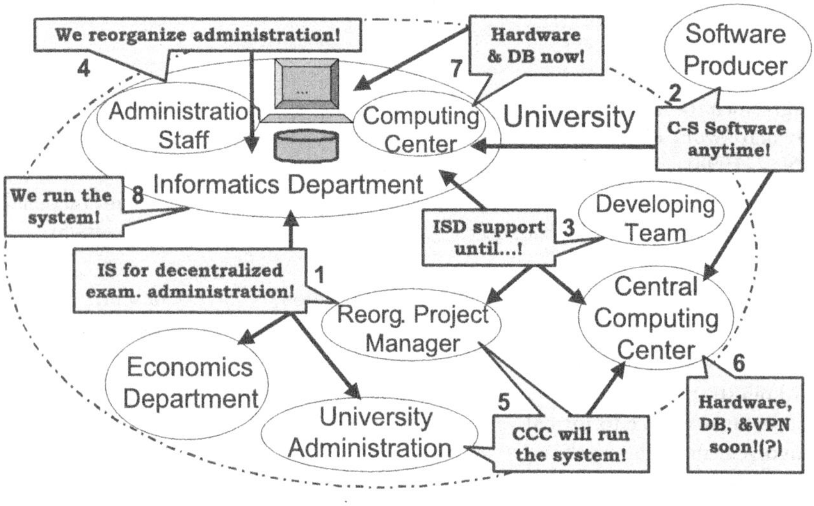

Figure 15.2
Actor network supporting the commitment "We run the system!", focusing on social actors and commitments for allocating resources

and sustained by signing a "goal agreement" between the departments, PUD, and the university administration in 1999.

2. *Client-server-software anytime!* The agreement between the university and the software producer (reached in early 1999) stipulates that the university may draw on the latest release as well as operational support as soon as it is ready for deployment. This commitment was boxed in a contract in July 1999. In addition, an employee of the software producer sets up a test installation at the informatics department (April 1999).

3. *ISD expertise and support limited until year 2000!* The engagement of the IS expert team had been based on (or boxed by) four single contracts with the PUD (totaling seventeen months between 1998 and 2000) with resources for only part-time consulting services and partly to manage/carry out the development and implementation under the formal guidance of the PUD. For various reasons (an unsatisfactory financial basis, project delays, short-term contract offers only), the IS expert team made clear (at project meetings, in a letter circulated to the social actors involved) that its expertise and support would not be available beyond the year 2000.

4. *The central computing center will run the system!* Although the central computing center has offered to run the system (i.e., to host the server and to provide a secure network for client access as well as user support) since 1998, it refused to engage seriously in the project (to allocate any resources) before the university administration along with PUD decided that the central computing center should provide this service and therefore will receive additional resources from the university. Due to difficulties in reorganization of the university IT services (at the same time another IT department was dissolved), the formal decision (i.e., the boxing) was delayed until October 1999.

5. *We reorganize administration!* The introduction of a new study program forces the informatics department to reorganize examination-administration procedures, which can only be accomplished with computer support. To avoid using some preliminary computer support and to combine reorganization with system introduction, departmental actors try to put pressure on the project. In November 1999, the IS expert team meets with the planner of the informatics department to agree on tasks, responsibilities, and a schedule for the implementation procedure in this department. For the next few months, introducing the computer support becomes a high priority on the daily agenda of the planner and other staff members (competing with the staff's commitments to a number of other pressing tasks). The IS expert team achieves a boxing by elaborating an accepted project plan (including role assignment, tasks, and schedules) for each organizational unit involved.

6. *Hardware, database, and virtual private network soon!(?)* In project meetings, the central computing center always promised to provide

the necessary hardware, database, and virtual private network shortly after it was officially assigned to run the system. The center's general responsibility was boxed in a "goal agreement" between the main stakeholders. However, because of complicated administrative procedures, a risk-avoidance strategy, the lack of personnel resources, the need to get acquainted with new technology, and other factors, the center failed to fulfill its assigned role. In addition, center administrators refused to agree to any kind of service agreement, fixed project plan or schedule, or any other kind of detailed contract. In short, a boxing of the commitment beyond the outspoken general intention was never achieved.

7. *Hardware and database now!* In April 1999, the software producer and the departmental computing center set up a test system in the informatics department accessible by a number of clients via local network. As the central computing center realizes its failure to provide the service assigned, one member brings in a machine, leaving the informatics department to install an operating system, the database, and the server software (provided by the software producer). To meet the pressing needs of the department, the IS expert team and the departmental computing center set up a stand-alone system ready to use in January 2000. Here, the boxing is the installation itself: due to the general role assignment, the departmental computing center has to maintain any system it sets up within the department.

8. *We run the system!* Facing the situation at hand, all departmental actors involved (head of department, department council, administration staff, head of examination committee, departmental computing center) agree that the department should run a computer-supported administration system of its own—at least until the central computing center is ready to take over. In March 2000, the IS expert team trains three members of the department administration in the use of the system. Right away the new users start to enter results of the examinations that have taken place in recent weeks. The PUD and university administration do not object to this, although the economics department—facing similar needs—is left without any computer support. However, the departmental commitment is based on oral agreements only (no formalized boxing) since, at this time, everyone thought the stand-alone system would be needed for a few weeks only.

Epilogue. In December 2000, PUD and the IS expert team have withdrawn their commitment for project coordination and assistance. However, the other actors involved are trying to continue, and so is the networking, so that there is no end to this story yet. In October 2000, the departmental administration is facing a number of operational problems: the technical situation is still the same (there is still no central service), but the departmental planner (as the organizational expert) left his job in April and the IS expert team finished its last contract in July. Some procedures turned out to be complicated, requiring an unacceptable degree of effort. The software producer sent a patch to ease the workarounds, but without secure networking facilities the producer is not allowed to log into the system and to provide online support. Rumors about the system's performance have started to spread. The enthusiasm of the new users is decreasing as operational problems become serious, and the lack of overall support turns out to seriously impede the motivation of the administration staff. After becoming obvious that the preliminary stand-alone installation lacks organizational support, it has drawn the critical attention of the work councils and data-protection experts.

Commitments in Distributed Systems Development (Case Discussion)

Taking part in this effort to get an information system up and running to support the university's examination administration taught us (the IS experts) a number of lessons. We assume some of these are characteristic of projects that are distributed in the sense that they involve a number of social actors from different, more-or-less independent organizational units:

- The experience of "missing links" to draw on necessary resources in due time is one of the major obstacles to accomplishing project tasks.
- With no executable power structures framing the project environment, the declared intentions of the social actors involved to support the project are not sufficient for allocating resources when they are needed.
- Selecting and accessing resources are critical success factors: a large part of the development work is to achieve stabilized relations between

all actors (humans and nonhumans) to create a network that eventually will support the use of the system.

Based on this experience, we adopted Latour's (1997) idea "that by following circulations we can get more than by defining entities, essences or provinces." We started to identify commitments—that is, social actors' intentions to allocate resources—as independent mobile actants, and we learned how they became boxed and how other social actors related to those boxes. Pursuing this approach, systems development emerged as a process of forming a network of associations aligning heterogeneous resources concentrated in a few places (e.g., computing center, departmental administration, software producer) that are connected with one another by (black)boxed commitments. In this way, we can now identify network structures (e.g., see figure 15.2) supporting the use of the system.

But the network established in this case is far from being sustainable. Some of the relations seem stabilized; the respective commitments for allocating resources (e.g., decentralization of examination administration, producer's provision of software and support) are boxed in a way that succeeding action draws on their output as "for granted" without opening the box—these boxes have become black. Other relations are not stable because the commitments themselves are not or might not be sustainable (ISD expertise, hosting assignment)—the respective boxes are black only for some period of time, but (maybe) not for the process as a whole. Instability of other relations might occur in case the allocation of resources turns out to be worthless after a period of time. The social actor's commitments are still there (e.g., by the informatics departments to run the system), but now stand-alone installation needs additional resources and commitments (e.g., a secure network access for the producer's online support)—that is, the networking must spread out further to stabilize the relations it already achieved.

Because we were mainly interested in project-management issues, we focused on the social actors bringing in their commitments to allocate resources. However, the software installed is also an actor "calling" for resources and respective commitments (to allocate hardware, network, trained users, workflow organization). It is also a blackbox of its own—that is, it is a mobile but unchangeable commitment to set up a client-server architecture. Here, ANT offers the potential to analyze the impact of commitments made in the past at some distant place, becoming relevant for the development project at stake by using existing infrastructure and IT devices. For example, the software imported by the university is "committed" to certain ideas about how to handle examination administration. It is a task of future research to examine the impact of these past and distant commitments and to suggest how project management could cope with them.

Networking for ISD Research and Practice

The key question posed toward the beginning of the chapter was the following: *How do systems developers recruit and mobilize (enough) allies to forge a network that will bring out and support the use of "the system"?* The answer provided here is that they reach out for commitments, thus aligning social actors and their resources in a network. From the corner of ISD research, what do we gain by applying this perspective?

First, focusing on boxing and circulating commitments as recurrent activities implies a different approach to analyzing development processes and setting up project agendas, especially in such distributed project environments where commitments cannot be achieved by wielding hierarchical power. On the one hand, systems development as networking must strive for stability of relations (especially by boxing commitments) so that other actors can rely on and are encouraged to take the next step—thus a sustainable structure for resource allocation can be created step by step. On the other hand (and at the same time), it must enable translation and transformation of network relations such as identifying necessary resources to be aligned, enrolling new actors, allowing actors to work with past commitments as resources, renewing or substituting commitments under changing conditions, and so on. Thus, focusing on commitments in ISD puts in more concrete terms what Lanzara calls "designing-in-action": "a practical, context-sensitive mode of design that feeds on the dynamic tension between the requirements of change and stability" (Lanzara 1999).

Second, with ANT's origin in analytic research, ANT-based framings of ISD elaborated so far have not been particularly useful for generating methods and guidelines for IS practitioners. By focusing on commitments, we can now use ANT to explain in more detail what actually contributes to the growth of networks supporting the system, what provides the "glue" for relating the distributed network elements, and what kind of objectives social actors should strive for to get a system up and running.

Third, this approach to framing the project inquiry can also be used to develop a methodological framework for analyzing ISD processes as well as guiding practitioners. Such a framework should elaborate on:

Microlevel analysis: events-commitments-events The whole process of systems development may be structured on the microlevel by identifying subsequent social events (meetings, activities) leading to one or more commitments. The links between these events are the boxed and circulated commitments as preconditions (required for the success of the event) and as postconditions (as a basis for future social events), forming a network of commitments as the development proceeds. The level of granularity for analysis is flexible; events come into focus according to the observer's subjective judgment of the commitment's importance for the development progress.

Project history as accumulation of commitments The accumulation of commitments represents the project history. It may be described by identifying the increasing number and complexity of boxes that become more or less "black" in the sense that the project budget and time constraints usually do not make it possible to disengage or expose the boxes as the development moves on. In addition, macrolevel models of the development process can be constructed by grouping several (kinds of) commitments, where each group represents a stage of the process as a whole. The networking approach allows for an evolutionary perspective—that is, process modeling is possible while the process is still going on.

Project management: commitments as milestones Certain (groups of) commitments may be interpreted as milestones, which makes it possible to plan and carry out project management: What kinds of commitments do we need to set up this system in this organizational context? Who can/must commit the required resources? What kind of process and what kind of preconditions do we need in order to achieve this? It is a requirement-driven approach, bringing into focus social actors, resources, and environmental conditions as the development moves on. Recurrent activities to achieve such milestones include the following: identifying the necessary resources to be aligned; enrolling new actors; calling for, boxing, and circulating commitments; allowing actors to work with past commitments as resources; and renewing or substituting commitments under changing conditions.

Methods and tools: computer support for process modeling The networking approach opens up a passage for a new generation of methods and tools. Given a number of empirical studies, it could be worth rethinking the issue of computer-supported process modeling based on events and commitments, possibly leading to new ways of supporting systems development and project management.

To sum up, systems development as networking brings into focus the developers' work to subsequently reach for commitments, thus aligning social actors and their resources in a network. This approach offers considerable potential for reflecting on and managing the phenomena related especially to distributed development environments. Future research applying this approach should provide empirical studies as a sound basis for developing new methods and tools for systems development, while relating its results to the existing knowledge of systems development processes.

Note

I wish to thank my colleague Bernd Pape for putting in most of the hard work necessary to keep the examination-administration project going and for having shared his extensive notes on project events within the project team (thus providing a sound basis for empirical research). Also, I thank Kalle Lyytinen and Volker Wulf for commenting on earlier versions, and I am grateful for the reviews and discussions at the "Sociotechnical Networks" minitrack of the AMCIS 2000, where the main idea of this chapter was first presented.

References

Atkinson, C. 2000. The "Soft Information Systems and Technologies Methodology" (SISTeM): An Actor Network Contingency Approach to Integrated Development. *European Journal of Information Systems* 9(2): 104–123.

Bowker, G., S. L. Star, W. Turner, and L. Gasser, eds. 1997. *Social Science, Technical Systems, and Cooperative Work: Beyond the Great Divide*. Mahwah, NJ: Erlbaum.

Damsgaard, J., and R. Scheepers. 1999. A Stage Model of Intranet Technology Implementation and Management. In *Proceedings of the European Conference on Information Systems*, 100–116. Copenhagen: Department of Informatics, Copenhagen Business School.

Gasson, S. 1999. A Social Action Model of Situated Information Systems Design. In *Proceedings of IFIP WG8.2 & WG8.6 Joint Working Conference on Information Systems: Current Issues and Future Changes* (1998), 307–326. Laxenburg, Austria: IFIP. Available at www.bi.no/dep2/infomgt/wg82-86/proceedings/index.htm

Jones, M. 1999. Information Systems and the Double Mangle: Steering a Course between the Scylla of Embedded Structure and the Charybdis of Strong Symmetry. In *Proceedings of IFIP WG8.2 & WG8.6 Joint Working Conference on Information Systems: Current Issues and Future Changes* (1998), 287–302. Laxenburg, Austria: IFIP. Available at www.bi.no/dep2/infomgt/wg82-86/proceedings/index.htm

Kling, R., and R. Lamb. 1999. IT and Organizational Change in Digital Economies: A Socio-Technical Approach. *Computer and Society* 29(3): 17–25.

Klischewski, R. 2000. Systems Development as Networking. In H. M. Chung, ed., *Proceedings of the 2000 Americas Conference on Information Systems* (August 10–13, Long Beach, CA), 1638–1644. Atlanta: Association for Information Systems.

Lanzara, G. 1999. Designing Systems In-Action: Between Transient Constructs and Permanent Structures. Keynote presentation, European Conference on Information Systems (Copenhagen, 23–25 June, 1999). Available at www.ecis99.cbs.dk/Lanzara%20Paper.htm; download 23 September 1999

Latour, B. 1987. *Science in Action: How to Follow Scientists and Engineers through Society*. Cambridge, MA: Harvard University Press.

Latour, B. 1991. Technology Is Society Made Durable. In J. Law, ed., *A Sociology of Monsters: Essays on Power, Technology and Denomination*. London: Routledge.

Latour, B. 1997. *On Recalling ANT*. Department of Sociology, Lancaster University. Available at www.comp.lancs.ac.uk/sociology/stslatour1.html

Latour, B. 1999. *Pandora's Hope: Essays on the Reality of Science Studies*. Cambridge, MA: Harvard University Press.

Law, J. 1997. *Traduction/Trahison: Notes on ANT*. Department of Sociology, Lancaster University. Available at www.lancaster.ac.uk/sociology/stslaw2.html

McMaster, T., R. T. Vidgen, and D. G. Wastell. 1999. Networks of Association and Due Process in IS Development. In *Proceedings of IFIP WG8.2 & WG8.6 Joint Working Conference on Information Systems: Current Issues and Future*

Changes (1998), 341–357. Laxenburg, Austria: IFIP. Available at www.bi.no/dep2/infomgt/wg82-86/proceedings/index.htm

Newman, M., and D. Robey. 1992. A Social Process Model of User-Analyst Relationships. *MIS Quarterly* 16: 249–266.

Robey, D., and M. Newman. 1996. Sequential Patterns in Information Systems Development: An Application of a Social Process Model. *ACM Transactions on Information Systems* 14(1): 30–63.

Vidgen, R. T., and T. McMaster. 1996. Black Boxes, Nonhuman Stakeholders, and the Translation of IT through Mediation. In W. Orlikowski, G. Walsham, M. Jones, and J. DeGross, eds., *Information Technology and Changes in Organizational Work* (IFIP Working Group 8.2, 1995, Cambridge, England), 250–271. London: Chapman & Hall.

Walsham, G. 1997. Actor-Network Theory and IS Research: Current Status and Future Prospects. In A. S. Lee, J. Liebenau, and J. I. DeGross, eds., *Information Systems and Qualitative Research*, 466–480. London: Chapman & Hall.

16

Participatory Organizational and Technological Innovation in Fragmented Work Environments

Bettina Törpel, Volker Wulf, and Helge Kahler

In this chapter we draw on observations and experiences that support the hypothesis that common participatory design (PD) suggestions presuppose a number of prerequisites that are absent in many work settings. Even though many work environments are unsuited for common PD measures, we think that they could be target environments for participatory organizational-technological innovations as well. Hence we suggest that the repertoire of PD be extended. We present ideas on how to proceed for two of the work environments of the OrgTech and InKoNetz projects.[1] Both projects have had the objective of improving cooperative work by improving the codevelopment of individual work processes, organizational structures, and technical infrastructures. One target environment of the OrgTech project, which we are reporting on here, has been the interorganizational collaboration between a steel mill and two engineering offices. One of the target organizations of the InKoNetz project, our second case in this chapter, has been a service network. The improvement of internal cooperation by improving the organizational groupware has been the focus of the project work (see Rittenbruch, Kahler, and Cremers 1998; Törpel 2000).

We first introduce common PD suggestions and principles. A closer look reveals that these measures and principles presuppose organizational features most of which are present in unionized traditional organizations (first section). Even most of the small organizations do not have these characteristics and hence the participation of their members in technological innovation processes has to take different forms (second section). In the context of outsourcing, business relations between organizations can become so tight that interorganizational working units in their own right result. We describe one case of close interorganizational collaboration where the need for participation in (inter)organizational-technological innovation emerged. Conventional PD measures are not applicable in this work environment without additional steps. One way to make the constellation amenable to PD is to take preliminary organizational steps; from the experience in the OrgTech project we mainly suggest forming an interorganizational semiautonomous group (third section). In our second case of a fragmented work environment, a network organization, fragmentation is present with respect to locality, work content, and work means and interests. Traditional PD suggestions are hardly applicable here. Our suggestion for a participatory approach to organizational-technological innovation in this organization is close to practices already performed. It consists of parallel local experimentation and integration at the organizational level on the basis of delegates (forth section).

The Implicit Target Environment for Common PD Suggestions and Principles

Participatory approaches to the development and introduction of computer applications have recently gained relevance. A variety of methods have been developed and successfully applied in practice. Reports of and comparisons between PD projects, collections of suggested and suitable methods, and compilations of criteria for successful participatory processes are abundant in the literature.[2] In this section we will first introduce a number of common PD measures followed by a collection of common PD principles.[3] The descriptions will serve as a background for our subsequent question if a special kind of target organization has to be assumed for PD.

Table 16.1 contains a selection and brief description of PD techniques that have been applied and reported on in the literature: workplace visits, work scenarios, future workshops and organizational games, mock-ups, cooperative prototyping, and ongoing design. Table 16.2 contains a list of and short introduction to some of the principles guiding PD:

Table 16.1

Visiting workplaces	As a means of enhancing real-life knowledge about the organization, the workplaces, the work practices, and the existing problems, interests, and conflicts, participants in PD processes spend time with members of potentially affected work environments, engaging in activities that seem suited, like observing, inquiring, interviewing, or scrutinizing relevant artifacts (see for example Bødker, Grønbæk, and Kyng 1993).
Elaborating work scenarios	Different typical work practices are reconstructed and integrated into an overall picture of the work tasks, the division of labor, and the cooperative structure to be supported by computer applications (see Holtzblatt and Jones 1993).
The future workshop and organizational games	Originally developed by Jungk and Müllert (1987), the future workshop was adapted to the special situation of gathering requirements in participatory processes for the design of computer applications at work (see Kensing and Halskov Madsen 1993). It is a means for brainstorming, for identifying shortcomings of the current state, and for developing visions; it proceeds by the steps of critique (present), fantasy (future), and feasible next steps (back to reality in the form of real-life solutions and action plans); the elaboration is structured by techniques of interaction. With a structure analogous to the future workshop, design work is acted out as a theatrical play in organizational games (see Ehn and Sjögren 1991).
Using mock-ups	Instead of using specification documents, mock-ups can serve as a means of experimenting with and evaluating potential organizational-technological alternatives in real-life settings. Mock-ups themselves are noncomputer artifacts, but as means for designing computer-related artifacts they serve to imagine computer system functionality; examples are cardboard screens or flipcharts with menus or file contents. They were developed in the context of the Utopia project (see Ehn and Kyng 1991). They allow for real-life experience, are easy to understand and inexpensive, enhance imagination of future solutions, and are fun to work with.
Cooperative prototyping	As revisable technical realizations of the functionality represented in the mock-ups, prototypes can serve as means for cooperative experimentation and modification with the potential functionality and realization of the prospective system (see Bødker and Grønbæk 1991).

Table 16.1 (continued)

Continued design of computer applications, work practice, and organization	Often, continued design is equated with tailoring as adapting or modifying technical solutions in use. Tailorable systems leave space for a variety of appropriations by providing the users with options to further design them in use. Continued design can also comprise more comprehensive activities (see for example Henderson and Kyng 1991; Wulf and Rohde 1995). The ongoing improvement of means, processes, structures, rules, and so on can be described in terms of spiral-like change processes, often called evolutionary (Floyd, Reisin, and Schmidt 1989). The affected organization members receive the opportunity to suggest and/or make changes in the form of feedback loops instead of being subject to linear processes (like the sequence of requirements definition, design, implementation, test, introduction, use, maintenance).

acknowledgment of diversity, impact of the future users, real impact, exchange and education, separation of interest groups, and protection of participants.

To meaningfully apply or realize single suggestions and principles or combinations in tables 16.1 and 16.2, the setting has to have certain features. Measures like the future workshop or organizational games, for example, require an opportunity to (often, regularly) meet somewhere. Locations have to be available, and it has to be possible to meet on a regular basis or to schedule meetings in advance. A certain continuity of participants is beneficial.

To elicit honest and to-the-point statements and contributions from the participants, regulations have to be present so that the participatory activities do not pose a danger for those taking part. This requires regulations within the organization, including employment contracts that protect workers. Often this is the case in unionized organizations, at least in organizations that have structures that represent worker interests. Sometimes this can be justified because of the public attention devoted to large and well-known organizations. To be able to elaborate typical work scenarios, at least some aspects of the work (content, means, procedures, collaboration) must be generalizable.

Table 16.2

Acknowledging diversity	Different perspectives, differences, and interests should be explicitly articulated. In negotiations all interests should count.
Impact of those who will work with the product	All perspectives and interests should have an impact on the innovation, independent of power structures and hierarchies. This often means that the powerless (typically workers) have more impact than usual.
Impact instead of token participation	Real impact should be granted in core areas instead of token participation in minor decisions with the major issues predefined by the powerful.
Exchange and education	Mutual learning should be promoted on all levels. Mutual learning between the different interest groups (hierarchy level, content areas, design vs. content, capital vs. labor, . . .) is especially encouraged. The participants should become qualified in the course of the participatory change process. For example, the workers who are the "work content specialists" will undergo steps qualifying them for technology design and development, and the technology specialists will undergo steps helping them understand the work content and context in question.
Separation of interest groups	For certain phases, interest groups of the participatory process might have to be separated. It is often stressed that fruitful work, for example in future workshops and organizational games, may rely on a homogeneity or compatibility of interests of the participants. Mostly workers and management are separated (see Bødker, Grønbæk, and King 1993, 165).
Protection of the participants	Participation should not be a disadvantage. Participants should get compensation for the work in the project. The normal work should be done without anybody doing extra work. The participants' statements should not endanger their status in the organization.

The separation of interest groups presupposes that these interest groups have to be identifiable and present. To settle certain conflicts these conflicts have to be present. In the PD literature the conflicts of capital versus labor, management versus workers, design versus use are often assumed. This presupposes an organization with a vertical and a horizontal division of work. With the different responsibilities and levels of the formal hierarchy, different perspectives and interests are then associated. The most important of these interest groups (like "capital" and "labor") have superregional organizations with regional and/or organizational branches that represent their interests. Within the organization their local representatives have a voice. National legislation warrants structures within the organization like committees in which the representatives negotiate relevant issues regarding matters of the organization and work.

Real impact requires that the results of the participatory process become implemented and that traditional power structures cannot overrule the conclusions arrived at in the participatory process.

Most PD measures are time consuming and require the presence of resources (time, money) and negotiation structures to allocate these resources. For example, participants will only be motivated to contribute to the process if they receive compensation for their work and if their ordinary work gets done while they are absent. To be able to meaningfully contribute to the process the participants need to be qualified, which also requires resources (money, time, educators,...). This can be provided if a clear border with defined channels for exchange, especially incoming and outgoing orders, separates the organization from the "outside world." If the organization provides a strong buffer between the market and the individual working within the organization, the outcomes of individual efforts do not have to compete in the market but contribute to the overall competitive strength of the organization. The relations between individual contributions to the organization and benefits from the organization are then largely regulated by the structure of the organization itself, contracts and rules, and, sometimes, the ownership of shares. If this is true, the organization might allocate resources for participatory measures regarding technology development, introduction, and maintenance.

Many of these organizational prerequisites were present in projects reported on in the literature. Bødker (1996, 217) states that even in "traditional" organizations, the feasibility of PD agendas is not always warranted; for example, the results of PD core groups often do not become sufficiently disseminated, the PD efforts lack continuity, management overrules PD decisions, the participants are not sufficiently compensated, or the participants do not get sufficient resources for measures qualifying them for the participation. In the rest of this chapter, we explore the possibilities of participatory organizational-technological innovation for organizational environments that do not meet the organizational criteria of traditional PD.

Participatory Shopping and Tailoring as an Alternative to Conventional PD in Small Organizations

Some crucial presuppositions for traditional PD are not in effect in many small organizations. Rather, besides being small, many small enterprises, especially in the high-end service sector, can be characterized as follows.

Usually each member of the organization is the only specialist for a particular field in the firm. The need to survive as an enterprise is obvious to everybody. Therefore, everybody usually feels a strong obligation to contribute to the success of the firm. Due to its small size, the organization can hardly serve as a buffer between the individual organization members and the "outside world." Rather, the market is always visible to everybody. Members who do not visibly contribute to the success of the organization have to leave. Many small organizations are highly dependent on incoming orders. Outsourcing has resulted in new forms of dependencies between large and small organizations. One of these forms is stable interorganizational collaboration (see below); another is the formation of networks of small companies. The ability to form and maintain flexible and mutually supportive professional networks of small and medium-size organizations has become a crucial success factor for small and medium-size enterprises. The relation between contributions to and benefits from the organization is regulated by the internal division of work. Usually small organizations try to keep administrative overhead low. In small organizations, capital or labor organizations are usually absent. Accordingly, the individual employees' interests are not represented by unions, interest groups, or negotiation structures of any kind. The decision to introduce technical means depends on the frequently low purchasing power of the firm, and the risks involved in purchasing new means have to be kept small.

There are also egalitarian small organizations, but many small organizations have a clear top-down organizational command structure, with powerful managing directors (usually the owners) and compliant employees (see Nett, Fuchs-Frohnhofen, and Wulf 2000).

The measures suggested in the PD literature (see table 16.1) are too expensive and time consuming for small enterprises. Robertson (1998, 210) concludes on the basis of a sample of small organizations in the field of design (not the design of information technology) that "none of the companies studied enjoyed the resources to engage in ... the canonical case of Participatory Design—where 'users and designers work together over a long period to craft a system uniquely suited to the tasks, practices and environment of its users.'" Rather, "small companies are purchasers of off-the-shelf technology and lack the infrastructure, and the economic means and justification, to design their own systems from scratch. They must make do with what is available within the marketplace and within their invariably tight budgets" (p. 209). "For the designers of systems within small companies," Robertson notes, "the challenge is selecting the best fit technology from what is available in the marketplace and adapting it to the local conditions. User participation in this process is crucial to the quality of purchasing decisions and the effectiveness of the adaptations" (p. 218). Robertson adds that "for people employed in design companies, participation in the shaping of their systems is rarely a question of the nature of their involvement in the development of software. Instead they rely on off-the-shelf-applications that have been developed somewhere else.... User participation in small companies focuses on such issues as shopping decisions, consumer rights and protection and the compatibility, tailorability and reliability of off-the-shelf applications" (pp. 207–208).

Some of these organizations want to be as participatory as possible in the development, introduction, and appropriation processes of their computer applications. The principles of traditional PD approaches can guide participatory shopping and tailoring. In small organizations it is possible for the diverse individual interests, perspectives, and work constellations to be taken into account and for everybody to have an impact on core decisions. Members can learn from each other and qualify themselves and each other in the processes of shopping and tailoring. The bottleneck is certainly resources; small offices have tight budgets and schedules. In hierarchical small organizations the managers are not inclined to accept participatory processes at all. With Robertson (1998), we hold that the options and constraints for PD in small organizations are special. This requires an adaptation of PD approaches and methods.

In the following pages, we will describe the work carried out in the OrgTech project and the InKoNetz project and attempt to integrate experiences and results (conclusion). The integrated organization and technology development framework (OTD; see Wulf and Rohde 1995; Wulf et al. 1999) served as a set of guidelines for these projects. The OTD process is characterized by a parallel development of workplace, organizational, and technical systems, by the management of (existing) conflicts by means of discourse and negotiation, and by immediate participation of the organization members affected. The change process is thought to be an ongoing one. For the work toward viable organizational-technological solutions in the application organizations of the OrgTech and InKoNetz projects, we recommended procedures and principles successfully employed in participatory processes of organizational-technical innovation. After a while, though, we realized that some of these proposals did not apply to the work environments in our projects. We had to change our strategy and look for PD methods better suited to the settings.

Case: A Participatory Approach to Organizational-Technological Innovation for an Interorganizational Collaboration

In this section, we examine the potential of PD in the case of the collaboration between three companies: MeltIt, a large steel mill, and Techno and Doku, two engineering offices (names of companies have been changed). All three companies are located in the German Ruhr area. In the following paragraphs, we will first describe the interorganizational cooperation and then introduce semiautonomous groups as an organizational measure to base PD measures on.

Techno and Doku have done subcontractual work for MeltIt in the field of maintenance engineering—for example, the construction of and documentation for steel furnace components. These business relationships have existed for more than a decade on different levels of intensity. When the OrgTech-project started, the cooperation had intensified after the steel mill had decided to outsource most of its maintenance engineering work.

Both Techno and Doku are "traditional" hierarchical, small organizations. In workshop discussions of the OrgTech project, the employees of Techno and Doku were often unsure whether to articulate individual positions (as opposed to "the official policy") or not.

MeltIt is a large unionized organization and hence meets most of the above-mentioned criteria that are implicit standards of traditional PD proposals. Within MeltIt, different departments compete for resources —for example, the operating units and central units are in a constant struggle with each other. Therefore, it was not possible to integrate MeltIt's plant operators into the OrgTech project. The consequence was that an important group of actors did not contribute to the processes initiated by the project.

A construction department within MeltIt coordinates the maintenance-engineering activities and manages the relations with the external engineering offices. The construction department is a central organizational unit. It is responsible for all maintenance activities of the mill and belongs to the mill's department of central services. This resembles the business cooperation between independent organizations. Typically, an order is created by the plant operator, who controls the production equipment and machinery in a plant and who is in charge of the production of the plant. Should a maintenance measure be necessary, the plant operator sends a request to the company-internal construction department for further processing. The transaction is either handled internally or referred to an external engineering office.

In the case of external subcontracting, an order will then be prepared by the internal construction department. The necessary information, documents, and drawings are transferred to the engineering office for further processing. Since order specifications can contain errors and sometimes need further clarification from the beginning, inquiries, further discussions, and extensive reordering of drawings are often necessary. Drawings and documents have to be found, coordination work has to be done, and contacts with other departments have to be initiated. This process of realignment of orders is tedious and time consuming and requires special knowledge of technical domains and knowledge related to the structure of MeltIt's physical and electronic archives (see Iacucci et al. 1998; Hinrichs 2000).

There is a mutual dependency. At the beginning of the project the bulk of the incoming orders of Techno and Doku were commissioned by MeltIt. But the tasks to be performed for MeltIt are so special and require so much knowledge related to MeltIt's equipment—especially its archives of technical drawings—that it would be more expensive and time consuming to commission anyone other than Techno and Doku to fill an order. Due to its volume of orders, MeltIt has been able to determine the conditions of the collaboration, for example in terms of the legal agreements, definition of work processes, and technical arrangements. This may be illustrated as follows. The amount of work done within the interorganizational structure has changed over time. How much of the maintenance construction is sourced out into engineering offices instead of being done within the steel mill has mainly depended on the policy of the steel mill and has been unpredictable for the engineering offices. At the beginning of the project, the steel mill tried to source out as much work as possible in order to reduce its fixed costs. Later on, the steel mill drastically changed its policy by trying to limit the amount of maintenance engineering in general and hence save short-term costs. The background for this policy was their initiative to replace old plants by new ones. The remaining maintenance-engineering work was supposed to be carried out by the internal construction department.

In an interorganizational collaboration, long-term company strategies can be diverse and conflicting. In the case of the collaboration between MeltIt, Techno, and Doku this even led to the introduction of incompatible technical applications endangering the cooperation. For instance, the director of one of the engineering offices decided to introduce an incompatible 3D CAD application because he believed that its functionality would open new markets for the engineering office. It became obvious that both engineering offices simultaneously have an interest in working with MeltIt and in collaborating with other business partners. These interests have sometimes been conflicting.

Interorganizational collaborations are nothing new but belong to the defined interfaces between traditional organizations and the "outside world," especially in the context of incoming and outgoing orders. Yet in this case we observed that the collaboration can acquire the status of a work environment in its own right, with an extreme interdependence among the performed work tasks, a stable collaborative objective, regulation by legal means like contracts, streamlined by a set of computer work means and with relative independence from other work environments.

There is not much of a formal (inter)organizational structure supporting the interorganizational collaboration. The resources for the cooperation and for process improvements have to be provided by the individual organizations. A framework of contracts developed by the legal department of the steel mill provides the legal setting for the interorganizational cooperation.

In general, the steel mill has more resources than the engineering offices. For PD processes that are meant to improve the working conditions for all parties involved, the inequality in terms of resources poses problems. The employees at Techno and Doku, for example, did not have enough resources (time, money) to participate continuously in the OrgTech project.

So far, it has been unusual to suggest PD measures beyond one single organizational context. For the collaboration between MeltIt, Techno, and Doku, PD suggestions would have to consider the combined status of a collaboration and a work environment with qualities traditionally restricted to organizations. Especially since this kind of collaboration can remain stable over long periods of time, we think that attempts to apply PD techniques used in single organizations so far, make sense. To make this a realistic scenario, it has to be acknowledged that the interorganizational collaboration forms a relatively stable working environment with regard to the services exchanged and the division of labor between the partners.

However, as long as the current status of the collaboration between MeltIt, Techno, and Doku remains unchanged, traditional PD measures are not applicable. In a constellation where one organization dominates the scene and where local decisions can be overruled by formally superordinate structures, participatory approaches cannot reach far. The prerequisite for employing PD measures might be an organizational step. We think that in order to install practices involving all potentially affected individuals in the processes of decision making and organizational-technological innovation, one way is to first enforce a status of relative autonomy of the interorganizational network. This could be realized by giving the group of individuals involved in the interorganizational collaboration the status of an interorganizational semiautonomous team (see Brödner 1985). A binding agreement should secure the semiautonomous status. The semiautonomous status means that the group has its own budget, defined areas of sovereign decision making, and a contact person mediating between the group and the three enterprises. Decision making regarding the interorganizational structure of the group and technological innovation should be in the hands of the group. Special resources for enabling the processes of organizational-technological innovation have to be allocated, and it also has to be guaranteed that the processes and outcomes are widely determined by the members of the semiautonomous group (see Nett, Fuchs-Frohnhofen, and Wulf 2000).

The formation of a semiautonomous team would allow for participatory processes regarding the structure of the collaboration and technological changes. An ongoing process of negotiation and improvement regarding work processes, structural-(inter)organizational changes, and suitable technology (continuous improvement process) makes a great deal of sense. We think that the traditional PD measures are applicable in this kind of constellation, even though this work environment does not meet the implicit standards for PD projects. For example, the oppositions of management versus workers or capital versus labor have played a subordinate role. We think that semiautonomous groups might also be amenable to other approaches to organizational-technological innovation beyond the scope of traditional PD.

Case: A Participatory Approach to Organizational-Technological Innovation in a Network Organization

SIGMA (name changed) is a training and consulting firm consisting of a network of about 200 freelancers.[4] As in the previous section, we will first describe the cooperation within the organization and then introduce our recommendation for participatory organizational-technological innovation, a continuous process of local experimentation and organization-wide integration allowing the organization members to change their work processes participatorily.

The members of the network live and work in locations throughout Germany. The founders established the enterprise in 1992 and are now its managing directors. The enterprise and its services are structured along the lines of projects, with each project having its specific objective, a specific time limit, and a specific composition of team members. Projects last only for a limited period of time, sometimes a few months, but typically not more than a few days. After finishing a training or consulting measure, SIGMA's members turn to new tasks and often form new teams.

Apart from a few employees whose work contributes to the infrastructure of the network (for example, administrative or office work), the network does not employ members on the basis of employment contracts. Instead, the individual members are freelancers. They pay a fixed percentage of their incomes from their training and consulting activities to the network in exchange for infrastructure (like finance, legal, and tax-related advice, contact with customers, organizational intranet software).

Working with SIGMA means having to provide one's own workplace, typically a home office with telephone, personal computer, Internet access, a variety of software programs, and a fax machine and other technical equipment.

The managing directors on the one hand and the freelancing trainers and consultants who work within the network and hold shares on the other have a fundamentally different status as innovative entrepreneurs: the directors manage a workforce of freelancers, while the freelancers manage their working capacity (Voß and Pongratz 1998).

SIGMA stresses its strength of being flexible. This means that the network is often able to quickly, unbureaucratically, imaginatively, and appropriately react to market changes with innovative services and products. As an organization, SIGMA reacts to the "global" market with ongoing changes in its spectrum of products and services. The organization reacts to the external market by creating an internal market. The individual organization members have to compete and succeed in both; they rely on finding customers or job offers. This means that most SIGMA members continuously extend their portfolios and offer their skills and potentials to a twofold (labor) market: the market within SIGMA and the "global" market outside. Both markets constantly change, and hence the portfolios of the SIGMA members also change. Organizations like SIGMA are the opposite of a buffer between the individual organization member and the outside market. Thus, organizations like SIGMA reinforce market forces with the result that individual work contents, incomes, and lifestyles directly and heavily rely on the market. The correspondence between request and individual portfolios can change rapidly.

Another factor enabling the flexibility of the organization is the flat hierarchy with the levels of managing directors, project managers, and regular project members, with the two latter positions varying over time. Informal relations of power, dependency, and subordination strongly structure the organization and the activities of its members. They exist along the lines of access to information, position in the flow of communication within and beyond the network, skills related to the commissioning of projects and winning of grants, contact to potential customers, membership in certain circles, domain of business activity (IT knowledge has had high status), and extent to which the network relies on a person or promotion from the management side. The criteria for the status of organization members keep changing, are constantly (re)negotiated, and are the objective of interpersonal and structural struggles. Hierarchy, subdivisions, and departments are partly replaced by "locality": coexisting, often partly overlapping units and circles keep developing and changing.

SIGMA does not have a clear border to the "outside world." Rather, the boundaries between SIGMA and the "outside world" are blurred.

For example, customers or participants in training or consulting measures easily change their status and become SIGMA members. The criteria for membership in SIGMA are often unclear.

Communication within and beyond the network in general and personal relationships between network members in particular are crucial factors for the work within SIGMA. Meetings of various levels of exclusivity and dedication of SIGMA members in their areas or of groups with overlapping interests take place frequently, typically in bars or restaurants. These meetings serve purposes like establishing relationships, exchanging experiences, and developing new business objectives.

For the network members, flexibility often means working conditions in accordance with their individual preferences and constraints (e.g., time budgets), having more responsibility for the projects they work in than "ordinary employees," and work based on motivation and self-determination. However, they trade this for disadvantages like less security concerning their future incomes or in cases of inability to work and the absence of contracts and formal codetermination possibilities. They work in a hybrid situation between being dependently employed and being autonomous freelancers.

As a legal form, SIGMA is a private liability company with a shareholder structure. The shareholders are the freelancers within SIGMA or associated individuals, and they participate in the business successes.

Capital and labor organizations, representatives, negotiation partners, and structures for decision making and negotiating are not present and would not be appropriate for the structures and problems in SIGMA. They do not fit into the organizational agenda, the organizational forms of decision making, and the interest spectrum of the freelancers.

SIGMA is an attempt to replace the command structure of "traditional" enterprises with self-organization, motivation, and the individual reactions to market forces. It is often said that it requires a high level of motivation and self-determination to succeed within a network like SIGMA. The possibility that self-determination will subliminally turn into "outside-determined self-determination" can never be ruled out (Voß and Pongratz 1998; Törpel 2000).

In traditional organizations, laws, rights, and explicit rules serve to regulate the internal cooperation; in SIGMA this is done by ever (re)negotiable statements, agreements, commitments, and rules, many of which are implicit, "locally" different, and subject to a permanent change process. They are specific for (subdivisions of) SIGMA and mostly beyond the scope of national legislation.

With an internal market and constantly changing roles (project director, normal team member, seeking a job, offering jobs) perspectives and interests are not easy to identify, either for outsiders or for organization members. Instead, perspectives and interests are typically changing fast, are fragmented and contradictory in themselves, and are sometimes subject to conflicts (e.g., conflicts of loyalty toward the directors, the organization as a whole, customers, potential project commissioners, and project partners). The clear and polar interests of capital versus labor have been replaced by a differentiated spectrum of individual interests, sometimes conflicting inter- and intraindividually. The opposition of capital and labor, "traditionally" an opposition between classes, for SIGMA members takes place in their "souls and hearts" (see Voß and Pongratz 1998, 152).

In organizations like SIGMA, some problems are due to the coexistence of nontraditional and traditional concepts. In SIGMA, this has been the case for the development and maintenance of their organizational groupware. SIGMA itself has an organizational approach and culture that rests on virtues like self-organization, flexibility, local responsibility, trust, transparency, and participation orientation, whereas the provider of their organizational groupware is a hierarchical and small enterprise, has followed a traditional (nonparticipatory) approach to systems development, and has delivered an inflexible, centrally maintained system. The groupware is basically an online-offline e-mail and bulletin-board system. It has to be maintained centrally; all changes and bug fixing have to be done at the office of the software provider; there is no local support for quick nonbureaucratic help; adaptation and tailoring of the system cannot be done by the users themselves; even smaller changes have to be exclusively carried out by the maintenance personnel at the provider's site. The development and introduction of the groupware was basically not a participatory process. The centralized approach caused problems and discontent, especially until individuals and groups were able to purchase individual and local solutions as more affordable and easy-to-use solutions became available on the market.

For the future, it is likely that SIGMA will buy an off-the-shelf groupware system. The adaptation of this system to SIGMA's specific needs would then be the task of the provider of the current groupware and some of SIGMA's IT specialists.

The past and current approaches to the procedure and to SIGMA's groupware system do not fit into SIGMA's approach of flexibility and self-organization. Communications with SIGMA members confirm our impression that SIGMA would benefit from a participatory approach to groupware development/purchase, adaptation, introduction, design-in-use, and so on. Yet the feasibility of participatory measures in the face of internal and external pressure (especially related to the market) is often doubted. A participatory procedure for SIGMA would have to be a special one with an impact on distribution and integration.

Traditional PD measures and principles are hardly applicable to SIGMA:

• Because SIGMA does not provide offices for most network members, workplace visits would have to take place quite often and in many different locations, since the temporary microsettings differ from each other and change over time. Future workshops, organizational games, gathering work practices, and working with mock-ups and prototypes are probably hardly feasible in a situation where members work in different locations and meeting space does not belong to the infrastructure provided by the organization. With possibly hundreds of permanently changing teams and tasks, the elaboration of work scenarios and the experimental cooperative use of mock-ups and prototypes would not only be tedious, but their results would be outdated before they have even been produced.

• Different interests and perspectives are present. But the interests are fragmented not only within SIGMA and its temporary groups but also among the freelancers themselves (see Voß and Pongratz 1998; Törpel 2000). Real impact cannot be guaranteed in an organization without formal employee rights and in the absence of formal rules. The realization of some principles relying on resources—like compensation necessity or learning/qualification—would have to be the objective of extensive negotiations. For freelancers, the motivation to contribute to the network beyond the immediate customer-paid tasks is low as long as they are not compensated for the network-related work. The prevention of disadvantages from individual activities and statements cannot be guaranteed in SIGMA because of the absence of an organizational buffer in favor of a double market. Most likely, it would be difficult to tell if the statements and activities of the individuals involved in a participatory process are honest and to the point or merely strategic in relation to the double market as perceived by the participants. Cyclical processes might be useful in new forms.

The following suggestions for one kind of participatory approach to organizational-technical innovation in SIGMA are based on the localized practice already existing. We think that this practice of organizational-technological innovation provides useful hints for participatory approaches suited for organizations like SIGMA.

One fact regarding organizational-technological innovation that deserves special attention in SIGMA is the diversity in the work means: almost every group, team, region, and individual has its own composition of devices and systems. Everything, including technology, is subject to informal inconsistent rules, relations, negotiations, and decisions and can be (re)negotiated at any time. Sometimes the outcomes have only regional validity; sometimes they have organization-wide impact. The current practice of technological innovation is local development and/or a combination of purchase and adaptation. The groupware has become an addition only used because an organizational guideline to use it for the internal communication had been enforced.

Given that the individual members of SIGMA own their work means, including computer applications, design processes are only necessary for purposes that are potentially of concern for more than one local work environment. By local work environments, we mean all work environments that are part of the network but not the network itself. Local work environments may themselves be distributed.

We recommend a continuous process of parallel local experimentation and network-wide collection of experiences, feedback, and integration into an overarching infrastructure consisting of a variety of local substructures. Instead of a project with time constraints and a limited number of participants, an ongoing process of contributions, discussion, and integration would be installed. We envision parallel local microprocesses of participatory systems development and introduction, network-wide possibilities for the exchange of local experiences and results, and network-wide consequences of the interplay between local experimentation and network-wide exchange.

Locally, the members of the work environments identify areas in which they need technical support and analyze their requirements in these areas. In some settings, new means will be designed and implemented; in others, off-the-shelf products will be purchased and adapted to the special local needs. In any case, the new product will be introduced, used for a while, and then evaluated, for example regarding its suitedness for local and network-wide work, or its usability. The local experiences are put into a communicable form.

The participants in the local experimentation select themselves, nobody is excluded or discouraged; individuals with different backgrounds regarding knowledge or experience are encouraged to participate. Locally, the participants are encouraged to mutually qualify each other for the process; non-IT professionals get an opportunity to learn approaches to systems (development), modeling, design, and so on, and IT professionals get a chance to learn more about the work environments in which the systems are to be integrated. For all participants the acquisition of knowledge relevant for the local development/introduction processes is encouraged.

Delegates from the local work environments exchange information on a regular basis, either in person or by technical means. The delegates exchange information on issues like

- Work environments within the organization in need of computer support
- Aspects of work in need of support
- The kind of computer support that might be needed
- Off-the-shelf solutions already on the market
- Solutions developed and/or introduced in working environments of the organization

- Possibilities for the generalization of these solutions, regarding the network as a whole or regarding the introduction in more than one local setting within the organization
- Network concerns like standards, network architectures, security, and bandwidths

The delegates could play a role comparable to the role of the user advocates described in Mambrey, Mark, and Pankoke-Babatz 1998. Having the background enabling them to take both the user and the designer perspective, user advocates serve as intermediaries between the users' needs and the designers' ideas. The delegates might have to switch between the user and designer (or shopper/tailor) perspectives as well. Additionally, their task would be to mediate between the worm's-eye view of the microsetting and the bird's-eye view of the network regarding technological equipment.

The delegates could elect a committee that would select good solutions and give them awards according to criteria like good design or choice, appropriateness of the solution (for the local environment or for the network), usability, potential for integration into the IT infrastructure of the network, appropriateness for bridging individual/local work environments, or involvement of a range of different perspectives/qualifications. Small systems that do not have much functionality besides integrating otherwise-disparate solutions should especially be encouraged. The awards should be significant.

The exchanges of the delegates should result in communicable suggestions for generalization, either regarding use in more than one local setting or regarding the integration into the network-wide infrastructure (systems, guidelines for use, organizational structures, rules). This also includes suggestions for the introduction and/or integration in the existing technical and organizational and local structures and infrastructures. These suggestions should be fed back to the members of the local work environments. In case of approval (approval criteria are to be negotiated), the solutions become generalized. The network should provide resources for local developments, education of local participants, network-wide exchange of the local delegates, and feedback loops between network delegates and local network members.

The result of this combination of local experimentation and network-wide distribution is an architecture with a variety of coexisting applications, possibly with overlapping functionality, ideally artfully integrated into the evolving work practice (Suchman 1994).

Conclusion

In this chapter, we have looked at "traditional" large and small organizations and at two new forms of collaboration, between organizations of different size and status as in the technical collaboration between MeltIt, Techno, and Doku, and between individuals as in the network organization SIGMA.

What used to be mere business relations between largely independent business partners (sometimes with severe power differences between the enterprises involved) seem to turn into interorganizational work environments with qualities of "cross-section organizations." In the case of the collaboration between MeltIt, Techno, and Doku, the collaborative work environment has become rather stable in terms of the contents and in terms of the persons and groups involved. The work processes in the hands of the different enterprises are strongly intertwined.

In collaborations like those within and beyond SIGMA, the contents and the individuals involved often keep changing. Sometimes the collaborations last longer, but mostly they are short. From the individuals' point of view, collaborations like those in SIGMA mean that they are part of various microsettings or "cross-section collaborations."

In interorganizational collaborations like the one between MeltIt, Techno, and Doku, PD efforts might benefit from acknowledging the relative stability of the working environment even though the units involved belong to different enterprises. The organizational measure suggested by the OrgTech project is the establishment of an interorganizational, semiautonomous team. This constellation would be amenable to traditional PD measures and other participatory approaches to organizational-technological innovation.

Participatory approaches in organizations like SIGMA might benefit from the diversity of the local environments as well as from the fact that these local environments belong to and form a network. Therefore, for

SIGMA we suggest replacing PD projects with parallel local experimentation and a network-wide collection of experiences, feedback, and integration into an overarching infrastructure consisting of a variety of local substructures.

From the experiences and results presented in this chapter, we conclude that it would be beneficial to reconsider central notions incorporated in traditional PD—for example, the notions of organization, interests, design, and projects.

The scope of the participatory approaches to organizational-technological innovation in both application environments reported here has been limited (see Törpel 2000). Certainly there are organizational factors and power issues that have kept relevant actors from engaging in PD practices. But PD may become even more attractive as soon as more feasible varieties appropriate for the emerging new organizational environments are available.

Notes

We would like to thank Yvonne Dittrich, Ralf Klischewski, Finn Kensing, Keld Bødker, Peter Mambrey, Bernhard Nett, Toni Robertson, and Hans-Jörg Burtschick for their invaluable comments on earlier versions of this chapter.

1. *InKoNetz* means "Integrated Cooperation Management in Network Organizations" (Integriertes Kooperationsmanagement in Netzwerkorganisationen); *OrgTech* means "Integrated Organization and Technology Development in Concurrent Engineering" (Organisationsentwicklung bei Einführung computerunterstützter Telekooperation in klein- und mittelständischen Ingenieurbüros). Both projects have been funded by the ADAPT Initiative of the Commission of the European Union and the MAGS, NRW.

2. See for example Greenbaum and Kyng 1991; Schuler and Namioka 1993; Kuhn and Muller 1993, a special issue on Participatory Design in the *Communications of the ACM*; Trigg and Anderson 1996, a special issue on Participatory Design in the journal *Human-Computer Interaction*; or the proceedings of the biannual "Conference on Participatory Design" (PDC); for historical accounts and overviews see for example Floyd, Reisin, and Schmidt 1989 or Clement and Van den Besselaar 1993. We realize that we largely equate PD with experiences, approaches, and suggestions from Scandinavia.

3. These lists are necessarily selective and cannot represent the entire range of methods ever employed. We are well aware that sensitivity for target organizations has been a serious topic in the PD community (see e.g. Clement, Kolm, and Wagner 1994; Bjerknes and Bratteteig 1995).

4. For a description and discussion of the approach of SIGMA, especially regarding the relationship between internal communication and groupware, see Rittenbruch, Kahler, and Cremers 1998.

References

Bjerknes, G., and Bratteteig, T. 1995. User Participation and Democracy: A Discussion of Scandinavian Research on System Development. *Scandinavian Journal of Information Systems* 7: 73–98.

Bødker, S. 1996. Creating Conditions for Participation: Conflicts and Resources in Systems Development. *Human-Computer Interaction* 11(3): 215–236.

Bødker, S., and K. Grønbæk. 1991. Design in Action: From Prototyping by Demonstration to Cooperative Prototyping. In J. Greenbaum and M. Kyng, eds., *Design at Work: Cooperative Design of Computer Systems*, 197–218. Hillsdale, NJ: Erlbaum.

Bødker, S., K. Grønbæk, and M. Kyng. 1993. Cooperative Design: Techniques and Experiences from the Scandinavian Scene. In D. Schuler and A. Namioka, eds., *Participatory Design: Principles and Practices*, 157–175. Hillsdale, NJ: Erlbaum.

Brödner, P. 1985. *Fabrik Zweitausend: Alternative Entwicklungspfade in die Zukunft der Fabrik*. Berlin: Edition Sigma.

Clement, A., P. Kolm, and I. Wagner, eds. 1994. NetWORKing: Connecting Workers in and between Organizations. *Proceedings of the IFIP WG9.1 Working Conference on NetWORKing* (Vienna, 16–18 June, 1993). Amsterdam: North Holland/Elsevier.

Clement, A., and P. Van den Besselaar. 1993. A Retrospective Look at PD Projects. *Communications of the ACM*, 36(4): 29–37.

Ehn, P., and M. Kyng. 1991. Cardboard Computers: Mocking-It-Up or Hands-on the Future. In J. Greenbaum and M. Kyng, eds., *Design at Work: Cooperative Design of Computer Systems*, 169–195. Hillsdale, NJ: Erlbaum.

Ehn, P., and D. Sjögren. 1991. From System Descriptions to Scripts for Action. In J. Greenbaum and M. Kyng, eds., *Design at Work: Cooperative Design of Computer Systems*, 241–268. Hillsdale, NJ: Erlbaum.

Floyd, C., W.-M. Mehl, F.-M. Reisin, G. Schmidt, and G. Wolf. 1989. Out of Scandinavia: Alternative Approaches to Software Design and System Development. *Human-Computer Interaction*, 4: 253–350.

Floyd, C., F.-M. Reisin, and G. Schmidt. 1989. STEPS to Software Development with Users. In *Lecture Notes in Computer Science* 387: 48–64.

Greenbaum, J., and M. Kyng, eds. 1991. *Design at Work: Cooperative Design of Computer Systems.* Hillsdale, NJ: Erlbaum.

Henderson, A., and M. Kyng. 1991. There's No Place Like Home: Continuing Design in Use. In J. Greenbaum and M. Kyng, eds., *Design at Work: Cooperative Design of Computer Systems*, 241–268. Hillsdale, NJ: Erlbaum.

Hinrichs, J. 2000. Telecooperation in Engineering Offices: The Problem of Archiving. In R. Dieng, A. Eiboin, L. Karenty, and G. De Michelis, eds., *Designing Cooperative Systems: The Use of Theories and Models*, 259–274. Amsterdam: IOS Press.

Holtzblatt, K., and S. Jones. 1993. Contextual Inquiry: A Partcipatory Technique for System Design. In D. Schuler and A. Namioka, eds., *Participatory Design: Principles and Practices*, 177–210. Hillsdale, NJ: Erlbaum.

Iacucci, G., R. Peters, O. Stiemerling, and V. Wulf. 1998. Telecooperation Systems in Engineering Companies Supplying the Metallurgy Industry: The Experience of the OrgTech Project. In G. Iacucci, ed., *Globalization of Manufacturing in the Digital Communications Era of the 21st Century: Proceedings of PROLAMAT '98—The Tenth International IFIP WG 5.2/5.3 Conference*, (September 9–12, 1998, Trento, Italy), 107–119. Dordrecht: Kluwer.

Jungk, R., and N. Müllert. 1987. *Future Workshops: How to Create Desirable Futures*. London: Institute for Social Inventions.

Kensing, F., and K. Halskov Madsen. 1993. Generating Visions: Future Workshops and Metaphorical Design. In J. Greenbaum and M. Kyng, eds., *Design at Work: Cooperative Design of Computer Systems*, 155–168. Hillsdale, NJ: Erlbaum.

Kuhn, S., and M. Muller, eds. 1993. Special Issue on Participatory Design. *Communications of the ACM* 36(4).

Mambrey, P., G. Mark, and U. Pankoke-Babatz. 1998. User Advocacy in Participatory Design: Designers' Experiences with a New Communication Channel. *Computer Supported Cooperative Work* 7: 291–313.

Nett, B., P. Fuchs-Frohnhofen, and V. Wulf. 2000. Obstacles to Tele-Cooperation in Engineering Networks of the Building Industry. In T. Cherkasky, J. Greenbaum, P. Mambrey, and J. K. Pors, eds., *Proceedings of the Participatory Design Conference (November 28–December 1, 2000, New York)*. Palo Alto, CA: CPSR Press.

Rittenbruch, M., H. Kahler, and A. B. Cremers. 1998. Supporting Cooperation in a Virtual Organization. In R. Hirschheim, M. Newman, and J. I. DeGross, eds., *Proceedings of the International Conference on Information Systems (ICIS) '98 (December 13–16)*, 30–38.

Robertson, T. 1998. Shoppers and Tailors: Participative Practices in Small Australian Design Companies. *Computer Supported Cooperative Work* 7(3–4): 205–221.

Schuler, D., and A. Namioka, eds. 1993. *Participatory Design: Principles and Practices*. Hillsdale, NJ: Erlbaum.

Suchman, L. 1994. Working Relations of Technology Production and Use. *Computer Supported Cooperative Work* 2: 21–39.

Törpel, B. 2000. Self-Employed Labor Meets Codetermination: Participatory Design in Network Organizations. In T. Cherkasky, J. Greenbaum, P. Mambrey, and J. K. Pors, eds., *Proceedings of the Participatory Design Conference (November 28–December 1, 2000, New York)*. Palo Alto, CA: CPSR Press.

Trigg, R., and S. I. Anderson, eds. 1996. Special Issue on Current Perspectives on Participatory Design. *Human-Computer Interaction* 11.

Voß, G., and H. Pongratz. 1998. Der Arbeitskraftunternehmer. Eine neue Grundform der Ware Arbeitskraft. *Kölner Zeitschrift für Soziologie und Sozialpsychologie* 50(1): 131–158.

Wulf, V., and M. Rohde. 1995. Toward an Integrated Organization and Technology Development. In G. M. Olson and S. Schuon, eds., *Proceedings of the Symposium on Designing Interactive Systems* (Ann Arbor, August 23–25, 1995), 55–64. New York: ACM Press.

Wulf, V., M. Krings, O. Stiemerling, G. Iacucci, P. Fuchs-Frohnhofen, J. Hinrichs, M. Maidhof, B. Nett, and R. Peters. 1999. Improving Inter-Organizational Processes with Integrated Organization and Technology Development. *Journal of Universal Computer Science* 5(6): 339–365.

17

Large-Scale Requirements Analysis as Heterogeneous Engineering

Mark Bergman, John Leslie King, and Kalle Lyytinen

Information systems development (ISD) has remained a high-risk proposition despite huge advances in computing and telecommunications technologies. Information systems projects in general, and large information systems projects in particular, continue to fail at an unacceptable rate (Abdel-Hamid and Madnick 1990; Myers 1994; Drummond 1996; Mitev 1996; Rosenwein 1997). While some portion of troubled ISD projects are turned around successfully, intensive research in the past has generated too little understanding of how to avoid failures in large systems development initiatives. From the growing incidence of failed projects, we conclude that advances in technologies are not sufficient to save large systems projects. Instead, large projects remain susceptible to failure until we learn to understand how technological, organizational, and institutional changes are interwoven in large systems and how systems developers should accordingly state and manage requirements for such systems.

Consider the following example. On March 11, 1993, the world was shocked by the sudden cancelation of the Taurus project, which the London Stock Exchange had been developing for more than six years. Taurus was expected to be instrumental in the radical restructuring of the securities trade, widely known as the Big Bang, by forming a backbone system for the London Stock Exchange. The project cost the Stock Exchange \$130 million, and securities companies invested \$600 million more (Drummond 1996). After years of alternating embarrassments and heroic efforts, Taurus was canceled before a single module was implemented because the required functionality and performance could never be delivered.

Although Taurus was a very complex project, involving novel technologies and massive organizational and institutional scale, ineffective project controls allowed requirements to change continuously throughout the project. Moreover, management ignored clear warning signs about organizational and technical risks, while powerful interests pushed for Taurus's development despite confusion over the system's purpose and design. There was little understanding of what the system was supposed to do and what stakeholders it should serve. In the end, advocates had an almost superstitious faith in the project, dismissing objections and proposals for modifications and clearer statement of the requirements with comments like "we have had all those arguments. Great idea but no, we have been arguing about it for twelve years, forget it" (Drummond 1996, 352). With the benefit of hindsight, the Taurus failure could have been averted by adjusting its course based on a more delicate and politically sensitive requirements engineering. But this was not done despite a well-known truism shared both in academia and industry that systematic requirements engineering is a keystone to a successful delivery of a large-scale system. The failure of Taurus can be partly attributed to the dismissal of this well-known fact, but we think there is more to learn. Taurus's failure was also due to the fact that we have poor knowledge about how to state and manage requirements for large systems that involve political and institutional elements.

Stating requirements for such systems is not just a technical exercise, but necessitates a new mind-set that we call *heterogeneous engineering* after Hughes (Hughes 1979a, 1979b, 1987). Heterogeneous engineering sees all requirements specifications as inherently heterogeneous due to the need to establish stable networks involving both social and technical elements through engineering (if the network is not stable the system fails!). As Law (1987, 112) puts this: "The argument is that those who build artifacts do not concern themselves with artifacts alone, but must also consider the way in which the artifacts relate to social, economic, political, and scientific factors. All of these factors are interrelated, and all are potentially malleable." Consequently, requirements engineers need to be seen as "heterogeneous engineers" who must successfully associate entities that range from people, through skills, to artifacts and natural phenomena.

In this chapter we will examine the problem of stating and managing requirements for large systems development initiatives qua "heterogeneous engineering." Our argument is twofold. First, we will argue that failures like the Taurus disaster happen not only because existing approaches to requirements engineering have not been adopted. We contend that current requirements engineering techniques used *alone* will not do the job. This is because they are based on a fallacious assumption that business problems and political problems can be separated from technical *requirements engineering* concerns of how to specify a consistent and complete technical solution to a business problem. In contrast, large-scale systems development initiatives involve a simultaneous consideration of business, institutional, political, technical, and behavioral issues. Second, based on behavioral theories of decision making, we argue that solutions and problems are intertwined and addressed simultaneously during a requirements engineering process. Thus, requirements engineering can be understood only by using theories of behavioral and institutional decision making along with applied technical understandings, but not only through the lens of rational technical "engineering."

This chapter is organized as follows. In the second section, we examine the received "view" of requirements engineering as outlined by the proponents of the current requirements engineering literature. Our conclusion is that though forming a necessary step toward an understanding of the difficulties involved in requirements engineering for technical change, the current view is insufficient alone to understand how technical requirements relate to the organizational and institutional "problems." Therefore, in the third section, we propose an alternative concept of requirements engineering that we call the *functional ecology of requirements*. In this view, requirements are not discovered but constructed as mappings between solution and problem spaces. The construction process involves a protracted "walk" between these spheres. The fourth section examines the implications of the functional ecology model. The fifth section concludes the chapter by considering some implications for both research and practice of requirements engineering.

Requirements Engineering Defined

The concept of a systems requirement has been relatively well known in the systems and software engineering literature since the mid-1970s. The concept was originally conceived to involve the stating of *what* the system is supposed to do before stating *how* the system produces the desired functionality (Ross 1977). The earliest concepts of systems requirements can be traced back to the work of Langefors (Langefors 1966) and to some early attempts to develop high-level systems description languages.[1] One reason for separating the *how* and the *what* has to do with the desire to achieve what we call a "responsibility push-back." By this we mean the desire to relegate the failure to develop or implement the system to the prior environment, which gave rise to the definition of the systems development task. Such attempts to move the "reasons" for failure to higher-level systems environments have been a continuing trend in software engineering and systems development since the mid-1970s. This has gradually shifted the interest of the software engineering and systems development communities from implementation considerations (like "structured programming," "structured design") into problems of how to define what the system is expected to do and what this involves. This is currently fashionably called *requirements engineering* (RE) (Kotonya and Sommerville 1998).

The main concept in requirements engineering is the desire to repeatedly create successful systems. The main interest in the requirements engineering literature is to explore ways of expressing and articulating the desire to develop the system—that is, how to define features of the new systems, or how to change current systems that will solve an identified business need, want, or desire (Loucopoulos and Karakostas 1995; Pohl 1996; Sommerville and Sawyer 1997). Therefore, the requirements engineering literature has concentrated on developing tools and methods that answer questions like the following: Whose desire? How to express the desire? Who and what define success and failure criteria for addressing the desire? For example, when doing user-centered design, the end users of the new or changed system are expected to define success and failure criteria (Pohl 1996; Noyes and Baber 1999). At the same time, knowledge of the current state of the art of system design can influence the choice of success and failure criteria. These can be seen as systems design constraints and opportunities, which can also affect—that is, change—the identified business wants, needs, and desires. In general, requirements in the received literature are seen to establish these success and failure criteria. The "received" definition is the IEEE standard 610.12 (Loucopoulos and Karakostas 1995, 2; Pohl 1996, 4), which defines *requirement* as:

1. A condition or capability needed by a user to solve a problem or achieve an objective.
2. A condition or capability that must be met or possessed by a system or a system component to satisfy a contract, standard, specification, or other formally imposed document.
3. A documented representation of a condition or capability as in 1 or 2.

Accordingly, requirements engineering denotes a set of methodologies and procedures used to gather, analyze, and produce a requirements specification for a proposed new system or a change in an existing system.

The Functional Ecology of Requirements

In this section we will create a schematic representation of RE from an *emergent functional perspective*. The term *functional* suggests that any RE analysis is done in pursuit of practical objectives for a given task domain, such as to make task accomplishment more efficient and/or effective. We use the term *emergent* to capture the evolutionary view of how organizational goals, problems, and solutions are constructed during the RE, as opposed to discovered, in alignment with a behavioral view of human decision making. Though this perspective is still in line with a prevailing model of technical rationality in which it is assumed that organizational goals are clear, it departs from it in how organizations and actors can approach these goals and what mechanisms are available for accomplishing these objectives.

A prevailing bias in the RE literature is the notion that requirements exist "out there" waiting to be captured by the systems analyst and then refined into a complete and consistent specification for the system that will subsequently be created (Davis 1993; Loucopoulos and Karakostas 1995; Macaulay 1996; Pohl 1996; Kotonya and Sommerville 1998).

Consequently, the main focus has been on formalizing the *content* of the system that will deliver the solutions and on how this meets the objectives of being complete and consistent. Continued disappointing experiences in large-scale systems development suggest, however, that the challenge is a good deal more complicated. In this section we provide an overview of what we call the *functional ecology of requirements*—a new perspective for developing RE strategies that explains the origins and sources of such complexity and seeks to offer some means of understanding the challenge we are facing on both conceptual and practical levels for stating requirements.

Requirements Analysis Framework

The crux of the ecological view is to adopt insights from the study of human decision processes and to use this to inform our formulation of the RE framework. We draw on two major sources in this endeavor that deviate considerably from the predominant "technical rationality" model. First, in any complex development initiative, including RE, we must take seriously Simon's theory of bounded rationality (Simon 1979, 1982, vol. 2, 160–176) in that we can never find an optimal, but at most a *satisficing* solution. Accordingly, RE processes should be analyzed and understood from the viewpoint of heuristics, limited search spaces, and the quest for increased intelligence during the RE process. This is what RE methods and tools seek to offer. But their problem is that they scale up poorly for large systems, and in addition they fail to recognize the type of complexity inherent in large-scale RE.

Second, we will draw on the institutional and behavioral theories of decision making that have, in past decades, studied complex organizational decision-making processes involving complex social, business, or political change (March and Olsen 1976; Lindblom 1979). These studies have shown that complex organizational decisions are not discrete events (i.e., bets) in which pros and cons are weighed and optimal decisions are rendered. Instead, organizational decision making forms protracted processes of iteration in which problems search for solutions, solutions search for problems, and decision makers search for decisions to be made (March and Olsen 1976). In organizational theory, this is described as the "garbage-can model." It is so named because of the relatively permanent nature of the cans in which different solutions, problems, and decisions are "thrown" within an organizational arena. Available experience from many large-scale RE and SE (e.g., software engineering) initiatives coincide with this view. The development of the World Wide Military Command and Control System (WWMCCS) of the 1970s and early 1980s formed a continued process of redefining this "can" over two decades. Hence, contrary to common assumptions underlying RE, RE decisions are implicated by solutions searching for problems rather than the other way around. The behavioral study of decision making has thus benefited from the transformation of the "problem → solution" construction to a new and more evolutionary view of iteration represented as "solution → problem → solution."

We will apply this model to the area of RE, and will therefore begin with an examination of the "solution space" of requirements, followed by an examination of the "problem space." This leads to the articulation of the requirements analysis process as an iterative "walk" between the solution and problem spaces. The main components of the framework are depicted in figure 17.1. The acronyms M and N in the figure describe how different components in the RE environment can be related to one another during a RE process (i.e., many to many). Below, each component and its relationships are explained in more detail.

Solution Space

The ecological view suggests that any RE process starts from an existing solution space that will be affected by a proposed new or changed system (see figure 17.1). This continuous construction and movement of the solutions is depicted by the rotating arrows around the solution space. The "existing solution" space we call the *current solution space*, denoted as S_t. Fundamentally, this space embodies a history of solved social, technical, and procedural problems and constitutes the legacy of previously solved organizational problems. The definition denies that solutions exist ahistorically. Instead, they are socially constructed and legitimized. Capabilities to produce such solutions must be acquired and maintained in the surrounding sociotechnical system. Therefore, the solution space is intimately related to the principals—that is, a set of actors who can represent themselves as capable of arriving at solutions to an identified

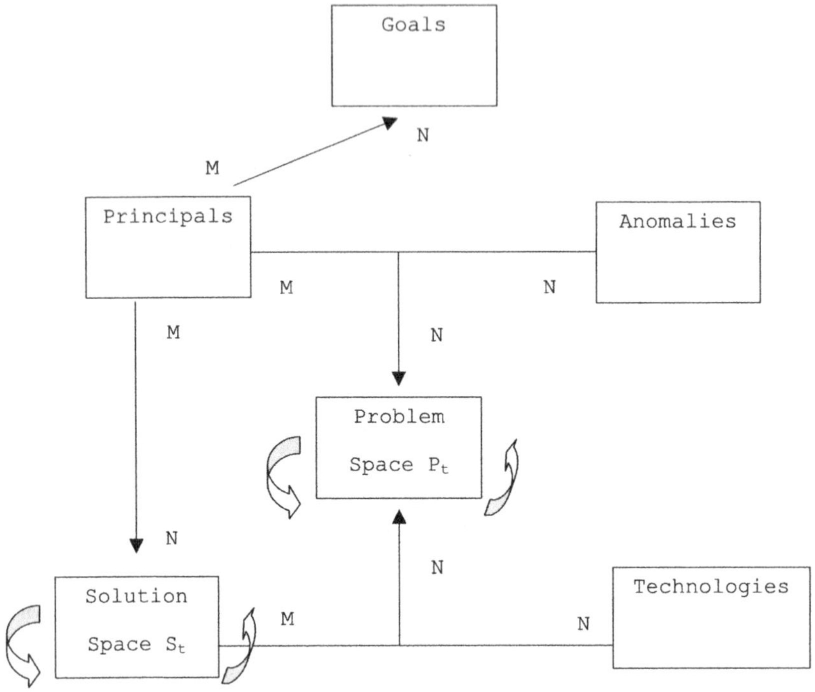

Figure 17.1
Requirements analysis framework

problem, or who possess specific skills that can result in specific solutions. The solutions are socially constructed in the sense that the principals must find solutions to fit their problems and thereby accept the legitimacy of a specific solution to their specific problem. Principals also have incentives to create their own solutions (e.g., goals) so they can influence the social system in which they reside and obtain resources. Accordingly, solutions often search for problems and not the other way around.

Working solutions form instantiations of one or more principals' successful attempts to adapt generic as well as custom technologies to suit specific business or social problems in a sociotechnical system. Hence, solutions embody new ways of carrying out organizational tasks with novel configurations of social arrangements and technical artifacts. Our

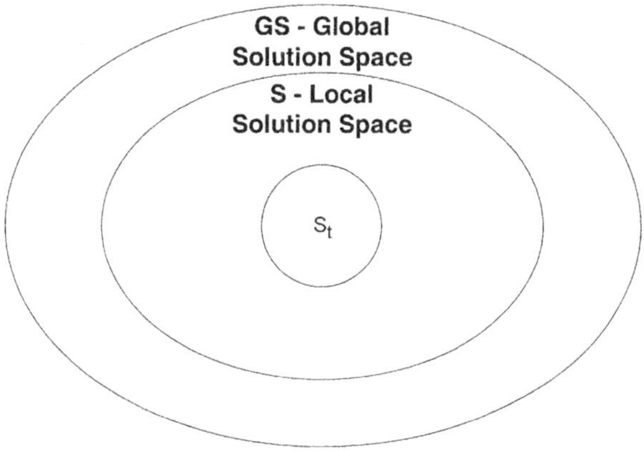

Figure 17.2
Solution spaces

concept of technology is thus a heterogeneous one in the sense that it covers both social and managerial innovations, and technical innovations that draw on properties and laws of the physical world (Law 1987).

In general, there is a M:N (e.g., many-to-many) relationship between technologies and solutions. Hence, any given technology can be used to solve many types of problems and the same type of technology can be used to solve many problems. Moreover, any given problem can be solved or approached (in the spirit of sociotechnical design) by the application of many types of technologies. This heterogeneity also provides a basis for the garbage-can model of organizational decision making: organizations can and often will throw several types of technologies into the "can" in their attempts to solve any given problem.

Organizations change over time, as do their solution spaces. We use the subscript *t* ($_t$) to denote a snapshot of the organizational workspace at time *t*. A *local solution space*, depicted by S in figure 17.2, is the current solution space and all locally accessible solution spaces that can be reached from the current solution space using available skills and resources offered by the principals.[2] A local solution space forms a subset of a *global solution space*, denoted GS. The global solution space is the space of all feasible solution spaces, including those not currently accessible from the local solution space and that require mobilization of all principals and technologies. Reasons for not being able to reach them can be due to lack of resources, lack of intelligence (i.e., this solution is not known or cannot be connected effectively to any known problem), cognitive bias, shifting goals, or incompatibility with organizational goal(s) or political structure. In general, a local solution space represents the range of all locally accessible solution spaces with regard to organizational resource limitations, but without regard to any particular proposed new product. A local solution space is a more general form of a product space (Davis 1993), but it contains the essential attributes and context of the product space.

Anomaly and Problem Spaces

The source of a problem is an *anomaly*—that is, a known existing inconsistency between the current solution space and a desired solution space.[3] We call the set of all such inconsistencies an existing *anomaly space*. An anomaly is only a potential problem, because not all anomalies are attended to as problems that need to be solved.

An anomaly, however, becomes a problem only when it is observed and acted on by a *principal with a standing to act*. Standing refers here to the power to define and legitimize an anomaly as a problem to be solved by collective action, and the demonstrated capability to mobilize means to address a defined problem.[4] A principal is thus assumed to hold organizational power—that is, to have access to means by which she or he can influence the others (Bacharach and Lawler 1980; Pfeffer 1981; Fairholm 1993). The exercise of standing is normally seen when an executive sets an organizational policy and objectives that provide a legitimization for a RE process. Standing can also be held by groups as well as individuals at different stages of the RE process that relate to possible rewards, incentives, or side effects of the possible system solution. Such standings are often held by "lower-level" participants in organizations like systems analysts. Standing can and also needs to be changed, and it can easily drift during a complex RE process. In the RE literature, principals are called *business stakeholders* (Wieringa 1996; Kotonya and Sommerville 1998).

Due to cognitive limitations, some anomalies are not recognized by actors with a standing, and thus are not acted on. Similarly, anomalies can be observed by principals as problems, but they choose not to act on them due to their resource constraints or difficulty in defining a solution space linked with the problem (e.g., goal failure). Such processes of inattention normally relate to observed high functional, technical, or implementation risks related to moving to a possible solution space (Lyytinen, Mathiassen, and Ropponen 1998). Anomalies can also turn into problems at later stages of RE, or further down in the design process due to learning by doing. In the same vein, principals can later drop problems out of consideration and reinterpret them as mere anomalies, or even beyond that if they change their goal sets, or observe high obstacles to moving from the current solution space to the target space.[5]

Although the underlying causes of anomalies can spring from many sources, the conversion of an anomaly to a problem is a social process we call *problematization*. Problematization begins long before a recognizable problem space has emerged in RE. It begins with a principal's decisions standing to act or not act on anomalies that turn them into problems. Often, these problematizations can start with the *metaproblems* of finding out what the problem is to which a solution can be applied. During this activity, principals determine and apply legitimizing reasons to change an anomaly into a problem. Legitimate reasons relate to the *goals* (see figure 17.1)—that is, desirable properties of those solution spaces that can be reached from the current solution space. Any principal can pursue several goals at the same time, and the same goals can be chosen by several principals.

An important capability of a principal with standing is thus the power to define particular characteristics of the problem space.[6] Such features can include who has a right to address that problem space, why this is regarded as the problem space, and so on. Moreover, as Fairholm (1993, 7) suggests, such power entails "*the ability to gain aims in interrelationship with others, even in the face of their opposition.*" Because the principals define the problems and, by implication, their solutions, they can be considered the most important systems design stakeholders.

The space of all problems implied by a current solution space S_t is called the *problem space*, denoted as P. A problem space (e.g., the space of all selected problems) is by definition always a subset of an anomaly space. Hence, a *proposed system problem space*, denoted by

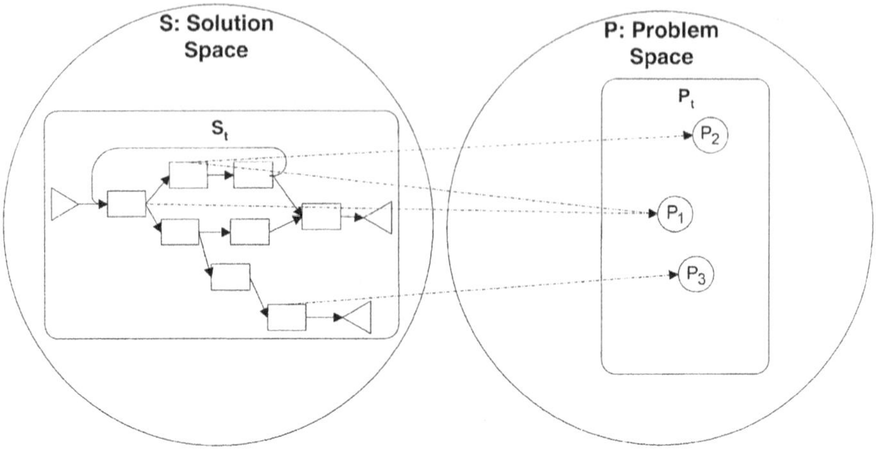

Figure 17.3
Solution and problem spaces

P_t, contains all the recognized and chosen problems by all the principals at time *t*.[7] All problems in P_t are contextualized by S_t[8] and are associated with a proposed new system or system change. Figure 17.3 shows this general relationship between S_t and P_t. The arcs in figure 17.3 represent the connection to the problems in P_t from their contextualizing source in S_t.

Also, as shown in figure 17.3, multiple solution sources can point to any one problem and any one solution source can lead to multiple problems. This corresponds to the M:N relationship between the solution space and problem space as depicted in figure 17.1. What this means is that it is possible for a single problem to have multiple contextualizing sources. Also, a single solution source can contextualize multiple problems.

RE in this characterization involves a deliberate *construction* of an ecology consisting of a solution space and a problem space.[9] The objective of RE is to reconcile all essential aspects of the solution space and the problem space, producing a specification for a particular solution space that can be achieved at some future time point $t + x$[10] that will mitigate or eliminate the identified problem space. This is an iterative process in which new information on both the solution space and the

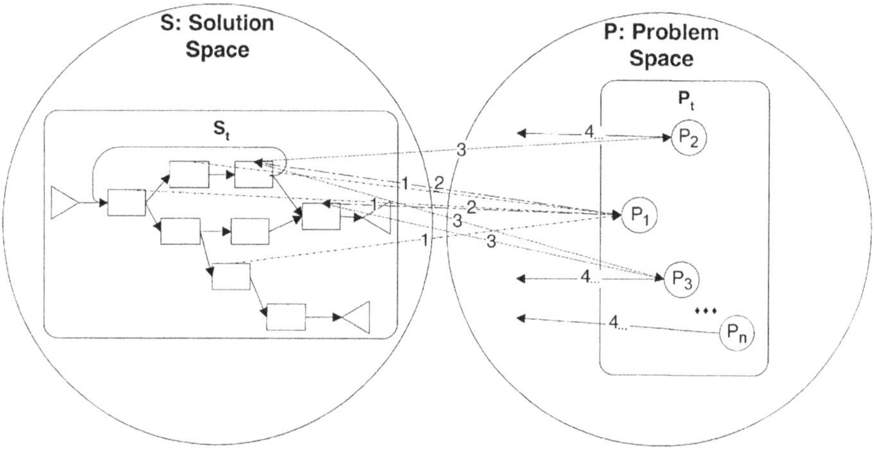

Figure 17.4
Problem blossoming

problem space is discovered, and in which decisions need to be made to restate both the solution space and the problem space in the direction of reconciliation. The specification is a product of a coevolutionary process of discovery and decision, in which both the solution space and the problems space are constructed. Although this process is influenced by many constraints arising from the environment itself (e.g., physical laws, technical choices, legal considerations, institutional influences, organizational goals and capabilities, market forces), it remains a social process of negotiation and inquiry that is constrained by bounded rationality and limited organizational resources.

Evolving the Problem Space: Problem Blossoming

The process of problematization frequently uncovers other anomalies that are deemed problems. This can trigger an iterative reconsideration of the current solution space in turn. This is the process of *problem blossoming*. Figure 17.4 shows this process in action. Arcs 1 and 3 (and beyond) in figure 17.4 present the identification of new anomalies. Arcs 2 and 4 (and beyond) present the identification of new areas of S_t that are now affected by the discovered anomalies.[11] If these anomalies become defined as problems, they become part of P_t.

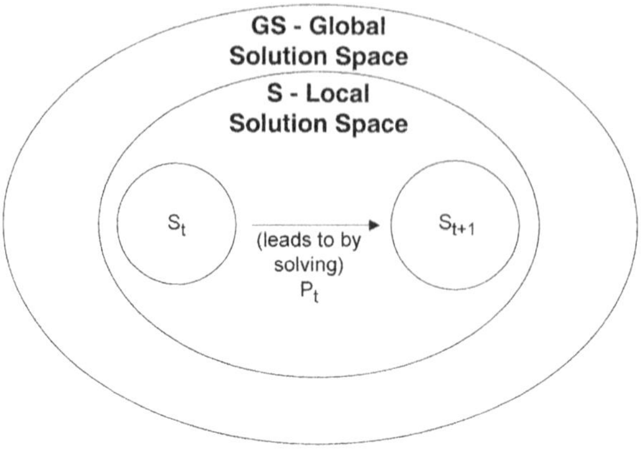

Figure 17.5
Solution space transformation

This iterative process can change the contents, and hence the structure, of the current solution space (S_t) as well as the problem space (P_t). This process can be iterated as long as the affected areas of S_t are being discovered and the corresponding anomalies, and resulting problems, are constructed. Once complete, or prematurely stopped by a principal with standing due to the fear of endless search, the resulting problem set is called P_t.[12]

Proposed Solution

A proposed solution, denoted as S_{t+1} (shown in figure 17.5), forms a subspace of the solution space that includes the reconciliation of S_t to P_t. Each part of a proposed solution must be reconciled with one or more problems in P_t. The process of reconciliation, changing S_t into S_{t+1} by solving for P_t, is called a *solution space transformation*, which results in defining a new local solution space, S.[13] During this process, constraints are seen as limitations of current organizational resources as well as limitations concerning the product IS, including people, artifacts, rules, processes, and the like.

The goal is to find an optimum path from S_t to S_{t+1}. This is seldom the case in any given requirements analysis effort, because (1) the prospect of attaining global solutions is quite remote, (2) systems analysts cannot foresee the future, and (3) their cognitive and resource limits

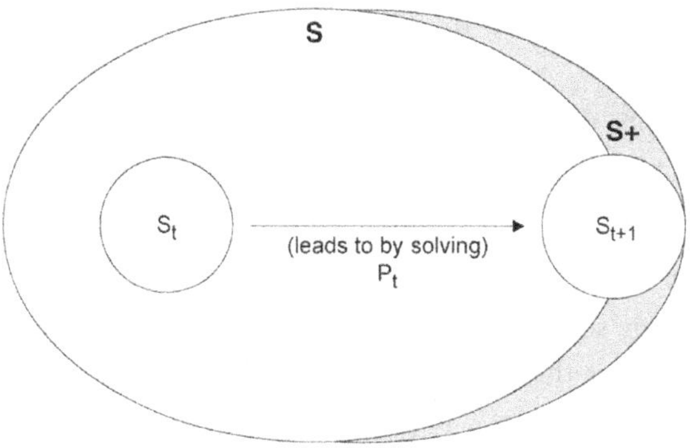

Figure 17.6
Expansion of solution space

make any analysis a suboptimal endeavor. Successful systems analysts therefore can, and often do, create additional complexity and difficulty in comprehending S. The task of the analyst is to find a traversable path from a current solution space to a new one (Haumer et al. 1999). This is accomplished by identifying problems that will arise during the process of transformation. In other words, the analyst's job is at the intersection of the solution spaces (and technologies embedded in them) and the problem space.

A possible outcome of the solution space transformation is to expand the local solution space, S. As shown in figure 17.6, solving P_t can lead to a S_{t+1} that expands S to S+. Expanding S means not only an expansion of the technical capability, but also an expansion of the organizational capability in that analysts do discover new information and gain new insights. Hence, an expansion of S can open previously unavailable opportunities. This process could even expand the GS, a general solution space, and thus demonstrate organizational learning and innovation in the sense that new solution "frames" have been created (Lyytinen, Rose, and Welke 1998).[14]

Redefining Requirements

At this point in the chapter, we can contrast our definition of requirements with the "received" definition that is common to the RE literature, as delineated in an earlier section:

1. A condition or capability needed by a user to solve a problem or achieve an objective.
2. A condition or capability that must be met or possessed by a system or a system component to satisfy a contract, standard, specification, or other formally imposed document.
3. A documented representation of a condition or capability as in 1 or 2.

Part 1 focuses on meeting some expressed desire of a principal with standing, usually the client or the system's intended user. Such requirements have been called "functional" requirements (Loucopoulos and Karakostas 1995; Pohl 1996). Part 2 departs from the issue of desire and addresses compliance with conditions set by social circumstances. Such requirements have been referred to as "nonfunctional" requirements (Loucopoulos and Karakostas 1995; Pohl 1996). Part 3 makes it mandatory that a requirement be represented in a document. In other words, if a requirement is not written up, or the equivalent, it is not a requirement. A good summary of the IEEE definition, accordingly, would be the following: *A requirement specifies a written want, need, or desire that solves a problem in the context of a set of constraints or a written constraint imposed by a formal document.*[15]

We depart from this nomenclature in two ways. First, we see requirements not as solutions to problems, but as a set of *relationships* between a solution space and a problem space. Solutions to problems are determined in design, not requirements. As such, requirements are no more fixed than the evolving understanding of the characteristics of the solution space and the problem space. Requirements in this sense cannot be *discovered*, but rather must be *constructed* by a search in the search space that covers all known mappings between the problem space and the solution space.[16] They are represented by the arcs, shown in figure 17.7, between the problem and solution spaces and where the problem space analysis postulates an alternative solution space for the problem set. We call this alternative solution space a *future solution space* (S′), represented by S′. S′ contains a proposed solution, S_{t+1} (originally from figure 17.5). Any given future solution space can, consequently, become the focus of the systems development or enhancement project. Requirements provide links to solution space contextualization and the problems

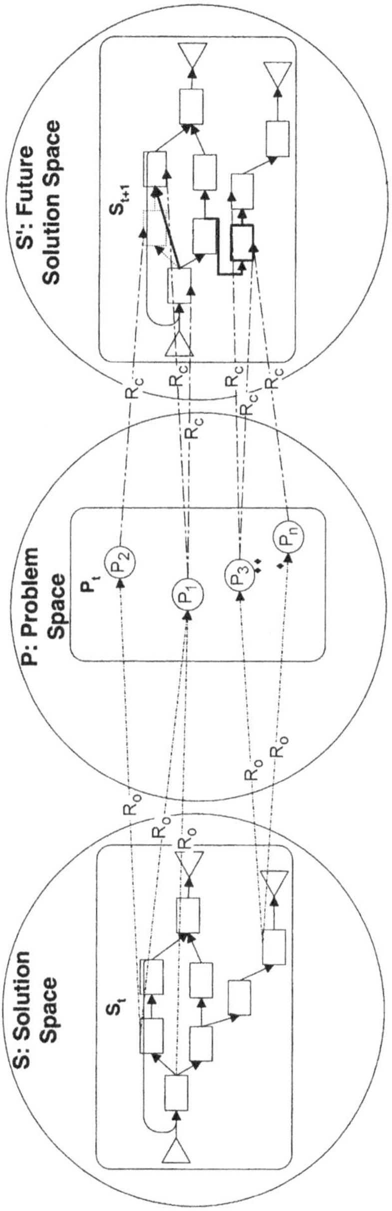

Figure 17.7
Requirements arcs

that truly need to be addressed by a future solution. Taken together, requirements become a contextualized rules framework in which a future solution can be constructed via project design.

Second, we apply insights from the functional ecology of requirements to redefine requirement types. We refer to what the literature calls a functional requirement as an *objective requirement*, denoted by R_o. An objective requirement is defined as a want, need, or desire that corresponds to a problem (e.g., P_n within P_t) as contextualized by a part or all of a current solution (e.g., S_t). A R_o is represented by an arc from a solution to a problem, as shown in figure 17.7.[17] In this way, R_o can be viewed as a relationship that comes from a solution looking for a problem.

We refer to what the literature calls a nonfunctional requirement as a constraint, denoted by R_c. A *constraining requirement*—for example, a *constraint*—is defined as a restraining condition imposed on a solution within S_{t+1} as contextualized by a problem within P_t.[18] A R_c is represented by an arc from a problem to a new solution, as shown in figure 17.7.[19] The third part of the IEEE requirement definition remains unchanged—that is, requirements must still be documented in some way for the principal(s).

Taken together, R_o and R_c fill in the arrows in the "solution → problem → solution" framework. Hence, figure 17.7 represents a model of the functional ecology of requirements.

Implications

An implication of the new requirements definition is that since solutions and problems are heterogeneous in nature, as discussed earlier, requirements are therefore heterogeneous in nature as well. This supports the earlier discussion of requirements as heterogeneous engineering (Hughes 1987; Law 1987). This also means requirements of one type can be related to, and hence, can affect requirements of other types.

Another implication of the new requirements definition is that, by transitivity, the principal(s) who own the problem(s) that are used to define a R_o or R_c are also the owners of that R_o or R_c. This point is needed to repair an ownership gap that appears between problems and requirements. Together, R_o and R_c form the basis of a *requirements specifica-*

tion. A requirements specification is the set of requirements selected for attention by the principal requirements owners. By induction, requirements owners are the primary stakeholders of the systems design. Also, by induction, since requirements are heterogeneous, the requirements specification is a heterogeneous, yet holistic, view of the project under consideration.

The activity of requirements analysis according to this new definition constructs a set of dynamic relationships between specific solution spaces and a specific problem space such that the specific principal's objectives are realized in the context of constraints. This definition is simple and clear, but its simplicity can be misleading. The challenge for researchers and practitioners alike is in the adjective *specific* that appears before the words *solution* and *problem.* We argue that most requirements analyses fail as a result of insufficient or incorrect specificity (i.e., level of detail and certainty) concerning the links between the solution and problem spaces. In fact, in many cases it can be extremely difficult to achieve such specificity due to problems of bounded rationality, changing environmental conditions, limited resources, problem blossoming, or political shifts among the stakeholders.

As noted earlier, multiple solution parts can point to one problem and any one solution part can lead to multiple problems. Hence, there is a M:N relationship between S_t and P_t. This suggests that there can be a nonlinear number of R_o arcs between the nodes of the two spaces. Similarly, a problem can affect multiple parts of a future solution, while multiple problems can point to the same part of a solution. Hence, similar to R_o, there is a many-to-many relationship between P_t and S_{t+1}. This allows for a nonlinear number of R_c arcs in relation to their sources. In short, requirements at a given time can be represented as the set of all the arcs, (R_o, R_c), that reflect the contextualized connections between the problem space and the current and future solution space.

The final set of requirement arcs between S_t, P_t, and S_{t+1} can be seen to form a network of interrelationships—for example, a *requirements web.* Any change to even a single part of S_t can affect a large number of problems in P_t. The change is nonlinear in size. Also, due to the reflexivity of the connections via problem blossoming from P_t to S_t, any such change can show up in other parts of S_t itself. Accordingly, any change in P_t can result in a nonlinear number of new or changed connections to S_t and S_{t+1}. Therefore, a small change in S_t or P_t could result in a nonlinear—that is, potentially explosive—change in the requirements (R_o, R_c).

In addition, a change in one requirement could have a nonlinear change effect on other requirements. This has been observed as the "cascade effect" of requirements change, and forms the source of a phenomenon that has been called *requirements shift* and *requirements creep* (Gause and Weinberg 1989; Pohl 1996). Also, in large-systems design, a nonlinear number of requirements connections coupled with nonlinear change effects can yield a very complex, yet delicate requirements web. This can, in turn, lead to "requirements paralysis"—that is, the rational fear of changing requirements due to the possible impact of a change.[20] This is supported by the observed failures in the Taurus project (Drummond 1996). The combination of requirements paralysis, bounded rationality, and organizational resource limitations can create the impression that any serious attempt to change requirements or to change their base problems or solutions would result in incurring spiraling costs that are simply too high for the current principals to pay. This can lead into a path of escalation—for example, increasing commitment to a failing course of action, if the project under consideration starts to falter (Keil and Montealegre 2000).

Another implication of recursive, reflexive, nonlinear requirements change is that *determining requirements also determines stakeholders*—for example, shifting requirements can shift the composition of the stakeholders. Shifts can even change who can be a stakeholder. This means the original principals of a project to implement a new or changed system may not be the final principals of the project. The implications of this can have profound effects on the process of requirements determination.

Conclusions

The functional ecology of requirements—that is, the intricate linking and evolution of solution and problem spaces vis-à-vis a set of principals—suggests that requirements are not solutions to problems. Rather, they establish links between solution spaces and problem spaces in a changing environment of environmental conditions, shifting principals, and evolution of organizational knowledge (what is a solution, what is a problem). Accordingly, requirements emerge through the identification of anomalies in the existing solution space that are declared by a principal with standing to be problems, followed by an effort to identify new solutions that would reconcile with those problems. Any effort to identify new links between solution and problem spaces can uncover information that alters perceptions of both the problem and solution space and the set of principals. Under this model, requirements are not waiting to be *discovered* by an analyst, but rather are systematically *constructed* through an iterative and evolutionary process of defining and redefining the problem and solution spaces (see also Iivari 1990a). The construction process is by definition imperfect and often inefficient due to bounded rationality, organizational resource limitations, uncertainty due to changing environmental conditions, and changing views of principals with standing while new information is discovered. Moreover, changes in the problem space will affect the solution space in nonlinear ways, with modest changes in one having the possibility of creating large changes in the other. The same holds in reverse. Thus, requirements analysis can be exceedingly difficult due to this instability, even in cases where organizational objectives are relatively clear.

We believe that an articulation of the functional ecology of requirements captures one key reason for the persistent failures in systems development, when the target system operates in complex domains. The crux of the ecology is the recursive and reflexive relationship between solution spaces and problem spaces, and the fact that each can influence the other in nonlinear ways. This creates a situation in which "real" problems and their corresponding "real" solutions can be impossible to pin down with confidence. In such situations, the temptation is strong to abandon the analysis and shift to old, (at one time) reliable heuristics and learning by doing in order to implement one feasible solution without ever really pinning down its requirements. Such a shift would correspond to a random walk from the current solution space to a new solution space. This signals a failure to state the requirements. In other cases, principals can simply declare a particular problem/solution space alignment to be real and proceed to implementation. We call this the "early-out strategy," and it was followed with disastrous consequences in the Taurus system. In the former case no specification is produced; in the latter it is likely that a bad specification will be produced and declared to be good by the powers that be. Either can be damaging to organizational welfare, but the latter is often more destructive because resources are consumed in a futile effort to build a useful system from bad specifications, and organizational confidence in systems development suffers (Markus and Keil 1994; Keil 1995).

As per the functionalist requirements model, care needs to be taken to minimize the chance that size and impacts of possible requirements will cascade effects. One possible way is to apply the concept of *separation of concerns* and *modularization* (Brooks 1995) at the heterogeneous level of the requirements web, not just the technical level. Such constructs can act as a "firebreak" to the "wildfire" of cascade failures at the points of modular connection. This strategy requires a more holistic approach in constructing a requirements specification. This corresponds to the construction of complex subassemblies as discussed by Simon (1996). Such subassemblies, as argued by Simon, allow for the creation of more stable and more highly complex systems. Complex subassemblies can be heterogeneous—that is, a system composed of different types of parts. Indeed, this technique can allow for different types of possible future solution combinations that may be difficult to see without such constructions.

A second method to be gained from this requirements model is the ability to identify "killer problems." A *killer problem* occurs when a problem that must be addressed for the system under consideration to be successful cannot be adequately addressed to deal with it. In other words, it is a gap between what is and what is wanted by one or more principals that is too wide to cross due to either (1) the cost of crossing the gap being too high for the current principals to pay, (2) it is simply not known how to cross it (e.g., outside the boundaries of GS), or (3) it is logically impossible to cross in that the resulting sociotechnical system will not stabilize. A killer problem could thus be a single problem or a web of interrelated problems in the spirit of heterogeneous engineering. The former are normally technical in nature, while the latter deals with heterogeneous elements in the solution space. Such problems combine functional, political, or technical issues and are thus extremely difficult to analyze and understand; as a result, they are often ignored. The main way to deal with a killer problem is to either reproblem (change the project by choosing alternative, solvable problem(s) where possible), partition the problem into subproblems that are solved one at a time ("muddling through"), or end the project.

Since requirements are relationships between problems and solutions, it is possible and likely for there to be *killer requirements* in large systems development initiatives. These are requirements that must be, but yet cannot be, adequately addressed for a system under consideration. We argue that these are either improper relationships or representations of contextualized killer problems. An improper relationship is one that creates an objective or constraint that cannot be met or that makes it impossible to meet one or more separate requirements. In this case, it may be possible to either drop the requirement or rework it such that the connection between the solution and problem (objective) or problem and solution (constraint) can still be realized and other conflicts mitigated. If such rework is not possible, this would indicate a gap that cannot be crossed between what is and what is wanted—that is, a killer problem. Unfortunately, such analyses are not normally done, and they rarely form part of a risk assessment.

The ability to uncover additional problems by problem blossoming makes it possible to discover killer problems, if they exist. Unfortunately, this could lead to a search in an exponential-size search space. There are at least two methods that can help deal with this problem. First, if separation of concerns and modularization are well applied, then the search space is reduced to the complex components and the combined system itself. This will tend to isolate such problems within these subdivisions or at the systems level, hence reducing the possible search space. Second, as problems are discovered by analysts, they tend to be quickly categorized in their level of difficulty to solve. Most problems in a new system have known solutions; otherwise the effort would be pointless. Some problems may not have obvious solutions, but usually there are known techniques to work around them. This leaves problems that people do not know how to solve once they are uncovered. These are potential killer problems, and they often relate to the heterogeneous nature of the RE activity—that is, to how the resulting sociotechnical system will stabilize. The list of these problems is likely to be rather small, but they are often "deadly enemies." As noted, these can also be some of the most tricky to either find or correctly identify. Still, being able to perform problem triage to identify the most serious problems should be part of a systems analyst's repertoire of RE techniques. We believe that applying the heterogeneous approach to systems analysis would allow analysts to discover more of these potential killer problems early in the project. In this sense, it can be considered a risk-reduction methodology.

This and other possible functionalist methodologies needed to deal with heterogeneous RE are the subject of future research. By improving the understanding of the complexity and uncertainty involved in performing RE, we should see an overall reduction in failed systems and a likely increase in the production of successful systems. In the end, this is the main goal of requirements engineering.

Glossary

Anomaly A known existing inconsistency between the current solution space and a desired solution space. An anomaly is only a potential problem, because not all anomalies are attended to as problems that need to be solved.

Anomaly Space The set of all anomalies associated with the system under consideration.

GS A *global solution space* is the space of all feasible solution spaces, including those not currently accessible from the local solution space and that require mobilization of all principals and technologies.

P The space of all problems implied by a current solution space S_t. A problem space (e.g., the space of all selected problems) is by definition always a subset of an anomaly space.

P_n A problem (1 of at least *n* problems) within P_t.

P_t A *proposed system problem space* is the space that contains all the recognized and chosen problems by all the principals at time *t*.

Principal A person with standing. Standing refers here to the power to define and legitimize an anomaly as a problem to be solved by collective action, and the demonstrated capability to mobilize means to address a defined problem. A principal is thus assumed to hold organizational power—that is, to have access to means by which she or he can influence the others.

Problem An anomaly that is observed and acted on by a principal with a standing to act.

Problem Blossoming The process of recursive problem determination. The process of problem determination (problematization) frequently uncovers other anomalies that are deemed problems. This can trigger an iterative reconsideration of the current solution space in turn. This, in turn, can lead to a further discovery of new anomalies, which can be deemed problems. This recursive process continues until all related problems are constructed or prematurely stopped by one or more principals.

R_c A *constraining requirement.* A constraining requirement, such as a *constraint*, is defined as a restraining condition imposed on a solution within S_{t+1} as contextualized by a problem within P_t. A R_c is represented by an arc from a problem to a new solution.

R_o An *objective requirement.* An objective requirement is defined as a want, need, or desire that corresponds to a problem (e.g., P_n within P_t) as contextualized by a part or all of a current solution (e.g., S_t). A R_o is represented by an arc from a solution to a problem. In this way, R_o can viewed as a relationship that comes from a solution looking for a problem.

S A *local solution space* is the current solution space and all locally accessible solution spaces that can be reached from the current solution space using available skills and resources offered by the principals.

S′ A *future solution space* is an alternative local solution space postulated from the problem space analysis for the problem set P_t. S′ contains a proposed solution, S_{t+1}.

S+ An expansion of the local solution space, S, due to an outcome of a solution space transformation. Expanding S means not only an expansion of the technical capability, but also an expansion of organizational capability.

S_t The *current solution space*, denoted as S_t. Fundamentally, this space embodies a history of solved social, technical, and procedural problems that constitutes the legacy of previously solved organizational problems.

S_{t+1} A *proposed solution* is a subspace of the future solution space, S′, that includes the reconciliation of S_t to P_t.

Solution Space Transformation The process of reconciliation—that is, changing S_t into S_{t+1} by solving for P_t.

Notes

1. For a good historical analysis, see Couger and Knapp 1974.

2. Those who are knowledgeable in possible-world semantics (or Kripke semantics; see e.g. Dowty, Wall, and Peters 1981) can see an immediate similarity with the set of solution spaces that can be reached from the current solution space and the concept of the accessibility relation R from any given possible world to

other possible worlds. The difference is that due to organizational learning, the set of possible solutions spaces accessible from the current solution space is not fixed but changes over time.

3. This is similar to DeTombe's simple definition of a problem (DeTombe 1994). It is also in alignment with the definition used in the RE literature (Kotonya and Sommerville 1998; Haumer et al. 1999).

4. This formulation does not exclude the possibility that the principal does not have these skills and capabilities available when the time to act occurs. We must, however, assume that there is some belief, among the actors involved, in such capabilities under the rational model; otherwise the principal should choose not to act at all. Within a political scenario, this is not necessarily the case. This suggestion is also derived from the idea that it is actors with solutions looking for problems rather than the other way round. Therefore, the demonstrated capability is important in any RE process.

5. These are known in the IS literature as abandoned projects or as the process of deescalation (Keil 1995; Keil and Montealegre 2000).

6. See Foucault's "those who have ability to define 'truth' are those who have power" (see Foucault and Gordon 1980, esp. 131–133).

7. The issue of "who gets to be a principal" is as important as "what is the problem." This issue is discussed throughout the rest of the chapter, but a more in-depth treatment is beyond the scope of the chapter.

8. A problem is understood within the context of the sociotechnical (e.g., organizational) ecology in which the solution space resides. Each problem is constructed, legitimized, and owned by one or more principals who reside in this ecology. Hence, all problems are ecologically situated (Suchman 1987), socially constructed (Berger and Luckmann 1966; March and Olsen 1976), and owned. Contextualization includes all these concepts.

9. In theoretical terms, a solution space is the subset of the local solution space (S) that is affected by as well as affecting the system change. In practical terms, a solution space can be represented as a model of this space—for instance, a (richly detailed) workflow or equivalent model.

10. For the sake of clarity, $t + x$ is replaced by $t + 1$ throughout the rest of the chapter. This is used to indicate the time of an operational future solution space.

11. For the sake of clarity, each anomaly in figure 17.4 has been defined into a problem.

12. Problem blossoming is similar to an aspect of Checkland's Soft Systems Methodology (SSM) (Checkland 1981; Checkland and Scholes 1990). However, problem blossoming is focused on problem discovery and identification of likely impacted parts of S_t. SSM, in contrast, focuses on the whole process of systems development. Problem blossoming and SSM share the basic components of iterative learning and discovery, as well as a recognition of the ability to change the current solution and problem spaces as per new insights.

13. This space, S, is similar to Davis's (1993, 42) *product space*, defined as "the range of all possible problem solutions that meets all known constraints."

14. We are using here the concept of frame as defined by Bijker (Bijker 1987). Bijker uses the term *frame* to denote a new aggregate of concepts and techniques employed by a community of problem solvers in its problem solving. Changes in frames embody "revolutions" and discontinuities in technology evolution. Such discontinuities are reflected in such elements as goals of technology use, theories and concepts, problem-solving steps and tools, and organizational and managerial principles related to problem-solving practices. An example of this is moving from structured programming to object-oriented programming.

15. Loucopoulos and Karakostas (1995), as well as most of the requirements engineering literature, transform a capability into functionality and a condition into a constraint (e.g., nonfunctionality). Functionality represents a want, need, or desire of one or more principals in S_t for a new capability to be made available in response to one or more of their problems in P_t. This corresponds with Gause and Weinberg's view on RE: a process to discover what people desire (Gause and Weinberg 1989). It is also in line with Graham's view, which focuses on what is needed by people (Graham 1998). A constraint represents a condition on a future solution in response to a problem.

16. The same observation has been confirmed by researchers advocating the spiral model of software development, which emphasizes the evolution and learning of requirements and the dynamic nature of mappings between requirements and implementations (see, e.g., Boehm 1988; Iivari 1990a, 1990b).

17. As discussed earlier, there could be many arcs from a solution source to a single problem. Still, each arc is an individual requirement. Also, the arrow on the arc (which is informational only) indicates that the node pointed to is contextualized by the node pointed from. In this case, a problem is contextualized by a solution.

18. A constraint does not originate in a formal document. It is rooted in one or more problems that are implied in the formal document. Since, by definition, these contextualizing problems come from a formal document, they must have principal representation and, thus, are part of P_t. But these problems are usually not clearly and specifically identified in most formal documents. This means they cannot be accurately represented within P_t. This is a source of potential requirements failure. The possibility exists of not truly solving the problems that the formal document wanted addressed by the project under consideration even if the constraints (or objectives) specified in a formal document are well met. In turn, this allows for the increased probability of an incorrect future solution, resulting in eventual deployment failure. All in all, this highlights the importance of constraints as traceable relationships, not just stated restrictions.

19. The lightened and bolded parts of S_{t+1} correspond to proposed changes in the solution space S_t in response to the problems in P_t.

20. See Bak's adding a grain of sand, causing an avalanche in a sandpile (Bak 1996).

References

Abdel-Hamid, T. K., and S. E. Madnick. 1990. The Elusive Silver Lining: How We Fail to Learn from Software Development Failures. *Sloan Management Review* 32(1): 39–48.

Bacharach, S. B., and E. J. Lawler. 1980. *Power and Politics in Organizations*. San Francisco: Jossey-Bass.

Bak, P. 1996. *How Nature Works: The Science of Self-Organized Criticality*. New York: Copernicus.

Berger, P. L., and T. Luckmann. 1966. *The Social Construction of Reality: A Treatise in the Sociology of Knowledge*. Garden City, NY: Doubleday.

Bijker, W. 1987. The Social Construction of Bakelite: Toward a Theory of Invention. In W. Bijker, T. Hughes and T. Pinch, eds., *The Social Construction of Technological Systems*, 159–190. Cambridge, MA: MIT Press.

Boehm, B. W. 1988, May. A Spiral Model of Software Development and Enhancement. *Computer*, pp. 61–72.

Brooks, F. P. 1995. *The Mythical Man-Month: Essays on Software Engineering*. Reading, MA: Addison-Wesley.

Checkland, P. 1981. *Systems Thinking, Systems Practice*. New York: Wiley.

Checkland, P., and J. Scholes. 1990. *Soft Systems Methodology in Action*. New York: Wiley.

Couger, D., and J. Knapp. 1974. *Systems Analysis Techniques*. London: Wiley.

Davis, A. M. 1993. *Software Requirements: Objects, Functions, and States*. Englewood Cliffs, NJ: Prentice Hall.

DeTombe, D. J. 1994. *Defining Complex Interdisciplinary Societal Problems: A Theoretical Study for Constructing a Cooperative Problem Analyzing Method: The Method COMPRAM*. Amsterdam: Thesis Publishers.

Dowty, D. R., R. E. Wall, and S. Peters. 1981. *Introduction to Montague Semantics*. Boston: Kluwer.

Drummond, H. 1996. The Politics of Risk: Trials and Tribulations of the Taurus Project. *Journal of Information Technology* 11: 347–357.

Fairholm, G. W. 1993. *Organizational Power Politics: Tactics in Organizational Leadership*. Westport, CT: Praeger.

Foucault, M., and C. Gordon. 1980. *Power Knowledge: Selected Interviews and Other Writings, 1972–1977*. New York: Pantheon Books.

Gause, D. C., and G. M. Weinberg. 1989. *Exploring Requirements: Quality before Design*. New York: Dorset House.

Graham, I. 1998. *Requirements Engineering and Rapid Development: An Object-Oriented Approach*. Reading, MA: Addison Wesley.

Haumer, P., P. Heymans, M. Jarke, and K. Pohl. 1999. *Bridging the Gap between Past and Future RE: A Scenario-Based Approach*. RE'99. Limerick, Ireland: IEEE Computer Society.

Hughes, T. 1979a. The Electrification of America: The System Builders. *Technology and Culture* 20(1): 124–161.

Hughes, T. 1979b. Emerging Themes in the History of Technology. *Technology and Culture* 20(4): 697–711.

Hughes, T. 1987. The Evolution of Large Technogical Systems. In W. Bijker, T. Hughes, and T. Pinch, eds., *The Social Construction of Technological Systems*, 51–82. Cambridge, MA: MIT Press.

Iivari, J. 1990a. Hierarchical Spiral Model for Information System and Software Development, Part 1: Theoretical Background. *Information and Software Technology* 32(6): 386–399.

Iivari, J. 1990b. Hierarchical Spiral Model for Information System and Software Development, Part 2: Design Process. *Information and Software Technology* 32(7): 450–458.

Keil, M. 1995. Pulling the Plug: Software Project Management and the Problem of Project Escalation. *MIS Quarterly* 19(4): 421–447.

Keil, M., and R. Montealegre. 2000. Cutting Your Losses: Extricating Your Organization When a Big Project Goes Awry. *Sloan Management Review* 41(3): 55–68.

Kotonya, G., and I. Sommerville. 1998. *Requirements Engineering: Processes and Techniques*. New York: Wiley.

Langefors, B. 1966. *Theoretical Analysis of Information Systems*. Lund, Sweden: Studentlitteratur.

Law, J. 1987. Technology and Heterogeneous Engineering: The Case of Portugese Expansion. In W. Bijker, T. Hughes, and T. Pinch, eds., *The Social Construction of Technological Systems*, 111–134. Cambridge, MA: MIT Press.

Lindblom, C. E. 1979. Still Muddling Through. *Public Administrative Review* 39: 517–526.

Loucopoulos, P., and V. Karakostas. 1995. *System Requirements Engineering*. London: McGraw-Hill.

Lyytinen, K., L. Mathiassen, and J. Ropponen. 1998. Attention Shaping and Software Risk: A Categorical Analysis of Four Classical Approaches. *Information Systems Research* 9(3): 233–255.

Lyytinen, K., G. Rose, and R. Welke. 1998. The Brave New World of Development in the Internet Work Computer Architecture (InterNCA): or How Distributed Computing Platforms Will Change Systems Development. *Information Systems Journal* 8(3): 241–253.

Macaulay, L. 1996. *Requirements Engineering*. London: Springer.

March, J. G., and J. P. Olsen. 1976. *Ambiguity and Choice in Organizations.* Bergen: Universitetsforlaget.

Markus, M. L., and M. Keil. 1994. If We Build It, They Will Come: Designing Information Systems That Users Want to Use. *Sloan Management Review* 35(4): 22.

Mitev, N. N. 1996. More Than a Failure? The Computerized Reservation Systems at French Railways. *Information Technology and People* 9(4): 8–19.

Myers, M. D. 1994. A Disaster for Everyone to See: An Interpretive Analysis of a Failed IS Project. *Accounting, Management, and Information Technologies* 4(4): 185–201.

Noyes, J. M., and C. Baber. 1999. *User-Centered Design of Systems.* London: Springer.

Pfeffer, J. 1981. *Power in Organizations.* Marshfield, MA: Pitman.

Pohl, K. 1996. *Process-Centered Requirements Engineering.* New York: Wiley.

Rosenwein, M. 1997. The Optimization Engine That Couldn't. *OR/MS Today* 24(4): 26–29.

Ross, D. 1977. Structured Analysis (SA): A Language for Communicating Ideas. *IEEE Transactions on Software Engineering* 3(1): 16–34.

Simon, H. A. 1979. Rational Decision Making in Business Organizations. *American Economic Review* 69(4): 493–513.

Simon, H. A. 1982. *Models of Bounded Rationality.* 3 vols. Cambridge, MA: MIT Press.

Simon, H. A. 1996. *The Sciences of the Artificial.* Cambridge, MA: MIT Press.

Sommerville, I., and P. Sawyer. 1997. *Requirements Engineering: A Good Practice Guide.* New York: Wiley.

Suchman, L. A. 1987. *Plans and Situated Actions: The Problem of Human-Machine Communication.* Cambridge, England: Cambridge University Press.

Wieringa, R. 1996. *Requirements Engineering: Frameworks for Understanding.* New York: Wiley.

V

Reorienting

Olav W. Bertelsen

How should social practice be expressed in software thinking? In different ways, this question underlies this section's attempt to reorient software knowledge away from formalized technical specification.

The title of the book, *Social Thinking—Software Practice*, assumes a relationship between theorizing about social matters and practical wrestling with the construction and use of computer-based artifacts. The assumed relationship implies that social science has the potential to inform software, though it is still basically separated from it. In other words, people working with software are considered unable to understand and handle the full impact of their work, so that they need guidance from philosopher-kings and social scientists. The argument of this section is that software needs no doctor. On the contrary, what is needed is action-oriented reorienting. Software is social. Software knowledge treats social issues as fundamental. Software-relevant social thinking cannot be produced in isolation from general software knowledge. The object of software knowledge has to be reconsidered, not by enrolling experts from other fields but by reorienting the production of software knowledge itself. Reorienting the production of software knowledge is the concern shared by the authors of this section.

Software is process. It is constructed in a design process by a group of people developing a vision, making a specification, implementing and deploying a system. More fundamentally, however, software is a process because the use of a specific computer artifact itself is a process involving constant change. Thus, software thinking and software practice have to be built on basic notions of dynamics and process, not only in understanding the social context of design and use, but also when it comes to the means provided for specification, for systems architecture, and for implementation. Social dynamics pervade all aspects of software and hardware.

The concern for material mediation in design, shared by the authors of this section, can be understood as a shift from discussion to construction. There is a dialectical relationship between desired futures and the material foundation of these futures. This is true not only in the sense that software-based artifacts must obey the laws of gravity, and so on, but more radically in the sense that the future is to be envisioned in a dialectical interplay with materials. Similarly, materiality plays a role in understanding the frontiers of new technology, in the sense that the virtual world spanned by software in the age of pervasive computing is to be rooted in, almost physically concrete, materiality.

The multiplicity and specificity of software is a concern in this section, directly pointing to the reorienting of software knowledge away from generalization by logical argumentation toward the analysis of concrete cases of software use and software design, and toward concrete action in design. General knowledge is considered less relevant as a resource for concrete action in design. The chapters in the section supply both rich case descriptions and concepts for understanding software and software knowledge within the general concern with specificity and heterogeneity.

Reorienting is about setting out in new directions, but it is also about rethinking what has been done in light of acquired insights. In various ways, the chapters in this section reframe the concepts of software and software knowledge on the basis of twenty years of use-oriented design.

Horst Oberquelle, in chapter 18, titled "Useware Design and Evolution: Bridging Social Thinking and Software Construction," introduces a concept of useware, reflecting and reinterpreting the growing concern for use in the software profession. He outlines a model of useware and useware design that is equally preoccupied with use and construction, taking dynamics of use as the focal point in moving beyond software engineering. By eliminating isolated specification, the role of separated social thinking is bypassed, or subsumed under concerns for bridging construction and use. Social thinking is integrated with software thinking in useware thinking.

In chapter 19, titled "Discontinuities," Olav W. Bertelsen and Susanne Bødker introduce the concept of discontinuities in (and around) design in order to provide a handle on action in the useware process, and to support new directions for artifacts mediating design. Theoretically based on activity theory, the chapter outlines three fundamental discontinuities in design, explained through examples from past and recent research and design projects. In line with Oberquelle, they argue that software cannot be understood meaningfully if it is not located in the web of activities of use and design.

Sara Eriksén, in chapter 20, "Localizing Self on Internet: Designing for 'Genius Loci' in a Global Context," takes contemporary constructionism as a starting point, in reviewing four design experiments emphasizing the role of the specifics of time and place. She employs the concept of genius loci as a way of identifying and dealing with context in relation to network applications as well as pervasive computing devices in general. Through her analysis of the specifics of the use of networked pervasive applications, she lays out a perspective for understanding human-computer interaction in these new situations.

In chapter 21, titled "Intent, Form, and Materiality in the Design of Interaction Technology," Thomas Binder discusses the mediational role of various sorts of material in bridging use and design in the useware process. With examples from projects he has participated in, he describes a reorienting within a conversational approach inspired by Schön from a focus on intentions to a focus on direct, material enactment in design. This reorienting is motivated by a concern for the discontinuity or fragility of intention when artifacts are brought from design to use, and by fruitful experience with tangibility as a central feature of an evolving "language" of design.

The move away from an ideal of software knowledge as an exact science toward concrete engagement in design and toward an analytic focus on specific cases in their own right implies a risk of falling into total relativism, denying propagation of any insights further than the one specific case looked at. The challenge, however, is that the production of software knowledge can become a catalyst for a new design-oriented, pragmatic epistemology. The reorientings in this section contribute to this new epistemology for an integrated field of software knowledge.

18

Useware Design and Evolution: Bridging Social Thinking and Software Construction

Horst Oberquelle

Since the advent of interactive software, the role of the "programmer" has been redefined several times. Now it is time to complement software constructors with useware designers who are able to provide users with usable and flexible environments.

The user-programmer of the early days was in an optimal situation. Being the user made it easy to respect the context of use, and being the programmer made it easy to build, understand, and adapt the software to changing needs. Usability was not an explicit issue. The transitions between the world of programming and technical and mathematical applications were easy.

Building software to support the work of others changed the situation considerably. It became necessary for programmers to build on knowledge about the context: people and their properties, tasks and their subtleties, as well as the organizational context and the organization of work. The lack of knowledge and the use of simplistic as well as mechanistic models or just prejudices about the context, especially about social behavior, tasks, and organizations, were among the reasons for the delivery of more or less "unusable" interactive software. For some time it went unnoticed that traditional requirements *engineering* implicitly determined usability. Getting the written requirements right seemed to be the problem. The emphasis on requirements *analysis* hid the creative measures taken by software engineers. Usability problems were encountered only after bringing the implemented "solutions" back into a use context.

Since the mid-1980s a great deal of research has been conducted on how to improve usability, especially in the Scandinavian tradition of informatics. With user participation as a starting point, a movement toward cooperative design got underway (Ehn 1988; Greenbaum and Kyng 1991; Kyng and Mathiassen 1997). Chapter 13 of the present book, by Bødker, Kensing, and Simonsen, comes out of this tradition.

Usability research in the United States emphasized analysis in the beginning, based on interdisciplinary knowledge of perception and cognition. The discussion of design was set in motion by the well-known book by Winograd and Flores (1986), which has *A New Foundation for Design* in its subtitle.

Designing appears in the title of Carroll's 1991 anthology, and Carroll, Kellogg, and Rosson (1991) also wrote about human-computer interaction (HCI) as a design science and wanted to base it on a design rationale that reifies the design process and its products. They saw clearly that scientific analysis and invention are intertwined in iterative software development processes. The mutual influence of tasks and artifacts ("task-artifact cycle") was another topic of concern.

In the scientific discussion in the field of HCI, the important role of design in software development was no longer debatable.

In 1990, Kapor published a first version of his *Software Design Manifesto*. It stated that usability was not a relevant aspect of software development practice and that the role of design should be taken seriously:

> The lack of usability and the poor design of programs is the secret shame of the industry.... And the most important social evolution within the computing professions would be to create a role for the software designer as a champion of the user experience.... The perspectives and skills that are critical to good design are typically absent from the development process, or, if present, exist only in an underground fashion.... One of the main reasons most computer software is so abysmal is not that it's not designed at all, but merely engineered. (Kapor 1996, 3, 5)

Since the early 1990s, usability has become an accepted issue in informatics/computer science, but it has not really found its proper place in practice. Several approaches to user-centered software engineering (usability engineering) have tried to provide relevant knowledge and methods for programmers to improve the usability of their products. But usability factors still seem peripheral to the central activity of software construction and remain a question of engineering:

> Ironically, the thing that will likely make the *least* improvement in the ease of use of software-based products is new technology. There is little difference *technically* between a complicated, confusing program and a simple, fun, and powerful product. The problem is one of culture, training, and attitude of the people who make them, more than it is one of chips and programming languages. We are deficient in our development *process*, not in our development tools. The high-tech industry has inadvertently put programmers and engineers in charge, so their hard-to-use engineering culture dominates. Despite appearances, business executives are simply not the ones in control of the high-tech industry. It is the engineers who are running the show. In our rush to accept the many benefits of the silicon chip, we have abdicated our responsibilities. *We have let the inmates run the asylum.* (Cooper 1999, 15)

Cooper vividly argues from a designer's perspective for a design orientation in software production, and that design is not only a question of the surface of software.

A new transition seems necessary but difficult to achieve: the design of usable software has to become a central issue and a new task for software practice, which must be separated from construction and needs special competence. The deficiencies impeding the new transition are manifold:

- The insight in industry that usability must be improved is only growing slowly. A declaration of users' rights (Karat 1998) brings the problem out into the public but does not solve it. The costs and time needed to produce more usable software will be somewhat higher for software companies, hence increasing time to market and costs of software for customers. But the ultimate cost of running inadequate software, in terms of the time needed for training and error correction, the frustration, sometimes leading to rage and illness of employees, the expense of help desks, and so on, will easily exceed the additional investment. Even software companies pay for inadequate software by running hotlines and paying for avoidable maintenance—if the costs are not shifted to customers. Detailed studies of the costs of (un)usability are unavailable.
- Knowledge of the social aspects of computers in use is not widespread. The number of competent people who can design for usability is small and must be dramatically increased. Traditional design competence (e.g., typography, graphic design, industrial design) is helpful but not sufficient. Winograd (1997) envisions "interaction design" as a new profession.

• A further challenge is the need to keep software "soft"—that is, to allow in a permanently running networked environment the coevolution of interactive systems and context. Flexibility and tailorability are new demands.

• A clear name for the new direction is missing. We need design competence for the sake of usability. *Software design* is somewhat misleading; this term has already been used for the technical construction of complex software and does not emphasize the new direction. *Usability engineering*, on the other hand, points in the right direction, but with the implication that the problem can be solved by engineering methods. This notion may have been necessary to convince engineers that usability is a problem to be tackled. Without going into a detailed discussion of narrow versus broad interpretations of *engineering*, I believe that a clear distinction is necessary between software as seen by programmers and software as experienced by users. *Interaction design* has many interpretations and does not focus on the artifacts that are designed.

This is the reason I propose to look at bridging the gap between "social thinking" and "software construction" under the provocative heading "Useware Design and Evolution." Having an adequate conceptualization and a trendy phrase is considered an important vehicle for bringing usablity into practice.

But obstacles exist as well: engineers will lose the right and the obligation (or even the burden?) of designing the "user interface." Cooper (1999) argues that their opposition is the most serious problem. I will return to this issue later.

What Is Useware?

Useware is a new term for interactive artifacts (software and hardware, printed material, organizational support) as they are designed for the user's perspective.[1] Useware offers users opportunities and services to be experienced individually. Useware is not a component or level of an interactive system, but an intergral view of an interactive system designed for a use context. There are several other notions relevant to aspects of useware, to useware design and use: system image (Norman

1986), information architecture, IT artifact, information appliances (Norman 1998), interaction design (Winograd 1996, 1997; Cooper 1999), designing user experience (Laurel 1986), and many more. But none focuses on all the relevant factors. What are these factors?

For analytic purposes, I will distinguish between three levels of useware, the conceptual, interaction, and representation levels, all of which have to be addressed in design.

The Conceptual Level

The conceptual world encompasses the artificial world a user interacts with. The new world has *spatial properties*. It introduces spaces, rooms, and other locations where materials may be found and actions can happen (see Winograd 1997). Spaces may be private or possessed by groups or be public. The perception of computers as places seems to be natural (Reeves and Nass 1996). Users experiencing the interaction in the mode of "first-personness" (Laurel 1986) feel as if they are in those places. The user enters the conceptual world as a *border subject*. Other users may also be present as border subjects in shared spaces ("inter-spaces"; Winograd 1997). Locations can be *connected*, making it possible to transfer material to other spaces or to exchange information between spaces. Users may move to other spaces.

The world contains *passive materials* that are meaningful for the users' activities: simple and compound documents with contents, collections of documents, containers for documents (defining places again for the contained material), organizers of material like lists, tables, hierarchies. Secondary documents like written plans, rules, and norms may be used to influence activities.

The conceptual world allows for *dynamic activities done* by *actors*. Users may perform operations on the contents of material or on objects with respect to their existence (create, copy, combine, destroy) and to space (move to other places and spaces, push and pull). These operations may range from simple manipulations via the application of tools to squeezing materials through complex machines or mechanisms. All these processes are initiated by a user, and she or he is responsible for the consequences. Sometimes the tools used may be experienced as natural extensions of the user and not as a property of the environment.

The conceptual world may contain *agents*, semiautonomous mechanisms that act on behalf of a person—for instance, as a surrogate carrying out repetitive, tedious actions or as a gateway for the cooperation or communication with other users while the possessor is absent or concentrates on other activities. Such agents are treated by users like all language-based reactive components—that is, like real people—and evoke social responses (Reeves and Nass 1996). Automated sequences of operations as well as so-called autonomous processes all have an initiator and should be under the control of certain users, making it possible to interrupt, continue, modify, and possibly terminate such processes. A person responsible for the actions of agents must be defined.

The conceptual world may have *other border subjects and neighbor worlds*. The existence of other users, their presence, activities, or absence must be known to every other user. Avatars are an approach to make the presence of other users visible inside the virtual world. Video connections are a different approach. Neighbor worlds not connected as artifacts may be connected by users on the border of several worlds. Different users may be connected by "interspaces" (Winograd 1997).

In the long run, the virtual worlds must be *integrated with the physical world*. They will become part of it from the users' perspective.

The basic properties of a conceptual world are explained by the notions and metaphors used to describe it. They have to be chosen carefully. One key property of a conceptual world should be that it is based on notions meaningful in the use context and not on technical notions as used in software construction, like files, modules, applications, and so on. One interesting approach to separate conceptual design from technical construction is the WAM approach of Züllighoven (Lilienthal and Züllighoven 1997), which proposes that user-centered designs be based on the notions of material, tool, and automaton. This approach has been gradually extended to cover aspects of a networked world.

The Interaction Level

Usually, we have limited opportunities at the user interfaces to perceive the conceptual world and to act in it by communication or actions. On the *interaction level*, we concentrate on the means that allow us to interact with the conceptual world.

The means must provide access to space and places, to materials and their contents, and must support the awareness of the presence and activities of others and their surrogate agents. The user must be permanently able to answer at least the following set of extended old "Nievergelt questions" (see Nievergelt and Weydert 1980).

Orientation questions

Where am I?

What is going on?

Who else is here?

What are they doing?

Influence questions

What can I do here?

Did I perform an action successfully?

How can I control running processes?

How can I communicate with others?

Navigation questions

How did I get here?

How can I find things?

How can I reach others?

Context-switching questions

Where else can I go?

Forms of access like windows, scrolling, zooming, and virtual reality as well as interaction techniques like commands, menus, forms, drag and drop, and so on can support users in their interaction with the conceptual world.

Besides directly supporting the user's perception and acting in the conceptual world, the interaction level may provide additional support for the coevolution of users and artifacts:

- Understanding the conceptual world (from help systems to help-desk connections)
- Supporting experimentation and error handling (e.g., by history keeping and undo mechanisms)

- Adapting the useware to user preferences and task necessities by the user
- Delegating routine actions (from action-sequence logging to macro definition)

The Representation Level

On the *representation level*, we deal with the surface questions of representing the conceptual and interaction level for perception of the user (from visualizations by traditional screens to mobile WAP devices to wall-sized whiteboards and on to audio presentations for blind people and to . . .) and her or his access by physical action using all kinds of traditional and novel input devices and techniques or speech input or . . .

The conceptual world should be experienced by the user using adequate multimodal perception, mainly the visual and auditory channels. In a networked conceptual world, focused perception as well as peripheral perception in the form of awareness mechanisms must be supported. Weiser and Brown (1997) stress the importance of "calm technology" in the future, technology that can be perceived at the periphery. Much work in the area of computer-supported cooperative work (CSCW) now develops awareness-support mechanisms.

A wide range of input techniques are available for identifying places, materials, pieces of contents, positions, and so on and to select appropriate actions.

Useware Experienced

From the users' point of view, the levels described above should not be experienced directly. Users should have a holistic experience of the useware they are interacting with or even "acting in" or "acting or communicating through." Useware is designed in a user-adequate way if users have the feeling of acting through the interface(s) (Bødker 1990) in a world they are acquainted with and that serves their purposes.

The three aspects of usability of ISO 9241, part 11 (ISO 1998), reflect this view of usability by calling for effectiveness (i.e., matching the task requirements with the functionality of the conceptual world), for efficiency (i.e., smooth interaction), and for pleasantness (i.e., the satisfaction of the users with the aesthetics of useware).

A special question concerns the integration of interactive systems into the physical environment, like portable electronic books, wearables, computers integrated into furniture, walls, and so on ("ubiquitous computing"; see Weiser and Brown 1997). Ubiquitous and calm technology will gain importance in the future. The distinction between hardware, software, and the surrounding physical environment is not important from a useware point of view. Useware design covers all the artifacts a user can experience.

Useware Design as an Activity

Useware design is a creative and mediating activity between social, informal, and situated use situations on the one hand and formal construction of artifacts that implement useware on the other. In chapter 19, Bertelsen and Bødker discuss this activity as dealing with different discontinuities.

Useware designers must speak at least two languages: the language of the use context and the language of software construction. They may also develop a third language—a language of form, as proposed by Binder in chapter 21.

The analogy to architecture is helpful but limited. Like an architect who has to understand the interests of clients and has to invent a solution and win clients' approval for it, the useware designer has to work with users. The architect does not personally build the building. Just as he or she gives the design to construction engineers and construction workers, the useware designer has to work with software construction. Supporting coevolution is a new challenge, as we will see.

Useware design has at least two key facets, as shown in figure 18.1, and bridges the use context and the construction context.

Interfacing with Users and the Use Context

Three activities can be distinguished that may be cyclically connected.

Understanding the Context of Use Understanding the social nature of useware in context is a prerequisite for its creation. The useware designer must understand that experience is an individual and social

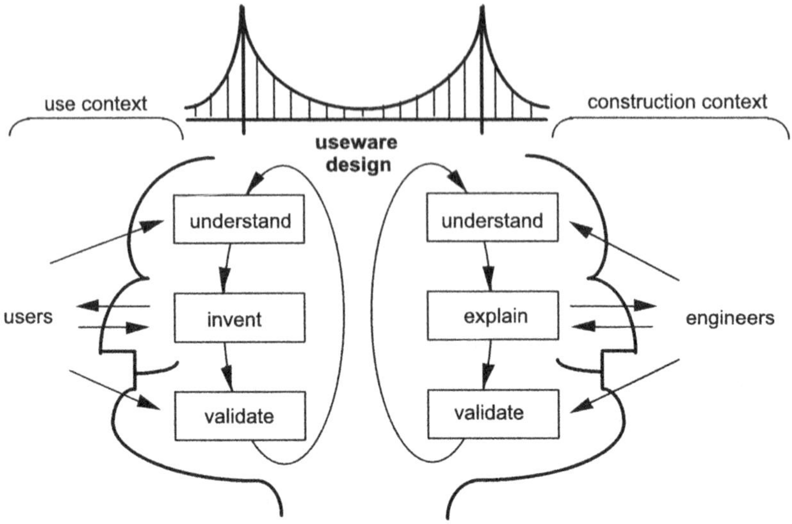

Figure 18.1
The two facets of useware design

phenomenon, which is situated, local, embodied, and emotional. Useware can only provide room for experience. Here the human and social sciences can be valuable for purposes of understanding use (perception, cognition, emotions, activities, situatedness, learning, social behavior ...). Ethnographic approaches have been especially successful in observing use situations.

Inventing Useware Useware design contains a creative component that is different from collecting wishes in feature lists (leading to the disease of "featuritis," one of the reasons for unusable software) or from plain imitation by taking metaphors too literally.

The design process usually has to work inside out: novel conceptual worlds with adequate interaction and presentation have to be invented. Sometimes they may be new combinations of well-known parts, variations of successful patterns; sometimes they will be extensions of existing worlds, or sometimes radically new worlds. The important message for this activity is that useware invention has to cover all three levels, from concept via interaction to representation, and is not just a question of surface polishing.

It will be based on the designer's experience, possibly utilizing a language of form (see Binder, chapter 21, this volume), and will be based on design rules evolving over time. It must be informed by knowledge of the technical aspects of software construction—analogous to the knowledge an architect must have about civil engineering and building materials.

Invention is guided by (often-implicit) values. Work science provides hints for the qualities useware has to have to support work. Other non-technical sciences can inform useware invention for other contexts. The creative arts can help to make useware enjoyable and may highlight a designer's style.

The designs must be presented in a form usable for testing, whether as sketches, mock-ups, prototypes, or executable versions combined with scenarios.

Validating Useware Designs The final test for the validity of a design is use. Designs should be tested with users as early as possible to avoid expensive construction work before the design is stable. The danger of not throwing away a prototype or version in which much work has been invested has often been described in the literature on rapid prototyping.

Teaching useware is part of the test. First, the conceptual model should be experienced in the artifact itself. The additional material must support the development of adequate mental models by the users. The introduction of useware in a context should be done or at least be observed by useware designers to give them direct feedback.

Interfacing with Software Construction

Three activities can be distinguished as well that may also be cyclically connected.

Understanding Software Construction The useware designer must have basic knowledge of the technical factors and challenges involved in the construction of complex software in networked environments. He or she can learn from successful construction efforts and available construction patterns. The important point here is that the construction perspective is different from the useware perspective and that it is not the task of the useware designer to explain the construction to users. Like the inhabitants of a well-designed house, the users will be interested in the functionality and comfortable access to it, not in the details of stability and material used internally. The useware designer even has to hide construction details.

Communication of Useware Designs to Software Construction The step from the informal to the formal is inevitable. Useware designers must communicate their designs to software construction. Whether this is done by sketches, mock-ups, formal specifications, scenarios, or person-to-person talk does not matter. A blueprint language for useware designs does not exist yet—and may never exist, at least not for novel designs. Formal specifications will not suffice to inform construction about the useware design. The useware designer must be in direct communication with construction.

Validating Constructed Useware Checking whether the communication of the step before was successful is necessary and is different from the validation of the design with users, although users may be helpful in testing executable prototypes or versions of implemented useware.

Useware Design: Qualifications and Power Relations

Useware design demands different qualifications.

- *Observation and listening* to the context is a prerequisite for understanding the needs of the context. Here methods from anthropology and ethnography are useful. They especially help in offsetting prejudices and misleading or simplistic mental models one might have about the practice of others.
- *Understanding* presupposes a conceptual and theoretical framework in which to interpret the observations. Social thinking is a prerequisite; activity theory can be used as a framework (see Nardi 1996).
- *Invention* requires imagination and creativity, which are not scientific qualifications but are based on experience and are close to artistic gifts.
- *Expressive competence* is necessary to explain useware to users as well as to engineers.
- *Communicative competence* is needed to fulfill the mediating role in both directions.

• *Mutual respect* is necessary in both directions, toward users and engineers.

The education of useware designers can partly occur in studios, as proposed by Kapor (1996) and Winograd (1997). But useware designers also need basic experience in software engineering as a foundation for cooperation with software engineers.

Useware design will be influenced by the relative power of the three groups: users, useware designers, and software engineers.

Users are the final evaluators. They may provide design ideas, but letting them design on their own may be problematic. Construction by users is more or less impossible, except for simple adaptations. Users will at least have power as customers in a growing market.

Designers should be in charge of the whole design activity, informed by users' ideas and by their knowledge of the engineering aspects. In a sense, the provocative rule "Listen to the users, but ignore what they say" (Borenstein 1991)—interpreted in a respectful way—stresses that users can provide important information, but design competence is an extra quality seldom found on the part of users. In Greenbaum and Kyng 1991, users are considered competent codesigners together with software engineers.

Design may be based on successful useware patterns and styles (language of form) as well as on design rules, which cannot be automated.

Designers have to decide whether the constructed software implements a useware design.

Software engineers are in charge of the construction process and are responsible for the technical quality of the software. Today almost all power rests with software engineers, who implicitly play the role of useware designers or who dominate useware designers with so-called technical necessities (see Cooper 1999). If useware design is an activity in its own right, a corollary of the above rule seems to be followed by software engineers: "Listen to the designers, but don't implement what they say." This corollary should only be true if designers say too much about software construction.

The idea of automating design rules and putting them into software generators is an attempt to avoid designers and appropriate design by the engineers. It keeps software engineers in charge. The economically sound idea of software reuse may also be a hindrance for innovative useware designs, if reuse means to use badly designed useware components again and again. A creative use and variation of technically successful software patterns may provide the necessary flexibility for software construction.

If the responsibility of software engineers is restricted to software construction, they may be relieved. This may motivate them to look for interesting new possibilities for software construction and for cooperation.

Whether the useware designer should have the same power as an architect supervising the construction of a planned building is an interesting question. For the near future, an equal-rights approach between users, designers, and engineers seems advisable.

Useware Design and Coevolution

One aspect of future useware has been mostly ignored so far. Useware of the future will be embedded and permanently running. Actual forms of use cannot completely be foreseen. At the same time, the feedback from the context (persons, tasks, organizations) will permanently call for adaptations. In the long run, useware and context will be intertwined in a relationship of coevolution. Henderson and Kyng (1991) argued for adaptable software long ago. Carroll has observed part of this as the inevitable task-artifact cycle (Carroll, Kellogg, and Rosson 1991). In general also, people and organizations will adapt by learning.

- Useware must be open for situated actions, offering opportunities related to the user's task, not just ever-growing collections of features (the disease of "featuritis").
- Useware must be adaptable in the sense of supporting preferences and routinization.
- Useware must be designed for evolution—that is, open for extensions and redesign.

This puts a new burden on users as well as on useware designers and software engineers. Adaptation and modification of useware make it more complex and require additional learning. Designing for evolution is almost without precedent in design: neither graphic nor product design nor architecture provide experiences from which to learn. Adaptivity and evolutionary rebuilding of complex running software are a challenge for software engineering as well. How can stable and at the same time open systems be constructed? The idea of pliant software (Harris and Henderson 1999) provides suggestive ideas for the challenge useware design and software construction will face in the future.

Conclusions

Looking at interactive software from a radically different, user-centered perspective is a necessary step in a rapidly changing networked, socially determined information world that connects increasing numbers of persons in manifold ways. The perspective of *useware design and evolution* is intended to support this change.

Useware design has been treated in scientific papers under different headings for many years. Useware design is still a challenge for software practice, drawing as it does on mixed competencies: social thinking, technical knowledge, and creative skills as well as communicative competence. Software production and introduction are social processes themselves with power relations that have to change.

To make useware design a respected activity in software production for social worlds, several shifts are necessary:

from: Applications as collections of features

to: Useware as networked conceptual worlds integrated into worlds of human practice

from: Interface for looking from the context into a "technical system"

to: Looking through the interface at conceptual worlds and their borders and acting there, including the social aspects of observing, monitoring, intruding, influencing other persons

from: Specifiable products that determine users' behavior

to: Evolving (malleable, pliant) infrastructures as spaces of opportunities with feedback/learning loops to use contexts

from: Users who have to learn "solutions" of engineers (acquiring "computer literacy") *to:* Engineers who have to build useware as it has been designed with users and can be understood by users

from: Requirements analysis as preparation for software construction and usability as an afterthought

to: Useware design at the forefront, software construction at the back end—two activities in their own right and with mutual respect

from: Software engineering

to: Useware design plus software construction plus evolution support

This is a tedious way to go. Will it happen? How long will it take? I personally believe that progress in this direction is possible, is necessary—if not inevitable. The notion of *useware* may be a vehicle to bring the problem better into consciousness and to speed up this process. Asking for *design and evolution* stresses two important problems of software practice.

Notes

I gratefully acknowledge constructive comments on earlier versions of this chapter by Olav Bertelsen, Thomas Binder, Austin Henderson, and Terry Winograd.

1. To the best of my knowledge, the term *useware* was first introduced by Detlef Zühlke in the context of forming the Useware-Forum in Germany, a joint activity of several scientific and engineering associations to promote usability (see Zühlke and Wahl 1999).

References

Bødker, S. 1990. Through the Interface: A Human Activity Approach to User Interface Design. Hillsdale, NJ: Erlbaum.

Borenstein, N. S. 1991. Programming as if People Mattered. *Friendly Programs, Software Engineering, and Other Noble Delusions*. Princeton, NJ: Princeton University Press.

Carroll, J. M., ed. 1991. *Designing Interaction*. Cambridge, England: Cambridge University Press.

Carroll, J. M., W. M. Kellogg, and M. B. Rosson. 1991. The Task-Artifact Cycle. In J. M. Carroll, ed., *Designing Interaction*, 74–102. Cambridge, England: Cambridge University Press.

Cooper, A. 1999. *The Inmates Are Running the Asylum: Why High-Tech Products Drive Us Crazy and How to Restore the Sanity*. Indianapolis: SAMS.

Ehn, P. 1988. *Work-Oriented Design of Computer Artifacts.* Stockholm: Arbetslivscentrum.

Greenbaum, J., and M. Kyng, eds. 1991. *Design at Work: Cooperative Design of Computer Systems.* Hillsdale, NJ: Erlbaum.

Harris, J., and A. Henderson. 1999. A Better Mythology for System Design. *Proc. CHI'99* (Pittsburg, 15–20 May 1999), 88–95. New York: ACM Press/ Reading, MA: Addison-Wesley.

Henderson, A., and M. Kyng. 1991. There's No Place Like Home: Continuing Design in Use. In J. Greenbaum and M. Kyng, *Design at Work: Cooperative Design of Computer Systems,* 219–240. Hillsdale, NJ: Erlbaum.

ISO. 1998. *ISO 9241-11: Ergonomic Requirements for Office Work with Visual Display Terminals (VDTs)—Part 11: Guidance on Usability.* Geneva: ISO.

Kapor, M. 1996. A Software Design Manifesto. In T. Winograd, ed., with J. Bennett, L. De Young, and B. Hartfield, *Bringing Design to Software,* 1–9. New York: ACM Press/Reading, MA: Addison-Wesley.

Karat, C.-M. 1998. Guaranteeing Rights for the User. *Communications of the ACM* 41: 29–31.

Kyng, M., and L. Mathiassen, eds. 1997. *Computers and Design in Context.* Cambridge, MA: MIT Press.

Laurel, B. K. 1986. Interface as Mimesis. In D. A. Norman and S. W. Draper, eds., *User Centered System Design: New Perspectives on Human-Computer Interaction,* 67–85. Hillsdale, NJ: Erlbaum.

Lilienthal, K., and H. Züllighoven. 1997. Application-Oriented Usage Quality: The Tools and Material Approach. *Interactions* 6(6): 35–41.

Nardi, B. A., ed. 1996. *Context and Consciousness: Activity Theory and Human-Computer Interaction.* Cambridge, MA: MIT Press.

Nievergelt, J., and J. Weydert. 1980. Sites, Modes, and Trails: Telling the User of an Interactive System Where He Is, What He Can Do, and How to Get to Places. In R. Guedj, ed., *Methodology of Interaction,* 327–338. Amsterdam: North-Holland.

Norman, D. A. 1986. Cognitive Engineering. In D. A. Norman and S. W. Draper, *User Centered System Design: New Perspectives on Human-Computer Interaction,* 31–61. Hillsdale, NJ: Erlbaum.

Norman, D. A. 1998. *The Invisible Computer: Why Good Products Can Fail, the Personal Computer Is So Complex, and Information Appliances Are the Solution.* Cambridge, MA: MIT Press.

Norman, D. A., and S. W. Draper, eds. 1986. *User Centered System Design: New Perspectives on Human-Computer Interaction.* Hillsdale, NJ: Erlbaum.

Reeves, B., and C. Nass. 1996. *The Media Equation: How People Treat Computers, Television, and New Media Like Real People and Places.* Cambridge, England: Cambridge University Press.

Weiser, M., and J. S. Brown. 1997. The Coming Age of Calm Technology. In P. J. Denning and R. M. Metcalfe, eds., *Beyond Calculation: The Next Fifty Years of Computing*, 75–85. New York: Copernicus/Springer.

Winograd, T. 1997. The Design of Interaction. In P. J. Denning and R. M. Metcalfe, eds., *Beyond Calculation: The Next Fifty Years of Computing*, 149–161. New York: Copernicus/Springer.

Winograd, T., and F. Flores. 1986. *Understanding Computers and Cognition: A New Foundation for Design*. Norwood, NJ: Ablex.

Winograd, T., ed., with J. Bennett, L. De Young, and B. Hartfield. 1996. *Bringing Design to Software*. New York: ACM Press/Reading, MA: Addison-Wesley.

Zühlke, D., and M. Wahl. 1999. Hardware, Software—Useware. Machinenbedienung in vernetzten Produktionssystemen. *Elektronik* 23: 54–62.

19

Discontinuities

Olav W. Bertelsen and Susanne Bødker

Classical systems development literature, be this from systems theory or from the so-called critical schools, suffers from too simplistic concepts of contradiction and difference. On the one hand, the harmony perspective understands design as the identification and implementation of the one best way, for the benefit of everybody, and on the other, the conflict perspective tends to understand design mainly as the battle between antagonistic parties.

Totally ignoring differences and conflicting interests leads to a problem of understanding and dealing with innovation. If design is believed to be the one best solution that can satisfy all, it becomes a frustrating mystery when various groups, such as users, refuse technically sound proposals for what seem to be irrational reasons. In this sense the conflict perspective is still relevant to systems design, although a too-strong focus on contradictions may lead to the misconception that design is merely a matter of negotiation between clear-cut interests.

If, however, designers and users are given the means to reflect on the nonidentical—the differences, divergences, and contradictions that they are surrounded by—the caricature of design from the trenches can be avoided, and the nonidentical used fruitfully in the creation of the future. The present discussion of discontinuities is aimed at providing such means for reflection.

This chapter discusses discontinuities in design, how they are mediated, and how they can become resources for innovation. We consider discontinuities in the relations between groups with conflicting interests as well as more subtle discontinuities within harmonious situations.

Discontinuities

We take discontinuities as the focal point for a change-oriented concern for design artifacts. The concept of discontinuity assumes a process—it is relative to an underlying movement. In this way, it makes explicit what is implicit in the concept of contradiction in activity systems (Engeström 1987); it activates the potential for movement and change of an activity. We see discontinuity as resources of design rather than a problem, because it makes it necessary for the participants to face a reconception and a change of action. We base our analysis of discontinuities in design on activity theory to maintain a manifest material focus. Discontinuity exists at a variety of levels, from the grand discontinuity between the old state of affairs and the unknown to come, to more subtle discontinuities like that between training in using a method and the actual use of the same method.

We identify three basic classes of discontinuities: between experience and desire, between parallel rooms, and between interpretation and implementation.

The fundamental discontinuity in design is between *experience and desire*. The historical transition that any design process invokes, presupposes mediation of the discontinuity between established state of affairs and a new situation to come, between discrete, possibly incommensurable, phases of the considered use practice. Design is what goes on in between two such discrete phases and is therefore stretched out between the need for radical change and gentle evolution.

Discontinuities between *parallel rooms* are basic features of design. Most importantly, the room of design practice is discontinuous from the room of use practice. But the discontinuities between parallel rooms are not only related to the heterogeneity of different groups involved in design. The discontinuity between parallel rooms also marks the course of practice exercised within a uniform group—for example, for a group of designers between learning a new method and using the new method in a project, or between building a new system and maintaining an old one.

Discontinuities between *interpretation and implementation* could also be discussed in terms of crystallization lag or as a dilemma of formulation. It is the discontinuity between decontextualized principles and concrete historical practice; between artifact and situation; between technical implementation and cultural interpretation. The basic flow in systems design goes from workplace studies over systems specification to implementation of a running software-based system. At some point in this process, the interpretability of the designed object decreases dramatically because the open specification has to be turned into unambiguous program code. This decrease leads to a lack of usefulness of the final system if not handled properly.

Before we go on to explore the concept of discontinuities in further detail, we outline our basic view on IT design and use and introduce a few theoretical concepts that our contribution is built on or that we are debating with.

Design as a Human Activity

We use the term *design* broadly to encompass the processes and activities through which future computer applications are shaped. Design is the process where users and designers (and others involved parties) co-construct a future everyday practice. Design is a multipractical activity, where the experiences, resources, tools, and so on of designers meet, and sometimes clash, with those of the users, and with other involved parties in a number of interlinked and partly overlapping activities. Design takes place in a boundary zone where heterogeneous practices meet to create the new, emphasizing the multivoiced nature of design (Bertelsen 1998).

Our theoretical framework is that of activity theory (Leontjev 1978; Engeström 1987; Bødker 1991; Bertelsen and Bødker 2000). The basic unit of analysis in activity theory is the systemic composition of a (collective) subject, an object of the motivated activity, and the social context—mediated by societally constructed artifacts: instruments, rules, and division of labor (often pictured as a triangular figure). Activity theory places computer applications, along with other artifacts, as mediators of human activity, making us focus on the context of use, instead of seeing computer use in isolation. Artifacts are seen as historical devices that reflect the state of practice up until the time they are developed. This practice in turn is shaped by the artifacts used, and so on. Thus to learn something about the present shape and use of an artifact, a historical analysis of artifacts as well as of practice is important. We can reflect on artifacts as objects in the world around us, or they can act as mediators of our interaction with the world, in which case they are not themselves objects of our activity (Bødker 1991).

Design is mediated by design artifacts—for example, systems development methods, programming tools, and analysis techniques, which occupy several positions in the web of activities of the specific design activity. Design artifacts are the objects of research and method development, and instruments in design and the education of designers. Generally, design artifacts are mediators of production and communication within or across different communities of practice involved in design, preferably facilitating shared understanding between the various parties. Ideally, design artifacts embody and communicate ideas, helping us let go of old conceptualizations and giving way for new ones (Bødker and Christiansen 1997); they lend themselves to various kinds of hands-on experience. Most importantly, design artifacts should, ideally, work as springboards for innovation, "a facilitative image, technique or socio-conversational constellation ... misplaced or transplanted from some previous context into a new...." (Engeström 1987, 287). Springboards do not come about smoothly or automatically, and they are not as such solutions to the problem one is facing. They are starting points that may lead to an expansive (or radically innovative) solution. Brown and Duguid (1994) claim that "design deals with border issues," emphasizing that design crosses, or lives on the boundaries of, several communities, with different practices, power and interests. The mediation by design artifacts of this border crossing led us to characterize design artifacts as being *boundary objects* (Star 1989) in the sense that they are always made subject to local interpretations by involved groups of users as well as of designers. At the same time, they must sustain the scrutiny of these local interpretations and maintain a role in the design process at large, with the flaws that we have pointed to here and discussed in much of our earlier work (e.g., Bertelsen 1998; Bødker 1998).

Since artifacts most often mediate in several activities, computer applications and other artifacts are situated in a web of activities. Each activity is conducted through actions of individuals, directed toward an object or another subject. Activity is what gives meaning to our actions, though actions have their own goals, and the same actions can appear in different activities. We use the concept *web of activities* to focus on a particular artifact in its multitude of uses (Bødker 1999). Engeström (1987) describes how an understanding of the development of an activity must be based on understanding of its tense relations to other activities—those producing the components of the studied activity and the activity being object—as well as potential future forms of the activity. Webs of activities can be very complicated, as well as very simple, involving just two activities; the later is the case in most of our examples. The analysis of webs of activities adds dynamics to the systemic relation of the activity to its surrounding activities, by focusing on the shift from one use of a particular artifact to another. The web of activities is, accordingly, a concept that can be used to analytically unfold the process and the shifts between focus and purpose of the action as it actually happens in the process. The contradictions of the activity system are, however, important for this analysis, because they help explain why certain shifts take place.

Engeström (1987) classifies contradictions in and between activity systems. The *primary contradiction* is the contradiction of commodity between use and exchange value. This double nature is a basic feature of the economic structure in capitalist culture; this contradiction permeates every single corner of the triangle and is the basic source of instability and development (Marx [1867] 1962, 49–55; Engeström 1987, 82–91). The *secondary contradictions* of an activity system are contradictions between, for example, the skills of the subject and the instrument, or between rigid rules and new flexible instruments. *Tertiary contradictions* are contradictions between the central activity and a culturally more advanced activity. Such contradictions can be generated by representatives from another culture introducing culturally more advanced objects or motives into the central activity. The obvious problem is to know what is more advanced without subscribing to a very deterministic idea of history. However, the concept of a culturally more advanced activity does not necessarily imply historical determinism; it can also be interpreted as actual or potential different ways of conducting the central activity. Thus, the conflict between the history-determinism, still present somewhere in the basis of activity theory and notions of heterogeneity (e.g., Star 1989), is not necessarily unsolvable. *Quaternary contradictions* are contradictions between the central activity and the neighboring activities—that is, (1) object activities where the immediate objects of the central activity are embedded, (2) instrument-producing activities where key instruments of the central activity are produced, (3) subject-producing activities educating the subject of the central activity, and finally (4) rule-producing activities like administration and legislation. An example of a quaternary contradiction is the contradiction between education of computer scientists at the university, focusing on mathematical formalization, and the central activity of computer scientists working as systems developers in industry.

The discontinuities discussed in this chapter are related to tertiary and quaternary contradictions in webs of activities, whereas primary and secondary contradictions primarily seem to be tensions within activities. Tertiary contradictions relate to the discontinuity between experience and desire, whereas parallel rooms and the discontinuity between interpretation and implementation are related to various quaternary contradictions.

Between Experience and Desire

In the early 1980s, researchers and the graphics workers' unions in Scandinavia worked together in the UTOPIA project on developing a vision for how graphics work in the future could be mediated by computer-based technology without jeopardizing quality of product and working life (Bødker et al. 1987; Ehn and Kyng 1987). The bottleneck turned out to be the discontinuity between graphics workers' experience with the existing technology and the researchers' experience with batch systems and character-based TTYs on the one hand, and the desired future where graphics workers would produce high-quality newspapers with not-yet-existing technology on the other.

To remedy the participants' lack of experience with electronic page makeup technology, graphic workers and researchers visited newspapers in the United States of America, where this new technology had been applied for some time and where graphics professionals been eliminated from the production. This trip was used both to get some idea of the new technology and as a generator of a negative vision of the new technology in use.

The UTOPIA project developed several techniques that, in different ways, address the discontinuity between experience and desire. The organizational game (Ehn and Sjögren 1991) was a way to explore a potential future work arrangement by role playing through hypothetical situations prepared on so-called situation cards for the specific game. Ehn and Sjögren (1991, 252) explain that "for all participants in a design group [the organizational game] serves as a means to create a common language, to discuss existing reality, to investigate future visions, and to make requirement specifications on aspects of work organization, technology, and education."

In this way the organizational game was not only a vehicle for experiencing the future, but also for the creation of means for the co-construction of desires for future technology. In a similar manner, the use of mock-ups (Bødker et al. 1987; Ehn and Kyng 1991) made it possible for the graphics workers to understand how it would be to work with the new technology, thus enabling them to criticize solutions and develop their own requirements for future tools.

The UTOPIA techniques can be analyzed in the terminology of developmental work research (Engeström 1987, and others), as being springboards and so on (Bisgaard et al. 1989; Bødker and Christiansen 1997). However, in developmental work research, development is talked about as the result of the inability of the current work arrangement to satisfy the needs of the practice considered. With respect to the design of computer-based artifacts, "needs" have to be understood in a broader sense, including the desire for cutting-edge technology. The desired future is not only the answer to the current misery, but is also an answer to desire.

It can be argued that the techniques developed in the UTOPIA project were resistive rather than innovative, that the aim was primarily to avoid the deskilling, unemployment, and inferior product that had been the result of the use of new page makeup technology in the United States of America. However, these techniques were followed by techniques more directly and exclusively addressing the issue of innovation—for example, the use of metaphors and future workshops (Kensing and Madsen 1991).

The discontinuity between experience and desire can be of different length. It is assumed by many design methods that the method eliminates the distance; SA/SD is an awkward example of this with the idea of smooth transitions from old physical system via old logical and new logical to new physical system. In other parts of the literature, it seems to be the goal to be as radical as possible (Hirschheim and Klein 1989) in a spectrum between supporting change and radical change. In the perspective of this chapter, we may argue that discontinuity between experience and desire ranges almost from the level of minor adjustments related to secondary contradictions within the considered use activity, to the all-embracing emancipatory project (driven by the eternal primary contradiction in commodity).

The development of new technology lies somewhere within this continuum. From a practical perspective, creativity can be enhanced by deliberately avoiding considerations over purpose, realism, or developmental directionality. The future workshop (Jungk and Müllert 1987) is a modest example of what Engeström (1987) refers to as springboards, somewhat based on Wartofsky's (1973) concept of tertiary artifacts—that is, artifacts outside the direct loop of production, effecting production through reshaping of modes of perception.

The techniques developed in the UTOPIA project, and its successors, not only deal with the issue of generating desirable visions for the future. Just as important was communication between users and designers through the establishment of a shared language and the rooting of design in the established course of practice. These issues are related to the mediation of the discontinuity between parallel rooms.

Between Parallel Rooms

The discontinuity between parallel rooms covers a broad range of discontinuities in design where the same object or artifact is synchronously dealt with in more than one context. Most obvious is the discontinuity between use and design.

In the festival project (Bertelsen 1996a, 1996b, 1998; Madsen 1996), the discontinuity between the parallel rooms of use and design was emphasized by a series of unfortunate circumstances. Ideally, the design process could have been a process of transforming artifacts from the domain into a new computer artifact by emulating the historical process of crystallizing activity into artifacts (Bertelsen 1996b). The artifact under transformation would bind the room of design to the room of use. Successive transformations of the artifact into specifications and prototypes would be assessed in terms of how well they would mediate simulated use. Due to organizational obstacles, however, activities ensuring the relevance of the transformed artifact in simulated use were canceled. At the end the design failed miserably, when brought into real use. Crucial features of the transformed artifact in use had disappeared, most importantly the lack of reminders for needed information on printouts from the system. The canceled activities were more or less derivatives of the organizational game.

Most of the above-mentioned techniques from the UTOPIA project address the discontinuity between the room of use and the room of design. The organizational game and the mock-up anchor the vision for a new organization of work or a new tool back into actual use, and they create a common language between users and designers. To some extent, these techniques also address a (partly temporal) discontinuity between the room of basic technology development and the room of application development. In the EuroCODE project (e.g., Grønbæk, Kyng, and Mogensen 1997), the aim was to develop new basic technology and application platforms. In this project, the development of specific applications for specific domains was used as a vehicle for development of the new basic technology. Thus, the EuroCODE project addressed the discontinuity between the room of technical innovation and the room of future application development, as well as the discontinuity between the room of in-house development and the room of product development.

In a recent project exploring the possible future roles of information technology in wastewater treatment work (e.g., Bertelsen and Nielsen 1999), we initially established an understanding, shared with wastewater workers and the plant managers, that rewriting was an important vehicle for the plant workers' understanding of wastewater data. In several cases, we saw how redundant rewriting was inserted in the daily routines to ensure that the workers actually looked at the numbers. However, after we had worked for a while with various design ideas based on integrating paper input with computing, the managers told us at a meeting that rewriting should be avoided because it did not guarantee that workers would think about the numbers. They gave examples that now seemed to be common knowledge among them, of how workers had rewritten numbers from obviously broken instruments without taking notice. This is another example of a discontinuity between parallel rooms—in this case divergence between the developing room of practice (or use), and the room of design. Independently of the design effort, people at the wastewater plant had developed a new understanding of the role of rewriting. This type of divergent discontinuity is impossible to avoid; they result from the "users'" unrestricted reconsideration of premises set by the "project group." In the case of the wastewater project, eliminating the discontinuity between users and designers would have made the new understanding of the uselessness of redundant rewriting less likely to occur.

Discontinuities between parallel rooms are not only a matter of discrepancies between groups. In the festival project, we saw that, due to the cyclic nature of their organization with one yearly event, festival workers had difficulties calling forth how it was to engage in festival work at other times of the year than the actual time. The same type of discontinuity between parallel rooms of the same praxis can be seen in relation to the role of design methods. The method is one thing in the room of training and rehearsal, and a very different thing during the course of a design project. In this sense, designers live in discontinuous rooms tied together by means of boundary objects; design artifacts should be suited to act as such boundary objects in between the parallel rooms of designers' practices. Bertelsen (1998) elaborates on the concept of boundary objects to cover this type of mediation across discontinuities between (possibly incommensurable) rooms of a homogeneous practice.

Oberquelle's depiction—in chapter 18 of the present book—of what he calls useware design as having a face oriented to use and a face oriented to technical construction can be understood in terms of a discontinuity between a concern for use and a concern for technical construction. Sjöberg and Timpka (1994) summarize a number of voices, or abstracted agencies, in participatory design: where they shift, and where they confront each other. This analysis points to the web of activities in design as being more complicated than the mere use-design relation. A computer artifact assumes positions in several of the activities of the web, and artifacts and material change character through transformation when moved between the positions. Looking at design and use as parts of webs of activities is to emphasize the big picture, but at the same time it provides a handle for systematic analysis of context, interdependencies, and contradiction at a very detailed level.

Between Interpretation and Implementation

The discontinuity between interpretation and implementation is pronounced in relation to computers in general. It is the discontinuity between the open interpretability in the cultural sphere and the closed nature of software running on digital computers. This discontinuity is instantiated in the discontinuity between decontextualized principles and concrete historical practice; between artifact and situation; between technical implementation and cultural interpretation.

Our study of an object-oriented source-level debugger, Valhalla (Bertelsen and Bødker 1998) illustrated how decontextualized principles and practice of use can collide: the debugger was based on strict object-oriented principles, in contrast to the textual view supported by traditional source-level debuggers. However, in debugging situations, the users we studied and interviewed most often worked with programs as text. The Mjølner BETA system, which the debugger is part of, is built on a conceptual framework emphasizing programs as models, but also focusing on static aspects of models rather than the dynamics of execution. However, a redesign workshop with users and designers of Valhalla showed that practical debugging depended on the possibilities for monitoring dynamics of execution; the debugger was conforming to principles rather than supporting established programming practice. The designers discussed whether programmers had, or should be allowed to have, a textual understanding of programs. The claim from one of the designers that "if you are working on the text, then you are working in a procedural [non-object-oriented] manner" was later moderated by another designer acknowledging that "the program text is a suitable means of navigation." However, it was emphasized that "the true object-oriented programmer" is not working on code text but on the structure of the program—that is, hierarchies, patterns, and objects. The views on the textual representation as well as the view on specific executions are only means of viewing the structure. The tool designers think that programmers need to understand their own work as constructing object-oriented structure, whereas the programmers, even when they are intimately familiar with the structure-not-text idea, continue to write program text, and work with the programs as if they were texts.

In the case of the Mjølner debugger, the discontinuity between interpretation and implementation takes shape in a contradiction between the way programmers work and the debugging tool. The object-oriented pioneers and programmers promote a norm for programming, "structure not text." This norm is a change instrument, open for interpretation and adaptation to a broad range of situations and practices; it is not a description of actual programming practice. The contradiction between tool and practice arises when the norm is implemented in a computer-based tool, and therefore closed for interpretation.

In general, the discontinuity between interpretation and implementation can be handled if it is identified in the basic flow of systems design, and then addressed systematically in order to make sure that implementation and decontextualization cover the needed interpretations. Cooperative prototyping (e.g., Bødker and Grønbæk 1996) is a technique that precisely mediates the discontinuity between interpretation and implementation by giving users access to the point in the flow of systems design where interpretability is sacrificed in order to construct the running software. Cooperative prototyping bypasses the discontinuity by subsuming the process of implementation under the process of interpretation.

End-user tailoring (MacLean et al. 1990; Mørch 1997; Trigg and Bødker 1994) is another approach to the discontinuity between interpretation and implementation aiming at opening the computer artifact for interpretations beyond the point of implementation by letting the user reshape the artifact to fit the needs of the situation. This approach is limited by the fact that users are users and not designers; they will not benefit from the total flexibility of a general programming environment.

In several ways, prototypes and other design artifacts that crystallize or capture use practice are idealized versions of this practice—idealizations, different from practice. This cannot be helped, because these design artifacts are constructed through reduction of the complexity of everyday activity. This is the reason Engeström (1987) proposes that the new activity, where for example the final computer application is used, will always be different from the one anticipated in the development process. Thus, the final closing of interpretation through implementation paves the way for a new kind of interpretation in the use of the computer-based artifact.

Conclusions

We have analyzed and discussed three fundamental discontinuities in design and pointed to how they have been approached by existing techniques. Theoretically, we have pointed to activity theory, in particular the concept of webs of activities, as a suitable basis for understanding discontinuities in design.

The discontinuity *between experience and desire* has mainly been addressed in terms of a need state. We experience a lack of techniques and concepts addressing innovation per se, without direct reference to needs in a specific practice. The discontinuity *between parallel rooms* has been analyzed in a way transcending the conflict perspective's focus on groups with divergent interests—for example, as a feature of designers' own practice. Our example from the wastewater project illustrated that decoupling of parallel rooms can be helpful in avoiding tunnel vision. The discontinuity between *interpretation and implementation* is addressed specifically by cooperative prototyping, but there is a strong need for further development, technically as well as conceptually, in order to accommodate this discontinuity.

In relation to practical design, we have shown that discontinuities are indispensable and fundamental features of design that will cause trouble if not addressed. We have, however, also shown that discontinuities are fruitful resources, both as driving forces and as analytic concepts. At a general level, this leads to the Marxo-Freudian conclusion that design artifacts should simultaneously bridge discontinuities and preserve and explicate them. The elimination of discontinuities—for example, when user representatives are so engulfed in a project that they become designers—is not very productive. Design artifacts should not be levelers, imposing the state of maximum entropy on design. As such, harmony is not important; use situations in design should be different from real situations in use, users should be different from designers, and so on. Design artifacts should not just bring use into design to eliminate problems, but rather to exploit the discontinuity of the displacement as a dynamic force.

Note

In the writing of this chapter, we have received useful comments from Sara Eriksén, Volker Wulf, Horst Oberquelle, Christina Nielsen, Marianne Graves Petersen, Marianne Dammand Iversen, and Preben Mogensen. Also thanks to the editors for initiating *Social Thinking—Software Practice* and to the group that organized the seminar. The Centre for Human-Machine Interaction has funded the writing of this chapter.

References

Bannon, L., and S. Bødker. 1991. Beyond the Interface: Encountering Artifacts in Use. In J. Carroll, ed., *Designing Interaction: Psychological Theory of the Human-Computer Interface*, 227–253. Cambridge, England: Cambridge University Press.

Bertelsen, O. W. 1996a. Contradictions in the Festival Project—Activity Systems, Obstacles and Dynamic Forces in Design. In *Proceedings of the 19th Information Systems Research Seminar in Scandinavia (IRIS 19)* (10–13 August 1996, Lökeberg, Sweden), 597–612. Gothenburg: Gothenburg Studies in Informatics.

Bertelsen, O. W. 1996b. The Festival Checklist: Design as the Transformation of Artefacts. In J. Blomberg, F. Kensing, and E. Dykstra-Erickson, eds., *PDC '96: Proceedings of the Participatory Design Conference*, 93–101. Palo Alto, CA: CPSR.

Bertelsen, O. W. 1998. *Elements to a Theory of Design Artifacts: A Contribution to Critical Systems Development Research*. Doctoral dissertation. DAIMI PB-531. Aarhus, Denmark: Aarhus University.

Bertelsen, O. W., and S. Bødker. 1998. Studying Programming Environments in Use: Between Principles and Praxis. *NWPER '98: The Eighth Nordic Workshop on Programming Environment Research* (Bergen, Norway, 14–16 June 1998). Bergen: Department of Informatics, Bergen University.

Bertelsen, O. W., and S. Bødker. 2000. Introduction: Information Technology in Human Activity. *Scandinavian Journal of Information Systems* 12(1): 3–14.

Bertelsen, O. W., and C. Nielsen. 1999. Dynamics in Wastewater Treatment: A Framework for Understanding Formal Constructs in Complex Technical Settings. In S. Bødker, M. Kyng, and K. Schmidt, eds., *ECSCW '99: Proceedings of the Sixth European Conference on Computer Supported Cooperative Work* (12–16 September 1999, Copenhagen), 277–290. Dordrecht: Kluwer.

Bisgaard, O., P. Mogensen, M. Nørby, and M. Thomsen. 1989. *Systemudvikling som lærevirksomhed, konflikter som basis for organisationel udvikling.* DAIMI IR-88. Aarhus, Denmark: Aarhus University.

Bødker, S. 1991. *Through the Interface: A Human Activity Approach to User Interface Design.* Hillsdale, NJ: Erlbaum.

Bødker, S. 1998. Understanding Representation in Design. *Human-Computer Interaction* 13(2): 107–125.

Bødker, S. 1999. *Computer Applications as Mediators of Design and Use. Doctoral dissertation.* DAIMI PB542. Aarhus, Denmark: Aarhus University.

Bødker, S., and E. Christiansen. 1997. Scenarios as Springboards in Design. In G. Bowker, L. Gasser, S. L. Star, and W. Turner, eds., *Social Science Research, Technical Systems, and Cooperative Work*, 217–234. Hillsdale, NJ: Erlbaum.

Bødker, S., P. Ehn, J. Kammersgaard, M. Kyng, and Y. Sundblad. 1987. A Utopian Experience. In G. Bjerknes, P. Ehn, and M. Kyng, eds., *Computers and Democracy—a Scandinavian Challenge*, 251–278. Aldershot, UK: Avebury.

Bødker, S., and K. Grønbæk. 1996. Users and Designers in Mutual Activity: An Analysis of Cooperative Activities in System Design. In Y. Engeström and D. Middleton, eds., *Cognition and Communication at Work*, 130–158. Cambridge, England: Cambridge University Press.

Brown, J. S., and P. Duguid. 1994. Borderline Issues: Social and Material Aspects of Design. *Human-Computer Interaction* 9(1): 3–36.

Ehn, P. 1988. *Work-Oriented Design of Computer Artifacts.* Falköping, Sweden: Arbejdslivscentrum.

Ehn, P., and M. Kyng. 1987. The Collective Resource Approach to System Design. In G. Bjerknes, P. Ehn, and M. Kyng, eds., *Computers and Democracy*, 17–58. Aldershot, UK: Avebury.

Ehn, P., and M. Kyng. 1991. Cardboard Computers: Mocking-it-up or Hands-on the Future. In J. Greenbaum and M. Kyng, eds., *Design at Work: Cooperative Design of Computer Systems*, 169–196. Hillsdale, NJ: Erlbaum.

Ehn, P., and D. Sjögren. 1991. From System Description to Script for Action. In J. Greenbaum and M. Kyng, eds., *Design at Work: Cooperative Design of Computer Systems*, 241–268. Hillsdale, NJ: Erlbaum.

Engeström, Y. 1987. *Learning by Expanding: An Activity-Theoretical Approach to Developmental Research*. Helsinki: Orienta-Konsultit Oy.

Grønbæk, K., M. Kyng, and P. Mogensen. 1997. Towards a Cooperative Experimental System Development Approach. In M. Kyng and L. Mathiassen, eds., *Computers and Design in Context*, 201–238. Cambridge, MA: MIT Press.

Hirschheim, R., and H. Klein. 1989. Four Paradigms of Information Systems Development. *Communications of the ACM* 32(10): 1199–1216.

Jungk, R., and N. Müllert. 1987. *Future Workshops: How to Create Desirable Futures*. London: Institute for Social Inventions.

Kensing, F., and K. H. Madsen. 1991. Generating Visions: Future Workshops and Metaphorical Design. In J. Greenbaum and M. Kyng, eds., *Design at Work: Cooperative Design of Computer Systems*, 155–168. Hillsdale, NJ: Erlbaum.

Leontjev, A. N. 1978. *Activity, Consciousness, and Personality*. Engelwood Cliffs, NJ: Prentice Hall.

MacLean, A., K. Carter, L. Lovstrand, and T. Moran. 1990. User-Tailorable Systems: Pressing the Issues with Buttons. In *Proceedings of ACM CHI '90 Conference on Human Factors in Computing Systems*, 175–182. New York: ACM Press.

Madsen, K. H. 1996. Initiative in Participatory Design. In *PDC '96: Proceedings of the Participatory Design Conference*, 223–230. Palo Alto, CA: CPSR.

Marx, K. [1867] 1962. *Das Kapital*. Vol. 1. Berlin: Dietz Verlag.

Mørch, A. 1997. Three Levels of End-User Tailoring: Customization, Integration, and Extension. In M. Kyng and L. Mathiassen, eds., *Computers and Design in Context*, 51–76. Cambridge, MA: MIT Press.

Sjöberg, C., and T. Timpka. 1994. Voices in Design: The Dynamics of Participatory Information Systems. In R. Trigg, S. I. Anderson, and E. Dykstra-Ericson, PDC '94: *Proceedings of the Participatory Design Conference*, 75–86. Palo Alto, CA: CPSR.

Star, S. L. 1989. The Structure of Ill-Structured Solutions: Boundary Objects and Heterogeneous Distributed Problem Solving. In L. Gasser and M. N. Huhns, eds., *Distributed Artificial Intelligence* 2, 37–54. Menlo Park, CA: Morgan Kauffman.

Trigg, R., and S. Bødker. 1994. From Implementation to Design: Tailoring and the Emergence of Systematization in CSCW. In R. Futura and C. Neuwirth, eds., *Proceedings of CSCW 94*, 45–54. New York: ACM Press.

Wartofsky, M. W. 1973. Perception, Representation, and the Forms of Action: Toward an Historical Epistemology. In M. W. Wartofsky, ed., *Models*, 188–210. Dordrecht: Reidel.

20

Localizing Self on the Internet: Designing for "Genius Loci" in a Global Context

Sara Eriksén

In this chapter, the notions of *software development*, *design*, and *use*—when I eventually get around to them—are employed in a broad and partly overlapping fashion. There is also a shifting signification, and an implicit tension in the text, between the meaning of these words in an imagined, ideal world and in the examples given, which come from "real-life" experience. The tension would not be there, however, if interrelationships did not exist that could be further explored between the ideal,[1] the experienced, and the subjectiveness that brings the two together. Herein lies the dynamic source of both social thinking and software practice.

Ideally, from the author's point of view, software development would always entail design.[2] The design and use of software would not only be slightly overlapping, but would be deliberately interwoven, and mutually informing, in everyday work practice. The relationship between software design practice and the actual everyday use of software would thus in many "best-practice" cases be rich and complex. With this approach, methods would not be limited to development, design, *or* use, but would normally be chosen in relation to all three, and would depend on considerations concerning the specific situation, the goals, the people involved and their skills and interests, and so on.

In real life, I have been exploring the politics and problems of trying to bring this ideal state to bear. More and more, I have come to see how this very process of problematizing may be understood as constitutive of both the ideal itself and the practice it is striving to inform, and how it is, basically, a profoundly social and cooperative endeavor. In this process, the concept of "self," versus "we," is central. Yet it is often strangely invisible in the official discourse about "what's going on."

In the following pages, my choice of method is to give a brief overview of what I see as the major shift during the past century in mainstream social theorizing, to compare this to recent and ongoing developments in information technology (IT) and software practice, and, finally, to bring these themes together in a brief personal narrative of experiences from four research-and-development projects I have been involved in during the past four years. The course of the narrative is strongly influenced by my choice of analytic tool. As I will note in the final section of the chapter, I have applied a metaphor borrowed from architecture and Greek mythology in an attempt to reconceptualize the relationship of "the user" to the development, design, and use of public information systems accessible via the Internet. The motivation for this, with respect to software practice, will, I hope, become clearer as the story develops. It is basically about making use of strong subjectivity[3] and the power of empathy, in both social thinking and software practice. It is an attempt to objectify and instrumentalize the actions, rather than the actors, in human-machine interaction.

The social science–based approach incorporated in this chapter is basically constructionist. It has been influenced, on the one hand, by the pragmatic philosophy of the later Wittgenstein, and on the other hand by Berger and Luckmann ([1966] 1991), Gergen (1985, 1991), Papert (1994), Lave and Wenger (1991), Engeström (1993), and Latour and Woolgar (1986). Other influences include ethnographic field methods and American ethnomethodology, the "work practice and technology" approach of Suchman and others, as well as feminist writings and gender research focusing on issues of strong subjectivity (Hartsock 1998; Smith 1988, 1990).[4]

My contribution to the process of understanding and intervening in software practice might best be characterized as an attempt at rethinking the conceptual modeling of software for Internet applications in order to bring subjectivity and concepts of "self" to the fore. That is, I am striving to highlight the importance of the complex, dynamic relationships between intentional action and specific time and place issues, thus bringing the user as an "I"—as well as the designer/developer, as a co-constructing "I"—more squarely into focus in software development, design, and use.

Localizing Self

The difficulty in focusing on what is being explored here—the invisibility of "self" in most discourse on the design, development, and use of IT—is mirrored in the ambiguous relationship between the title of this section and its contents. For, though I am addressing the issue of localizing self, what follows is not primarily about me, *my* self: Sara Eriksén, the author of this text, researcher, mother of two children, one-time consultant/ systems developer, and so on. Yet it is precisely this sense of awareness and recognition of one's own identity as a conscious human being, an individual with a history of one's own, this sense of existence in space and time, this awareness of self, and intentionality in action, that I am attempting to bring to reason, as it were.[5] Thus, what follows is not a microautobiography but rather a brief and sketchy historical overview of social reasoning during the past hundred years, and of what I interpret as past and ongoing attempts at "localizing self" in this discourse.

In the past century, mainstream social theorizing has gradually shifted from attempting to gain legitimacy through adopting ideals, models, methods, and concepts of validity from the natural sciences, to exploring and challenging even the concept of "scientific facts," and the ways we construct and understand the world we live in (Callon and Latour 1981; Latour and Woolgar 1986; Pickering 1992; Latour 1993, 1999; Smith 1988, 1990; Suchman 1987). This has involved not only an extensive rethinking of what is observed, and how, but also reconceptualizing the observer—unscrewing the Big Leviathan, in the words of Callon and Latour—and developing notions of dynamic, co-constructive relationships between the observer(s) and the observed. The "pragmatic turn" is an expression often used to describe the philosopher Ludwig Wittgenstein's shift from studying the formal rules and logic of language (in his earliest work) to exploring the construction of meaning through language *use*, and understanding formal rules as interpretations of rules, and rule following as *practice* (Johannessen 1990). During the past century, we seem, gradually, to have been making something of a "pragmatic turn" in social thinking. New scientific methods, such as ethnomethodology (Garfinkel 1967), have evolved and are now widely in use for focusing on human activity and studying the "ongoing co-construction of reality" (Karasti 2000; Blomberg and Trigg 2000). Feminism, and, more recently, gender research, have contributed in important ways to the deconstruction of the rationalist view of "the world as is," and to the development of new understandings of subjectivity, intersubjectivity, and multiperspectivity (Hartsock 1998; Smith 1988, 1990; Benhabib 1992).

We have come a long way. When the American pragmatist William James claimed, at the beginning of the twentieth century, that "true ideas are those that we can assimilate, validate, corroborate, and verify,"[6] the heresy, for all believers in objective reality, was the introduction of "we" into such a serious matter as the truth.[7] That was a hundred years ago. Yet, in 1999, Latour wrote, "from the trenches of the Science Wars," of a scientist friend asking him, hushed and embarrassed, but very seriously, "Do you believe in reality?" (Latour 1999, 1).[8]

In this chapter, I am attempting to explore how we might get beyond the trenches, to more fertile ground; I am concerned with how "believing in reality" and "believing in realities" might be fruitfully managed within the same framework of understanding. Stepping up out of the trenches, from my point of view, means making explicit the identity of the observer as a strong—but nonsovereign—subject, situated *within* the "reality" that is being observed. In doing this, we may actually be strengthening the argument for considering, and making use of, coexisting "realities." By acknowledging and exploring the concept of "self," and localizing ourselves as subjects in the world we are inquiring about, we can begin to take into serious account the concept of "other selves," and the powerful concept of co-construction.

The dialogical philosophy of Martin Buber explores "self" in this direction, as I understand it. In *Ich und Du*, Buber (1956) makes a clear distinction between the two primary word pairs I-You and I-It. The primary word I-You (whether expressed as I, or as You) can only be spoken with the whole being, according to Buber, whereas the primary word I-It can never be spoken with the whole being. The existence of

I and the speaking of I are, from this point of view, one and the same thing. When a primary word is spoken, the speaker enters the word and takes his or her stand in it.[9] The "I"—the understanding of self and others—is different, depending on whether it enters into dialogue with a "You," or only observes or reflects on an "It." The "You" is forever running the risk of becoming an "It"—and thus diminishing the scope of the "I"—as we strive to objectify, to step back from the world we live in and observe it.

But academic narratives—the formalized kinds of discourse—of software theory, as they are cultivated in subject areas such as computer science, informatics, and so on, do not encourage making the narrator visible as a "self." In stark contrast to this "objective," formal discourse, everyday work practice in software development projects and software maintenance work, as well as software use, are riddled with "war stories" (Orr 1996), where the narrator may not only be visible but in many cases may be something of a hero. These openly subjective anecdotes and stories are an important part of how knowledge and experience are shared among systems developers and scientists.

In interdisciplinary areas such as human-computer interaction (HCI) and computer-supported cooperative work (CSCW), words like *co-construction*, *situatedness*, *context*, and *user-centered* are commonly used. But *I*, *me*, *myself*, and *you*, when used at all, seem to represent what Buber calls the primary word combination I-It—as does the frequent, but noncommittal, use of *we*.

There is a basic problem here that I am trying to make visible, a problem that is often underestimated, or even totally ignored, in software theory *and* practice. Take, for instance, the seemingly emancipated discourse and work practices[10] within the field of participatory design. Goals, and methods of reaching them, are discussed. Elaborate arguments are developed and presented in favor of various methods, and in favor of flexibility in applying them. Agreements are made about how to proceed. But basically, we continue to act within the scope of, and according to, our different understandings of ourselves and the world we live in.[11] These worldviews may be profoundly different. There is a built-in ambiguity and potential for future disagreement in our contracts from the start. This should not come as a surprise to us. After all, we design and develop software in a world of many "realities"; we talk and write of "co-construction" and argue about the various roles and alternative understandings of agency, and mediation, and translations. Yet in practice, and in theorizing, we keep striving for clear and unambiguous wording, for unconditional representation, for detailed specifications—as though, basically, we still believed in the "rational man" and in "the one-and-only real world." In many cases, we find ourselves all too easily slipping into using ethnomethodology as a magnifying glass, pushing our faces up flat against work practices in a specific workplace and believing that, somehow, if we just get close enough to the "real" world out there, translations, mediations, interpretations, and all other possible sources of ambiguity will go away. Stubbornly, we continue to look for the one-and-only reality, even though we profess to be studying co-construction, and even when we know that, according to some of the best-known and most influential philosophers and social psychologists of the past century and more, ambiguity is the very place to begin exploring (see, for example, the writings of philosophers, social scientists, and social psychologists such as Hegel, Mead, Vygotsky, Beauvoir, Wittgenstein, and Buber[12]).

We are haunted, still, it seems, by the ghost of the Big Leviathan.[13]

The Internet and the Wireless Boom

Paradoxically, the Big Leviathan may lose his remaining, most vital screws, and finally be forced to give up his ghost, not so much because of radical shifts in social theory, but rather as an effect of violent repercussions from recent and ongoing technological developments.[14] In the following, I will, at least initially, leave the issues of subjectivity, and of "localizing self," out of the picture for a while, and take a look at "reality" from a position that I perceive to be somewhat closer to the Leviathan's singular and objective point of view.

The widespread use of the Internet and the World Wide Web has evolved interdependently with an expansive production of Internet/intranet applications. This development has been more rapid, and more pervasive, than anyone could have anticipated. In only a few years, the world of software practice and use has changed radically.

On the one hand, a vast number of diverse software applications now exist, as well as an enormous amount and variety of information that can be accessed through them. On the other hand, more and more people can access them, at any time, from anywhere, and for any number of different reasons and purposes.[15]

The rapid development and diversification in the use of new information and communication technologies actually leads to further challenges. The "from anywhere" has not only become a question of the geographic location of the user. The answer to "Where from?" now includes a growing variety of tools for communication, such as cellular phones, personal digital assistants (PDAs), laptop computers, Web tablets or so-called surfboards, and the like. These tools make use of new types of software and protocols—for example, Wireless Application Protocol (WAP), Short Message Services (SMS), and voice message services. This in turn puts new and more diverse demands on the applications, packaging, transportation, and presentation of information. Thus, there is a proliferation of directions and dimensions to be handled in software practice.

Today, speaking of "the use situation" or "the user," as though such an entity could be envisioned in one basic scenario with a limited number of variations, is, in most cases, unrealistic. Yet the importance of addressing the concrete, contextual aspects of the specific use situation, the "this is me, here and now, and where-do-I-go-from-here" issues of IT in use, has not been diminished by this development. The users, on the contrary, are becoming more obvious, more diverse, and more demanding, as active co-constructors of the technologies in use.

The Global Context

Turning to my own experience, in the research-and-development projects I have been involved in, I have repeatedly come up against a problem in software practice that is hardly new. It bears a marked resemblance to a well-known problem in academic theorizing, concerning the risk of losing your foothold—your sense of self in the world—during the transition from specific to general, from local to universal, and concerning what guidelines to follow in order to get there safely and legitimately.

This includes, of course, the fundamental questions of "Where, precisely, is 'there'?" and "Is that where I want to go?"—that is, "What can I accomplish from there?" Here, I have paraphrased these problems, very broadly, as "the global context." By this, I am referring to issues of local versus global. "The global context" is a seemingly simple concept with enormous built-in tensions. Seriously juxtaposing local and global in software practice means managing layers of complex connectivity and actability while attempting to survive in a tradition of extreme reductionism. It means basing one's understanding of the world, at all levels, on one's participation in it. It means, to put it in feminist and Marxist terminology, retaining the unity of science and political practice (Hartsock 1998). *Global*, without claiming to be synonymous with *universal*, indicates a broad scope and wide range, and, in some sense, an overview. *Context* indicates a complex web of interrelationships, and a situatedness in time and space. The real challenge comes in fitting the two concepts together and making sense of the picture.

Formalization processes in traditional systems development by and large involve generalizing through reductionist abstraction rather than associative connection. This tends to lead to a disassociation of software design from issues concerning complex interrelationships between human intentional action and time and place, issues that may be crucial for the meaningful use of the resulting software. Thus, the primary focus on formalization processes in traditional software design and development makes programming easier, but makes software introduction and use in the workplace and work practice more problematic. Basically, a computer program is of course a formalization, but it needs to be designed to be meaningful in use—that is, to be understood by those who will be affected by it, and, ideally, to be interpretable in ways that make it susceptible of further design and development in actual use contexts. This means that during the software formalization process, there must be an openness toward, and methods for managing, multichoice, multimode solutions. There are issues of future interpretability and accountability at stake. In the very process of formalization, of decontextualization, measures must be taken, and means must be provided, for future recontextualization and reinterpretation in use (Dittrich 1998). The formalization process itself must be recognized as part of an interpretative process.

The growing diversity of information and communication technologies in use may be the development that finally forces us to undertake the "pragmatic turn"[16] in software formalization processes.

Designing for "Genius Loci"

In the following paragraphs, as a way of trying to substantiate and interrelate the various themes developed in this chapter, I will recount, in an extremely simplified fashion (as storytellers are prone to do), some lessons learned from four research-and-development projects I have been involved in during the past four years. The first two examples provide background. Through these experiences, I gradually developed the idea of using the concept of "genius loci" as a metaphor for focusing on and exploring a cluster of interrelated concerns for designers of public service applications for Internet use. The last two examples may be seen as the beginning of an exploration of this metaphor as a possible analytic tool for software practice. As for the metaphor itself, *genius loci* is Latin and means the "spirit of the place." The metaphor is further discussed in the final section of this chapter.

Each of the four research-and-development projects referred to here has centered around notions of rapidly developing information technologies as inherently conducive to communication, interaction, and cooperation. "Globalization" has generally, in these contexts, been a relatively unproblematized concept, like "information societies." The implicit assumption has been that the ongoing development is something you want to be a part of, make use of, and contribute to—above all, an ongoing, worldwide, but highly selective, development you do not want to be left out of (like someone missing the train[17]).

Yet in each project we have had to face and come to terms with issues of the situatedness and context of use. Often, these have surfaced as recurring problems around the striving for standardization of information content, structure, and interface design.

Universal Standards vs. Designing for a Local Context: The ATTACH Project

In the first project, we came to what I see, in retrospect, as a successful compromise. Five European nations (six different regions) were involved. At the outset, in January 1996, it was an accomplishment, the magnitude of which today is hard to grasp, for all the partners to reach an agreement about using the Internet as a common basis for developing public service information kiosks in the ATTACH project.[18] By December 1998, when the project came to an end, considerable effort had been put into developing a handbook and formalized standards for the user interface; relevant issues included what icons to use, shape and size of buttons, recommended text formats, and so on. However, the products developed at each site looked entirely different. None actually conformed to the suggested standards. All worked and were in use locally. And, despite the apparent disparity in the interface design between them, they were all based on Internet solutions, making use of design ideas developed and shared in cooperation between the partners during the three years' duration of the project. Together, we had developed an initial vision about a platform, which we each proceeded to explore and make use of in different ways, choosing different design solutions for the interface according to what seemed most relevant in the context of each site, and influenced by what was already there to start with. In Ronneby, my home site, this design-to-fit-the-context even carried through to the five individual kiosk solutions. In one case, for instance, the resulting "kiosk" consists of a PC mounted in an old wooden cupboard with its doors flung wide open, inviting passersby to explore the local Web site for information about ongoing exhibits, activities, and opportunities in the town and its surroundings. The cupboard is conveniently located inside the entrance of an old wooden house open to the public in the popular spa park. Similarly, in each of the other four kiosk locations in Ronneby, the individual physical "kiosk" has been given an appropriate shape of its own.

Thus, one of the lessons I learned from the ATTACH project was that although the power of symbols may be universal, symbols themselves are not inherently so. It seems that symbols gain their very power from, and in complex relation to, their local use and context. This became apparent in the local applications developed within the ATTACH project, and in how poorly they corresponded with the formal interface standards we had established within the same project—yet how well they fit into, and worked in, the local contexts. In the ATTACH project, this just "happened" as we went along. It was basically considered a bit of an embarrassment for the project board and coordinators that we had not managed to enforce the standards we had set up, and that the various applications lacked a common look and feel—a universal brand identity, as it were. Yet the issue of being more deliberate and aware of this need for local connectivity in design, and more consciously making use of it, is what I now began to explore and elaborate on as the notion of designing for "genius loci."

Designing for "Genius Loci" as Community-Based Co-construction: The One-Stop Service Project

In the second project, One-Stop Service,[19] a participatory design approach was used for developing practices and standards for coordinating, structuring, and linking public service information online at different levels.[20] The aim was to allow comprehensive, easy, and useful Internet access to national, regional, and local information sources in ways that would take into account where the question was coming from, and some of the explicit intentions of the individual user. The idea was to develop an overall coherence and quality to public services online that could to be of real, everyday use to employees within public service administration at all levels, as well as to "citizens in general." This was seen as a basic condition for at least two reasons: first, to guarantee in-depth quality in the development of the decentralized, linked-together information structure, and second, to guarantee continuing quality, in use and life-cycle design and development, of public service information and interactive services online.[21] Because of my experiences from past and ongoing parallel research projects focusing on computer support in one-stop shops, a third reason for using participatory design here was equally obvious: to, finally, more seriously, begin to realize the visions of integrated, comprehensive computer support for front-office work.

This project ended in December 1999. It resulted, among other things, in a number of the most commonly used blanks in local public administration being made available online jointly from the five municipalities in the county of Blekinge. It also resulted in a prototype for linking local, regional, and national information according to various "themes" considered to be of interest to citizens looking for public service information online. One such theme was "divorce"; another was "I want to study at the university"; yet another was "we're expecting a baby."

One of the lessons learned from this project was that the "common citizen" being addressed via the developing online public services was still to some extent a traditional bureaucratic construct. This citizen-user was on the one hand one dimensional and nonspecific, on the other hand multifaceted, in that each sector of public administration had a different view of him or her. Yet our attempts at localizing this user on the Internet, in the sense of offering integrated information relevant for the life event (the "theme") as well as for the municipality, county, and region where this person indicated they stood at present, were at least a step toward reconceptualizing the citizen-user and personalizing the information for them, in cooperation across organizational borders. The differing views, the different types of understandings and underlying assumptions about the citizen-user that surfaced in this cooperative work between different public service agencies, began to bring out a more complex, multidimensional picture of who it was that was being addressed as public service information went online.

Somewhere along the line in this project, I began more deliberately to combine and explore the notions of designing for "genius loci" in a global context and of localizing "self" on the Internet. Shouldn't we, as citizens, and the communities to which we feel we belong, be more actively and consciously involved in defining our relevant profiles and needs? Shouldn't we, in fact, be more actively involved in designing public service? And finally, in this process, shouldn't we be constructively designing our goals, our lives, and ourselves?[22]

By this time, I was beginning to see the idea of designing for "genius loci" as a possible label for a long-term, co-constructive, community-based project. It encompassed, but was no longer confined to, interface-design questions such as the look and feel of buttons on the screen, or what various physical access points to public service online looked like and where they were located (in old wooden cupboards in spa parks, in futuristic stainless steel kiosks in airports, or whatever). Designing for "genius loci" seemed to be about more than this. It needed further exploring. I was beginning, by now, to see it as a possible conceptual tool for grasping, bringing to the surface, and dealing with important issues of context, complexity, multiperspectivity, and politics in the design and development of software.

Deliberately Designing for "Genius Loci" from the Outset: The Entrance-Net Project

The third project, the Entrance-net project, seemed, when we planned it in the fall of 1999, an ideal first project for deliberately exploring the concept of designing software for "genius loci." Here, two master's students from the MDA program[23] and seven first-year students from the systems engineering program at the Blekinge Institute of Technology were to work together during the spring of 2000, developing a prototype of an information system especially designed to address the needs of visitors entering at one of seven different entrances to the combined business and university complex at the Soft Center in Ronneby. The system would also be made accessible via the Internet. However, the main challenge was that the graphical interface to each local, public physical-access point to the system, in each entrance in the Soft Center, was to be designed for the "genius loci" of that exact location. In the Entrance-net application, helping the visitor with "localizing self" in the system would, basically, be a seemingly simple and straightforward matter of making clear at the local interface the user's physical location in the building, showing the digital version of the "you-are-here" spot, and indicating how to get from that spot to whereever you wanted to go in the Soft Center area. Beyond this, there were ambitions to design a system to match, mirror, and support both the physical architecture of the buildings in the area and the multitude and variety of activities continually being carried out there.

The questions addressed in this project included the following: How can the design of the building, the entrance itself, the lighting, the physical signs and symbols, and the way people move through each entrance, be taken into account in the design of the interface to, and the interaction with, the information system aiming to support the needs of the visitor to the building? How can these local features be catered to at the same time that the system is designed for access from anywhere via the Internet? How can this "anywhere" include designing for support of communication via Short Message Services, e-mail, voice mail, chat, and so on? That is, how can specificity, diversity, and generality be tailored to one and the same application, without losing sight of one or the other? What are the implications for software practice of thus specifically addressing both the local and the global possibilities in one and the same application?

In some sense, in this project, we were trying to force the issues that in recent computer-supported cooperative work (CSCW) and human-computer interaction (HCI) literature have often been played out through avatars in the virtual world back out into the complexity of the "real" world, where software design, through each specific user, can be made as tangible and accountable to its surroundings, as can a brick wall, a glass-and-steel entrance door, or an elevator button.

One important source of inspiration in the Entrance-net project was Thomas A. Markus, architect and author of *Buildings and Power* (1993), who visited the university during the spring of 2000 and played an active part in our design discussions. Markus writes about how buildings—like words—do not automatically *have* meaning, they *convey* it. Thus

> just as meaning in language needs a speaker and a listener who are members of the same language-using community, so buildings and their texts acquire meaning when the subject (an observer, user, reader) experiences a building or a text about it, when the two worlds intersect. Subject and object are embedded in—neither free of nor determined by—their historical societies. The first world is an outer, visible one (which is, of course, the result of its author's inner world) and the second an invisible, inner world. At this intersection the Cartesian boundary between object and subject dissolves. So our study of meaning will have to embrace three domains: the building, the text, and the experiencing subject, all in a language-using society. (Markus 1993, 5)

Both in his writing and in our discussions, Markus used a professional language that not only allowed for the presence of experiencing subjects, but relied on it and made use of it. Here, designers and users were co-constructors of meaning, and as such were dependent on each other. Here, empathy was not a bad word, but rather a prerequisite to accomplishing good design. What would it take to develop such a professional standpoint in software design practice? How can we go about seeing ourselves, and our role of co-constructors, in what we do?

As may be imagined, the ambitions in the Entrance-net project were far greater than the time and resources actually allotted to it. By the end of the spring semester, there was a prototype of an information system for Soft Center visitors running on the university server (although not available for actual visitors), and all the students involved in the project had passed their respective exams. In this sense, the project had been successful.

But the attempt to deliberately design for "genius loci" from the start in a multiorganizational setting like the Soft Center had also succeeded in bringing to the surface a number of political issues that repeatedly stalled and delayed the project throughout the spring. Although the students had initiated, and kept in continual contact with, a group of representatives of the various interested parties for the prototype they were developing, it was unclear who actually "owned" the idea and was willing to take long-term responsibility for the continued development of the system. The internal information infrastructure in the various organizations involved was not geared to cooperation across organizational boundaries. Despite the inspiring mix of student and business cultures at the entrances to the Soft Center, in the joint library InfoCenter, and in the cafeteria, there was a lack of a core sense of "we" to build on, beyond the various organizational hierarchies, in developing a joint information system on the Internet/intranet. To me, this seemed to emphasize that on the one hand "localizing self" on the Internet, and on the other hand relating to others, and thereby to various possible groupings of "we," in presenting oneself to the rest of the world, were interrelated problems, and could be explored on both individual and organizational levels.

Many of the issues initially addressed in the Entrance-net project were actually never really grappled with. The prototype was not developed beyond an initial mapping onto the Internet of the horizontal floor plans and vertical sectional drawings of the Soft Center buildings, with links to various organizational databases for information about who could be found in what office, or reached by what e-mail address. No serious attempts were made to design alternative interfaces for WAP or SMS access to the prototype, for instance. There was no time for this. However, we explored the concept of designing for "genius loci" in connection with developing WAP applications in other projects. My final example is from one such project.

Designing for "Genius Loci" as a Way of Locating Future Users: The Cellular Phone Bus Timetable

The fourth example I have chosen to relate here is a student project that ran in parallel with the Entrance-net project, during the spring of 2000. This project had a much narrower and more clearly delimited focus from the start. Two third-year students in the MDA[24] program chose to develop a prototype for a WAP-based bus timetable as the basis for their bachelor's thesis. Their problem, at the outset, was a not-uncommon one these days: how do you go about finding "users" for an entirely new product, which does not yet exist, provided you want to ground your design in some kind of experienced needs by using participatory design methods? They started, as students often do, by brainstorming together, and then by interviewing fellow students. But after we had had a discussion about exploring the possibilities of concepts like designing for "genius loci," they decided that they should look for the "spirit of the place" for bus timetables. They went to the main bus station in town and interviewed people waiting for buses. They looked at how people used the timetables on display. They made mock-ups of personalized bus timetables on cellular phones and asked people at the bus station to try them out and suggest changes to make them work better.

They discovered that, although a WAP-based bus timetable was an entirely different artifact from a traditional bus timetable, and could encompass novelties like information about individual instances of delays in normal bus traffic, people who ride buses and use traditional bus timetables have a lot of imagination and could contribute useful and relevant ideas for the new product. Not only that, but they became aware of the fact that designing a new product would also mean having to design a new information infrastructure to support it in the existing bus-traffic system. A system would have to be in place for locating buses and keeping track of delays, a system that could continuously update the information on the Internet. This information about the current state of the local traffic could be useful for the bus drivers to have access to, as well.

In this project, I believe the concept of designing for "genius loci" helped the students locate possible future users in such a self-evident place that they had initially overlooked it entirely. More than that, thinking about "genius loci," and trying to define it, also seems to have helped them see beyond the design of the artifact itself and begin to discern important infrastructural relationships to be considered and perhaps redesigned to support the personalized bus timetable.

Closing Discussion

Perhaps the most self-evident things in everyday life are the hardest to perceive and address in designing for the future. To me, it seems as though the existence of "self" is one of these self-evident[25] but invisible basics that tend to get lost when focusing too narrowly and exclusively on formalization processes, as examplified, for instance, in traditional software development. Yet the use situation—the ultimate goal for which software is designed and developed—would not exist if there were not an "I, me, myself" involved at that end. Nor would there be any software to use, if there did not exist an "I, me, myself" of the systems developers who must interpret, conceptualize, and sensitively decontextualize—while catering to the needs of future recontextualization in use—the problem area in focus during the design-and-development process.

The realization that trying to adequately address and understand the contextual aspects of the actual use situation is important for the design of usable software is not new. The need to understand more about the user and the use situation has led to the development of what are, by now, fairly well-established traditions in software engineering science and practice, such as participatory design and user-centered design. More than a decade ago, Lucy Suchman (1987) juxtaposed plans and situated action and examined IT design in light of the largely unexplored relationship and tension between them. However, the rapid development during the 1990s of the Internet and the World Wide Web has in turn led to an expansive development of Internet/intranet applications. Diverse issues surrounding what applications and information can be accessed, by whom, and how are changing the world of software practice. And still, "I," "me," "myself," "you," and "we" are largely unexplored relationships in the discourse pertaining to software practice.

The "I, me, myself" self I refer to here, in quotation marks, is no more subtle, or less complex, a conceptual construction than the individual user using the individual IT artifact. It is the "I" who may well get up in a moment or two and walk away/move to a different application in disgust, saying something under their breath like "I can't get anything useful out of this stupid thing!" "I" is a specific person, in a specific place, at a specific time, with the intention of accomplishing something through an action of "my" own. What I have been trying to do, here, with the hyphenated "I," "me," "myself," "my," is to focus intently, not only on the situatedness, but also on the constructive subjectiveness, of intentional action. The problem, for the designers of modern IT, is at once simple and incredibly complex. We are faced with having to seriously consider the specificities of human intentional action, and take seriously the "I, me, myself"—and "we"!—of the subject with a goal. Yet, at least since the days of Hobbes, we have not been developing very good tools, metaphors, and methods for managing the diversities and ambiguities that this multiperspective approach assumes and opens up toward.

What about "genius loci"? It is a concept I have borrowed from architecture and Greek mythology in order to visualize the importance of returning from "out of time, out of space" objectivity to the subjective, messy complexities of everyday life, where specific places and points in time, and people and their individual intentions, make a difference. As noted earlier, "genius loci" means the "spirit of the place." As I have heard architects use the term, it seems to refer to something important—though hard to put into words—to which good design must be made accountable.

For me, "genius loci" implies a place where the subjective and objective meet and define each other in and through action. In Greek mythology, the lusty mingling and mating of mortal gods and godly mortals was a common theme, often resulting in the birth of new and powerful constellations.

My aim has been to bring the notion and location of an active "self"—in time as well as in space—more squarely into focus when considering "the user" and "the use situation" in software design and development. Pinpointing a specific place, its physical design, and what it means to the people passing through it and their actions, has been a part of this endeavor.

Thomas A. Markus, architect, author of *Buildings and Power* (1993), and cosupervisor in the Entrance-net project (the third of the four examples presented above) writes about how buildings—like words—*like software?*—do not automatically *have* meaning, they *convey* it. This implies both mediation and interpretation, in design *and* in use, for which means must be provided, and that must be cared for and cultivated. But while the aim of abstractions is simplification, disinvolvement, and, ultimately, objectivity, acts of mediation and interpretation are always subjective, their very accomplishment being dependent on empathetic involvement.

Today, we are increasingly faced with the need to design for diverse and changing contexts, for space, place, mode and mobility, for local and global considerations. We need to find ways of conceptually modeling complex dynamic relationships between intentional action and specific time and place issues, and to bring these conceptualizations to bear in software design and development practice, as well as in everyday use of IT. My main contribution here has been an attempt to focus and address the increasing complexity of the design projects we are faced with by turning to the concept of strong subjectivity, and of localization of "self," as a previously vastly underestimated resource for deliberately co-constructive design, development, and use of IT.

Notes

Thomas A. Markus, author of *Buildings and Power*, visited Ronneby in the spring of 2000 and cosupervised the students working with the Entrance-net project described above. His enthusiasm and wise questions and comments were invaluable both for the project he supervised and for more serious reflection on subjectivity as a central issue in design. Special thanks to Yvonne Dittrich, Olav W. Bertelsen, Thomas Binder, and Ralf Klischewski for insightful feedback on various drafts of this chapter.

1. "The ideal" might be replaced here by "the model," "the plan," "the vision," "the goal," "the dream," "the theory," and so on—that is, whatever you believe you are striving to approximate, match, or achieve. See for instance Naur 1985; Suchman 1987; Smith 1988, 1990; Stolterman 1991; Hartsock 1998.

2. Some methods currently in use for software development, such as extreme programming (XP), explicitly aim at supporting simultaneous designing and code writing, "designing-as-you-go-along." When applying XP, programmers

strive to develop a communal ownership of evolving concepts and code by working in pairs, having daily, informal morning meetings to share and coordinate their ideas and work (Beck 1999; compare Naur 1985, on programming as theory building).

3. Strong subjectivity—which concerns a specific individual's concept of "self," of identity, and of the power to act—is one of the central concepts under construction in this chapter and in my research in general at present. It has been emphasized by, and adds emphasis to, design issues concerning public information systems and their relationship to and dependancy on conceptualizations of "the individual user," "user groups," "people," and "the public." See more below.

4. The notion, here, of "strong subjectivity" is inspired by Hartsock's views on the feminist standpoint (see Hartsock 1998, 78–81, as in her quoting of Weeks 1996, 101: "This project of transforming subject-positions into standpoints involves an active intervention, a conscious and concerted effort to reinterpret and restructure our lives.... A standpoint is a project, not an inheritance; it is achieved, not given"). However, although I agree with Hartsock's argument (Hartsock 1998, 79) that subjects are defined by their relations with others, I do not share her conviction that a conscious standpoint—here, "strong subjectivity"—can only be achieved by a collective subject, or group. On the contrary, the only way I can understand Hartsock's persistent defense of the concept of "objectivity" is by rethinking the power of "objectivity" as energy, ability to act—that is, by developing a reflective process of dialogically objectifying action, rather than rationally objectifying people. In this project, I see no emancipatory potential or power, unless we are able, ultimately, to take a stand, and take action, as individuals. Otherwise we lose the power of co-construction. Hence the importance of "localizing self."

5. Compare Horkheimer ([1947] 1996, 128): "The crisis of reason is manifested in the crisis of the individual, as whose agency it has developed.... The individual once conceived of reason exclusively as an instrument of the self. Now he experiences the reverse of this self-deification.... At the moment of consummation, reason has become irrational and stultified. The theme of this time is self-preservation, while there is no self to preserve. In view of this situation, it behooves us to reflect upon the concept of the individual."

6. William James, quoted in Dewey 1988.

7. R. Ross, in the introduction to Dewey 1988.

8. This candid question from a very serious scientist may have triggered Latour's choice of a teasingly ambiguous title for the book in which it is quoted: *Pandora's Hope: Essays on the Reality of Science Studies* (1999).

9. Compare Wittgenstein on language use; also compare the ongoing debate within gender research about subjectivity and the possible interpretation of it as being "a positioning in language" (Benhabib 1992, quoting Judith Butler). However, Benhabib strongly disagrees with Butler. This debate seems partly to

be going on in the trenches, from where the possibility of gaining insight into alternative understandings of language use is limited by restricted horizons and heavy armament on both sides.

10. In this context, I will not attempt to differentiate "discourse" from "practice." In my reality, they are intermingled and interdependent, like "theory" and "practice."

11. This point was nicely made, and brought more directly to my attention, in a guest lecture by Jim Nyce, a contributor to this book, during his visit to Ronneby, Sweden, September 19, 2000.

12. This clustering of names does not mean I claim they share the same perspective—far from it—although Hegel seems to have had a profound influence on Mead, and probably on the others as well. It is precisely the many differences, the alternative, coexisting perspectives, in the ways we explore and co-construct the world we live in, that I am trying to bring to the fore here. (As an example, to emphasize this point, see Hood Holzman 1996 for an interesting discussion of basic differences between Mead's and other American pragmatists' primarily communicationist approaches, based on notions of human action and interaction, and Vygotsky's cultural-historical, dialectical approach, based on concepts of more structurally-anchored-in-context activity.)

13. The Big Leviathan, an ambiguous beast from the start, represents both evil powers and the sovereign will of God in the Old Testament. The metaphor is used by Thomas Hobbes in his treatise *Leviathan* (1651), where, in defense of secular monarchy, he presents his theory of the sovereign state. In Latour's words, this involves "[calling] back Socrates" Body Politic to become a Leviathan of *this world*, a monster and a half, composed only of "unhampered" individuals half-dead, half-alive, "without trappings, without clothes, without relatives and friends'" (Latour 1999, 263). Latour repeatedly returns to the metaphor of the Big Leviathan in problematizing the traditional split between power, knowledge, and reason in scientific theorizing. He uses what might be called a deconstructionist approach in his attempt at focusing "*the very act of smashing practice into bits*" (Latour 1999, 267). But here I am attempting to use a constructionist approach by focusing on "localizing self" in theorizing about practice. Basically, I believe we are fighting the same ghost.

14. A fittingly mechanical death for such a ghost, if so, I would say. Latour's Leviathan is markedly mechanical, much more so than Hobbes's. Compare Callon and Latour 1981, "Unscrewing the Big Leviathan: How Do Actors Macrostructure Reality and How Do Sociologists Help Them Do So?" See also my discussion earlier in this chapter about the ongoing, piece-by-piece deconstruction/ reconstruction of reality, the actor and the observer. A mechanical worldview, quite logically, would, metaphorically speaking, need to be taken apart screw by screw.

15. Less often talked about, perhaps, and probably growing at least as fast, are the vast numbers of people on earth who, for economic and/or other concrete

reasons such as illiteracy, lack of electricity, lack of public access to computers, lack of experience and guidance, lack of energy and initiative because of starvation, and so on, do not have computer access. (Thus spake the author, not the Big Leviathan—our realities differ.)

16. See my earlier discussion of Wittgenstein's so-called "pragmatic turn" (Johannessen 1990), and the discussion of an ongoing "pragmatic turn" in social theory.

17. Inge Lytje's example, in discussing the power of metaphors during a lecture on software design in Ronneby, March 31, 2000.

18. ATTACH is an acronym for the EC project *Advanced Trans-European Telematics Applications for Community Help*, UR 1001, 1996–1998.

19. One-Stop Service was a one-year cooperative regional project that ran from January through December 1999 and involved local and regional public service administration as well as local and regional offices of the central Swedish government in the county of Blekinge, Sweden. The project was funded by the National Board for Industrial and Technical Development (NUTEK).

20. The participatory design approach, in this case, involved a number of employees from various levels and sectors of the Swedish public service administration, but, beyond that, no representatives of "citizens" at large.

21. "Design in use" is how I usually think of and refer to this life-cycle design-and-development issue. The ambiguity of the expression is deliberate.

22. See Ekelin 2000.

23. MDA is the Swedish acronym for the interdisciplinary master's program at the Blekinge Institute of Technology called *People, Computers, and Work*, where computer science and human work science are combined in educating systems developers for the future.

24. See note 23.

25. No pun intended.

References

Beauvoir, S. de. [1948] 1994. *The Ethics of Ambiguity*. New York: Carol Publishing Group.

Beck, K. 1999. *Extreme Programming Explained: Embrace Change*. Reading, MA: Addison-Wesley.

Benhabib, S. 1992. *Situating the Self: Gender, Community and Postmodernism in Contemporary Ethics*. (In Swedish translation by Annika Persson, *Autonomi och Gemenskap. Kommunikativ etik, feminism och postmodernism.*) Gothenburg: Daidalos.

Berger, P., and T. Luckmann. [1966] 1991. *The Social Construction of Reality: A Treatise in the Sociology of Knowledge*. London: Penguin.

Blomberg, J., and R. Trigg. 2000. Co-constructing the Relevance of Work Practice for CSCW Design: A Case Study of Translation and Mediation. *Occasional Papers from the Work Practice Laboratory*. Vol. 1, No. 2: 2000. Department of Human Work Science, University of Karlskrona/Ronneby, Ronneby, Sweden.

Buber, M. 1956. *The Writings of Martin Buber*. Edited by W. Herberg; translated by R. G. Smith. New York: Scribner.

Callon, M., and B. Latour. 1981. Unscrewing the Big Leviathan: How Do Actors Macrostructure Reality and How Do Sociologists Help Them Do So? In K. Knorr and A. V. Cicourel, eds., *Advances in Social Theory and Methodology*. London: Routledge and Kegan Paul.

Dewey, J. 1988. *Reconstruction in Philosophy and Essays 1920: The Middle Works of John Dewey 1899–1924*. Edited by J. A. Boydston; textual editor, B. A. Walsh. Carbondale: Southern Illinois University Press.

Dittrich, Y. 1998. *How to Make Sense of Software: Interpretability as an Issue for Design*. Research Report 19/97. Department of Computer Science and Business Administration, University of Karlskrona/Ronneby, Sweden.

Ekdahl, P., E. Guldbrandsen, C. Mörtberg, L. Trojer, and G. H. Aas. 1999. *Möten mellan retorik och verkligheter*/The encounter between rhetoric and realities. Department of Human Work Science, University of Karlskrona/Ronneby, Ronneby, Sweden.

Ekelin, A. 2000. Mapping Out and Constructing the Needs: A Pilot Study of On-Line Public Services and Citizens' Involvement. Work in progress report in T. Cherkasky, J. Greenbaum, P. Membrey, and J. K. Pors, eds., *PDC 2000 Proceedings of the Participatory Design Conference, New York*, 258–260. CPRS Computer Professionals for Social Responsibility.

Engeström, Y. 1993. Developmental Studies of Work as a Testbench of Activity Theory: The Case of Primary Care Medical Practice. In S. Chaiklin and J. Lave, eds., *Understanding Practice: Perspectives on Activity and Context*. Cambridge, England: Cambridge University Press.

Eriksén, S. 1998. *Knowing and the Art of IT Management: An Inquiry into Work Practices in One-Stop Shops*. Doctoral dissertation, Department of Informatics, Lund University, Lund, Sweden.

Eriksén, S. 1999. *Globalization and "Genius Loci"; From Intentional Spaces to Purposeful Places*. Working paper for UK-/Nordic workshop held in Ronneby April 15–16, 1999 on the theme "Social Theory and ICT." See http://www.brunel.ac.uk/research/virtsoc/nordic/eriksen.html (2001-07-30).

Garfinkel, H. 1967. *Studies in Ethnomethodology*. Oxford: Polity Press/Blackwell.

Gergen, K. 1985. The Social Constructionist Movement in Modern Psychology. *American Psychologist* 3: 266–275.

Gergen, K. 1994. *Realities and Relationships: Soundings in Social Construction*. Cambridge, MA: Harvard University Press.

Giddens, A. 1991. *Modernity and Self-Identity: Self and Society in the Late Modern Age*. Stanford, CA: Stanford University Press.

Goffman, E. 1959. *The Presentation of Self in Everyday Life*. Garden City, NY: Doubleday Anchor Books.

Hartsock, N. 1998. *The Feminist Standpoint Revisited and Other Essays*. Boulder, CO: Westview Press.

Hood Holzman, L. 1996. Pragmatism and Dialectical Materialism. In H. Daniels, ed., *An Introduction to Vygotsky*. New York: Routledge.

Horkheimer, M. [1947] 1996. *Eclipse of Reason*. New York: Continuum.

Johannessen, K. S. 1990. Rule-Following and Intransitive Understanding. In B. Göranzon and M. Florin, eds., *Artificial Intelligence, Culture and Language: On Education and Work*. Berlin: Springer Verlag.

Karasti, H. 2000. Co-constructing Shared Understandings of Work Practices for System Design: The Interplay of Views. *Occasional Papers from the Work Practice Laboratory*, Vol. 1, No. 1: 2000. Department of Human Work Science, University of Karlskrona/Ronneby, Ronneby, Sweden.

Latour, B. 1993. *We Have Never Been Modern*. Cambridge, MA: Harvard University Press.

Latour, B. 1999. *Pandora's Hope: Essays on the Reality of Science Studies*. Cambridge, MA: Harvard University Press.

Latour, B., and S. Woolgar. 1986. *Laboratory Life: The Construction of Scientific Facts*. 2nd ed. Princeton, NJ: Princeton University Press.

Lave, J., and E. Wenger. 1991. *Situated Learning: Legitimate Peripheral Participation*. Cambridge, England: Cambridge University Press.

Linstead, S., and R. Grafton-Small. 1990. Theory as Artifact: Artefact as Theory. In P. Gagliardi, ed., *Symbols and Artifacts: Views of the Corporate Landscape*. New York: Aldine de Gruyter.

Markus, T. A. 1993. *Buildings and Power: Freedom and Control in the Origin of Modern Building Types*. London: Routledge.

Naur, P. 1985. Programming as Theory-Building. *Microprocessing and Microprogramming* 15: 253–261.

Orr, J. 1996. *Talking about Machines: Ethnography of a Modern Job*. Ithaca, NY: Cornell University Press.

Papert, S. 1994. *The Children's Machine: Rethinking School in the Age of the Computer*. New York: Harvester Wheatsheaf.

Pickering, A., ed. 1992. *Science as Practice and Culture*. Chicago: University of Chicago Press.

Rosen, M., W. Orlikowski, and K. Schmahmann. 1990. Building Buildings and Living Lives: A Critique of Bureaucracy, Ideology and Concrete Artifacts. In P. Gagliardi, ed., *Symbols and Artifacts: Views of the Corporate Landscape*. New York: Aldine de Gruyter.

Smith, D. 1988. *The Everyday World as Problematic: A Feminist Sociology.* Oxford: Open University Press/Milton Keynes.

Smith, D. 1990. *The Conceptual Practices of Power: A Feminist Sociology of Knowledge.* Boston: Northeastern University Press.

Stolterman, E. 1991. *Designarbetets dolda rationalitet. En studie av metodik och praktik inom systemutveckling*/The Hidden Rationale of Design Work: A Study in the Methodology and Practice of System Development. Doctoral dissertation, Department of Informatics, Umeå university, Umeå, Sweden.

Suchman, L. 1987. *Plans and Situated Actions: The Problem of Human-Machine Communication.* New York: Cambridge University Press.

Weeks, K. 1994. Subject for a Feminist Standpoint. In S. Makdisi, C. Casarino, and R. Karl, eds., *Marxism beyond Marxism.* London: Routledge.

21

Intent, Form, and Materiality in the Design of Interaction Technology

Thomas Binder

In a pioneering Swedish textbook on interaction design, Löwgren and Stolterman (1998) have polemically suggested that information technology (IT) be seen as the *material without qualities*. They do this with reference to the many attempts among software designers to come to grips with their design material (Winograd 1996). But the suggestion is also paraphrasing the title of Robert Musil's book *The Man without Qualities* (Musil [1930–1943] 1995). Musil was writing in the 1920s in an attempt to capture modernity as purified intentionality, in which structure and form have evaporated. The mirroring of IT and its embedding in a design discourse of intent and instrumentality in the emblematic image of the twentieth-century modern man are perceptive and far from coincidental. With this double anchoring of software design in a heritage of purified instrumentality and a striving for a workable notion of quality, the authors hit on the tune to which much concern with the emerging new field of design is played. But taken literally, the statement is misleading. Information technology (or rather, as I will argue by the end of this chapter, interaction technology) has—like any other class of artifacts—a "materiality." This "materiality" is not only shapable; it is also only through the "objectness" of the artifact that we as designers can hope to convey anything from setting to setting.

From my personal journey through design projects aiming at informing the skilled work of industrial technicians and operators, the issues of "materiality" and embodiment seem to emerge out of a simple and straightforward engagement with what it means to be informed. Having taken a starting point in participation and work practice, it has become increasingly clear that what we can channel with IT is not information with any guaranteed resemblance to what the "receiver" perceives. Rather, it is cues and clues for a constructing-sense-of-the-world that is basically not unlike the design process itself (Reddy 1979). I will argue that this implies an urgent need to escape a dominant utilitarian discourse of design that is centered on intent and instead engage in a more open-ended inquiry into what I will call the formation of artifacts.

I will develop my argument in three steps following retrospectively my own movements in the field. First, I will look at the fragile nature of the matrices in which we have been considering IT. From my own experience of working with information systems for the industrial shop floor, I will pinpoint the breakdown, not only of a unifying intentionality, but also of any kind of smooth transition from (design) intentions to lived-in practice. With a detour to Herbert Simon's "science of the artificial," I will look at how both I and the Scandinavian environment, which I see myself as a part of, have had difficulty coming to grips with this insight without losing sight of the distinction between artifact and context. Second, I will dwell on what—with a reference to Donald Schön—I call a more conversational approach to designing. With a starting point in a design project where we developed concepts for an industrial personal digital assistant (PDA), I will look at how leaping into design from a contextual inquiry runs the risk of adopting uncritically some of the technological "forms" already embedded in this context. Finally, I will consider how recent attempts to look for tangibility perhaps open a route to a new language of formation in the design of IT artifacts.

Taking IT Design beyond Bounds

For a number of years I was designing hypermedia-type shop-floor information systems for various industrial settings.[1] We wanted to use the then-new option of multimedia presentations to provide a richer and less abstract type of information for industrial workers directly on the shop floor. We designed the POSTI information system for postal workers and technicians working with automatic letter-sorting machines. POSTI contained information on maintenance, troubleshooting, and repair designed to soften the boundaries between the two groups and between novices and experienced workers. Later we designed the SPRING multimedia-based training package, meant for on-the-job training of machinists setting up spring coiling machines (Binder and Passarge 1996). As a design group we all had our roots in the Scandinavian tradition of collaborative design. We developed a way of working where we involved experienced workers extensively in the design work. We worked with industrial partners. These had typically organizational goals, such as reducing the division of labor or reducing time for off-line training. We saw our work as creating systems that facilitated such organizational change.

Our basic idea of what information to provide had two sources. First, we had an image of the type of industrial work we were to inform as being highly dependent on experienced practice, and we wanted to mirror this by making room for content generated by experienced workers in a format that avoided generalizations and was rich with examples. Slide shows and later small video sequences recorded with master craftspeople became the content backbone of our information systems. Second, we worked from the idea that having free access to instructional information on the shop floor would enable the users of the system to take turns with tasks they had little or no previous experience with. One can say that in our own understanding, we were creating an odd "Trojan horse." We saw the opportunity to create an artifact that could initiate change by making skill acquisition possible on the floor. At the same time, we were convinced that the information our system provided had to be generated by skilled workers on the same shop floor. Put differently, we took a fairly conventional idea of knowledge-based systems and tried to translate it into an environment where relevant information seemed to be documentation of best practice. We also envisioned mixed groups of users who could access information whenever they found it relevant. If, as designers within that framework, we had the role of "documenters" and "system architects," the people we worked together with were both "domain experts" and "users."

We were quite successful in setting up a participatory design process in these design projects, but a number of our initial assumptions became increasingly questionable as we gained experience in the field. Our idea of documenting best practice seemed straightforward, but our dialogue with the experienced workers in the field turned out to be much more of a design process in itself (Binder 1995). The workers did not agree among themselves as to what should count as best practice. At first we saw that as an indication of a large variance in actual work practice, but even if this is still true to some extent, I increasingly came to see the dialogue as a genuine construction process where "stories" of appropriate practice emerged. This spilled over onto an understanding of the role of the designer. We tended to see ourselves as the information systems designers that worked with domain expert and users who provided and evaluated information content. But as we continued to see a pattern where core "users" seemed to take on authorship of the systems, we started to wonder what our contribution was.

When we began to look more closely at our systems in use, we learned that what we had was much less than a fully negotiated information system put in place. In the POSTI project, the physical setup of the information system became a matter of contention among technicians and operators. Where should the POSTI system be placed? Should it be on wheels, have a keyboard, and so on? These turned out to be concrete questions through which not only the system itself but also the symbolic value attached to it had to be settled. And negotiations were not definitive. To the extent that we could follow what happened after we left, it seemed as if the POSTI system continued to be moved around and reinterpreted. The only thing that seemed fixed (and important) was the simple fact that something new was there.

With the SPRING application, continuous reinterpretation appeared to go even deeper. In a follow-up study of how the hypermedia material was used by inexperienced machinists, we found that even the informational content had to be reconstructed in light of both the social setting of use and the experiential horizon of the machinist (Meier 1998). A pattern very similar to what we had seen when we created the application together with experienced machinists of reinventing practice appeared to recur in use.

Designing the Artificial: Change Agency or World Making

Herbert Simon (1976) was among the first to articulate a broader concept of design that has been highly influential for our way of looking at the development of information systems. For Simon, the core competency of professionals is to design artifacts that interface between different systems in order to meet certain goals. This calls, according to him, for a science of the artificial, where scientific rigor is applied to the intricate network of societal means and ends. Simon's approach created the foundation for a discourse on systems design in which intent became the central issue. In Scandinavia, the participatory design tradition argued for a multiplicity of legitimate intentions that have to be incorporated into the process of design. With such notions as "user involvement," and "sociotechnical systems design," information systems designers have tried to broaden both the scope and the methodological approach of designing (Greenbaum and Kyng 1991). Such positions can, however, still be inscribed in a rationalistic design discourse of intentionality.

What is more problematic, though, is that the increasing sensitivity to the multitude of interests and perspectives engaged in "implementing technology" seems to have blurred the distinction between artifact and context (Binder 1996a). In the discussion on differentiating between computer science and informatics, authors such as Rolf (1992) have argued for a design orientation in informatics, which takes seriously the designer's role as change agent enrolled in a particular project with social goals. This position has been developed in dispute with a dominant self-image among technologists of being not in the realm of social discourse. For Rolf, the principal distinction to make is consequently the distinction between designing and producing. This in itself does not set him apart from Simon, but as he develops his views on design, the actual artifact seems to disappear behind the call for accounts of intended change. Bødker (1999) seeks to reinstate the artifact in the discussion of the design and use of computer applications. Taking her starting point in the activity-theory perspective on mediation, she sees computer applications as mediators enabling or restricting various ways of engaging with the world. Seeing these mediating artifacts as historical devices crystallizing work practices of the time they were made opens up for an analysis distinguishing (although only vaguely) design from actual use. But because she appears to apply an almost all-encompassing notion of artifacts, she does not in my view manage to differentiate design project (in terms of change agency) from evolving practice.

From this standpoint, our work on shop-floor information systems is also conventional. We started out with an organizational intention of having operators take responsibility for maintenance tasks. From this initial goal, we set in motion a process by which relevant task-specific information could be documented and channeled to the operators. If the system we designed had been a support system for office work or an instructional system for assembly-line workers, we may never have been confronted with the puzzling questions about the artifact we designed. The fact that we went for a participatory design process can be seen as an attempt to deal with the apparent complexity of the social context. By defining our collaborators as users and domain experts, we had carved out roles for them that established a firm playground for arbitrating between intentions.

What emerged was different. Our movement outside the established informational formats of, for example, text-based instructions that we could comprehend and control and into the much more ambiguous formats of multimedia documentation, came to illuminate in a practical manner how information has to be interpreted and appropriated to make sense. Similarly, the fact that our system was to be placed in an environment on the shop floor where information technology was still rare, made the actual instances of use highly uncertain. Our framework of participatory design was, in this setting, not unlike what Donald Schön ironically labeled "the negotiation of the platonic republic" (Schön, in Binder 1996b). We believed (like most other systems designers) that through the process of participation, we could manage to negotiate these new issues on the level of exposing and negotiating interests. What we did not see was that we had entered a new realm of form that we were incapable of addressing directly.

The writings of Simon still have relevance for the expanded notion of designing as the crafting of artifacts interfacing people and things. As Dahlbohm (forthcoming) also argues, Simon points out the immediate relevance of inquiring into the specific ways artifacts get designed and successively may change social constellations. What we have to realize is, however, that the bodiless concept of systems design is highly dependent on the bureaucratic installation of a regime of form. Such a regime has been in place in the long historical period of monolithic technological development in many areas of social life (Banta 1993), but taking this kind of systems design outside traditional bounds immediately reveals the unsettled issues of formation.

Providing Windows Rather Than Systems

The shop-floor information systems tended to become "overdesigned" as self-contained sociotechnical systems. The growing number of open-networked infrastructures with multiple points of access invites new types of applications. The image of information "browsers" providing access to a large and—to the design—external mass of information paves the way for new types of IT artifacts. After some years of working mainly with a tool perspective on IT support, I had the opportunity to make a design-oriented exploration of PDA-type interfaces for service technicians at industrial process plants. I worked at the time at an industrial manufacturer of actuators, sensors, and controls.[2] In a number of design projects, we had sought to develop a concept of local inspection and control based on portable interfaces, labeled SMARTTOOLS. This effort was only partly successful for several reasons. The notion of local inspection of, for example, a motor drive or a motor-controlled valve never became fully satisfactory. The components were always interconnected with other components and could hardly be said to be functionally located at one particular spot. That each component typically has associated instantiations that turn up in control panels or monitoring units did not make the picture clearer. Furthermore, the tool metaphor as adapted from Ehn (1988), although easily understandable, was difficult to put in place because it presupposes a "nice fit" between the technicians' task and the often-unknown state of the inspected components. This seductiveness of the chosen metaphor even had repercussions for our own approach to design. My colleagues and I entered the design projects from a usability engineering perspective (we were a usability design team within corporate research) (Bagger-Nielsen, Buur, and Binder 1997). The search for tools gave us too much of an easy ride in matching usability needs on the side of the technicians with sought-after qualities of the portable interfaces without being sufficiently challenged by the overall environment in which these tools were going to be used.

The industrial PDA project gave us an opportunity to reconsider what kind of information distribution we could think of for technicians operating in as IT rich an environment as a process plant. We named our device the SMARTWINDOW to indicate that what we were looking for was an artifact that could provide the technicians with a particular view of the environment in which they were working. The starting point was still human-centered design, with a mix of user workshops and anthropologically inspired fieldwork as the recurring steps in the design process. Where in other design projects we had identified core users early on and had mainly focused on understanding their task, in this project we sought to widen our outlook. The window metaphor in itself called for an understanding of the environment of which our device was to produce a view. We searched for some of the structuring images that already exist in the setting. The control room "panopticon" is one such strong structuring image. Most information technology somehow links up with this unifying image of global monitoring and control. However, this did not exhaust the environment as an information system. The group of operators and technicians continuously retell stories of the moment-to-moment operation based on strolls through the plant. These stories are typically based on carefully matching redundant information collected from sensors on the spot, visual inspection of processes, and a general alertness to smell, sound, and so on in various "regions" of the plant. Even patterns of action seem anchored in an overlay of these systems of information both scattered all over the plant and (for some parts) concentrated in the control room. What stood out from these encounters with work practice at the plant was that technicians more or less lost IT support when they were working outside the control room (or had to connect to it by mobile phones). Seeing the SMARTWINDOW as a down-scaled portable control room that enables the technician to keep in touch with the overall network of sensors, actuators, and controls seemed a reasonable route to take.

Based on simple physical mock-ups of the SMARTWINDOW, the technicians and operators we worked with developed a number of video scenarios that envisioned some prototypical examples of how the SMARTWINDOW could be used. We carried these scenarios from plant to plant, and had them evaluated at workshops with participants from different types of plants (Binder 1999). This became an example-driven specification process that enabled us to work with detailing the design without needing to abstract a more generic concept or go into detailed task analysis. We supplemented the participatory engagement with users and use, with an examination of what we called *interaction style* (Øritsland and Buur 2000). Earlier we had been working with stylized user characters as a way to grasp diversities among users, but we had found that this quickly led us into a mix of different task profiles and societal stereotypes. To avoid this, we tried to bring together a sort of distilled image of interaction style from science fiction literature. With Flash Gordon from the 1960s, Spock from the 1970s, and Neuromancer Molly from the 1980s, we had an encapsulated style history that we could map to the things we found in the plant environment (Bødker, Nielsen, and Petersen 2000). This led us to the production of what we called *interaction style sheets*. The style sheets were poster collages bringing together significant words, textures, and images that to us conveyed a certain sense of the dynamics of interaction. We worked mainly with three different interaction style sheets derived from both field studies and sci-fi literature. All these were made up to date and can roughly be categorized as "organic" and "cyborg-like," "system-oriented" and "hands off," and finally "tool-like" and "sportsgear-like." The interaction style sheets worked quit well as inspiration for interaction design.

We ended the project with mock-ups, interaction prototypes, and a functional prototype, where we used an existing PDA interfaced to a simple SCADA system and a few sensors and actuators to demonstrate that we had a viable concept.

Conversational Design

If the Scandinavian tradition of participatory design for the most part can be said to be contained within an instrumental discourse on systems design, the SMARTWINDOW project can be seen as an attempt to establish usability design or interaction design as a design field in its own right. Within this new field, we attempted to establish a focus on shaping issues that derived their relevance from an inquiry into the context of use and a more freestanding examination of interaction "gestalt." The prize for this free zone is, however, high and continues to threaten the newly won freedom of the interaction designer. We are still struggling with the utilitarian notions of "use" and "user," and by giving up aspirations for sociotechnical systems design we are also blackboxing both the existing system of tasks and overall IT design.

By picking up on ongoing developments toward miniaturized and mobile interfaces and by choosing "the window" and "the control room in the pocket" as guiding images, we had an opportunity to deal with a less formatted context of future use. We did, however, also inherit the underlying assumptions of the feasibility of global and coherent views on the industrial process, and could hardly struggle with more detailed conceptions like alarm-driven operator action. We wanted to be more modest in our aspirations and confined ourselves to the realm of technicians fixing the plant. Within this area we could pursue a user-centered design approach being safeguarded from larger issues of systems functionality (which we by and large presumed). But as I see it, our approach is still vulnerable to Schön's criticism of the participatory designer negotiating the platonic republic of agreed-on use.

Schön's own concept of designing is not foreign to engagement with context. He suggests what he called *conversational design*, where the designer engages in a reflective dialogue with "the materials of the design situation" (Schön 1988). He was not particularly in dispute with participatory design. His project was from the outset somewhat similar to Simon's, seeking grounding for the design professions (Schön 1987). But unlike Simon, he saw the designer as engaged in a basically outward loop of engagement with the environment. He did not accept Simon's notion of the design problem as an externally generated starting point rooted in societal needs or objectives. For Schön, the setting of the problem is intrinsically connected to the generative cycle of constructing and perceiving the world. In this cycle, nothing can be seen before the designer projects herself onto the situation. By framing the situation and eventually imposing order on it, the designer enters into a constructive relationship in which images of the new can evolve. The introduction of the "materials of the *design* situation" is important here, to grasp the significant distinction from Simon's perspective on design. Simon and

Schön can be said to agree that the designed artifact is a human construct that may or may not turn out to be feasible when translated into new interfaces between various systems. But where Simon seems much in line with the participatory design tradition when assuming that the designer has direct access to reason on the problems of the context, Schön propagates a different kind of modesty, by introducing the representational issues of design. For Schön, the designer must be understood as herself situated in a reflective cycle with the materials at hand.

From the POSTI and SPRING projects to the SMARTWINDOW project, we moved along the axes laid out by both Simon and Schön. The shop-floor information systems can retrospectively be seen as confusing the designed artifact with aspirations on the part of the designer (and users) with respect to the future of work. The SMARTWINDOW project takes more seriously the need to differentiate between the artifact interfacing among various subsystems (i.e., the overall instrumentation of the plant and the particularities of plant maintenance), and the larger context of use. The SMARTWINDOW device has, however, the strong imprints both of existing technological systems and of the work practice of plant technicians.

Along the lines laid out by Schön, the SMARTWINDOW project was a move toward a more conversational approach to design and participation. As designers we were more explicitly molding our conceptions of the new device, and we were deliberately seeking an open conversation by handing it over to a mixed community of potential "users." Our inquiry into interaction styles can be seen as an attempt to come to grips with an extended language of representations. Still, it is somewhat obscure how we distinguish between the envisioned artifact and the representations crafted in the materials of the design situation.

Seen from a "bird's-eye" perspective, the design projects are all struggling with how to locate IT, and they are based on the assumption that different people and different jobs call for different informational perspectives on the same overall information ecology. In the shop-floor information systems projects, emphasis was on tailoring information to a particular context of use. The lessons learned were that this issue could not be dealt with without looking at the particular embodiment of the artifact designed. The SMARTWINDOW project corresponds to this insight by taking as its starting point the way a freely movable interface can be embodied and put in place in a larger environment. In this way, the physical shaping of the new device becomes the prime design material with which the designer and his collaborating users engage in a constructive dialogue. What is not clear from the projects is the status of dealing with these issues of embodiment. Is the actual physical setup in which the IT is enacted just another design parameter to consider? Or is it that embodiment is also an essential feature of IT that we have been neglecting in the past? The projects do not answer this question, because they have both limited themselves in scope to consider merely the provision of information to particular localities. A more radical approach would have to also call into question the more fundamental issues of overall information systems design.

The PUCKETIZER: Getting Hands on the "System"

In a recent design project—the PUCKETIZER project (Nilsson et al. 2000)—we wanted to take the conversational design approach further.[3] We wanted to see if we were able not only to add to but also to confront more fundamental issues of conventional systems design. We again wanted to work with the apparent tension between local inspection and maintenance and centralized control as we had found it in the process plants of the SMARTWINDOW project. This time we wanted to position our design project in such a way that we could work with the overall system of plant monitoring and control. We were inspired by the growing literature on ubiquitous computing starting with Weiser 1991, and we wanted to rival the idea of centralized and hierarchical control. In terms of our own design thinking, we also wanted to overcome the fixation we felt we still had on the notions of "users" and "use."

As in earlier projects, we worked closely with people in the field. We established a collaboration with a large wastewater treatment plant and decided to work mainly with process operators rather than technicians to get away from a potential fixation with discrete tasks. From the outset, we did not have any clear understanding of a problem we were going to solve. What we had were a number of examples from earlier projects on the shortcomings of conventional control. As a baseline for our design activities, we assumed a not-so-distant future where we can expect to have a multitude of input and output devices.

In the first part of the project, we followed a number of process operators during a normal working day and obtained extensive video footage, with the camera as a very visible third party in the on-the-spot conversations (Binder 1999). From the early visits we edited small video documentaries that we brought back for discussion with the group. After further visits we started to edit what we called *type scenarios*, which in our view expressed some interesting aspects of the work at the plant (Buur, Binder, and Brandt 2000). The image that emerged was that the entire plant could be seen as one large composite interface to the process of water treatment. Dealing with upcoming problems such as pump breakdown or clotting of pipes is generally a collaborative effort that often involves experimentation. Leaving traces of ongoing or newly finished activities seemed to be a widespread practice. Alarm handling, which is a well-supported feature of the monitoring and control systems, played a relatively minor role. As we ended the fieldwork we had six to eight small video stories that we had negotiated with the plant operators. They depicted plant monitoring as a rather fluent and ad hoc activity that has to deal with a plant that never seems to be in any simple sense "just up and running." We still did not have a well-defined problem to solve. But we had started to get a sense of a new environment and had developed a representation of this environment with our edited videos.

In the second part of the project, we moved in a variety of props generated from more-or-less generic IT building blocks. We introduced the idea of movable displays of varying sizes. The displays could be positioned at various locations where there was a need to view electronically collected data. We suggested movable sensors that would allow for flexible instrumentation, so that monitoring could be established with increasing intensity in areas that were particularly troublesome. And finally, we suggested new input devices that could work in the entire plant, much the same way that mouse and keyboard do on the computer. All our suggestions were brought up in workshops with the process operators, and we supplemented them with images of how we could imagine "dressing up" the operators, the plant, or the operator areas to accommodate these building blocks. We used simple cardboard mock-ups as representations of the different designs to provide a sense of size, portability, and so on (Brandt and Grunnet 2000).

From the discussions with the process operators and our own attempts to sketch different concepts in more detail, it seemed promising to concentrate on a design where the operators establish temporary interfaces according to the day-to-day concerns of the plant. We also wanted to minimize the number of devices that the operators would need to carry around with them. We ended up detailing a personal device that would keep operators connected but still leave much of the interaction with the plant to semistationary devices. This led us to design a device called the *Personal Bucket Organizer* (PUCKETIZER). With this device, the operators can collect items for a particular view of the process in a "bucket" and would later be able to monitor relations between the items when "pouring" the contents of the bucket into a display.

The functionality and interaction of the PUCKETIZER were again developed in a number of scenarios created and acted out in front of the video camera in the plant. The video scenarios formed the representational medium in which we could share with the operators the emerging design. We ended the design project by making a scaled-down functional model of the device. This not only functioned as proof of concept but also provided us with a way to more closely examine the viability of the design as a prototypical model for other interactive systems.

Beyond Information and Software

This account of design projects over a decade is likely to resemble that of many other designers. In the POSTI and SPRING projects, we were already sensitized to the challenged issued by Winograd (1996) and others to be true designers of the virtual world of the users. We did exercise our prototyping skills and engaged seriously with the people in the context we designed for. But we failed to see that although our job was to prepare the software, we were dealing with a setting where "the delivery platform" was not self-evidently encompassing anything like a "world."

We were stuck with the idea that what we provided was information that, through unproblematic encoding and decoding, would convey our "intent" to the "users." Form and materiality were left out of the equation. This prevented us from realizing that our artifacts are basically form, in-formed by our intentions and restricted by the subject matter. What we learned as we saw our designs appropriated on the shop floor was that this form had to evoke yet new intentions over which we could hardly have any control.

We moved with our field into the new world of mobile informatics, and we sought modestly to carve out a niche for ourselves as interaction designers. This taught us more about design at large. We came to work with the physical embodiment of new devices, and we learned to engage with a larger repertoire of design representations. But as we took to heart the new self-image of the architect-designer, we also fenced ourselves in in a reservation for user consent that left us out of touch with the design of the larger technological structures.

The recent interest in graspable user interfaces (Fitzmaurice, Ishii, and Buxton 1995) and tangibility (Ishii and Ullmer 1997) holds promise for a future in which software and systems thinking are again searching their bodies in the mixed-media environments of everyday life. These environments are likely to resemble the artificial world of, for example, the process plants we have engaged with. If this is the challenge, we may as well give up the concept of IT. All technologies we can think of today have an element of in-formation, and *interaction design* is certainly a good label for a dominant design issue in the shaping of technology. Replacing the concept of information technology with interaction technology will, however, at least for the present encourage designers in the field not to let themselves be trapped in the outdated opacities of an older regime of form. This will also leave the questions of how to deal with the immateriality of software and its lack of quality behind us. Instead it will inevitably put software designers back into the larger community of engineers, architects, and others struggling with interaction technology and trying to come to terms with a full-bodied notion of "the science of the artificial."

Notes

1. From 1990 to 1994 I worked in the department of Human Resource Development at the Danish Technological Institute. We were a mixed group of video photographers, computer scientists, and engineers working with interactive video and hypermedia applications for public and private clients. The group came out of linear video production for industry, and it was among the first groups in Denmark to make a larger hypermedia installation for workplace learning at the Danish Postal Services (the POSTI project). This project was later followed by an EU-financed project, SPRING, aimed at facilitating shop-floor learning in the European spring industry.

2. The work reported on the SMARTTOOL and SMARTWINDOW projects was carried out in 1995 and 1997 when I was a member of the User-Centred Design Group at the Danish company Danfoss. The User-Centred Design Group was at the time part of Corporate Research and collaborated extensively with students and researchers from different universities.

3. The PUCKETIZER project came out of our work at the Interactive Institute. In the Space and Virtuality Studio we inititiated the project as part of a collaboration with groups at Danfoss and the department of Computer Science at Aarhus University during 1998–1999. We wanted to explore how notions of "space" and "place" might change as mobile and configurable operator interfaces are introduced in industrial process plants.

References

Bagger-Nielsen, K., J. Buur, and T. Binder. 1997. From Usability Testing to User Dialogue. *Proceedings of the International Ergonomics Association Conference* (Tampere, Finland).

Banta, M. 1993. *Taylored Lives: Narrative Productions in the Age of Taylor, Veblen, and Ford.* Chicago: University of Chicago Press.

Binder, T. 1995. Designing for Workplace Learning. *AI & Society* 9: 218–243.

Binder, T. 1996a. Designers in Dialogue. In D. Vinck and J. Perrin, eds., *The Role of Design in the Social Shaping of Technology.* COST A4, EU Commission, Luxembourg.

Binder, T. 1996b. Learning and Knowing with Artifacts: An Interview with Donald Schön. *AI & Society* 10: 51–58.

Binder, T. 1999. Setting the Stage for Improvised Video Scenarios. *Proceedings of the CHI 1999 Conference* (Seattle), 230–231. New York: ACM Press.

Binder, T., and K. T. Nielsen. 1996. Industrial Culture and Design Methodology. In F. Rauner and L. B. Rasmussen, eds., *Industrial Cultures and Production.* London: Springer.

Binder, T., and L. Passarge. 1996. Supporting Reflection and Dialogue in a Community of Machine Setters: Lessons Learned from Design and Use of a Hypermedia Type Training Material. *AI & Society* 10: 79–88.

Bødker, S. 1999. *Computer Applications as Mediators of Design and Use.* DAIMI PB-542. Aarhus, Denmark: Aarhus University.

Bødker, S., C. Nielsen, and M. Petersen. 2000. Creativity, Cooperation, and Interactive Design. *Proceedings of the DIS 2000 Conference.* New York: ACM Press.

Brandt, E., and C. Grunnet. 2000. Evoking the Future: Drama and Props in User Centered Design. *Proceedings of the Participatory Design Conference 2000* (New York). Palo Alto, CA: CPSR.

Buur, J., T. Binder, and E. Brandt. 2000. Taking Video beyond "Hard Data" in User Centred Design. *Proceedings of the Participatory Design Conference 2000.* Palo Alto, CA: CPSR.

Dahlbom, I. B. Forthcoming. The Idea of an Artificial Science. In I. B. Dahlbom, S. Beckman, and G. B. Nilsson, eds., *Artifacts and Artificial Science.*

Ehn, P. 1988. *Work Oriented Design of Computer Artifacts.* Stockholm: Arbetslivscentrum.

Fitzmaurice, G. W., H. Ishii, and W. Buxton. 1995. Bricks: Laying the Foundations for Graspable User Interfaces. *Proceedings of CHI'95*, 442–449. New York: ACM Press.

Greenbaum J., and M. Kyng, eds. 1991. *Design at Work: Cooperative Design of Computer Systems.* Hillsdale, NJ: Erlbaum.

Ishii, H., and B. Ullmer. 1997. Tangible Bits: Towards Seamless Interfaces between People, Bits, and Atoms. *Proceedings of Conference on Human Factors in Computing Systems* (CHI '97) (Atlanta, March 1997), 234–241. New York: ACM Press.

Löwgren, J., and E. Stolterman. 1998. *Design av Informationsteknik—Materialet utan egenskaper*, Lund: Studentlitteratur. (In Swedish.)

Meier, Flemming. 1998. *Læring er indviklet i praksis! Et speciale om læringsbegreber, uformelle læreprocesser og fjedervikling.* Report Series 63. Roskilde, Denmark: Roskilde University Center. (In Danish.)

Musil, R. [1930–1943] 1995. *The Man without Qualities.* New York: Knopf.

Nilsson, J., T. Sokoler, T. Binder, and N. Wetcke. 2000. Beyond the Control Room: Mobile Devices for Spatially Distributed Interaction on Industrial Process Plants. *Proceedings of the Conference on Handheld and Ubiquitous Computing 2000.* London: Springer.

Øritsland, T., and J. Buur. 2000. Taking the Best of Company History: Designing with Interaction Styles. *Proceedings of the DIS 2000 Conference.* New York: ACM Press.

Reddy, M. 1979. The Conduit Metaphor. In A. Ortony, ed., *Metaphor and Thought*. Cambridge, England: Cambridge University Press.

Rolf, A. 1992. Sichtwechsel—Informatik als Gestaltungswissenschaft. In W. Coy, F. Nake, J.-M. Pflüger, A. Rolf, J. Seetzen, D. Siefkes, and R. Stransfeld, eds., *Sichtweisen der Informatik*. Wiesbaden: Vieweg.

Schön, D. A. 1987. *Educating the Reflective Practitioner*. San Francisco: Jossey-Bass.

Schön, D. A. 1988. Problems, Frames, and Perspectives on Designing. *Design Studies* 9(3).

Simon, H. A. 1976. *The Science of the Artificial*. Cambridge, MA: MIT Press.

Weiser, M. 1991. The Computer for the 21st Century. *Scientific American* 265(3): 94–104.

Winograd, T. 1996. *Bringing Design to Software*. New York: Addison-Wesley.

Contributors

Urs Andelfinger
Accenture, Frankfurt/Main, Germany

Gail Bader
Ball State University
Department of Anthropology

Eevi Beck
University of Oslo
Department of Informatics

Mark Bergman
University of California, Irvine
Department of Information and Computer Science

Olav W. Bertelsen
University of Aarhus
Department of Computer Science

Thomas Binder
Swedish Interactive Institute
Space and Virtuality Studio

Keld Bødker
Roskilde University
Department of Computer Science

Susanne Bødker
University of Aarhus
Department of Computer Science

Yvonne Dittrich
Blekinge Institute of Technology
Department of Software Engineering and Computer Science

Anne Eerola
University of Kuopio
Department of Computer Science and Applied Mathematics

Sara Eriksen
Blekinge Institute of Technology
Department of Human Work Science and Media Technology

Geraldine Fitzpatrick
University of Queensland
CRC for Enterprise Distributed Systems Technology

Christiane Floyd
University of Hamburg
Department of Informatics

Marina Jirotka
Oxford University
Computing Laboratory

Helge Kahler
Fraunhofer Project Agency
New Media in Education
Sankt Augustin, Germany

Victor Kaptelinin
Umeå University
Department of Informatics

Finn Kensing
The IT University of Copenhagen
Design and Use of Information Technology

John Leslie King
University of Michigan
School of Information

Ralf Klischewski
University of Hamburg
Department of Informatics

Mikko Korpela
University of Kuopio
Computing Center

Philip Kraft
State University of New York at Binghamton
Department of Sociology

Paul Luff
King's College, London
Management Centre
Work, Interaction and Technology Research Group

Kalle Lyytinen
Case Western Reserve University
Weatherhead School of Management
Department of Information Systems

Anja Mursu
University of Jyväskylä
Department of Computer Science and Information Systems

Hans-Erik Nissen
Lund University
Department of Informatics

Jacob Nørbjerg
Copenhagen Business School
Department of Informatics

James M. Nyce
Emporia State University
School of Library and Information Management

Horst Oberquelle
University of Hamburg
Department of Informatics

Kari Rönkkö
Blekinge Institute of Technology
Department of Software Engineering and Computer Science

Jesper Simonsen
Roskilde University
Department of Computer Science

H. Abimbola Soriyan
Obafemi Awolowo University
Department of Computer Science and Engineering

Bettina Törpel
Fraunhofer Institute for Applied Information Technology
Sankt Augustin, Germany

Chris Westrup
University of Manchester
School of Accounting and Finance

Volker Wulf
International Institute for Socio-Informatics
Bonn, Germany

Index

Abstract, 16. *See also* Formal
data types, 120
mathematics, 11
models, 257
representation of the workplace, 106 (*see also* Representation)
Abstraction, 106, 116, 146, 156, 244, 432, 443. *See also* Formalization
shared, 146, 152, 156
Accountability, 432
Actant, 312. *See also* Actor-network theory; Agent
Action, 60, 62, 395, 458
communicative, 128
situated, 20, 53, 192, 441
Action research, 248–249, 268, 299–301, 306
Activity, 209, 289, 297, 411
analysis, 287
boundary-crossing, 296, 300
creative, 399
development, 309
design, 463
documentary, 118
dynamic, 395
information systems development 288
mediating, 399 (*see also* Activity theory)
multipractical, 411
networks, 287, 290 (*see also* Activity theory)
situated, 19, 120, 404
social, 243, 309
use, 309
users', 293, 412–413
Activity theory, 18, 47–48, 55, 61, 155–156, 287, 289, 402, 411, 421, 455. *See also* Developmental work research
Actor, 17, 24, 190, 290, 292, 297, 309, 311, 312, 314, 324, 327, 363
Actor-network theory, 311–312, 320, 325. *See also* Actant; Agent
Adaptability, 404. *See also* Customization; Flexibility; Tailorability
Aesthetics, 398
Agency of technology, 17
Agent, 24, 56, 396. *See also* Actant; Actor-network theory
Allopoietic machines, 80
Ambiguity, 430
Anchoring, 271
Anthropology, 402, 458
Appropriation, 456, 465
Architecture, 399
Artifact, 455
computer, 10, 11
design, 410, 412, 422
mediating, 455 (*see also* Activity theory)
technical, 21
symbolic, 21
Artful integration, 352
Artificial intelligence, 74

Automotive supplier, 192
Auto-operational form, 21, 24
Autopoietic machine, 80
Awareness, 149

Background
 of software development, 171, 190, 192, 195
Best practice, 95, 205, 425, 453–454
Black box, 313, 315–319, 322, 324, 460. *See also* Actor network theory
Border object, 10
Border subject, 395
Boundary object, 198, 412, 418
Boundary zone, 411
Bus timetable, 440

Care giving, 165–166
Care taking, 291
Categorization, 162–163, 166–167, 170, 172–174. *See also* Classification
Category, residual, 153, 161, 166–167, 171–172, 190. *See also* Categorization; Classification; Heterogeneity
Change, 16, 51–52, 101, 236–237, 246, 257, 263, 267, 278, 410, 453
Choices, 25, 255
Classification, 79
Cleanroom, 247
Co-construction, 427–428, 443
Coevolution, 394, 399, 404
Cognitive science, 74
Collaboration, 127. *See also* Computer-supported cooperative work
 interdisciplinary, 49, 100, 119, 131 (*see also* Communication, interdisciplinary; Interdisciplinary)
 interorganizational, 337, 340, 342
Collaborative systems, 141. *See also* Computer-supported cooperative work
Commitment, 17, 278, 315–327. *See also* Actor network theory
Common sense, 42
Communicating sequential processes, 120–123, 126–128, 130
Communication, 117, 280, 86
 between developers and users, 60, 219, 415
 interdisciplinary, 115, 130
 mathematical theory of, 80
 means of, 290
 problems, 212
Communities of practice, 10, 412
Community, multidisciplinary, 146
Competence, 402
Computational model, 17
Computer artifact, 10, 11
Computer-based networks, 309. *See also* World Wide Web
Computers
 networks of humans and, 14 (*see also* Actor network theory)
 in use, 9, 393
Computer-supported cooperative work (CSCW), 53, 112, 143, 146–147, 153, 155, 181, 205, 208–210, 245, 249, 287, 398, 429, 438
Computing, 6–7, 11–12, 170
Conceptual
 framework, 186, 270
 ground, common, 64, 280
 world, 395–397
Concrete, 16. *See also* Abstract
Conflict, 83, 395
Conflicting interests, 84, 87, 256, 409. *See also* Politics; Power
Connotational, 81
Constructionism, 426
Constructive criticism, as a form for social science contribution, 59–60
Constructive proof, 260
Constructivism, 80–81, 224
Context, 9, 162, 171
 dependency, 190
 economic, 245
 global, 432
 local and interactional, 120

organizational, 115, 205–206, 218–220, 245, 257, 267
project, 198
social, 8, 51, 115, 187, 211, 411
of software development, 205–206, 210, 211
of use, 224, 396, 433, 459
Contextual design, 51
Contradictions, 409, 413
Contradicting interests, 256
Control, 216
Coordination, 125–128, 223
means of, 290
Creativity, 402, 416
Critical theory, 259
Cultural
assumptions, 34, 39
domain, 33
interpretation, 96
Cultural-historical psychology, 56. *See also* Activity theory
Cultures, 79
organizational, 297
Customization, 309. *See also* Adaptability; Tailoring

Data-intensive applications, 118
Data model, 118
Decision process, 362
Decomposition, 116
Deconstruction, 1
Denotational, 81
Descriptive, 91. *See also* Interpretative reason
Design, 24–25, 102, 114–115, 132, 141, 146–147, 151, 154, 244, 267, 269–270, 409–422, 453–457. *See also* Participatory design
activity, 463
artifact, 410, 412, 422
collaborative, 453
cooperative, 295, 299, 392–406
conversational, 460–462
database, 118
decisions, 154
and development, 37–38
discipline, 155
implications, 113
interaction, 393–395, 451, 457, 465
material, 452, 459
methods, 416
orientation, 393
practice, 244, 410
process, 24, 115, 120, 150, 367, 387, 400
projects, 269
science, 392
scope, 24, 27
socio-technical, 365
of technology, 116
use-oriented, 388
user-centered, 293, 299
utilitarian discourse of, 452
Design in use, 254, 348
Designer, 100, 150, 454–455
Designer's notepad, 100
Deskilling, 413
Development. *See also* Information system, development; Software development; Systems, development
cooperative, 295
distributed, 311
evolutionary, 182, 188, 258
experimental, 267
user-centered, 295
Development process, 393. *See also* Process; Software process
iterative and evolutionary, 191, 144
Developmental work research, 415. *See also* Activity theory
Dialectical, 15, 27, 76, 388
Dialogue, 12, 103–105, 152, 460, 462, 428
Discipline, 146, 202. *See also* Science
design, 155
engineering, 259
informatics, 392
information systems, 301
Documentary method, 230, 238
Domain knowledge, 32–33, 39

Ecological, 270, 362, 382n
Edge dwellers, 157

Education, 30
Emancipatory, 77, 416
Embedding
 auto-operational form, 24
 computer artifacts, 7
Embodiment, 461–462, 465. *See also* Tangibility; Ubiquitous computing
Empathy, 426
Empirical
 methods, 245
 research, 243–260
Engineering, 15, 76, 244, 394
 discipline, 259
 questions, 35
Engineering office, 339
Enterprise information systems, 14
Epistemology, 175, 229–231, 259, 389. *See also* Feminist theory; Gender research; Research, methodology
Ethic, 82, 87, 106, 243, 246, 255–258. *See also* Responsibility
Ethnographer, role of the, 97–99
Ethnographic. *See also* Workplace, studies
 account, 115
 analyses, 132
 methods, 84, 293, 299, 426
 practice, 105
 record, 99–101
 techniques, 271
Ethnography, 36, 42, 96–97, 249, 252, 256, 400, 402
 contributions of, 36, 98
 function of, 35
 industrialization of, 115
 as a method, 102
 quick and dirty, 115, 228
 as a technique, 95
 two formulations of, 106
 of use, 31
Ethnomethodologically informed ethnography, 170, 172, 228, 238–239, 249
Ethnomethodology, 48, 96, 112–113, 174, 229, 256, 426, 428, 430
 limitations of, 54
Examination administration, 316
Experimentation, 247, 267, 344, 349
Experiments, 247, 249
Extreme programming, 434n

Featuritis, 400
Feminist theory, 174, 428. *See also* Gender research
Festival project, 417–418
Financial trading floor, 123
Flexibility, 86, 394. *See also* Adaptability; Appropriation; Customization; Tailorability
Foreground
 of software development, 189, 192, 195,
Form, 7, 34, 465
 auto-operational, 7
 operational, 7
 language of, 401, 403
Formal, 402. *See also* Abstract
 language, 224
 methods, 244
 model, 24, 118, 120
 notation, 129–131
 theory, 11
Formalization, 23, 432, 441. *See also* Abstraction
Freelancer, 344

Gender research, 428. *See also* Feminist theory
Genius loci, 433–443
Globalization, 215, 433
Great divide, 310
Grounded theory, 170–171, 174. *See also* Research, qualitative; Research, methods
Groupware, 347–348

Hermeneutic, 77, 169–170, 174
Hermeneutic/dialectical, 15, 27, 76
Heterogeneity, 161, 166–167, 411, 414. *See also* Categorization; Category, residual
Heterogeneous engineering, 358

Hierarchies, 256, 335–336. *See also* Politics; Power
Historical
practices, 419
transition, 410
History,
analysis, 412 (*see also* Activity Theory)
of a project, 224
Human-computer interaction, 53, 245, 287, 392, 429, 438
Hypermedia, 452

Ideal, 425
Identity, 427
Immateriality of software, 465. *See also* Embodiment; Material
Immutable mobile, 315–316. *See also* Actor network theory
Improvement, 182, 246, 249–250, 255, 257, 259, 274. *See also* Method, improvement; Software process improvement
Incremental, 188
Informal, 402. *See also* Abstract; Concrete; Formal
communication, 218
cooperation, 209, 223
developer-user interactions, 217
practices, 120, 211–213
Informatics, 309, 392
Information appliance, 395. *See also* Tangibility; Ubiquitous computing
Information architecture, 395
Information processing, 288
Information system, 81, 288, 309
development, 274, 287–288, 292, 310, 357 (*see also* Development; Software development; Systems development)
development methods, 314
education, 301
practice, 263, 298
Information theory, 74
Informational objects, 22
Inscriptions, 100
Instrumentality, 451–452, 459
Integration, artful, 352
Intelligibility, mutual, 233
Intentionality, 426, 451–452, 455, 465
Interaction analysis, 252. *See also* Ethnomethodology
Interaction design, 393–395, 451, 457, 465
Interaction style, 459, 461
Interactive
systems, 141
technology, 451–452
workplace systems, 13
Interdisciplinary, 146, 191, 202. *See also* Communication, interdisciplinary
capabilities, 200
collaboration, 48, 100, 119, 131
understanding, 200
knowledge, 392
Interests, 17, 83, 348, 358, 421, 454–456. *See also* Politics
conflicting, 84, 87, 409
contradictory, 256
Interpretation, 20, 86, 104, 169–170, 397, 410–412, 419, 432, 443, 454, 456. *See also* Localizing; Representation
Interpretative reason, 103. *See also* Descriptive
Intervention, 36–37

Knowledge
domain, 32–33, 39
formation, 105
how, that, 119

Laboratory research, 257
Language, 84, 104. *See also* Communication; Interpretation; Notation; Representation
common, 415–417
of form, 401, 403
formal, 129–131, 224
everyday, 72
natural, 129
professional, 72

Language (cont.)
programming, 22, 187
of representation, 461
universal modeling, 116
use, 427
Learning, 86–87
mutual, 270, 335
Legislative reason, 101, 170. *See also* Prescriptive
Leitbilder, 244
Leviathan, 427, 430
Life cycle, 188, 297, 309, 435
Local
experimentation, 344, 350, 352
interpretations, 412
Locales, 147–149, 151, 155, 202
framework, 147–151
Localizing, 349, 427, 436–443, 461–462
Logic, 11
Logical/empirical, 15, 76

Management
practices, 206
processes, 288
project, 189, 200, 310, 326
Management information systems, 205–206, 208–209
Material, 395
design, 452, 459
Materiality, 388, 451
Meaning, 438
Measurement, 209, 217, 245
Mediation, 10, 56
Metaphors, 72–75, 82, 145, 270, 396, 433, 457
Method, 181, 298, 357; *See also* Research methodology; Ethnography; Ethnomethodology; Grounded Theory; Software development; System development; Software process improvement
adaptation, 339
of design, 416, 455
change, 236
development, 257–258, 412
dissemination, 267–269
ethnographic, 84, 102, 297, 299, 426
empirical, 77–78, 229–231, 243, 245, 247
formal, 244
improvement, 300–301
information systems development, 314
qualitative, 151, 209, 250 (*see also* Interaction analysis)
quantitative, 247, 256
as a resource for action, 270
software engineering, 182, 247 (*see also* Cleanroom)
usefulness of, 258
Methodological
choices, 259
discourse, 175
framework, 326
problems, 246, 250
Misinterpretation, 224. *See also* Interpretation
Mobile, immutable, 315–316
Mobility, 443
Mode of operation, 290
Model, 22, 24, 115, 146, 244. *See also* Form
abstract, 16
computational, 17
data, 118
formal, 24, 118, 120
organizational, 223
semiformal, 119
in social science, 48, 219
Modeling, 16, 22, 111–112, 116–117, 125–131, 170. *See also* Model; Formal; Languages, formal
exercise, 119
process, 321
representations, 219
as situated action, 120
techniques, 116, 118
of workplace conduct, 128
Motronic systems, 192
Multidisciplinary community, 146
Multiple rationales, 199
MUST, 51, 155, 269–286, 301

Mutual
intelligibility, 233
learning, 270, 335
understanding, 78–79, 85, 103–105

Natural science, 255
Network, 17, 311–313, 344, 350. *See also* Actor-network theory
of humans and computers, 14, 311
Networking, 305, 311, 324. *See also* Actor-network theory
Notation, 120
diagrammatic, 131
formal, 131
semiformal, 131

Objective/realist, 16
One Stop Services, 435
Operation, 18–19, 80. *See also* Activity theory
Operational form, 18–21, 27
Operational (re-)construction, 22–23
Organizational
boundaries, 439
change, 263, 453
context, 115, 205–206, 218–220, 245, 257, 267
cultures, 297
environment, 310
informatics, 309
model, 223
relations, 216
Orientee, 81
Orienter, 81

Pairwise programming, 194
Partial
perspective, 174
truths, 99
Participatory design, 38, 41–42, 52, 69, 167, 181–182, 205, 208–209, 226, 245, 249, 258–259, 269–286, 295, 299, 309, 331–353, 339, 419, 429, 435, 440, 451, 453–456. *See also* Scandinavian approach
Participatory engagement, 459
Patient care, 291
Personal digital assistant, 457
Personal integrity, 282
Perspective, 83, 188, 454. *See also* Interests
construction, 401
different, 259, 335–336
partial, 174
sharing, 310
users' and developers', 60, 10, 351
useware, 401
Physical sciences, 257
Place, 141, 145, 148, 395, 426, 442–443
Plans and situated action, 441
Political, 270, 439
Politics, 190, 199, 425. *See also* Conflict; Interests; Power; Stakeholder
Postal workers, 452
Power, 190, 199, 366, 402–403
balance, 70, 83
games, 216
structure, 309, 335–336
Practice, 405. *See also* Work practice
analytic, 161
bad, 249
contingent, 128
design, 115, 244, 410
development, 181
distributed, 227, 250, 252
everyday, 411
formal, 211, 213–214
heterogeneous, 411
historical, 419
idealizations of, 421
informal, 120, 211–213
information systems, 263, 298
interactional, 120
interpretative, 118, 120
joint, 156
localized, 349
management, 206
organizational, 117
programming, 419
reflection on, 173
reflective, 190–192, 201
of seeing, 164, 168

Practice (cont.)
situated, 128, 145
social, 8, 72, 115, 117, 238
social sciences, 49, 52, 64, 114, 164
software, 5–6, 57, 64, 82, 141, 200, 206
software design, 157
software development, 1, 36, 49, 52, 117, 182, 238, 249, 392
use, 1, 410
Pragmatic turn, 427–428, 433
Prejudice, 170
Prescriptive, 144. *See also* Legislative reason
Problem
domain, 118
framing, 190
and solution, 29, 35, 143–144, 359, 363–374
solving, 190
wicked, 143, 150, 190
Process. *See also* Development; Information system, development; Software development; Software process; Software process improvement
control, 209
management, 288
modeling, 321
open-ended, 271
Programmer, 219, 391
Programming, 13, 58–59, 213–214, 419–420
environment, graphical, 237
extreme, 434
as a human activity, 187–188
languages, 393
pairwise, 194
paradigms, 22
practices, 419
as theory building, 187
Project, 198
context, 198
environment, 325, 327
experience, 189
management, 189, 200, 310, 326
Props, 463
Public information systems, 426, 434–435

Qualitative. *See also* Ethnography, Ethnomethodology; Grounded Theory; Research
methods, 151, 209, 249–250
research, 245
Quantitative
measurements, 209, 217, 245
methods, 247, 250, 256
research, 245
Quick and dirty, 115, 228

Radio station, 271
Rationalistic
discourse, 455
tradition, 12
Rationality, 40
technical, 361–362
Realities, 426
Reality construction, 226
Reflective software development, 248
Reification, 10
Reorientation, 168
Representation, 116, 398, 461. *See also* Language, formal; Model; Modeling; Notation
abstracted, of the workplace, 106
tools, 270
of user work practices in design, 267
Requirements, 132, 231–239
analysis, 116, 129, 143, 287, 297
design, 297
engineering, 97, 100, 117, 223–225, 358–380, 391
handling, 223, 252, 209
functional ecology of, 359, 361–362, 376
originator, 233
specification, 189
techniques, 153
Research. *See also* Ethnography, Ethnomethodology, Grounded theory; Epistemology

action, 248–249, 268, 299–301, 306
empirical, 228, 243, 245, 247, 255
gender, 428
information systems, 298
interests, 77–78, 83–84
issues, 202
method, 84, 102, 245, 271, 296, 299, 313, 426
methodology, 174, 243, 255–258, 302, 313 (*see also* Feminist theory)
qualitative, 249–250, 256
quantitative, 151, 209, 245, 247, 250
questions, 303
traditions, 75
Researcher, relationship between and researched, 259
Residual category, 153, 161, 166–167, 171–172, 190. *See also* Categorization; Classification; Heterogeneity
Responsibility, 360, 393. *See also* Ethic
Rooms, 395, 410

Satisficing, 143, 362
Scandinavian approach, 39, 167, 181, 226, 453. *See also* Participatory design
Science. *See also* Discipline
of the artificial, 455
design, 392
natural, 255
physical, 257
social, 46–47, 49, 52, 64, 132, 164, 182, 245, 255, 400
Self-reflection, 176
Semi-autonomous groups, 340–343
Service network, 331
Shared abstraction, 146, 152, 156
Shared spaces, 144–145
Shop floor information system, 452
Situated
action, 20, 53, 192, 441
activity, 12, 19, 91, 120, 404
practice, 128, 145
Situatedness, 190, 199, 433
Skill, 249, 453. *See also* Deskilling
Small and medium-size enterprises, 337–338
Social
actor, 309, 311, 314
context, 8, 51, 115, 187, 211, 411
dynamics, 388
ecology, 368n
practice, 8, 72, 115, 117, 238
relations, 37
sciences, 46–47, 49, 52, 64, 114, 132, 164, 182, 245, 255, 400
setting, 99
systems, 363, 455
world, 147–149
Social thinking
as situated activity, 91
limited impact of, 70
impact on software practice, 50–51
models and concepts in, 48
Sociotechnical, 69
design, 365
Soft systems methodology, 69, 155, 370n
Software, construction, 392–406
Software crisis, 186, 199, 244
Software design manifesto, 392
Software development, 115, 223. *See also* Development; Information system development; Systems development
background of, 171, 192, 195
context, 205–206, 218–220, 245, 257, 267
as cooperative work, 249
distributed, 223, 227, 231–239, 250–252, 311
foreground of, 189, 192, 195
goal of, 57–58
organization of, 216
practice, 1, 36, 49, 52, 117, 182, 238, 249, 392
process, 223
as a social activity, 243

Software engineering, 115, 185–186, 199, 201, 205, 208–210, 229, 244, 255, 288, 360, 403, 441
 education, 201
 methods, 182
Software engineering laboratory, 247
Software enterprises, 71
Software knowledge, 387
Software practice, 5–6, 64, 57, 82, 141, 200, 206
 as an activity, 57
 as an intertwined sociotechnical, 200
Software process, 387. *See also* Development process; Process
 evolutionary, 191, 182, 188
 incremental, 188
 iterative, 144, 150, 191
 spiral model, 188, 372
 waterfall model, 188
Software process improvement, 216, 257. *See also* Change; Improvement
Software producers, 79
Software system, 292
 failures, 69, 357
Spaces, 395, 442–443
 shared, 144–145
Specification, 116, 212
Stakeholders, 188, 190, 194, 310, 358, 366. *See also* Interests; Politics
 maps, 317
Standardization, 166–167, 433
 in work practices, 215
Steel mill, 331–339
Stockbrokers, 123
Subjective/constructivist, 16
Subject-object dichotomy, 312
Subjectivity, strong, 426, 443. *See also* Feminist theory; Gender research
Sustainable information technology, 270
Systemic, 17
Systems. *See also* Information Systems
 design, 151
 development, 106, 309, 357, 360
 development as networking, 311
 engineering, 115
 interactive software, 13, 18, 141
 social, 288

Taboo, 165–168
Tailorability, 394. *See also* Adaptability; Flexibility
Tailoring, 347, 420. *See also* Appropriation; Customization
Talkaboutable, 239
Tangibility, 461. *See also* Information appliance; Ubiquitous computing
Tasks, 61–63
Tax-audit solutions, 276
Technical discourse, 40
Technology, 365
 as agent, 17
 rigid, 119
 as structure, 17
 in use, 229
Terminology, 78
Theories
 formal, 11
 of inquiry, 77
Theory building, 226
 collaborative, 188, 223, 233
 extended, 187, 198, 200
 interdisciplinary, 188
Therapists, 84
Thinking
 operational, 19
 software as bodily action, 8, 72
Translation, 98
 of qualitative data, 146
Trust, 106
Truth, 428
 partial, 99

Ubiquitous computing, 399, 462. *See also* Information Appliance; Tangibility
Understanding, 150, 154, 250, 256, 259, 399. *See also* Collaboration; Communication; Common Language
 of computer-use situations, 173
 lack of, 84

mutual, 78–79, 85, 103–105
of social needs, 157
Union, 167, 331
Universal modeling language, 119
University hospital, 273
Usability, 218, 351, 391–406, 457, 459
Use, 462
activity, 309
computer in, 9, 393
context, 181, 201, 224, 396, 433, 459
design in, 254, 348
ethnography of, 31
language, 427
local, 434
meaningful, 432
oriented design, 388
practice, 1, 410
qualities, 182
situated, 399
situation, 430, 441–442
understanding of, 51
User, 79, 85, 150, 293, 430, 453, 462
advocates, 352
-centered, 293, 295, 441
-friendly, 205, 209
involvement, 455
organization, 216, 219
-oriented, 205, 250
-oriented design, 250, 388
participation, 270, 388
requirements, 205, 218
User's
activity, 293, 412–413
perspective, 60, 10, 351
rights, 393
work, 219
Useware, 391–406, 418
Utilitarian discourse of design, 452
UTOPIA, 414–416

War stories, 429
Wastewater treatment plant, 417–418, 462–464
Web portal, 437. *See also* Hypermedia; World Wide Web
Wicked problems, 143, 150, 190
Work, 120, 237
activities, 287
development, 211, 297
invisible, 171
situation, 206
Work practice, 141, 145, 238, 271, 333, 451
in design, 267
evolving, 352, 451, 458
situated, 145
Workarounds, 253
Workplace
representation of the, 106
studies, 111–112, 114, 119–120, 123, 246
systems, interactive, 13
World Wide Web, 201, 430. *See also* Computer-based networks; Hypermedia; Web portal

Made in the USA
Monee, IL
05 November 2026

67806919R00272